Force Majeure and the Law: Acts of God in Comparative and Historical Perspective

Thomas D. Musgrave

LONDON AND NEW YORK

First published 2025
by Routledge
4 Park Square, Milton Park, Abingdon, Oxon OX14 4RN

and by Routledge
605 Third Avenue, New York, NY 10158

Routledge is an imprint of the Taylor & Francis Group, an informa business

British Library Cataloguing-in-Publication Data
A catalogue record for this book is available from the British Library

Library of Congress Cataloging-in-Publication Data
Names: Musgrave, Thomas D., author.
Title: Force majeure and the law: acts of God in comparative and historical perspective/Thomas D. Musgrave.
Description: Abingdon, Oxon [UK]; New York, NY: Routledge, 2025. | Includes bibliographical references and index. |
Identifiers: LCCN 2024051711 (print) | LCCN 2024051712 (ebook) | ISBN 9781032875927 (hardback) | ISBN 9781032875934 (paperback) | ISBN 9781003533450 (ebook)
Subjects: LCSH: Vis major (Roman law) |
Vis major (Civil law)–England. |
Vis major (Civil law)–France. | Contracts (Roman law) |
Contracts–England. | Contracts–France. | Comparative law.
Classification: LCC K875 .M87 2025 (print) | LCC K875 (ebook) |
DDC 346.02/2–dc23/eng/20241104
LC record available at https://lccn.loc.gov/2024051711
LC ebook record available at https://lccn.loc.gov/2024051712

ISBN: 978-1-032-87592-7 (hbk)
ISBN: 978-1-032-87593-4 (pbk)
ISBN: 978-1-003-53345-0 (ebk)

DOI: 10.4324/9781003533450

Typeset in Galliard
by Deanta Global Publishing Services, Chennai, India

Force Majeure and the Law: Acts of God in Comparative and Historical Perspective

This book examines how the Roman, French and English legal systems have each dealt with the issue of unforeseen, supervening events which have rendered the performance of contractual obligations either impossible or fundamentally different in nature, sometimes known as Force Majeure or Acts of God. Although the Roman, French and English laws of contract have each developed legal rules which address this issue, the approach adopted by each system is significantly different from that of the others. The thesis of this book is that the response of a legal system to unforeseen, supervening events derives primarily from the nature and structure of that legal system as a whole, and then, within that broader context, from the salient characteristics of that system's particular law of contract. The work compares the differing nature and structure of the Roman, French and English legal systems, and their respective laws of contract, in order to demonstrate how this is so.

The book will be a valuable guide for academics and researchers working in the areas of Comparative Law, Legal History, Legal Theory and Contract Law. As the English approach to unforeseen, supervening events is very different from that of the French, the book will be of benefit both to English and to French practitioners as they seek to understand how supervening events are dealt with across the Channel. It will also appeal to law students as a guide for studying comparative law.

Thomas D. Musgrave is an Honorary Fellow at the University of Wollongong, Australia, and a Member of the Law Society of Ontario.

To my daughter Fiona Maree,
the apple of my eye.

Contents

Acknowledgements

The publication of this book is the culmination of many years of research and study on the subject of unforeseen, supervening events. I wish to thank the many people at the University of Wollongong, Australia, who assisted me in bringing it to fruition. I thank two of my former Deans, Professor Colin Picker and Professor Stuart Kaye, for their help and encouragement. I am grateful to the librarians and staff at the University, and in particular to Renee Grant, the research librarian. The University provided me with a number of research grants, for which I am very grateful. The Law Society of New South Wales also provided me with a research grant, and I thank the Law Society for that grant.

I owe an enormous debt of gratitude to my four research assistants, Anne Thomas, Jacob Hand, Elise Blanc and Elizabeth Donoghue, who were extremely helpful in the making of this book. Anne assisted me in the early stages, Jacob and then Elise in the middle stages and Elizabeth in the final stages. I am blessed to have had such excellent research assistants and I am very, very grateful to each of Anne, Jacob, Elise and Elizabeth for their research.

I also want to thank a number of my friends and colleagues for their encouragement and support. In this regard I thank Brian Leslie, Lynn Shephard, Scott Grattan, Greg Rose, Andrew Kelly, Charles Chew, Margaret Bond, Gaye Nicholls, my brothers Ian and Bruce and my daughter Fiona Maree. I also want to thank my daughter for her patience and good humour in repeatedly helping me to navigate my way through the intricacies of the computer.

Finally, and above all, I want to take this opportunity to thank *la femme de ma vie*, Jean Zhao, for her sustaining love and unwavering support throughout the writing of this book.

TDM

Abbreviations

Roman Law

D – Digest (*Corpus Iuris Civilis*)
I – Institutes of Justinian (*Corpus Iuris Civilis*)

French Law

Ass. Plén. – Cour de cassation, assemblée plénière

Bull. civ. ass. plén. – Bulletin des arrêts de la Cour de cassation (assembée plénière)

CA – Cour d'appel
CCC – Contrats Concurrence Consommation
CE – Conseil d'état
Cass. Civ. 1er – Cour de cassation, première chambre civile
Cass. Civ. 2e – Cour de cassation, deuxième chambre civile
Cass. Civ. 3e – Cour de cassation, troisième chambre civile
Cass. com. – Cour de cassation, chambre commerciale
Cons. const. – Conseil constitutionnel
Chron. – Chronique

D. – Recueil Dalloz
DH – Recueil hebdomadaire de jurisprudence Dalloz (années antérieures à 1941)
DP – Recueil périodique et critique mensuel Dalloz (années antérieures à 1941)

Gaz. Pal. – Gazette du Palais

JCP G – Semaine juridique (La), Edition générale

LPA – Petites Affiches (Les)

rapp. Petit – rapport Petit
RDC – Revue des contrats
Req. – Cour de cassation, chambre des requêtes

RLDC – Revue Lamy Droit Civil
RTD civ. – Revue trimestrielle de droit civil

S – Recueil Sirey

T. com. – Tribunal de commerce
T. confl. – Tribunal des conflits
TJ – Tribunal judiciaire

English Law

AC – Appeal Cases
Aleyn – Aleyn's Reports
All ER – All England Law Reports
All ER Comm – All England Law Reports (Commercial Cases)
App. Cas. – Appeal Cases

B & A – Barnewell & Alderson's King's Bench Reports
B & Ald – Barnewell & Alderson's Reports
B & S – Best and Smith's Reports
Bing – Bingham's Reports
Bos & Pul – Bosanquet & Pullen's Common Pleas Reports

CA – Court of Appeal
Camp – Campbell's Reports
Ch or ChD – Chancery Division
Co Rep – Coke's Reports

Doug – Douglas' King's Bench Reports

E & E – Ellis & Ellis' Queen's Bench Reports
East – East's Term Reports, King's bench
El Bl & El – Ellis, Blackburn & Ellis
ER – English Reports
EWCA – England and Wales Court of Appeal
EWCA Civ. – England and Wales Court of Appeal, Civil Division
EWHC – England and Wales High Court
EWHC (Comm) – England & Wales High Court (Commercial Court)
Ex – Exchequer

H & N – Hurlstone & Norman's Reports
HL – House of Lords

Jenkins – Jenkin's Exchequer Reports
Jones W – W Jones, King's Bench and Common Pleas Reports

KB – King's Bench Division

Leon – Leonard's Reports
LJKB – Law Journal, King's Bench

LLLR – Lloyd's Law Reports
LlL Rep – Lloyd's Law Reports
Lloyd's Rep. – Lloyd's Law Reports
LR – Law Reports
LR App. Cas. – Law Reports, Appeal Cases
LR CP – Law Reports, Common Pleas
LR KB – Law Reports, King's Bench, New Series
LR QB – Law Reports, Queen's Bench

M & W – Meeson & Welsby's Reports

QB or QBD – Queen's Bench Division

SC – Session Cases
Stark – Starkie's Nisi Prius Cases
Style – Style's King's Bench Reports
Swan – Swanston's Reports

Taunt – Taunton's Common Pleas Reports
TR or Term Rep – Term Reports

UKHL – United Kingdom House of Lords
UKSC – United Kingdom Supreme Court

WLR – Weekly Law Reports

Other

CLR – Commonwealth Law Reports (Australia)

DLR – Dominion Law Reports (Canada)

ICJ – International Court of Justice

OJ C – Official Journal of the European Union, Communications

UNTS – United Nations Treaty Series

Table of Cases

France

Note: French cases are not generally known by the names of the parties. They are listed below in chronological order. Where there is a name to a case, as occurred in the earlier cases, the names of the parties are put in brackets at the end of the citation, and are italicised.

Other Cases

Australian cases

Canadian cases

International Court of Justice

Table of Roman Law Texts

I–Institutes of Justinian (*Corpus Iuris Civilis*)

Table of Legislation

UK Statutory Instruments

France

Table of Treaties

Introduction

For he makes his sun to rise on the evil and the good, and sends rain on the just and the unjust. *

Matthew 5:45

Unforeseen supervening events have traditionally been referred to in the Common Law as 'acts of God'. This expression has been in use in English legal terminology since at least the fourteenth century.[1] In contemporary terminology, an 'act of God' has a very precise and restricted legal meaning, usually describing uncontrollable and overwhelming natural forces, such as an earthquake or a tsunami. But in the earliest cases, the phrase was used to describe someone's death.[2] The death of a testator, for example, was referred to in *Shelley's Case* as an act of God.[3]

However, by the late sixteenth century the phrase had been widened to describe a diverse range of unforeseen events resulting in supervening impossibility.[4] In his *Maxims of the Law*, published in 1597, Francis Bacon (1561–1653) considered madness, tempests, thunder and lightning, floods and the collapse of cottages due to the lack of workmen to repair them, to be acts of God.[5] Lord Mansfield declared in the 1785 case of *Trent and Mersey Navigation v Wood* that an act of God 'was natural necessity, as winds and storms, which

---

* World English Bible (Matthew 5:45) See biblegateway/com/versions/World-English-Bible-WEB/

1 *Anonymous* (*Case XVIII*) (1355) Jenkins 95, 145 ER 68.

2 *Anonymous* (1428) Jenkins 95, 145 ER 68; *Anonymous* (1453) Jenkins 90, 145 ER 64; *Anonymous* (1485) Jenkins 170, 145 ER 111; *Anonymous* (1490) Jenkins 180, 145 ER 120.

3 (1579–1581) 1 Co. Rep. 88b, 93b; 76 ER 199, 206.

4 *Laughter's Case* (1595) 5 Co. Rep. 21b; 77 ER 82; *Blumfield's Case* (1596) 5 Co. Rep. 86b; 77 ER 185; *Keighleys' Case* (1609) 10 Co. Rep. 1392; 77 ER 1136; *Williams v Lloyd.* (1624) Jones W. 179, 82 ER 95.

5 Francis Bacon *Maxims of the Law* (Volume IV of *The Works of Francis Bacon*) London: C. Baldwin, Printer, 1819, Regula V, 33, 35, 36.

DOI: 10.4324/9781003553450-1

arise from natural causes, and is distinct from inevitable accident'.[6] He elaborated on the meaning that same year in the case of *Forward v Pittard*:

> Now what is the Act of God? I consider it to mean something in opposition to the act of man: everything is the Act of God that happens by His permission: everything by His knowledge.[7]

The first of these two definitions limits an act of God to natural events which were both unforeseen and overwhelming in their intensity. The second definition is much broader in scope and has a definite theological ring to it.

Lord Manfield's observations did not bring clarity to the parameters of the phrase, as English judges continued to use the term indiscriminately. In the 1859 case of *Hall v Wright*, for example, an unspecified debilitating illness, without hope of recovery, was referred to by Pollock CB as an 'act of God'.[8] This disparate usage has led some to conclude that there is actually 'no consistent judicial approach to what is an act of God in law'.[9]

Although French law does not refer to an 'act of God' as a legal term of art, the same notion that unforeseen supervening events should be attributed to the acts of God can be found in eminent French legal sources.[10] Jean Domat (1625–1696), the great French jurist of the seventeenth century, declared:

> Accidents happen either by the act of man, such as a robbery, a fire; or by a pure effect of the providence of God and of the ordinary course of nature, such as thunder, lightning, a shipwreck, an inundation; or by an

---

6 *Trent and Mersey Navigation v Wood* (1785) 4 Doug 286, 290; 99 ER 884, 886, 25 April 1785). Insurance companies refer to 'acts of God' in this narrow sense, as do exculpatory clauses in contracts, which are known as 'force majeure' clauses.

7 (1785) 1 TR 28, 33; 99 ER 953, 956.

8 (1859) 120 ER 695, 705: 'By the act of God the contract has become void'. Pollock CB was one of the dissenting judges. See pages 162–163 *infra*, where this case is discussed in detail. Lord Hobhouse defined an act of God, in *Transco Plc v Stockport MSC* (2004) 2 AC 1, at paragraph 59, as being a 'metaphorical phrase (like 'fate') with a religious origin used to describe those events which involved no human agency and which it was not realistically possible for a human to guard against...'.

9 C.G. Hall 'An Unsearchable Providence: The Lawyer's Concept of Act of God' (1993) 13 *Oxford Journal of Legal Studies* 227, 228. One of A.P. Herbert's fictional characters, a junior barrister, made a submission to the House of Lords that their decisions should be considered as acts of God: A.P. Herbert 'Dahlia, Ltd. v Yvonne (Act of God)' 314, *Uncommon Law* London: Methuen & Co., Ltd., 1935.

10 As Hall points out, although the Romans gave 'special consideration' to those adversely affected by supervening events (which for them included 'not only natural forces but also seizure by enemy forces and violence from pirates and armed robbers') they did not in general ascribe such supervening events to the actions of the gods: Hall, op. cit., 228. But there is at least one reference in the Digest of Justinian which does in fact do so: 'Higher force, which the Greeks term "the force of God" should not be a source of loss to the lessee if his crops are damaged more than is bearable...': D.19.2.25, per Gaius.

effect proceeding partly from a natural cause, and partly from the act of man, such as a fire which happens by stacking up hay before it is well dried.[11]

Similarly, the great French jurist of the eighteenth century, Robert Joseph Pothier (1699–1772), made reference to the intervention of God in such circumstances. Pothier referred to an unforeseen supervening event as *vis divina*, or divine force:

> The debtor of specific things is never answerable for accidents, and cases of inevitable necessity (*cas fortuits et la force majeure, vis divina*) until he is guilty of improper delay; ... at least unless he has subjected himself to the loss arising therefrom by particular agreement; or unless the accident is occasioned by some preceding fault of his own.[12]

It is evident from these examples that the whole mentality of those times, whether in Catholic France or in Protestant England, was to frame human events within the context of the will of God.[13]

In the Common Law the concept of an 'act of God' figures in a number of areas, including bailments, torts and contract law. This book will consider the impact of acts of God only within a contractual context. In this regard, it will examine how acts of God have been dealt with by the Roman, French and

---

11 Jean Domat *The Civil Law in Its Natural Order* (translated by William Strahan) volume 1, Boston: Charles C. Little and James Brown, 1850; reissued by Fred B. Rothman & Co., Littleton, Colorado, 1980, 621.

12 Robert Joseph Pothier (translated by William David Evans) *A Treatise on the Law of Obligations, or Contracts* (Volume 1) Philadelphia; Robert H. Small, 1826, 74, paragraph 142. French private law utilises the term *créancier* for the person who initiates a civil claim, and *débiteur* for the person against whom a claim is made. These terms translate into English as 'creditor' and 'debtor'. 'Creditor' and 'debtor' will therefore be the terms employed in this study with regard to French cases. In English law the person who initiates a civil claim has traditionally been known as the 'plaintiff' and the person against whom a claim is made as the 'defendant'. However, in 1998, by virtue of section 2.3 of the Civil Procedure Rules 1998 No. 3132 (L.17), the term 'plaintiff' was replaced by the term 'çlaimant'. This change came into effect on 26 April 1999. The term 'plaintiff' will therefore be employed in this study with regard to English cases decided before 26 April 1999, and the term 'claimant' for cases decided after 26 April 1999.

13 Another very good example of this mentality can be seen in the comments of Alexandre Dubois, the curé de Rumégies, in response to the crisis of the French royal succession in 1712: '*En un an de temps, il y eut quatre dauphins en France; et Louis XIV, surnommé le Grand, a eu la douleur de voir mourir son fils, son petit-fils et son arrière-petit-fils, de sorte que, de quelque côté qu'on puisse voir la France, le doigt de Dieu est sur elle*'. ('In a single year there were in France four living dauphins, and then, in that same year, Louis XIV, known as Louis the Great, had the painful misfortune to witness the deaths of his son, his grandson and his great-grandson, so that from whatever angle one might consider France, it was clear that the hand of God was upon her'.) Quoted in Olivier Chaline '*L'Année des Quatre Dauphins*' Paris: Flammarion, 2009, 9.

English legal systems. In Roman law acts of God were referred to as *vis maior* or *casus*, and in French law as *force majeure*. In English contract law acts of God are no longer referred to as such, but rather as 'frustration'.[14] The terms *vis maior*, *force majeure*, and frustration will therefore be utilised throughout this study to refer to supervening events in each of their respective laws of contract.

But the term 'acts of God' has been deliberately chosen as the title of this book, because of the poignancy of the phrase, which is lacking in the other terms. An act of God is unique in contract law because it cannot be attributed to any human action or omission on the part of the contracting parties. As Treitel notes, when an act of God occurs, both parties are 'equally the victim of an event for which … neither is responsible'.[15] An act of God is truly outside the competence and control of the two contracting parties; it is something which has suddenly overtaken them and has come upon them as an inexorable and overwhelming external force. To call such an occurrence an act of God would seem to be wholly appropriate.

In the 1886 case of *Pandorf & Co v Hamilton, Fraser & Co.* Lord Esher sought to exclude any theological aspects from the meaning of an act of God:

> I shall not now enter into a discussion, which at one time was rather rife, as to what was the exact meaning of the term 'the act of God'. In the older, simpler days I have myself never had any doubt but that it did not mean the act of God in the ecclesiastical and biblical sense, according to which almost everything is said to be the act of God, but that in a mer-cantile sense it meant an extraordinary circumstance which could not be foreseen and which could not be guarded against.[16]

But when an act of God occurs which prevents the realisation of a contract, one or both of the parties may suffer disastrous consequences, resulting per-haps in the failure of their business, the incurring of crippling financial loss, or some other ruinous outcome, for which neither is responsible. The contract-ing parties are certainly the helpless victims of an act of God in 'the mercantile sense', as Lord Esher asserts, but they will very often also go on to question why this has happened to them in the 'ecclesiastical and biblical sense'. Those who suffer, as Fontana notes, 'look for a reason for their suffering'.[17] 'Why has this happened to me?' they wonder, aghast. This is a question which the law cannot answer.

---

14 The phrase 'act of God' is now usually narrowly circumscribed to refer only to natural disas-ters.

15 Sir Guenther Treitel *Frustration and Force Majeure* (third edition) London: Sweet & Max-well, 2014. 550.

16 (1886) 17 QBD 670, 675.

17 David Fontana *Is Christianity Good For You?* Alresford, Hants: John Hunt Publishing Ltd., 2009, 170.

The law does, however, provide the necessary framework for sorting out the adverse consequences which inevitably ensue when an act of God occurs. But the law has often appeared to be 'at a loss to know what justice requires' in this situation.[18] This confusion arises because of the unique character of an act of God. Contract law is premised largely on the principle of personal responsibility.[19] When a contract goes awry, the inquiry will ordinarily focus on fault and intent: 'Who was to blame? What did they intend?'[20] But when an act of God intervenes to frustrate a contract, the contracting parties no longer 'appear as responsible agents but rather as the helpless victims of outside forces'.[21] How is the law to deal with such a situation, when the usual standards of justice do not apply?

This uncertainty in knowing how to proceed is compounded by the difficulty in determining the exact parameters of an act of God. Should the law intervene only when a supervening event has rendered performance impossible by one of the contracting parties, or should intervention occur when performance is still possible, but the nature of the contract has fundamentally changed? If it is the latter case, what are the criteria for determining when the nature of a contract has fundamentally changed? The law must also formulate some method of apportioning the loss between the two innocent parties, or determine which of them must bear the loss.

The Roman, French and English laws of contract have each developed legal rules that address these issues. But the approach adopted by each system is significantly different from that of the others. Moreover, the response to supervening events has differed within both the French and English laws of contract over the course of time. Even the understanding of what constitutes a supervening event has differed from one legal system to another.

The reason behind these widely divergent approaches to supervening events derives, first, from the nature and structure of the legal system as a whole, and then, within that broader context, from the salient characteristics of the system's particular law of contract. As Harris and Tallon make clear, the 'study of a particular legal situation cannot be conducted in isolation from its institutional context'.[22] This is especially true in the domain of contract law, where the various principles of the law are intimately connected to each other, so that a change to one of those principles necessarily effects a change in one or more of the others.[23] This means that the various differing ways in which the three legal systems have each dealt with unforeseen supervening events can only be understood through an examination, first, of the general character of the legal

---

18 Lon L. Fuller *The Morality of Law* (revised edition) New Haven: Yale University Press, 167.
19 Id., 162–167.
20 Id., 167.
21 Id., 167.
22 Donald Harris and Denis Tallon (editors) *Contract Law Today: Anglo-French Comparisons* Oxford: Clarendon Press, 1989, 39.
23 Treitel, op. cit., vii.

system as a whole, and second, of its respective law of contract. This pertains not only with respect to the differences which exist in the current approaches to supervening events, but also with respect to the changing ways in which supervening events have been dealt with within the legal system. Only by knowing in former times how a legal system dealt with supervening events in its broader legal context can one understand how and why that system now deals with supervening events in its present broader legal context. As a result, this book is necessarily in large measure a work of legal history.[24]

The primary focus of this book has been on the French and English legal systems. French law and English law both emerged as recognisable legal systems at more or less the same time in the Middle Ages. The two legal systems developed over the centuries within the same broad currents of European thought, religion, science and morals.[25] In spite of this, the two systems are profoundly different from each other. French law belongs to the Civil Law tradition, which encompasses virtually all of the modern states of contemporary Europe, and which is derived in large part from Roman law. French law has traditionally been held up as an exemplar of the Civil Law tradition.

English law, on the other hand, stands apart from the Civil Law tradition, and is the exemplar of a very different legal system, viz. the Common Law. The Common Law developed quite separately from the rest of continental Europe and was largely uninfluenced by Roman law. Although England has been for several millennia a part of the wider European civilisation, sharing many of the common attributes of that European civilisation, in the domain of law English law has been, and remains, fundamentally different from the Civil Law tradition of continental Europe. The focus on English law and French law, both in their broad contours and in their specific approach to supervening events, thus makes for a very apt comparison. This is not the case with Roman law, which preceded both the English and the French legal systems, with the result that a comparable chronological examination is not possible. Moreover, the ancient world within which Roman law developed presents an entirely different context from that in which both French and English law developed.

This book was initially intended to comprise only two parts, viz the French part and the English part. But it soon became apparent that there would need to be an introductory part on Roman law, given that Roman law has formed the foundational basis of much of the Civil Law of France, including almost all of French contract law. It is thus only possible to fully understand the historical development of French law, and the nature and structure of the French law of contract, by having some prior knowledge of Roman law. Moreover, although Roman law did not exercise any great influence on the development

---

24 As Carl Sagan memorably observed: 'You have to know the past to understand the present': goodreads.com/quotes/194992-you-have-to-know-the-past-to-understand-the-present
25 R.C. van Caenegem *Judges, Legislators and Professors* Cambridge: Cambridge University Press, 1987, 2.

of English law, it did interact in various ways with English law,[26] and it was certainly a powerful influence on Blackburn J. when he first formulated the doctrine of frustration in *Taylor v Caldwell*.[27] It is therefore also necessary to review Roman law in order to fully understand its role in the formation of the doctrine of frustration. The material set out in the Roman law section is there simply to facilitate a better understanding of the French and English laws, which is the study's main purpose.

This book is divided into three unequal chapters. The first, smaller chapter addresses Roman law, and the second and third much larger chapters address French law and English law, respectively. The chapters are structured so as to analyse each legal system in both a vertical and a horizontal manner.[28] The vertical perspective entails a focus on the attributes of the particular legal system under consideration. This will involve an examination of the historical development of that legal system, its broad and general nature and structure, the salient characteristics of its law of contract and finally the approach of that system to the problem of supervening events. This study will only consider the general law with regard to supervening events, and will not focus on *force majeure* clauses. A *force majeure* clause is a clause which provides for the adjustment or termination of the contract when certain specified events affecting the performance or outcome of the contract occur.[29]

The horizontal perspective comprises the comparative aspect of this book. At appropriate points throughout the chapters, comparisons are drawn between the particular subject matter under discussion within that particular legal system and the comparable subject matter within one of the other two legal systems. These comparisons range from a broad analysis of the fundamental differences of the three legal systems to much more specific comparisons of differing aspects of their individual contractual structures and processes. The horizontal perspective will have increasing prominence as the book progresses from chapter to chapter, until it culminates in the Conclusion. Chapter 1 is

---

26 In this regard see, for example, the comments made by Tindell CJ in 1843: 'The Roman law forms no rule, binding in itself upon the subject of these realms: but, in deciding a case upon principles, where no direct authority can be cited from our books, it affords no small evidence of the soundness of the conclusion at which we have arrived, if it proves to be supported by that law, the fruits of the researches of the most learned men, the collective wisdom of ages and the groundwork of the municipal law of most of the countries in Europe': *Acton v Blundell* (1843) 12 M & W 324, 353; 152 ER 1223, 1234.

27 (1863) 3 B&S 826; 122 ER 309.

28 The idea for describing the examination of the subject matter in terms of vertical and horizontal perspectives comes from D.J. Ibbetson 'Natural Law and Common Law' (2001) 5 *Edinburgh Law Review* 4, 20. Ibbetson, however, used the terms to describe a different process of comparison from the one being used here.

29 Although this book does not deal with *force majeure* clauses, there are actually a number of references throughout the book to such clauses. In this regard see pages 2 fn.6, 99 fn.322, 103, 106, 108, 111–112, 126, 204.

entirely vertical in structure, because it simply presents an introductory review of Roman law. Chapter 2, on the other hand, is both vertical and horizontal, because not only does it analyse French law but it also draws comparisons between French law and its Roman law forebear. Chapter 3 is more horizontal still, because it analyses English law and draws comparisons between English law and both Roman and French law. The Conclusion is the most horizontal of all, highlighting the contrasting attributes of frustration in English contract law with those of *force majeure* and *imprévision* in French law, which issue from the different nature and structure of their legal systems and the different characteristics of their respective laws of contract.

1   Roman Law

'Nam homo proponit, sed Deus disponit'. *
Thomas à Kempis

The Development of Roman Law

The history of Rome extends over a period of some 1,200 years, from its purported founding in 753 BC to the 'fall' of Rome in 476 AD. The history of Rome can be divided into three distinct periods: viz. the Monarchy, from 753 BC to 510 BC; the Republic, from 510 BC to 27 BC; and the Empire, from 27 BC to 476 AD. During this time Rome grew from a small town into the capital of an extremely large and diverse empire. By the third century AD the Roman Empire encompassed the entire Mediterranean basin, the Near East and all of western and central Europe up to the Rhine and Danube rivers.

Roman law remained relatively undeveloped until the 'formative period'. The formative period occurred during the final one hundred fifty years of the Republic, i.e. from approximately 177 BC to 27 BC.[1] Following on from the formative period Roman law then reached its most highly developed state. This occurred during the 'classical period', from 27 BC to 235 AD.[2] The mature Roman law was comprised of three parts, viz. the *ius civile*, the *ius honorarium*, and the *interpretatio*.

In 451 BC the first written laws were enacted. These laws were referred to as the Twelve Tables, and are thought to have simply reproduced the pre-existing customary laws in written form. No complete text of the Twelve Tables has survived, although much of its content has been found from other

* Thomas à Kempis *De Imitatione Christi*, Lipsiae: Sumtibus et typis Car. Tauchnitii 1840. See Hathi Trust Digital Library/catalog.hathitrust.org/Record
1 Barry Nicholas *An Introduction to Roman Law* Oxford: Clarendon Press, 1962, 34.
2 John P. Dawson *The Oracles of the Law* Westport, Connecticut: Greenwood Press, Publishers, 1968, 101.

DOI: 10.4324/9781003533450-2

sources.[3] Together with customary law the Twelve Tables constituted the *ius civile*, i.e. the general or common law of Rome, which provided the foundational basis for subsequent developments in the law.

Executive power in the Republican period was exercised by two elected Magistrates, known as Consuls. The Consuls held office for a one year period, and each had power to veto the decisions of the other. The Consuls exercised their authority by issuing edicts, in which they set out their orders and declared the policies which they intended to pursue.[4] In the early days of the Republic the Consuls alone exercised full executive authority in all spheres of life, including that of the law. However, over time additional magisterial offices were created in order to deal with certain specific matters, thereby lightening the duties of the Consuls. The subordinate magistrates exercised full executive power within their specific jurisdictions, although their decisions were subject to veto by the Consuls.

In 367 BC the office of the Praetor was created to administer the *ius civile*. The Praetor was elected for a one year term. In 242 BC the office of a second Praetor was created, and the administration of the civil law was divided between the two Praetors.[5] The Praetors did not have the authority to create new law.[6] Their function was rather to declare the law and to give effect to it by the grant of a remedy as set out in the appropriate form of action.[7]

During the later period of the Republic great innovations were made to Roman law, by which it developed in sophistication and complexity. Very few of these innovations occurred by way of statutory enactment. They occurred instead largely as the result of the manipulation of legal remedies by the Praetors. Roman law was conceived in terms of remedies rather than rights. This meant that a remedy would be available only where there was an appropriate form of action.[8] In the early Republican period there were a very limited number of forms of action, known as the *legis actiones*, and these actions were very rigid and technical in nature. However, by the latter half of the second century BC a more flexible legal procedure, known as the formulary system, replaced the rigid *legis actiones*, and remained in place throughout the classical period. Under this system the Praetors were empowered, after hearing the claims and defences of the litigating parties, to draft forms of action, which exactly defined the issues between the parties, in a set of words known as a *formula*.

3 Peter Stein *Roman Law in European History* Cambridge: Cambridge University Press, 1999, 4.
4 Nicholas, op cit., 17, 18.
5 Id., 4. The two Praetors were known as the *praetor urbanus* (the Urban Praetor) and the *praetor peregrinus* (the Peregrine Praetor).
6 Aldo Schiavone *The Invention of Law in the West* Cambridge, Massachusetts: The Belknap Press of Harvard University Press, 2012, 137.
7 Stein, op. cit., 9.
8 Alan Watson *The Spirit of Roman Law* Athens, Georgia: The University of Georgia Press, 1995, 8.

Although the Praetors did not have the authority to create new law, they were authorised to draft new forms of action. They were thus in effect able to create new causes of action, resulting in claims for which there was no precedent.[9] In such cases the Praetors maintained that 'the claim justified a remedy, and so the law must provide it'.[10] The Praetors always acted as though they were simply implementing the existing law, but in fact they were able to create new law through the grant of new legal remedies. This new law was disguised, because the new remedies were always justified on the basis that they were simply an implementation of the existing *ius civile*. The Praetors were thereby able to introduce legal innovations into the law through the grant of new remedies, while at the same time purporting to uphold the integrity of the *ius civile*.[11]

The Praetors effected the changes to the law primarily through an instrument known as the Praetor's Edict. At the beginning of his term of office each Praetor would issue a comprehensive declaration setting out his policies with regard to the granting or withholding of remedies in given circumstances, as well as model *formulae* for the remedies set out, and standard *formulae* for the enforcement of the *ius civile*. The Praetor's Edict was valid only for the Praetor's term of office, i.e. for one year, but usually most of the Edict was adopted by succeeding Praetors in their Edicts.[12] The Praetor's Edict thus 'acquired the character, though not the form, of a legislative document'.[13] These developments in the law came to be known as the *ius honorarium*, or magisterial law.[14] The *ius honorarium* became the vehicle by which Roman law was fundamentally transformed from the rigid structure of the Twelve Tables into the complex and flexible law of the classical period.

As Roman law became more and more complex, a class of legal experts emerged, who were known as 'jurists'. From the second half of the third century BC onwards the jurists began to play an increasingly important role in developing and explaining Roman law. The jurists were not interested in theoretical generalisations, and their contributions were essentially practical in nature. One of their most important functions was to give advice on specific legal problems that had arisen in actual cases. They advised the Praetors on the contents of the Edict, and whether a new remedy should issue in a novel case. Litigants and their advocates also relied on the jurists when preparing their cases.[15] The jurists drew up legal documents, such as wills and contracts, using their knowledge of the law to ensure that the documents achieved the legal effect desired and no other.[16] The persuasiveness of a jurist's opinion

---

9 Nicholas, op. cit., 20, 21.
10 Stein, op. cit., 9.
11 Schiavone, op. cit., 139; Stein, op. cit., 10.
12 Watson, op. cit. (fn. 8), 3; Nicholas, op. cit., 21.
13 Nicholas, op. cit., 22.
14 Id., 21; Stein, op. cit., 8.
15 Nicholas, op. cit., 29.
16 Stein, op. cit., 13.

depended solely on the strength of that individual's reputation. The writings of the most reputable jurists were reproduced in collections, and over time this resulted in the production of a large body of legal literature.[17] This body of legal literature became extremely influential, and comprised the third part of Roman law, known as the *interpretatio*, or juristic interpretation.

The juristic literature which has survived can be broadly classified into four categories, viz. the expository textbook, the commentary, the monograph and the problematic work.[18] Of these four types, it is the problematic work which best illustrates the nature of Roman law. This type of writing was casuistic and disputatious in nature. The jurist would focus on finding the most pragmatic solution to the specific legal problem which had arisen in a particular case. In arriving at a solution the jurist would analyse conflicting approaches, classify exceptions and draw distinctions. It was the problematic work, as Nicholas notes, which gave Roman law 'its extraordinary richness of detail'.[19]

The Classical Period

During the second and first centuries BC the Republic was beset with ongoing civil wars and power struggles amongst contending generals and populist strongmen. Peace was eventually restored in 27 BC with the victory of Octavian, or Augustus Caesar as he is better known. It is from this date that the Republic effectively ceased to exist and the Roman Empire began.[20]

The reign of Augustus re-established stability and inaugurated a period of some two hundred years of peace, known as the *Pax Romana*. During this time the Empire enjoyed a level of peace and prosperity which enabled it to grow and flourish. This was particularly true in the second century AD when the Empire was governed by a succession of strong and effective emperors. The period of the *Pax Romana* corresponds very closely with the classical period of Roman law, when the law reached its apogee.

During the classical period Roman law continued to develop in sophistication and complexity. But this now occurred by way of refinement rather than by way of further innovation. The Praetor's Edict, for example, which had been the primary instrument for innovation, became more or less fixed in the final years of the Republic, with very few alterations from year to year.[21]

The process of this ever increasing refinement occurred largely through the activity of the jurists, who became the primary agents for legal development and who so honed the law through their writings that Roman law reached

17 Id., 13; Nicholas, op. cit., 29.
18 Nicholas, op. cit., 33.
19 Id., 33.
20 Nicholas, op. cit., 9.
21 In the early second century AD the Emperor Hadrian ordered that the Edict be rendered into permanent form, thereby ensuring that there could be no further developments to the law by this means: Stein, op. cit., 14

its most advanced state. In the Republican period the jurists had been independent men who participated in public life, but in the period of the Empire they increasingly came to be employed within the Imperial Chancery and were amongst the Emperor's most preeminent officials.

From the middle of the second century AD the Emperors had become empowered to make law, so that their enactments now constituted an additional source of law, known as *constitutiones*. Because the Emperor was a magistrate, he was empowered to issue edicts within his sphere, setting out his policies or issuing orders. As the sphere of the Emperor was unlimited, he was able to issue edicts on any topic to which he turned his attention.[22] As a result, the law set out in the writings of the jurists came to be known as *ius*, and that of the Emperors as *lex*. The *ius* became the common law of Rome and the *lex* its legislation.

The *Corpus Iuris Civilis*

Throughout the fourth century AD the situation in the Empire was one of more or less continuous deterioration. Several of the Emperors, such as Constantine the Great, were able to forestall the Empire's decline, but their efforts amounted only to temporary reprieves. The Empire's decline was mirrored in the decline of the law during this period.

By the end of the fourth century Rome was on the point of collapse. It was constantly beset from without by invasions, whilst from within ongoing political and economic crises wracked the state and not infrequently led to chaos. In 410 AD Rome was sacked by the Goths, and in 476 AD the last Emperor, Romulus Augustulus, was overthrown by Odoacer, a Germanic chieftain. This date is traditionally considered to mark the end of the Roman Empire.

But the fall of Rome did not actually mark the end of the Roman Empire in its broader context. In 395 AD the Empire had been divided for administrative purposes into two halves, the Western Empire and the Eastern Empire. The fall of Rome signalled only the collapse of the Western Empire. The Eastern Empire survived, and came to be known as Byzantium. It comprised the territories of Greece, the Balkans, the Anatolian Peninsula, the Near East and Egypt. Byzantium continued to exist until 1453 AD, when Constantinople was conquered by the Ottoman Turks.

In 527 AD Justinian became the Emperor of Byzantium. The many achievements of his long reign, from 527 AD to 565 AD, mark him out 'as the greatest of the Byzantine Emperors'.[23] Justinian wanted to re-establish the Roman Empire to its former grandeur. His programme for doing so involved, *inter*

---

22 Alan Watson *Roman Law and Comparative Law* Athens, Georgia: The University of Georgia Press, 1991, 25.
23 Paul J. du Plessis *Borkowski's Textbook on Roman Law* (sixth edition) Oxford: Oxford University Press, 2020, 22.

alia, a project to restore Roman law to the complexity and sophistication it had attained at its zenith, i.e. during the classical period.

Justinian's efforts to revitalise Roman law began in 528 AD, when he commissioned a group of legal experts, under the direction of his Chancellor Tribonian, to produce a new and up-to-date compilation of the *constitutiones* from the time of Hadrian up to his own reign.[24] Justinian's Commission completed this project relatively quickly, and the new Code entered into force in April 529 AD. A second updated version of the Code was promulgated on 16 November 534 AD.[25]

Justinian then turned his attention to a much more ambitious project, one that had never been attempted. He ordered Tribonian and his Commission to edit the vast array of juristic literature, with a view to compiling the very best elements from it into a Digest.[26] The chosen extracts were to be arranged systematically by titles, according to their subject matter, and the titles would be organised into books.[27] These selected juristic extracts would then become a part of the codified law of Byzantium.[28]

The Commission took three years to complete its work. The Digest came into force on 16 December 533 AD.[29] The Commission chose extracts from the writings of thirty-nine jurists, extending from the first century BC to the fourth century AD. The great majority of extracts came from the classical period, between 100 and 250 AD. As the extracts selected were taken from a period ranging over some three and a half centuries, there were inevitably passages that contradicted each other, both as a result of differences of opinion between jurists and as a result of legal changes occurring in response to historical developments. Although Justinian had authorised the Commission to alter extracts in order to eliminate differences and to better reflect the law of sixth century Byzantium, many inconsistencies still remained in the final version. In some cases, attempts by the Commission to alter passages led to additional discrepancies between the texts.[30]

The Digest and the Code were the two largest and most important parts of Justinian's reforming work, which later came to be known as the *Corpus Iuris Civilis*.[31] The Digest and the Code were supplemented by two other parts of the *Corpus Iuris*, the Institutes and the Novels. The Institutes were essentially an elementary textbook designed for law students. While Tribonian's Commission was still working on the Digest, Justinian ordered that a law

---

24 Hadrian lived from 76 AD to 138 AD. He was Emperor from 117 AD.
25 Nicholas, op. cit., 42.
26 *Digesta* in Latin, *Pandectae* in Greek.
27 The Digest contains fifty books.
28 Schiavone, op. cit., 6.
29 Nicholas, op. cit., 41.
30 Id., 43.
31 The Body of Civil Law. The *Corpus Iuris Civilis* will hereafter be referred to as the *Corpus Iuris*.

textbook also be produced. A short book was then prepared which sum-marised the basic principles of Roman law, and which became known as the *Institutiones Iustiniani*.[32] The Institutes of Justinian were completed in 533 AD, and promulgated with the force of law. The Institutes comprised the third part of the *Corpus Iuris*.[33] The Novels were the fourth part of the *Corpus Iuris*. After the promulgation of the *Corpus Iuris* Justinian continued to issue additional imperial edicts until his death in 565 AD. These edicts, known in Latin as *novellae constitutiones*,[34] were later added to the *Corpus Iuris* as its fourth part.

The great reforming work of Justinian preserved almost all that is now known of the classical law of Rome, when the law was at its apogee. The clas-sical law which remains is to be found almost entirely in the Digest, and very little exists elsewhere. Had not the Digest been compiled this law would have been lost. However, the selective preservation of parts of the juristic litera-ture and the compilation of these excerpts into a codified form had the effect of radically transforming the nature of the classical Roman law. Thus, while 'essential documents were at least partially saved, the links and contexts each of them had actually developed in were erased'.[35] The result, as Schiavone elo-quently put it, is the tantalising knowledge of the existence of a 'vast garden', which, however, can only be narrowly glimpsed 'through a single window'.[36]

The Roman Law of Contracts

Classical Roman law, as noted above, was radically distorted by its transfor-mation into codified form. Nevertheless it is abundantly evident from the extant writings of the jurists that the classical law was pre-eminently 'a law of movement'.[37] It was never considered to be an instrument of equilibrium, and in dealing with it the jurists were not for the most part concerned with stating what the law was. There are thus very few definitions to be found in the Digest.[38] The classical jurists were much more interested in the changes which the law could bring about in certain situations, and thus they analysed the law with regard to when and how a 'particular legal situation would come

---

32 The Institutes of Justinian.

33 The Institutes of Justinian will hereafter be referred to as the Institutes.

34 The New Edicts.

35 Schiavone, op. cit., 11.

36 Id., 10.

37 F.H. Lawson *A Common Lawyer Looks at the Civil Law* Ann Arbor: University of Michigan Law School, 1953, Reprinted by William S. Hein & Company Buffalo, 1988, 96.

38 In fact, Javolenus went so far as to declare that '[e]very definition in civil law is dangerous; for it is rare for the possibility not to exist of it being overthrown': D.50.17.202 (*The Digest of Justinian* (Latin text edited by Theodor Mommsen, with the aid of Paul Krueger; English translation edited by Alan Watson) Philadelphia: University of Pennsylvania Press, 1985, vol-ume 4, 969.)

into existence and how it would disappear'.[39] This orientation focused the attention of the jurists on the law relating to contracts, because by its nature a contract is an instrument which effects change.[40]

As a result the law of contracts is the most original and most admired aspect of Roman law.[41] However, in Roman law there was no single law of contract, whereby general legal principles and rules could be applied to a variety of agreements. There were instead various individual contract types, each of which had its own format and its own procedural peculiarities. Contracting parties therefore had to ensure that their particular agreement conformed to a particular contract type, in order to guarantee its enforceability at law. The Institutes set out four distinct categories of contract, which were classified as real, verbal, literal and consensual contracts.[42] The verbal and literal contracts were formal contracts, whereas the real and consensual contracts were informal contracts.[43]

The earliest contract type in Roman law was the *stipulatio*, which was the most important contract in the category of verbal contracts.[44] As du Plessis notes, the origins of the *stipulatio* are obscure, 'but appear to predate the Twelve Tables'.[45] When parties contracted by *stipulatio*, they had to comply with a formal act, in which they exchanged specific words comprising formalised questions and answers. Under this procedure the promisee would solemnly demand of the promisor whether he agreed to be bound by the terms of his promise, setting out the terms of the promise. The promisor would then solemnly agree that those were indeed the terms of the contract. Thus the promisee would pose the question 'Do you solemnly promise ...' and then state the act to be done by the promisor, whereupon the promisor would declare 'I do solemnly promise' and repeat in exactly the same words the act to be done by him.[46]

---

39 Lawson, op. cit., 96, 97.

40 Id., 98.

41 Watson, op. cit. (fn. 22), 122.

42 The four categories are set out in the Institutes in the above mentioned order, even though the verbal contracts, and in particular, the *stipulatio*, are the earliest of the contract types: Lawson, op. cit., 113.

43 Nicholas, op. cit., 165.

44 The *stipulatio* was by far the most important of the verbal contracts. There were two other specialised verbal contracts, viz. the *dotis dictio* and the *iusiurandum liberti*. See A.M. Prichard *Leage's Roman Private Law* London: MacMillan & Co Ltd. 1961, at pages 331 and 332, for a full description of these two verbal contracts.

45 du Plessis, op. cit, 294.

46 The inverted formal structure of the *stipulatio* required the promisee rather than the promisor to articulate the promise, so that it was the promisor who agreed to the declaration of the promisee. By inverting the ordinary way in which such a transaction would normally occur, i.e. by making the promisee rather than the promisor declare the promise, and the promisor then to agree that this was indeed what he was promising, the *stipulatio* thereby ensured that the content of the promise was defined in a precise and exact manner, and guaranteed that

The *stipulatio* was a formal contract because exact words had to be used, viz. '*spondesne?*' on the part of the promisee, and '*spondeo*' on the part of the promisor.[47] If the parties used other words, the *stipulatio* would not be valid because the parties had failed to conform to its formal requirements.[48] The *stipulatio* had to be concluded verbally between the parties face to face, which meant that they could not contract by correspondence.[49] Although the *stipulatio* placed a legal obligation only on the promisor, this arrangement was not considered to be a *nudum pactum*. In Roman law a *nudum pactum* was a gratuitous promise on the part of the promisor, which had not yet been accepted by the promisee. However, once the promisee did accept the promisor's promise, this constituted an enforceable agreement, even though only the promisor had undertaken an obligation.

The growth of the Roman Empire, and the consequent increase in trade and commerce throughout the Empire, gave rise to the emergence of the second category of contract types, the consensual contracts. The consensual contracts became a part of Roman law in the first century BC. There were four consensual contracts: sale (*emptio venditio*), hire (*locatio conductio*), partnership (*societas*) and mandate (*mandatum*), which together covered the majority of commercial activities.

Unlike the *stipulatio*, the consensual contracts required both parties to perform, in the sense that there were obligations incumbent on both parties. Moreover, the consensual contracts were informal in nature, again unlike the *stipulatio*. This meant that they could be created by the parties without any requisite formalities, which made them extremely flexible. They could be made either orally or in writing, and could be concluded *inter absentes* by means of messengers.[50]

---

attention would not be diverted from 'a dangerous pledge': Sir Henry Maine *Ancient Law* (tenth edition) London: John Murray, Albemarle Street, W., 1920, 340, 341.

47 The verb *spondere* means 'to promise on one's oath'.

48 Nicholas, op. cit., 160. However, as du Plessis points out, during the Republic the formal requirement that the words '*spondesne?*' and '*spondeo*' be used was relaxed to permit the use of other synonyms, such as '*promittisne?*' and '*promitto*' (Do you promise? I promise). Moreover, by the time of the classical period, languages other than Latin were also permitted: du Plessis, op. cit., 296.

49 Watson, op. cit. (fn. 22), 53; Lawson , op. cit. , 116, 117.

50 Roman law was the first legal system to develop such formless contracts, and by doing so greatly facilitated commercial activities throughout the Empire: P.D.V. Marsh *Comparative Contract Law: England, France, Germany* Aldershot: Gower Publishing, 1993, 2. The contract of sale was by far the most significant in this regard: Id., 2. Maine explains the importance of the informal nature of the consensual contracts as follows: 'In the intercourse of life the commonest and most important of all the contracts are unquestionably the four styled consensual. The larger part of the collective existence of every community is consumed in transactions of buying and selling, of letting and hiring, of alliances between men for purposes of business, of delegation of business from one man to another; and this is no doubt the consideration which led the Romans, as it has led most societies, to relieve these transactions from

Although the consensual contracts were informal and flexible in nature, those who entered into them still had to fulfil certain requirements in order to claim that they had concluded a contract of this type. Agreement between the parties was essential for a valid consensual contract to come into existence. Although the consensual contracts were not defined, their various parameters were worked out over time, and each came to have its own particular characteristics and governing rules. Thus, for example, if a contracting party alleged that he had entered into a contract of sale he had to prove the incidents of such a contract, which required an agreement between the parties with respect to a specific thing at a fixed price.[51] If the agreement specified only that 'a reasonable price' be paid for the thing, the agreement would not qualify as a contract of sale.[52]

The real contracts comprised the third category of contract types. The real contracts, like the consensual contracts, were informal in nature, and could therefore be validly agreed upon between the contracting parties without requisite formalities. However, they differed from the consensual contracts in that they did not become effective upon the simple agreement of the parties, although agreement was essential. For contractual obligations to arise it was also necessary that one party deliver a corporeal thing to the other. Only when this occurred would a real contract become legally binding. There were four real contract types, viz. *mutuum*, which was a loan for consumption; *commodatum*, which was a loan for use only; *depositum*, which was the handing over of a thing for safekeeping and not for use; and *pignus*, which was the giving of real security by transfer of possession, otherwise known as a pledge.[53]

Mutuum was the oldest and most important of the real contracts. Like *stipulatio*, it was a unilateral contract because only one party, the borrower, was bound by a legal obligation. In *mutuum* the borrower actually obtained ownership of the thing transferred, and was then obliged to repay to the lender goods of an equivalent kind, quality and quantity.[54] This meant that *mutuum* could be used only with respect to goods which were generic and fungible in nature, such as grain or money. *Mutuum* was the standard contrac-

---

technical incumbrance, to abstain as much as possible from clogging the most efficient springs of social movement': Maine, op. cit., 345.

51 I.3.23.1. (*The Institutes of Justinian* (fifth edition) (translated into English by J.B. Moyle) Oxford: Clarendon Press, 1913, 144.)

52 Nicholas, op. cit., 165.

53 Id., 168. The holder of the thing pledged as a result of *pignus* obtained possession of the thing, whereas the holders of the thing obtained as a result of *commodatum* and *depositum* did not acquire possession and held only on the basis of detention. A possessor was able to protect his possession by recourse to legal remedies but a detentor was not. Under Roman law a detentor had no legal relationship to the thing, even though he held the thing under his physical control: Nicholas, op. cit., 107–116; Reinhard Zimmermann *The Law of Obligations* Oxford: Oxford University Press, 1996, 190, 205, 220, 221.

54 P.J. Thomas *Introduction to Roman Law* Deventer: Kluwer Law and Taxation Publishers, 1986, 91.

tual means for loaning money. Because *mutuum* required only the repayment of the equivalent amount of money loaned, interest was factored in by means of a *stipulatio*.

The remaining three real contracts were concerned with bailment type situations. *Commodatum* involved the gratuitous loan of a particular thing by the lender to the borrower for use by the borrower. Ownership remained with the lender, and the borrower was obliged to return the same thing to the lender at the conclusion of the agreed period. *Depositum* involved the physical transfer of a tangible movable thing from one person to another, with the transferee holding the thing gratuitously for the transferor until such time as the transferor indicated that he wanted it returned to him, at which point it would then be transferred back.[55] *Commodatum* and *depositum* both had to be gratuitous; otherwise, they would fall within the category of hire. *Pignus* arose when the contracting parties agreed that a tangible thing, which could be either a movable or an immovable, would be handed over by the debtor to the creditor as security for a debt. The debtor retained ownership of the thing, and the parties agreed that the thing would be handed back to the debtor upon payment of the debt.

The fourth category of contract types was the literal contract. Like the verbal contracts, such as the *stipulatio*, the literal contract was a formal contract. However, very little is known of the original literal contract, which disappeared relatively early in Roman legal history. Although the literal contract (or perhaps something quite different from the original) was reintroduced by the compilers of the *Institutes*, this subsequent creation of the literal contract was artificial and unimportant.[56]

The Institutes had classified the various contract types into four categories, but there was also a fifth category, which was not addressed in the Institutes. The existence of numerous contract types, each with their own peculiar requirements, could easily create uncertainty. Although there might be no doubt that an agreement had been concluded between the parties, it might nevertheless be unclear what category of contract type they had entered into.[57] This led to the emergence of the so-called 'innominate contracts'. The common attribute of these innominate contracts was that each party would promise to perform something for the other in a *quid pro quo* arrangement.[58] Originally these arrangements were considered to be *nuda pacta*, and therefore not enforceable at law. But over time, and certainly by the time of Justinian, such agreements of mutual promise had become legally enforceable, in those situations where one party had performed and the other had not.[59] As a result the innominate

55 Id., 93.
56 See Nicholas op. cit., at pages 196–198, for a detailed account of the literal contract.
57 Nicholas, op. cit., 189.
58 Lawson, op. cit., 131; Thomas, op. cit., 114.
59 du Plessis, op. cit., 310.

contracts became yet another category of contract, which would be enforced whenever there had been an agreement between the parties and there had been part performance by one of them.[60] The four most common agreements within the category of innominate contracts actually did have specific names, viz. *transactio, permutatio, precarium* and *aestimatum*. The *transactio* was a compromise, i.e. an informal settlement of a legal action, the *permutatio* was a contract of exchange, the *precarium* was a grant of the use of property for a time, and the *aestimatum* was an agreement to give property to another under the obligation to pay an estimated price or return the goods.[61]

Each contract type, as Lawson points out, 'stands by itself' and contains elements that are not found in the other contract types.[62] All of the contract types were addressed at some point or other either in the Institutes or the Digest. However, the two most important contract types, viz. the *stipulatio* and the contract of sale, were given much more attention in the Institutes and the Digest than any of the others.[63]

Liability for Breach of the Contract Types

Across the many contract types, liability for breach varied from contract to contract. The contract types were divided into two broad categories, those which were *stricti iuris*, i.e. 'in strict law', and those which were *bonae fidei*, i.e. 'in good faith'. In general, those contracts which were unilateral in nature, such as the *stipulatio*, were *stricti iuris* in nature, whereas those contracts which were bilateral in nature, such as the contract of sale, were *bonae fidei*.[64] *Stricti iuris* contracts were the older types of contract, and can be traced back to the *ius civile*, whereas '*bonae fidei* contracts were introduced through the *ius honorarium*'.[65]

When a contracting party failed to perform his obligations under a contract *stricti iuris,* liability arose automatically. As an obligation *stricti iuris* was created in accordance with the formal exigencies of the law, the judge was bound

---

60 Thomas, op. cit., 115.

61 Ronald J. Scalise Jr. 'Classifying and Clarifying Contracts' (2016) 76 *Louisiana Law Review* 1064, 1071, 1072. See also du Plessis, op. cit., 310–313.

62 Lawson, op. cit., 147.

63 Id., 150.

64 Nicholas, op. cit., 163. As Nicholas points out, at page 164: 'The idea of good faith does inevitably fit more easily with bilateral contracts than with unilateral contracts. For in a bilateral contract the duties of one party are the counterpart of the duties of the other. In arriving at his decision the judge must strike a balance, and in doing so he can readily take account of matters of good faith. In a unilateral contract, on the other hand, the duty of the defendant has no counterpart in a duty of the plaintiff. The judge has no balance to strike'.

65 du Plessis, op. cit., 258.

to observe and apply the law in a strict and formal manner.[66] Thus, the simple breach of the contractual obligation gave rise to liability without more.[67]

In an action involving the breach of a contract *bonae fidei*, on the other hand, liability for breach arose only when there was a failure to perform in good faith. In order to determine whether good faith was lacking Roman law developed the concepts of *dolus, culpa* and *custodia*.[68] The meaning of *dolus* is fraud or bad faith, and that of *culpa* fault or negligence.[69] Fault and negligence were equated in Roman law with a failure to perform in good faith, even if there had not been actual bad faith on the part of the defendant. This was because the debtor had failed to act as a 'reasonable man' in the circumstances, and had thus failed 'to conform to the objective standards of good faith and the care shown by the reasonable man'.[70] In Roman law the concept of the 'reasonable man' was expressed in terms of the *bonus paterfamilias*, i.e. 'the good father of his family'.

Roman law divided the category of *culpa* into several subcategories. There was *culpa lata*, which amounted to gross fault or negligence, and was little different from *dolus*. There was also *culpa levis,* which constituted a lesser degree of liability. *Culpa levis* could be either *culpa levis in abstracto* or *culpa levis in concreto*. *Culpa levis in abstracto* involved the failure to perform up to the standard of the abstract reasonable man i.e. the *bonus paterfamilias*.[71] *Culpa levis in concreto* involved the failure to render the 'care which the particular individual habitually shows in his own affairs'.[72] Whether a debtor was liable for *culpa levis* of either the abstract or the concrete varieties depended upon the contract type in question.

In the classical period liability could also arise as a result of failing in the duty of *custodia*. The failure to exercise *custodia* was a form of strict liability incumbent on the debtor with regard to the care of a thing. '*Custodia* originated at the time when Romans looked upon consequences as evidence of negligence: if a thing was stolen, then due care had not been taken of it'.[73] Thus, when a debtor failed to exercise *custodia* he became liable, whether or not he had exercised reasonable care. A debtor was liable for ordinary theft, for example, howsoever it occurred, and no matter what measures he had taken to

---

66 Thomas, op. cit., 75; du Plessis, op cit., 258.
67 In the first century BC the debtor was permitted to raise the defence of fraud in a *stricti iuris* action. Before this time, the debtor would be held strictly liable for his failure to perform, even if he had entered into the *stipulatio* as a result of the fraud of the creditor: Nicholas, op. cit., 164.
68 Nicholas, op. cit., 170.
69 Id., 170.
70 Id., 170.
71 Id., 170.
72 Id., 170.
73 Prichard op. cit., 327.

prevent it.[74] However, by the time that the *Corpus Iuris* was drafted, *custodia* had ceased to be a basis of liability. The combined influence of Christianity and Greek philosophy had produced a different understanding of contractual liability, in which a debtor could not be held liable for breach of contract unless he had been at fault.[75]

Vis Maior

The debtor could avoid liability if he could prove that his contractual obligations either were or had become objectively impossible to perform, without fault on his part. This principle was set out in the Digest in the maxim '*Impossibilium nulla obligatio*'.[76] The principle included both legal impossibility and physical impossibility. The impossibility to perform could be either an inherent aspect of the contract or it could arise as a result of a supervening event.

Impossibility of performance *ab initio* would arise when the purported contract contained an inherent defect which immediately rendered performance impossible. When there was initial impossibility, no contract would come into existence.[77] The Institutes declared that a *stipulatio* would be invalid when the promisor stipulated for the delivery of a thing that did not or could not exist:

> Anything, whether movable or immovable, which admits of private ownership, may be made the object of a *stipulatio*; but if a man stipulates for the delivery of a thing which either does not or cannot exist ... the contract will be void.[78]

The section then goes on to state that a *stipulatio* would also be invalid when the promisor stipulated for the delivery of a thing which was sacred or religious in character, thinking that the article in question was capable of human ownership, or which was public, thinking that it was private, or a thing which he was incapable of owning, or which was his already.[79] The common element

---

74 Nicholas, op. cit., 170.

75 Thomas, op. cit., 80.

76 'There is no obligation to do anything which is impossible'. D.50.17.185, per Celsus.

77 As Buckland and McNair state, 'When the impossibility is known to the parties at the time of agreement, it is clear that the essentials of a contract are lacking; when they were not aware of the impossibility, it is usual in our law to base the nullity of the contract on mistake': W.W. Buckland and Arnold McNair *Roman Law and Common Law* Cambridge: Cambridge University Press, 1936, 178.

78 I.3.19.1 The unedited text reads as follows: 'Anything, whether movable or immovable, which admits of private ownership, may be made the object of a stipulation; but if a man stipulates for the delivery of a thing which either does not or cannot exist, such as Stichus, who is dead but whom he thought alive, or an impossible creature, like a hippocentaur, the contract will be void'.

79 I.3.19.2.

was the impossibility of fulfilling the promise *ab initio*. When this occurred the *stipulatio* would be invalid. Initial impossibility occurred as a result of a mistake on the part of the debtor, rather than as the result of a supervening event. A *stipulatio* which was invalid from the outset by reason of the impossibility of the obligation would not become valid even if the obligation in question subsequently became possible of performance. An impossible condition annexed to an obligation would also invalidate the *stipulatio*.[80]

Impossibility of performance could also occur as the result of a supervening event, which did not involve any fault on the part of the debtor. In such circumstances, the debtor was relieved of liability for his non-performance, even when the contract was *stricti iuris*, such as the *stipulatio*.[81] Supervening events which rendered performance impossible without fault on the part of the debtor were referred to as '*vis maior*' or '*casus*'. The term *vis maior* is usually translated as 'superior or irresistible force'. It can also be translated as 'inevitable accident' or an 'act of God'. The term '*casus*' can be translated as 'fall, overthrow; error; accident, chance, event; occasion; danger, risk; death'.

There is no definition of either *vis maior* or *casus* in the *Corpus Iuris*. The absence of any definition was characteristic of the Roman jurists, who were much more interested in working out the resolution of specific legal problems than in defining legal concepts.[82] Almost all of the references to *vis maior* or *casus* which appear in the *Corpus Iuris* deal with identifying and analysing their consequences in specific situations. Most references in the Digest involve some type of catastrophe, and include both natural disasters and manmade events. The jurist Ulpian, for example, set out a series of catastrophes, of both the natural and manmade varieties:

> Accidents to and deaths of animals which occur without culpability, flights of slaves which are not habitually under guard, armed robberies, riots, fires, floods, and attacks of pirates are no one's fault.[83]

Fires and floods are frequently noted throughout the Digest as natural disasters which amount to *vis maior*.[84] The death of animals is also mentioned.[85] Other natural disasters include the following: the unexpected death of a

---

80 I.3.19.11.
81 A debtor in the classical period who would otherwise be liable in *custodia* was also excused in such circumstances.
82 See pages 11 *supra, and 32-33 infra*.
83 D.50.17.23, per Ulpian.
84 *Fires and Floods:* With regard to fires, see D.2.13.6.9, per Ulpian; D.3.5.21, per Gaius; D.4.4.11.5, per Ulpian; D.13.6.18, per Gaius; D.18.1.58, per Papinian; D.39.2.24.4, per Ulpian; and D.50.17.23, per Ulpian. With regard to floods, see D.7.4.23, per Pomponius; D.18.6.11, per Scaevola; D.39.2.24.3, per Ulpian; D.39.2.24.4, per Ulpian; D.39.3.2.6, per Paul; and D.50.17.23, per Ulpian.
85 *The Death of Animals:* D.50.17.23, per Ulpian.

slave,[86] shipwreck,[87] the collapse of a house or building,[88] the cracking apart of the earth,[89] landslide,[90] earthquake,[91] storms[92] and the force of the wind[93] and the hazards of navigation.[94] The various manmade disasters enumerated by Ulpian, viz. the unforeseen flight of slaves, armed robbery, attack by pirates or enemies and riots, are noted as instances of *vis maior* or *casus* throughout the Digest.[95]

The Institutes also discuss *vis maior*, albeit without referring to the concept by name, and only in the context of the *stipulatio* and the contract of sale. The Institutes point out that a *stipulatio* would be invalid not only when there was initial impossibility of performance but also when the *stipulatio* could not be performed by virtue of supervening impossibility:

> Conversely, a *stipulatio* which originally was perfectly good may be avoided by the thing, which is its object, acquiring any of the characters just specified through no fault of the promisor.[96]

The reference to 'characters just specified' in this passage was the same as that set out in the passage dealing with initial impossibility, viz. the delivery of a thing which does not or cannot exist, or which is sacred, religious or public in character, or which the promisor was incapable of owning, or which was his already.

The Institutes also discussed supervening events in the context of the contract of sale. Although *vis maior* is not explicitly referred to, it is clear that the concept is being invoked. The relevant passage refers to a number of specific situations in which the vendor will not be liable, provided there was no fault on his part:

---

86 *The Unexpected Death of a Slave*: D.4.4.11.5, per Ulpian; and D.13.6.18, per Gaius.
87 *Shipwreck*: D.2.13.6.9, per Ulpian; D.4.9.3.1, per Ulpian; and D.13.6.18, per Gaius.
88 *The Collapse of a House or Building*: D.3.5.21, per Gaius; D.28.5.8, per Julian; and D. 39.2.24.4, per Ulpian.
89 *The Cracking Apart of the Earth*: D. 4.4.11.5, per Ulpian.
90 *Landslide*: D.18.6.11, per Scaevola.
91 *Earthquake*: D.39.2.24.3, per Ulpian; D.39.2.24.4, per Ulpian; and D.39.3.2.6, per Paul.
92 *Storms*: D.4.6.38, per Ulpian; D.18.1.78.3, per Labeo; D.39.2.24.4, per Ulpian; and D.39.3.2.6, per Paul.
93 *The Force of the Wind*: D.7.1.12, per Ulpian; D.18.1.58, per Papinian; and D.39.2.24.4, per Ulpian,
94 *Hazards of Navigation*: D.4.6.38, per Ulpian.
95 *The Unforeseen Flight of Slaves*: D.4.4.11.5, per Ulpian; D.13.6.18, per Gaius; and D.50.17.23, per Ulpian.
    Armed Robbery: D.13.6.18, per Gaius; and D.50.17.23, per Ulpian.
    Attack by Pirates: D.4.9.3.1, per Ulpian; D.13.6.18, per Gaius; and D.50.17.23, per Ulpian.
    Attack by Enemies: D.13.6.18, per Gaius.
    Riots: D.50.17.23, per Ulpian.
96 I.3.19.2.

... if a slave dies, or is injured in any part of his body, or if a house is either totally or partially burnt down, or if a piece of land is wholly or partially swept away by a river flood, or is reduced in acreage by an inundation, or made of less value by a storm blowing down some of its trees, the ... vendor is not responsible and does not suffer for anything not due to any design or fault of his own.[97]

The specific events referred to in this paragraph are also referred to in various passages in the Digest, in which they are specifically indicated to be instances of *vis maior*.

Although the terms '*vis maior*' and '*casus*' were the terms most used throughout the *Corpus Iuris* to refer to supervening events, various other terms were also used. *Casus maior*, for example, is a term which is sometimes used instead of *vis maior*. *Casus minor*, on the other hand, is a term not found in the *Corpus Iuris*. The term *casus minor* was coined in the nineteenth century in order to denote those supervening events in relation to *custodia* which, unlike *vis maior*, did not exempt the debtor from liability.[98] Some Roman law scholars use the term *casus minor* to indicate events, such as theft, which could have been prevented by the debtor, had he taken the appropriate measures. They are thereby able to differentiate such events from those which come within the category of *vis maior*, which were considered unpreventable.[99]

The term '*casus fortuitus*' also appears at various points throughout the Digest. This term is likewise used by some scholars to denote an event which could have been prevented by the debtor had he taken the appropriate measures. In other words, some scholars use the term '*casus fortuitus*' as a synonym for the term '*casus minor*'. Thomas, for example, declares as follows:

The practical consequence in classical law was that these debtors were liable for their *mala fides* as well as for *casus fortuitus*, an accident; e.g. if performance became impossible because the thing in question was stolen and there was no negligence on the part of the debtor.[100]

---

97 I.3.23.3.
98 The term '*casus minor*' was first used by J. Baron 'Die Haftung bis zur höheren Gewalt' (1892) 78 *Archiv für die civilistische Praxis* 203 et seq: 'Thus one can say that "liability for *custodia* implied a liability for lesser accidents (*casus minor*), i.e. ... a liability for any loss not to be attributed to *vis maior*"'. Quoted in Reinhard Zimmermann *The Law of Obligations* Oxford: Oxford University Press, 1996, 193, fn. 56.
99 See, for example, A.-E. Giffard et Robert Villers *Les Obligations dans le Droit Romain et dans l'Ancien Droit Français* Paris: Dalloz, 1970, 334. Zimmermann notes that this understanding of liability with regard to *custodia* is the 'prevailing view' amongst contemporary Roman law scholars: Zimmermann, op. cit., 193.
100 Thomas, op. cit., 79. See also pages 93 and 103. Giffard et Villars also distinguish between *vis maior* and *casus fortuitus* as two types of unforeseen and external accident of differing severity. See for example, Giffard et Villars, op. cit., 334, where they employ the term '*cas*

The problem with using *casus fortuitus* in this way is that there are some passages in the Digest in which the term is clearly used as an alternative for *vis maior*. One such example is the following:

> Often it happens that deposited property or monies are at the risk of him with whom they are deposited, for example, if this has been expressly agreed. But, also if someone has offered himself as a depositee, the same Julian writes that he assumed the risk of the deposit, so that he is liable not only for fraud, but even for fault and *custodia*, not, however, for an act of God (*non tamen casu fortuitos*).[101]

In this passage, *casus fortuitus* is clearly used as the equivalent of *vis maior* rather than as some contrasting lesser category of external but preventable accident.

Zimmermann challenges the idea that there exists some lesser category of external but preventable accident, whether it be referred to as *casus minor* or *casus fortuitus*. He argues that *custodia* did not originally involve a 'category of liability' but rather 'the content of an obligation'.[102] That obligation was the guarantee to keep an object safe.[103] But the obligation was binding upon the debtor only insofar as it was humanly possible to perform. In situations which were beyond the control of the debtor, i.e. situations involving *vis maior*, the debtor would therefore not be held to his obligation.[104]

The Risk of Loss

The risk of loss was an integral aspect of *vis maior*. When contractual performance became impossible through no fault of either contracting party the law then had to determine which of them would bear the loss. The resolution of this issue was particularly important when it involved the destruction of the object of the contract. In fact, the Roman jurists were much more interested in addressing this particular question, given the differing degrees of liability of the various contract types, than they were in specifically addressing the concept of *vis maior*.[105] Their primary focus was usually to determine which party

---

fortuit', i.e. the French translation of *casus fortuitus*, as the equivalent French term for *casus minor*.

101 D.16.3.1.35, per Ulpian. See also D.39.2.24.3, per Ulpian: 'Does this stipulation cover only such injury as arises through illegal actions or any sort of injury originating externally? Labeo, at least, writes that no action can be brought over injury caused, say, by earthquake or the force of a river or any other accidental event (*quo casu fortuito*)'.

102 Zimmermann, op. cit., 194.

103 Id., 194.

104 Id., 194.

105 C.G. Hall 'An Unsearchable Providence: The Lawyer's Concept of Act of God' (1993) 13 *Oxford Journal of Legal Studies* 228, 229.

would be liable and who would therefore bear the loss of the object, in various circumstances. *Vis maior* would often be referred to in such analyses simply as one of the possible variables.

The two consensual contracts of sale and hire involved the transfer of an object from one of the contracting parties to the other. So too did the four real contracts, viz. *mutuum, commodatum, depositum* and *pignus*. It was therefore necessary to know upon whom the risk of loss would fall in each of these contract types should the object be destroyed by *vis maior*. As has been observed above, the two most important contract types in Roman law were the *stipulatio* and the contract of sale, and it was with regard to these two contract types that the Roman jurists devoted the most attention.

Two elements had to be satisfied for a contract of sale to be 'perfected', viz. that the parties had to agree on the object of the sale and the sale price.[106] Until this occurred the risk of loss fell upon the seller. However, once the parties had agreed on the object of the sale and the sale price the contract of sale then became 'perfect' and the risk of loss was borne by the buyer.[107] The issue is dealt with extensively in the Institutes:

> As soon as the contract of sale is concluded – that is, as we have said, as soon as the price is agreed upon, if the contract is not in writing - the thing sold is immediately at the risk of the purchaser, even though it has not yet been delivered to him... The vendor is not responsible and does not suffer for anything not due to any design or fault of his own.[108]

Thus, should some catastrophe constituting *vis maior* intervene before delivery could be effected, the loss of the object was to be borne by the creditor rather than the debtor. The purchaser would therefore still be required to pay for the object even though he would not receive it. The passage in the Institutes continued as follows:

> And if a slave who has been sold runs away, or is stolen, without any design or fault of the vendor, one should look to see whether the latter expressly undertook to keep him safely until delivery was made; for, if he did this, the loss falls upon him, though otherwise he incurs no liability: and this is a rule which applies to all animals and other objects whatsoever.[109]

In other words, the risk of loss before delivery would be borne by the debtor, i.e. the seller, only if the contracting parties had explicitly so agreed. Otherwise,

106 du Plessis, op cit., 271.
107 Id., 271.
108 I.3.23.3.
109 I.3.23.3.

it would be borne by the purchaser. This was known as the rule of *periculum emptoris*, which means 'the risk is on the buyer'.

The *Corpus Iuris* provides no explanation why the loss should fall on the purchaser rather than on the vendor, in the event of *vis maior*. However, this rule may have had its origin in the effect of *vis maior* on the *stipulatio*. As the *stipulatio* was a one-sided arrangement, in which the promisor undertook to do something for the promisee without any corresponding obligation on the part of the promisee, it would be natural to assume that the promisee would suffer no loss should performance of the *stipulatio* become impossible as a result of *vis maior*.

It was also possible to create reciprocal obligations by way of the *stipulatio*. This was done by drawing up two *stipulationes*. One of the contracting parties would be the promisor in the first *stipulatio*, and the other contracting party the promisor in the second *stipulatio*. In this way a sale could be concluded. The promisor in the first *stipulatio*, i.e. the vendor, would promise to transfer the ownership of a certain thing to the promisee, i.e. the purchaser. In the second *stipulatio*, the promisor, i.e. the purchaser, would promise to pay a certain amount of money to the promisee, i.e. the vendor. If the object of the first *stipulatio* was destroyed by *vis maior*, this relieved the promisor, the vendor, of his obligation to deliver the thing to the promisee, the purchaser.[110] The question then arose as to whether the promisor of the corresponding *stipulatio* was still obliged to fulfil his obligation, even though he would not now receive the object as promisee in the corresponding *stipulatio*. As Buckland and McNair note, this 'question is nowhere directly answered, either way' in the *Corpus Iuris*.[111] But by virtue of the fact that the *stipulatio* was a *stricti iuris* contract, it may very well have been the case that the promisor of the second *stipulatio*, the purchaser, was still obliged to honour his promise. Thus, in situations where a sale had been concluded on the basis of two corresponding *stipulationes*, and the thing to be sold had been destroyed by *vis maior*, the purchaser, who was the promisor in the second *stipulatio*, still had to pay the purchase price, and therefore bore the loss of the object which had been destroyed. If this was indeed the practice, then when the contract of sale came to replace corresponding *stipulationes* as the normal way of buying and selling, the rule that the purchaser was to bear the loss in the event of *vis maior* would have been continued with respect to contracts of sale.[112]

---

110   See, for example, D.45.1.23, per Pomponius: 'If by reason of a legacy or as a result of a *stipulatio* you owe me a certain man, you will not be liable to me after his death, except where it was your fault that you did not give him to me when he was still alive. This happens if you either failed to give him when requested or killed him'; D.45.1.33, per Pomponius: 'If Stichus has been promised to be given on a certain date and dies before that date, the promisor is not liable'; D.45.1.37, per Paul: 'If I stipulate certain monies, for instance, those which are in a strongbox, and these are lost through no fault of the promisor, we are owed nothing'.
111   Buckland and McNair, op. cit., 180.
112   Id, 178–180.

The contracts of *locatio conductio, mutuum, commodatum, depositum* and *pignus* also dealt with the transfer of goods from one party to another and therefore required rules to assign the risk of loss in the event of *vis maior*. The contract of *locatio conductio* was divided into three subcategories, viz. agreements for the hiring of a thing in order to use it, in return for a monetary payment (*locatio conductio rei*); agreements for the hiring of one's labour, in return for a monetary payment (*locatio conductio operarum*); and agreements in which one party contracted either to make something for the other party from material supplied by the other party, or to work upon that material in some way for the benefit of the other party (*locatio conductio operis (faciendi)*). The risk of loss as a result of *vis maior* will be examined by contrasting the approach taken in the *locatio conductio rei* and the *locatio conductio operarum*.[113]

In the contract of sale, counter-performance could still be demanded by the party who could no longer himself perform, when the non-performance was the result of *vis maior*, by virtue of the rule of *periculum emptoris*.[114] When *vis maior* intervened in contracts of hire, counter-performance could also be demanded if the contract was *locatio conductio operarum* (i.e. the hire of one's labour), but could not be demanded if the contract was *locatio conductio rei* (i.e. the hire of a thing). The rule allocating the risk of loss in the contract of the hire of a thing was known as *periculum locatoris*, and the rule allocating risk in the hire of one's labour was known as *periculum conductoris*.[115]

Under a contract *locatio conductio rei* the thing hired could be either a movable or an immovable. Thus the contract could involve either the hiring of a chattel, or the renting of a building or field. Should the thing to be hired be destroyed while still in the possession of the person letting it out, the hirer was relieved of his obligation to pay for it.[116] On the other hand, if the hirer already detained the thing, and it was destroyed without fault on his part, i.e. as a result of *vis maior*, the hirer was relieved of liability, and was not required to pay for the period in which he was unable to use the thing hired.[117] In this regard the Institutes declared as follows:

> Where a man has either given or promised hire for the use of clothes, silver, or a beast of burden, he is required in his charge of it to show as much care as the most diligent father of a family shows in his own affairs; if he do this, and still accidentally lose it, he will be under no obligation to restore either it or its value.[118]

---

113 For a detailed analysis of the risk of loss in the case of the *locatio conduction operis (faciendi)* see Zimmermann op. cit., 401–404.
114 Zimmermann, op. cit., 370.
115 Id, 370, 401.
116 Prichard, op. cit., 362.
117 Thomas, op. cit., 106.
118 I.3.24.5.

The same rule applied with regard to the renting of a building or field. Thus, should a rented building 'be swallowed by an earthquake', or rented cornfields destroyed by a marauding enemy army, the hirer would not be required to pay the rent when he had suffered the loss of the thing hired as a result of *vis maior*.[119] It was therefore the owner who bore the loss, because he could not enforce the counter-performance from the hirer.[120]

The situation was reversed when the contract of hire was *locatio conductio operarum*, i.e. one which involved the hiring of a person's labour. In such contracts the party being hired, i.e. the labourer, was entitled to demand counter-performance from the hirer, i.e. the employer, when the labourer was unable to perform as a result of the intervention of *vis maior*. Thus, the risk was upon the employer in cases of earthquake, invading armies and such like.[121] But of course the non-performance by the labourer had to be without fault on his part; otherwise, he would be liable for non-performance. Whether or not the illness of the labourer came within the ambit of *vis maior* is unknown.[122]

The risk of loss was also of fundamental importance in the four real contracts, all of which involved a thing as their object. However, *mutuum*, i.e. the loan for consumption, was qualitatively different from the other three real contracts, and this difference had important consequences in the allocation of the risk of loss. Under the contract of *mutuum* title to the thing was transferred to the party receiving it, which thereby entitled him to consume it or otherwise use it as he saw fit. The borrower was therefore under an obligation only to return property of an equivalent kind and amount to the lender. This meant that there was no question of who should bear the risk in case of destruction or loss as a result of *vis maior*. The 'borrower' naturally assumed the risk of loss for property which was his own, and which was in his possession.

The arrangement in a contract of *mutuum* was thus fundamentally different from the situation which pertained in the other three real contracts. In the loan for use only (*commodatum*), deposit (*depositum*) and pledge (*pignus*), the title of the thing transferred remained with the transferor. Possession was transferred to the transferee in the case of *pignus*, and detention in the case of *commodatum* and *depositum*. If the borrower did not exercise the requisite duty of care towards the thing in contracts of *pignus*, *commodatum* and *depositum*, he was responsible for the loss or damage of the thing. But the borrower could escape liability if he could demonstrate that there had been *vis maior*.

119 Zimmermann, op. cit., 369, 370.
120 However, not all inevitable accidents came within the rule of *periculum locatoris*. Risks which were an integral aspect of the process of farming, such as situations in which crops were destroyed by worms or weeds, were to be borne by the farmer, i.e. the hirer: Zimmermann, op. cit., 370, 371. In this regard see D.19.2.15.2, per Ulpian.
121 Zimmermann, op. cit., 386. This is provided for in the Digest at D.19.2.38, per Paul: 'A man who leases out his labour should receive wages for the entire term if he is not responsible for his labour not being rendered'.
122 Id., 386.

There is a telling passage in the Institutes, contrasting liability for loss in *mutuum* and *commodatum*:

> So too a person to whom a thing is lent for use *(commodatum)* is laid under a real obligation, and is liable to the action on a loan for use. The difference between this case and a loan for consumption *(mutuum)* is considerable, for here the intention is not to make the object lent the property of the borrower, who accordingly is bound to restore the same identical thing. Again, if the receiver of a loan for consumption *(mutuum)* loses what he has received by some accident, such as fire, the fall of a building, shipwreck, or the attack of thieves or enemies, he still remains bound: but the borrower for use *(commodatum)*, though responsible for the greatest care in keeping what is lent him – and it is not enough that he has shown as much care as he usually bestows on his own affairs, if only someone else could have been more diligent in the charge of it – has not to answer for loss occasioned by fire or accident beyond his control, provided it did not occur through any fault of his own.[123]

The references to fire, the collapse of a building, shipwreck and the attack of thieves or enemies are clearly instances of *vis maior*, but with regard to *mutuum*, these instances will not avail the borrower, because the thing transferred has become his property. With *commodatum*, on the other hand, the borrower would be able to escape liability if he could demonstrate that the loss or damage of the specific thing borrowed occurred as a result of the instances set out in the above passage, and without any fault on his part.

There was another difference between *mutuum* and the other three real contracts, which also had a bearing on the issue of *vis maior*. With *mutuum*, the thing which was transferred to the transferee was necessarily generic in nature, and the obligation of the transferee was simply to return to the transferor generic goods of the equivalent amount and quality. This was in contrast to the other three real contracts, in which a specific thing was loaned or bailed to the borrower, and the borrower was required to return that specific item. In Roman law generic goods were held not to perish.[124] *Vis maior* therefore could not apply to the contract of *mutuum*, because performance could never become impossible.[125]

123 I.3.14.2.
124 Thomas, op. cit., 92.
125 Id., 92.

Summary

Roman private law developed into the most advanced and sophisticated legal system in the ancient world, and was far superior to any other legal system then in existence. Its development can be attributed in large measure to its capacity for continuous innovation. These innovations did not occur through major legislative interventions. They occurred rather through the additions and alterations to the Praetor's Edict, and as a result of the analytical refinements effected by the jurists in their *interpretationes.* Roman law thus developed over a period of several centuries into the intellectually rich and sophisticated legal system which it became through a process of gentle, albeit ongoing, accretion.[126]

Equally important in the development of Roman law was the fact that it evolved at the hands of practical men. The Praetors and the jurists were motivated primarily by pragmatic considerations to resolve actual problems as and when they arose. Neither Praetors nor jurists were concerned with formulating general principles or abstract concepts, which are conspicuously absent from Roman law.

The pragmatic character of Roman law is eminently reflected in the Roman law of contracts. In its early stages Roman law had only one type of contract, viz. the *stipulatio*, which adequately addressed most contractual needs. But over time, with the increasingly complex nature of Roman society, the expansion of Empire, and the growth of trade and commerce, the *stipulatio* became unable to respond to novel types of contractual arrangements. It was therefore sheer practical necessity which prompted the emergence of the other types of contractual arrangements in Roman law. Each new type of contract 'arose subsequent to *stipulatio* when, for whatever reason, a *stipulatio* was inappropriate or inefficient for that type of situation and when there was a societal need'.[127] All of these new contract types, unlike the *stipulatio*, were defined by their function rather than by form, thereby demonstrating that they were each originally formulated to deal with a specific situation for which *stipulatio* was unsuited.

The essentially pragmatic nature of Roman law was also manifested in the high degree of conceptualisation and the lack of generalisation in the law of contracts.[128] Conceptualisation is the process of defining ever more precisely the exact parameters of a particular contract type, and being able to distinguish those parameters from other contract types, in order to determine which contract type was appropriate in a particular fact situation. Generalisation, on the other hand, is the process of identifying elements common to all contract

---

126 Watson, op., cit. (fn. 8), 124.
127 Id., 127.
128 Id., 146.

types, in order to derive general principles which are integral to all contractual arrangements.

Conceptualisation was vitally important in Roman contract law because of the nature of the Roman *formulae*, or actions. It was necessary for a creditor, in prosecuting his case, to proceed by way of the *formula* which correctly addressed his particular circumstances. If he chose the wrong *formula* – for example, by proceeding in an action on a contract of sale, when the contractual arrangement between him and the debtor was actually one of hire – his case would be dismissed and he would not be able thereafter to recommence proceedings with another action on the same facts.[129] It was thus essential to determine the exact parameters of the various contract types, because this was the basis for knowing how to proceed with the correct action. As a result, the jurists concentrated their efforts on conceptualisation, i.e. on determining the exact parameters of each contract type. On the other hand, they expended virtually no effort in identifying the common elements of the various contract types, as this served no purpose in the actual functioning of the law. Consequently Roman law never developed a general law of contract, and the various contract types remained distinct and sharply delineated from each other, with their own particular characteristics and requirements..

One of the most distinctive and individualised aspects of the contract types was that of liability. As has been seen, liability was strict when the contract in question was *stricti iuris*, but only arose in a *bonae fidei* contract when one of the contracting parties was at fault. The test of fault, however, differed from contract type to contract type. Liability therefore might or might not arise for a given standard of conduct depending on the type of contract in question. But whatever the standard of liability for a given contract type, liability would not arise when the purported obligation was actually an impossibility, or when, without fault on the part of the debtor, some supervening event had occurred which prevented him from performing his contractual obligation.

Vis maior was thus the antithesis of contractual liability, whatever the type of contract. The jurists, given their pragmatic approach, sought to identify specific situations in which *vis maior* would arise, and so relieve a debtor of liability. In this regard they produced lists of natural disasters and manmade events which they considered would qualify, frequently referencing each other in order to buttress their conclusions. But no jurist ever produced a definition of *vis maior* which addressed the common and essential elements of the items on their various lists.

Although *vis maior* was not defined in the *Corpus Iuris*, fundamental elements of the concept can be gleaned from the language used by the jurists and from the specific examples to which they refer. *Vis maior* clearly had to be something which could not be resisted by the debtor. This can be ascertained from the very term itself, which translates into 'superior' or 'irresistible force'.

---

129 Id., 90.

Vis maior was also an event which had to have been unforeseen by the parties when they concluded their contract. Moreover, its occurrence had to render performance by the debtor impossible. *Vis maior* was not extended to those situations in which the debtor could still perform, although the intervening situation had rendered that performance more onerous.[130] This conclusion is reinforced by reference to the way Roman law dealt with the consequences of *vis maior* involving reciprocal *stipulationes*. If it was indeed the case, as seems highly likely, that when *vis maior* intervened to destroy the subject matter of one of the two reciprocal *stipulationes*, this relieved the debtor of that *stipulatio* of his obligation, but did not relieve the debtor of the corresponding *stipulatio* of his obligation.[131] In other words, Roman law did not permit a contract to be terminated when a fundamental change of circumstances had occurred in cases when performance by the debtor was still possible. This reflected the essentially pragmatic nature of the Roman law jurists. Restricting *vis maior* to situations of impossibility of performance ensured that identifying *vis maior* would be simple and straightforward, and would avoid the complexities involved in trying to determine what exactly amounted to a fundamental change in circumstance.

---

130 Buckland and McNair, op. cit., 185.
131 See pages 28 *supra*.

2   French Law

'Non, l'avenir n'est à personne. Sire, l'avenir est à Dieu'.*
                                                     Victor Hugo

The Historical Background to French Law

After the fall of Rome in 476 AD Western Europe experienced a period of considerable retrogression. This period is known as the Dark Ages, and lasted for some five hundred years. The law, such as it was, was either Germanic customary law or a much debased Roman law. In either case the law was primitive and undeveloped, reflecting the societal conditions of the time.

In France the debased Roman law applied in the southern part of the country, where the majority of the population were romanised Gauls. In the northern part, occupied mainly by Franks and other Germanic peoples who had migrated there, Germanic customary laws applied. France was thus divided into two quite different legal regimes. South of the Loire was the *pays de droit écrit*: that part of France in which a simplified Roman law applied. North of the Loire was the *pays de droit coutumier*: that part of France in which differing customary laws applied from region to region.

In the eleventh century, Western Europe began to emerge from the Dark Ages. This period is sometimes referred to as the First Renaissance. Towns grew up, trade and commence expanded, universities were established and learning flourished. It was during this period that the law began to develop into a more sophisticated form. This occurred as a result of the discovery in northern Italy of a copy of the Digest, which up to that point had been completely unknown in Western Europe.[1] The discovery of the Digest was of monumental importance, because it 'represented the only part [of the *Corpus*

---

* Hugo, Victor 'Napoléon II' *Les Chants du crépuscule* Bruxelles: Mélines, Cans et Compagnie 1842. Source gallica.bnf.fr/Bibliothèque nationale de France

1 In spite of Justinian's great codifying project, the *Corpus Iuris* never really became an effective part of the Byzantine legal order. This was due in large measure to the fact that the *Corpus Iuris* was written in Latin, and hence incomprehensible to a majority of the Greek-speaking population of Byzantium, including its legal class. See Barry Nicholas *An Introduction to Roman Law* Oxford: Clarendon Press, 1962, 45, for a detailed account of the fate of the *Corpus Iuris* in Byzantium.

DOI: 10.4324/9781003533450-3

Iuris] that directly featured the thinking of the great Roman jurists'.[2] As such, it provided a rich source of legal ideas and arguments, and encapsulated the fertility and dynamism of the classical Roman law.

This superior law was first expounded and developed largely within an academic context. The Civil Law which eventually emerged from the study of the Digest was a legal system in which academic influences exercised the greatest impact. Ironically, the very deficiencies of the Digest, viz. the inconsistencies and the contradictions found in its extracts, ensured that it was studied assiduously by the most acute legal minds. The scholars of the Middle Ages considered the *Corpus Iuris* to be 'the single authoritative expression of right order'.[3] It therefore followed that the Digest necessarily had to be the expression of 'rational harmony'.[4] The Digest was in reality no such thing. But given the *zeitgeist* of the Age the defects of the Digest now became its virtues:

> Had it been a simple, systematic, closely coherent statement of sixth-century law, it could not have been so successfully adapted to the evolving needs of medieval society (and still less to those of later centuries). But, as it was, it provided an almost inexhaustible fund of solutions to practical problems which, while they presupposed a broadly consistent framework of principles, yet contained sufficient divergences and conflicts to enable the jurist to choose the solution best fitted to current needs.[5]

As a result, the Roman law of the Digest was continuously honed by the jurists of the medieval and early modern periods. Their scholarly efforts over several centuries produced a greatly modified legal system, which became known as the *jus commune*. Although originating in Roman law, the *jus commune* was significantly transformed from the law of the Digest. Whereas Roman law had been a system of specific and discrete legal categories and had functioned casuistically through the resolution of individual cases in a pragmatic manner, the *jus commune* emerged as a rationally coherent system of general rules and abstract legal principles. The *jus commune* became the basis upon which the modern Civil Law would be formulated.

---

2 Aldo Schiavone *The Invention of Law in the West* Cambridge, Massachusetts: The Belknap Press of Harvard University Press, 2012, 13.

3 Id., 47. The Middle Ages are often referred to as the 'Age of Authority'. In this Age of Authority the *Corpus Iuris* was considered to be the ultimate expression of legal authority, as the Bible was of theological authority, and the writings of Aristotle of philosophical authority.

4 Nicholas, op. cit. (fn. 1), 47.

5 Id., 47.

The Emergence of the French Legal System

From the sixteenth century French jurists began to express the hope that the deep divisions in French law would be done away with, and that a single, unified legal system would one day replace the plethora of diverse laws then in place. French jurists increasingly turned their attention to the problem of creating a unified legal system.

Jean Domat (1625–1696) was the foremost French jurist of the seventeenth century. As a young man Domat had studied both law and geometry, and his goal was to reorder and systematise the entire Roman law of the Digest on a geometric pattern. In his *magnum opus, Les Lois Civiles dans leur Ordre Naturel*, he did precisely that, eliminating those aspects of the Digest which were obsolete or superfluous, and reorganising all of the remaining rules in a concise and logical manner.[6] In doing so he completely transformed the unstructured law of the Digest into the logical and structured *jus commune*.

This reordering of the Roman law was continued in the eighteenth century by the great French jurist Robert Joseph Pothier (1699–1772). Pothier was a hereditary magistrate as well as a law professor at the *Université d'Orléans*. Pothier's most famous work was his *Traité des Obligations*, published in 1761. The French law of obligations was drawn almost entirely from Roman law, which was the law in effect both in the *pays du droit écrit* and in the *pays du droit coutumier*. In the *Traité des Obligations* Pothier elaborated on the common elements which pertained to every type of obligation, whatever their specific characteristics. In doing so he synthesised the law of diverse obligations into a single, unified body of law. The *Traité des Obligations* was translated into many languages, including English, and became influential throughout all of Europe. Thereafter, Pothier produced a series of legal treatises, each of which addressed a specific topic, in which the applicable law was set out in clear and simple terms. When he died in 1772 Pothier had published works on virtually every aspect of French law, both Roman and customary, making an enormous contribution to their clarification and systematisation.[7]

In the eighteenth century the notion of a unified legal system was conceived in terms of codification. Codification meant the adoption of comprehensive legislation which would deal in a rationally organised and exclusive manner with a particular area or areas of the law.[8] Once codified, the law would become a complete statement of the legal rules with regard to that particular subject matter. All legal problems had to be resolved through the application of those codified rules.

---

6 *Les Lois Civiles dans leur Ordre Naturel* was published in 1689.
7 Paul Viollet *Histoire du Droit Civil Français* Darmstadt: Scientia Verlag Aalen, 1966 (réimpression de la 3me édition du '*Précis de l'Histoire du Droit Français*' Paris, 1905) 255.
8 O.F. Robinson, T.D. Fergus and W.M. Gordon *European Legal History* (second edition) London: Butterworths, 1994, 248.

Domat and Pothier had done much to promote the goal of a single, unified legal system throughout France, and their scholarly works laid the foundations for its attainment.[9] But the actual process of codification only began with the onset of the French Revolution in 1789. In the following ten years there were three failed attempts at codification. It was only in 1799, when Napoleon assumed power as the First Consul, that real progress took place. Napoleon saw himself as a lawgiver in the tradition of Justinian, and he brought his considerable energy to bear on the realisation of a single, codified legal system. Napoleon, as Horne points out, was 'himself in no way a revolutionary, but a reformer and a moderniser'.[10] He was prepared to make use of whatever was required to serve his ends, whether it be from the *ancien régime* or the revolution.[11] Napoleon appointed a Drafting Commission of four experts.[12] The Commission was under pressure from Napoleon to draft the provisions of the Code as quickly as possible, and responded by producing a draft Code within a remarkably short period of time.

The *Code civil des Français* was enacted on 31 March 1804.[13] It contained 2,281 articles. The Code addressed the most important aspects of private law, viz. the law of persons and the family, the law of property, the law of successions, and the law of obligations. It was divided into three unequal books: 'Persons', 'Things' and 'The Different Ways In Which One May Acquire Property'. The third book was the largest of the three books. The law of persons and the family was set out in the first book, the law of property in the second book, and the law of successions and obligations in the third book.[14]

The Commissioners used Roman law to provide the conceptual structure of the *Code civil*. When drafting the articles they referred both to Roman law and

---

9 Jean-Louis Halpérin *L'Impossible Code Civil* Paris: Presses Universitaires de France, 1992, 64–66.

10 Alistair Horne *The Age of Napoleon* London: Phoenix, 2005, 31.

11 Id., 31.

12 The Commission was under the direction of the second Consul, Jean-Jacques-Régis de Cambacérès (1753–1824). The four Commissioners were Jean-Etienne-Marie Portalis (1746–1807), François Denis Tronchet (1723–1806), Félix-Julien-Jean Bigot de Préameneu (1747–1825) and Jacques de Maleville (1741–1824). Two of the Commissioners were from the North and were practitioners of customary law, and two were from the South and were practitioners of Roman law. All four had studied Roman law at university: Robinson, Fergus and Gordon, op. cit., 257. Napoleon paid Portalis a backhanded compliment when he declared: '*Portalis serait l'orateur le plus fleuri et le plus éloquent s'il savait s'arrêter*'. ('Portalis would be the most accomplished and eloquent of speakers if only he knew when to stop'.)

13 Four additional codes were subsequently produced during Napoleon's regime, viz. the *Code de Procédure Civile* (the Code of Civil Procedure, 1807), the *Code de Commerce* (The Commercial Code, 1808), the *Code Pénal* (the Criminal Code, 1811) and the *Code d'Instruction Criminelle* (the Code of Criminal Procedure, 1811).

14 Given that the Code was to be the sole and exclusive source of law on the subject matter which it addressed, all prior law now covered by the *Code civil* was abrogated, by virtue of Article 7 of the *Loi du 30 ventôse, An XII (21 mars 1803)*. The *Loi du 30 ventôse, An XII* remains in effect to this day.

to the customary laws, seeking to strike a balance between the two.[15] As the law of contractual obligations had long been based on Roman law both in the *pays du droit écrit* and in the *pays du droit coutumier*, this part of the Code was drawn almost exclusively from Roman law. The Commissioners made extensive use of the works of Pothier in drafting the articles on contractual obligations. Many of these articles, particularly in the section on General Principles, paraphrased or even simply reproduced *verbatim* passages from his works.

The *Corpus Iuris* had emphasised that the law was comprised of two fundamentally different parts, viz. private law and public law. The very first paragraph of the Digest set out this fundamental duality:

> There are two branches of legal study: public and private law. Public law is that which respects the establishment of the Roman commonwealth, private that which respects individuals' interests, some matters being of public and others of private interest.[16]

Jurists of the medieval and early modern periods accepted this categorisation of the law into two unlike parts as axiomatic, and it became established as a basic principle of the *jus commune*. The explanation for this was that the substantive rules of private law and public law could not be premised on the same theoretical foundations. In private law the legal interests of individuals had to be formulated on the basis of equality, whereas in public law the interest of the public outweighed the interest of the private individual, and the law therefore had to be formulated on this basis.[17]

The *Corpus Iuris* dealt almost entirely with private law, and as a result the *jus commune* which developed from the Roman law was also concerned only with private law. But the emergence in the early modern period of increasingly centralised nation-states gave rise to the need for a developed body of public law, and as a result principles of public law began to be formulated in the seventeenth century. The French revolutionaries decided that the judges of the private law courts should not adjudicate on matters of public concern, and ensured that they would not do so by enacting Article 13 of the *Loi des 16 et 24 août sur l'organisation judiciaire*, 1790:

> The judicial functions are distinct from the administrative functions and shall always remain separate from them: the judges shall not, on pain of forfeiture, interfere in any way whatsoever with the activities of the

---

15 K. Zweigert and H. Kötz *An Introduction to Comparative Law* (3rd revised edition, translated by Tony Weir) Oxford: Clarendon Press, 1998, 87.

16 D.1.1.1. This distinction between private law and public law was similarly underscored on the first page of the Institutes: 'The study of law consists of two branches, law public, and law private. The former relates to the welfare of the Roman State; the latter to the advantage of the individual citizen': I.1.1.4.

17 J.H. Merryman *The Civil Law Tradition* Stanford: Stanford University Press, 1985, 92, 93.

administrative bodies, nor summon before them administrators as a result of their activities.[18]

As a result, the French executive was exempt from the private law courts of France. This necessarily followed from the notion that private law and public law comprised two fundamentally different parts of the law. The executive would be governed not by the private law, but by public law, and therefore a separate court system had to be set up, which would administer the public law.

There are thus in France two separate substantive bodies of law, one of which deals with private law, and the other with public law. These two substantive bodies of law are each applied in a separate court system, and do not always reflect the same legal principles, given their different orientations.[19] The supreme court of the private law court system is known as the *Cour de cassation*, and that of the public law courts the *Conseil d'Etat*. Jurisdiction between the two court systems is determined by a court known as the *Tribunal des conflits*.[20]

The Generalisation of Contract Law

The gradual modification of the Roman law of the Digest into the *jus commune* transformed Roman law over time into something significantly different

---

18 *Les fonctions judiciaires sont distinctes et demeureront toujours séparées des fonctions administratives. Les juges ne pourront, à peine de forfaiture, troubler, en quelque manière que ce soit, les opérations des corps administratifs, ni citer devant eux les administrateurs pour raison de leurs fonctions.* Article 13 remains in force to this day.

19 Bernard Rudden *A Sourcebook on French Law* Oxford: Clarendon Press, 3rd edition, 1991, 119, 120.

20 The *Cour de cassation* currently comprises six Divisions, viz. *la Première Chambre Civile* (the First Civil Division), *la Deuxième Chambre Civile* (the Second Civil Division), *la Troisième Chambre Civile* (the Third Civil Division), *la Chambre commerciale, économique et financière* (the Commercial Division), *la Chambre sociale* (the Labour Division) and *la Chambre criminelle* (the Criminal Division). The *Cour de cassation* is composed of a total of 128 judges, divided more or less equally amongst its six Divisions. A Chief Justice, referred to as the *Premier Président* presides over the Court as a whole. Each division also has its own presiding judge, known as the *Président*. The Court will sit in plenary session (*l'Assemblée plènière*) in a number of circumstances, including those instances when a decision of the Court may overturn previous case law, or when the case at hand involves a matter of legal principle. When the Court sits in *Assemblée plènière* it is comprised of nineteen judges, including each of the divisional presiding judges and the senior trial judges, as well as a trial judge from each of the divisions.
      The *Conseil d'Etat* is divided into four divisions, viz. the *Secrétariat général* (the General Secretariat), the *Section du Contentieux* (Court Division), the *Sections Consultatives* (Consulting Divisions), and the *Section du Rapport et des Etudes* (the Reporting Division). The *Secrétariat général* oversees the management of the *Conseil*. The *Section du Contentieux* adjudicates on public law cases brought before the *Conseil*, and is itself made up of ten subdivisions, each of which is composed of three judges and ten public servants. The *Sections Consultatives* are comprised of five subdivisions (each of which is specialised in a particular field), whose role is to advise the judges of the *Section du Contentieux*. The *Section du Rapport et des Etudes* ensures obedience to the decisions of the *Conseil d'Etat*.

from the original. This transformation is particularly evident in the domain of contract law. As seen above, it was the law of contracts which was the most important and innovative part of Roman law. As a result it was the Roman law of contracts upon which the mediaeval and early modern jurists most focused their attention. Consequently, it was this part of the law which became the most honed area of Roman law as it was transformed into the *jus commune*. The mediaeval and early modern jurists considered contractual obligations to be 'the typical sort of obligation'.[21] Grotius (1583–1645) emphasised the fundamental importance of contractual obligations when he declared that 'the mother of the Civil Law is that obligation which arises from mutual consent'.[22] The centrality of the law of contract persists to this day. As Bénabent notes, contractual obligations are 'at the heart of the private law and enliven all the disciplines of the law'.[23]

As has been seen, the Romans did not possess a unified law of contract which applied to all agreements, but rather only a series of discrete contract types, each of which had its own particular characteristics and requirements, to which the contracting parties had to conform in order to bring an action under that particular contract type.[24] But during the long period of transformation into the *jus commune*, the Roman law of discrete contract types was converted into a generalised law of contract.

Much of this transformation occurred as a result of the influence of the Canon Law on the Civil Law. The Canon Law was the law of the Church, and was administered in separate ecclesiastical courts. Christianity had become the official religion of the Roman Empire in 380 AD. It spread throughout the Roman Empire, eventually becoming the religion of almost the entire population of Europe. The impact of Christianity on Roman law is evident in the *Corpus Iuris* itself. As Riccobono points out, 'almost everything in the *Corpus Iuris* that is substantially new as compared with the laws worked out by the Roman jurists is the result of Christian ethics'.[25] One example of this is the disappearance of *custodia* as a basis for liability. A debtor could be held liable only when he had been at fault, and not otherwise, in accordance with Christian ethics.

During the Middle Ages the Church was the largest institution throughout Europe, and it commanded universal respect and obedience. The Canon Law

---

21 Thomas Glynn Watkin *An Historical Introduction to Modern Civil Law* Aldershot: Dartmouth Publishing Company Limited/Ashgate Publishing Ltd., 1999, 307.
22 Hugo Grotius *De Jure Belli ac Pacis Libri* Tres (translated by Francis W. Kelsey) (Volume Two, Book I, Prologomena, 15, paragraph 15) Oxford: The Clarendon Press, 1925.
23 Alain Bénabent *Droit des Obligations* (20e édition) Paris: LGDJ, Lextenso, 2023, 33.
24 See page 16 *supra*.
25 S. Riccobono *La Codificazione dell'imperatore Giustiniano* Milano *Vita e Pensiero*, 1934' Idem, *L'Influenze del Cristianismo* ..., Scientia, 1909, Vol. V, 19, 1, as quoted in Amleto Giovanni Cicognani (translated by Joseph M. O'Hara and Francis Brennan) *Canon Law* (second edition) Philadelphia: The Dolphin Press, 1935, 47.

governed not only the internal functioning of the Church, but was the law applicable to matrimonial affairs, personal property, and certain criminal matters. The ecclesiastical courts could also exercise jurisdiction over other legal matters, which normally fell within the jurisdiction of the secular courts, if certain conditions were met. Thus, with regard to contractual matters, the ecclesiastical courts exercised jurisdiction whenever a contracting party had taken an oath to strengthen his promise to perform, which was a common practice in the Middle Ages. As a result, the ecclesiastical courts heard many contractual cases, and greatly influenced the development of contract law.

Because the breach of a promise under oath amounted to a mortal sin which put the debtor in danger of damnation, the ecclesiastical courts enforced the performance of oaths in all circumstances, whatever the type of contract. The canonists went even further, by asserting that every breach of promise, whether or not made under oath, amounted to a sin, because it was a form of lying. According to the canonists, even those contractual promises not under oath which had been breached should be enforced by the secular courts.[26] Eventually the secular courts accepted this position.

By insisting that agreements were enforceable whatever the nature of the contract, the canonists created the notion of a contract based solely upon consent. Although consent had been the one common element in all of the Roman contract types, it alone had not been sufficient to create any of the contract types. The adoption of consent as the sole criterion of a legally binding contract undermined the formal requirements of the various Roman law contract types. It then necessarily followed that the discrete formal requirements of the Roman law contract types had to be abandoned as a criterion for determining contractual validity. Consent became the basis upon which a valid and enforceable contract would be made, whatever the nature of that contract.[27]

By the sixteenth century the doctrine of consensualism had become an accepted part of the *jus commune*. In his *Traité des Obligations* Pothier defined a contract on the basis of consent, and in so doing expressly rejected the Roman law contract types:

> The principles of the Roman laws respecting the different kinds of agreements, and the distinction between contracts and simple agreements, not being founded on the law of nature, and being indeed very remote from simplicity, are not admitted into our law.[28]

---

26 K.W. Ryan *An Introduction to the Civil Law* Brisbane: The Law Book Co. of Australasia Pty. Ltd., 1962, 37; Zimmerman, op. cit., 542.

27 Ryan, op. cit., 37.

28 Robert Joseph Pothier (translated by William David Evans) *A Treatise on the Law of Obligations, or Contracts* (Volume 1) Philadelphia; Robert H. Small, 1826, 3, 4, para. 3. Evans translated Pothier's *Traité des Obligations* in 1806. His work comprised two volumes. The first volume was the actual translation of Pothier's *Traité des Obligations*, and the second was

The necessity of consent as the essential basis of all legally binding contracts found expression in the *Code civil* in former Article 1108, which listed it as the first of the four requirements of a valid contract:

Four conditions are essential for the validity of a contract:

- the consent of the party who binds himself;
- his capacity to contract;
- a definite object which forms the subject of the agreement;
- a legal cause for the obligation.[29]

The canonists also asserted that good faith was an essential element in the performance of all types of contracts. This recognition of good faith as the underlying basis of all contracts eliminated the Roman law distinction between contracts which were *stricti iuris* and those which were *bonae fidei*.[30] Good faith also became a part of the *Code civil*. Former Article 1134 affirmed that contracts had to be performed in good faith.[31]

The reference in former Article 1108 to a 'legal cause' as one of the four essential conditions of a valid contract was yet another contribution of the canonists. Although the concept of *iusta causa* had been a part of Roman law, it did not play a significant role in the Roman law of contracts.[32] It was the canonists who transformed a relatively minor aspect of Roman law into an essential

---

a commentary by Evans himself, in which he applied legal principles propounded by Pothier to the Common Law. Hereafter Evans' translation of Pothier's *Traité des Obligations* will be cited as follows: Pothier (Evans). This citation will refer to the first volume unless otherwise noted. Reference will also always be made to the original French version of the *Traité des Obligations*. This particular extract can be found in Robert Joseph Pothier (M. Dupin: éditeur) *Oeuvres de Pothier: Traité des Obligations* Paris: Pichon-Bechet, Successeur de Bechet Aîné, Librairie, 1827, 4, para. 3. The French version of the *Traité des Obligations* will hereafter be cited as Pothier (Dupin).

29 *Quatre conditions sont essentielles pour la validité d'une convention: le consentement de la partie qui s'oblige; sa capacité de contracter; un objet certain qui forme la matière de l'engagement; une cause licite dans l'obligation.*

30 F.H. Lawson *A Common Lawyer Looks at the Civil Law* Ann Arbor: University of Michigan Law School, 1953, Reprinted by William S. Hein & Company Buffalo, 1988, 150; Peter Stein *Roman Law in European History* Cambridge: Cambridge University Press, 1999, 199.

31 Former Article 1134 reads as follows: Agreements lawfully entered into have the force of law for those who have made them. They cannot be revoked except by mutual consent, or for reasons which the law authorises. They must be performed in good faith. (*Les conventions légalement formées tiennent lieu de loi à ceux qui les ont faites. Elles ne peuvent être révoquées que de leur consentement mutuel, ou pour les causes que la loi autorise. Elles doivent être exécutées de bonne foi.*) See pages 66–68 *infra* for a discussion of good faith as it has been subsequently developed in French jurisprudence, and its recognition in current Article 1104 as a provision of 'public order'.

32 See Nicholas, op cit. (fn. 1), at pages 117 and 118 for a discussion of the role played by *iusta causa* in Roman law. See also. Paul J. du Plessis *Borkowski's Textbook on Roman Law* (sixth edition) Oxford: Oxford University Press, 2020, 259–260.

condition of all French contracts.[33] Domat and Pothier then expounded this canonist doctrine in their writings,[34] and it was written into the *Code civil* as an essential condition of all contracts.[35]

'The classical explanation of cause in French law', as Ryan states, 'is that the cause of an obligation is the immediate and direct end which a contracting party has in view in incurring the obligation'.[36] The concept of cause answered the question why a contracting party had agreed to become contractually bound, in order to ascertain what advantage that party sought to achieve. In a contract of sale, for example, the end which the purchaser had in mind in becoming contractually bound was to obtain the object, in exchange for the purchase price.[37]

The notion of cause was also used as a device to determine those circumstances in which a contracting party need not fulfil his contractual promise. Ordinarily, contractual obligations had to be performed, whatever the nature of the agreement. In canonist terms, it would be a sin for the contracting party not to fulfil his contractual obligations. However, in certain circumstances a contracting party might legitimately be excused from performing his contractual obligations. Cause became the instrument to determine when this would be so. In this context, cause had a distinctly moral tone. Thus, a party would not be required to keep his contractual promise, for example, when the cause was illegal, immoral or contrary to public policy.[38] This was also the case when the other contracting party had declared that he would not fulfil his obligation, or was unable to do so by virtue of some supervening event.

Once the concept of a contract had been generalised to the extent that all contracts could be defined by certain common characteristics such as consent, good faith and cause, it was then possible for jurists to formulate other and more extensive rules which also applied to the contract in its generalised sense. Domat observed in his *Lois civiles* that there were certain common elements which applied to all contracts:

33 Barry Nicholas *The French Law of Contract* (second edition) Oxford: Clarendon Press, 1992, 118.
34 Jean Domat *The Civil Law in Its Natural Order* (translated by William Strahan) volume 1, Boston: Charles C. Little and James Brown, 1850; reissued by Fred B. Rothman & Co. Littleton, Colorado: 1980, 161, 162, paragraphs 148, 149 (hereafter referred to as Domat (Strahan)), Jean Domat *Les Loix Civiles dans Leur Ordre Naturel* (Tome I) (seconde edition) Paris: Chez Pierre Aubouin, Librairie de Messeigners les Enfans de France, Pierre Emery & Charles Clouzier – Quay des Augustins à l'Ecu de France, 1697, 64, 65, (titre 1, section 1, paragraphes V et VI) (hereafter referred to as Domat); Pothier (Evans) op. cit., 22–25, paragraphs 42–46; Pothier (Dupin) op. cit., 24–28, paragraphs 42–46.
35 Former Article 1108 *supra*.
36 Ryan, op. cit., 47.
37 Salène Rowan *The New French Law of Contract* Oxford: Oxford University Press, 2022, 109.
38 In this regard see former Article 1133: '*La cause est illicite, quand elle est prohibée par la loi, quand elle est contraire aux bonnes moeurs, ou à l'ordre public*'. ('Cause is illegal when it is prohibited by the law, and when it is contrary to morality or public policy'.)

... there are many rules which agree to all the kinds of covenants, such as those which concern their nature in general, the ways in which they are formed, the interpretation of such as are obscure or ambiguous, and some others; these kinds of common rules shall be the subject-matter of the first title, which shall be of covenants in general.[39]

Domat then proceeded to set out the various common rules which applied to all contracts, taking up some thirty-five pages to do so.[40]

This generalising trend reached its apogee in Pothier's *Traité des Obligations*. Pothier wrote his celebrated *Traité des obligations* with a view to setting out those characteristics which were common to all contracts. Pothier had noted that although the different types of contracts in Roman law were each characterised by aspects which were peculiar to that contract type alone, all contracts nevertheless had certain characteristics in common.[41] He resolved to ascertain all of the common elements that were present in every type of contract, to describe and classify those common elements, and to enumerate the obligations which flowed from them.[42] The *Traité des obligations* sets out in great detail all of the elements which comprise the common characteristics of contractual arrangements.

Pothier situated the category of contract within the wider category of an agreement (*convention*). He noted that a contract 'is a particular kind of agreement: to understand the nature of a contract, we should therefore previously understand the nature of an agreement'.[43] An agreement he defined as follows:

An agreement is the consent of two or more persons to form some engagement, or to rescind or modify an engagement already made.[44]

A contract, Pothier continued, was a particular kind of agreement, viz. an agreement the 'object of which is the formation of an engagement'.[45] Pothier then proceeded to define a contract as follows:

An agreement by which two parties reciprocally promise and engage, or one of them singly, promises and engages to the other, to give some particular thing, or to do or abstain from doing some particular act.[46]

39 Domat (Strahan) op. cit., volume 1, 160, paragraph 143, Domat, op. cit., 61 (Livre I, Introduction).
40 Id. 160–196.
41 Anon. 'Life and Writings of Pothier' (1834) 12 *American Jurist and Law Magazine* 341, 378.
42 Id. 378.
43 Pothier (Evans) op. cit., 3, paragraph 3; Pothier (Dupin) op. cit., 4, paragraph 3.
44 Id., 3, paragraph 3; Id., 4, paragraph 3.
45 Id., 3, paragraph 3; Id., 4, paragraph 3.
46 Id., 3, paragraph 3; Id., 4, paragraph 3.

Pothier's definition applied to all types of contract, whatever their nature. His definition illustrates the culmination of the generalising process, and was reproduced virtually word for word in former Article 1101 of the *Code civil*:

> The contract is an agreement by which one or several persons bind themselves, towards one or several others, to give, or to do, or not to do, something.[47]

By virtue of this definition, a contract could be either bilateral, in which case, as former Article 1102 declared, 'the contracting parties bind themselves reciprocally',[48] or it could be unilateral, in which case, as former Article 1103 declared, 'one or more persons are bound towards one or more others, without on the part of the latter there being any obligation'.[49] This metamorphosis of the specific and very different Roman law contract types into the uniform and generalised law of contract in French law represents one of the most profound and fundamental transformations of Roman law into modern Civil Law.

However, the emergence of a generalised law of contract which was applicable to all types of contract did not result in the disappearance of the specific contracts. Although all contracts were now subject to the generalised law of contract, the Roman law categorisation of contracts into specific types remained as an integral part of the *jus commune*. Thus a generalised law of contract applied equally to all contracts whatever their nature, but the specific contracts, or 'nominate contracts' as they are referred to in the *Code civil*, continued to be also subject to their own particular rules. These particular rules would take precedence over the generalised law in the event of a conflict between the two.[50]

The writings of Domat and Pothier exemplify this approach. In his *Lois civiles* Domat first set out a generalised law of contracts, and then proceeded

---

47 Le contrat est une convention par laquelle une ou plusieurs personnes s'obligent, envers une ou plusieurs autres, à donner, à faire ou à ne pas faire quelque chose.

48 Former Article 1102: Le contrat est synallagmatique ou bilatéral lorsque les contractants s'obligent réciproquement, les uns envers les autres.

49 Former Article 1103: Il est unilatéral lorsqu'une ou plusieurs personnes sont obligées envers une ou plusieurs autres, sans que de la part de ces dernières il y ait d'engagement. The French unilateral contract is simply the Roman law *stipulatio*, converted into a good faith contract and shorn of its verbal formalities. In the Common Law the French unilateral contract would not be a binding legal contract, unless it was under seal, because of the lack of consideration on the part of the promisee. The Common Law unilateral contract is unlike a French unilateral contract, because it is 'a promise in return for an act'. In other words there is consideration on both sides. In French law such a contract would be considered a bilateral contract.

50 This was based on the Latin maxim '*Specialia generalibus derogant*', i.e. the specific derogates from the general, or, in other words, when both general and specific rules apply to a legal issue, the specific rules take precedence over the general rules. See Marie Laure Fouché 'Les Règles Spéciales Dérogent aux Règles Générales' https://fouche-avocat.fr/les-regles-speciales-derogent-aux-regles-generales/.

to enumerate the contract rules which applied to the specific contract types. After writing his *Traité des Obligations*, Pothier likewise subsequently devoted himself to producing treatises which addressed the particular rules applying to the various specific contracts, in works such as the *Traité du Contrat de Vente* and the *Traité du Contrat de Louage*, amongst others.

This combination of a generalised law of contract which applies to every type of contract, and individualised rules which apply to the various nominate contracts, was readily incorporated into the *Code civil*.[51] The Commissioners, under considerable pressure from Napoleon to produce the Code as quickly as possible, responded by borrowing in large measure from the works of Pothier, and to a lesser extent, from Domat. This was particularly true with regard to the general law of contractual obligations, which was originally addressed in former Articles 1101 to 1369 of the *Code*. As Dupin points out, former Articles 1101 to 1369 virtually read as a continuous analysis of Pothier's *Traité des obligations*, and in some articles even the very words of Pothier were reproduced *verbatim*.[52] Pothier's influence on the contractual rules relating to the nominate contracts was also very significant. The various nominate contracts set out in the *Code civil* are based to a considerable degree on the treatises of Pothier dealing with those same nominate contracts, to the extent that a majority of the articles in these various sections resemble, if not replicate, the dispositions in the corresponding *Traités* of Pothier.[53]

---

51 In this regard see former Article 1107, which reads as follows:

> *Les contrats, soit qu'ils aient une dénomination propre, soit qu'ils n'en aient pas, sont soumises à des règles générales, qui sont l'objet du présent titre.*

> *Les règles particulières à certains contrats sont établies sous les titres relatifs à chacun d'eux; et les règles particulières aux transactions commerciales sont établies par les lois relatives au commerce.*

(All contracts, whether or not they have a specific denomination, are subject to the general rules that are set out in this title.

Special rules for certain contracts are set out in the titles that relate to each of them; and the special rules for commercial transactions are set out in the laws that relate to commerce.)

This article has now been replaced by Article 1105, which reads as follows:

> *Les contrats, qu'ils aient ou non une dénomination propre, sont soumis à des règles générales, qui sont l'objet du présent sous-titre.*

> *Les règles particulières à certains contrats sont établies dans les dispositions propres à chacun d'eux.*

> *Les règles générales s'appliquent sous réserve de ces règles particulières.*

(All contracts, whether or not they are specifically named in the present Code, are subject to the general rules set out in this subtitle.

Special rules for certain contracts are set out in the dispositions which apply to each of them.

The general rules apply subject to these special rules.)

52 M. Dupin, the editor of *Oeuvres de Pothier: Traité des Obligations* op. cit., wrote a separate biography of Pothier's life and works, which he entitled *Dissertation sur la Vie et les Oeuvrages de Pothier*, which served as an Introduction to the *Traité*. Dupin's biography comprises pages iii–cl of the volume. The citation is to page cxiv.

53 Dupin, op. cit., cxiv.

The Autonomy of the Will

Throughout the nineteenth century and well into the twentieth century French contract law was dominated by the theory of '*l'autonomie de la volonté*', i.e. the theory of the autonomy of the will. This theory reflected in a legal context the preponderant influence of liberalism and *laissez-faire* in French society during this period.[54] The theory purported to answer the question why a contract should create legally binding obligations between the contracting parties. It did so by asserting that a contracting party was bound because he freely chose to be bound.[55] In other words, it was by exercising his free will that an individual created legal obligations to which he was then subject.[56]

This proposition led to the assumption that contractual obligations, whatever the nature of the contract, must necessarily derive from the concurring wills of the contracting parties, and would become legally binding upon them because they had freely assented to those contractual obligations.[57] The concurring joint wills of the contracting parties thus became the touchstone not only for the formation, but also the legal content, of their contract. The crucial concomitant to the theory was that the judge could have 'no power to revise a contract when it seemed unjust to him'.[58]

The origins of the theory can be traced back largely to the influence of Pothier.[59] Pothier had declared in his *Traité des Obligations* that a contract was legally binding because it involved 'the concurrence of intention of two persons'.[60] He reiterated this formulation in his *Traité du Contrat de Vente,* in which he defined a contract of sale as follows:

> The consent of the parties, which is of the essence of the contract of sale, consists in a concurrence of the will of the seller, to sell a particular thing to the buyer, for a particular price, and of the buyer, to buy from him the same thing for the same price.[61]

---

54 Rowan, op. cit., 21.

55 Muriel Fabre-Magnan *Droit des Obligations (1 – Contrat et engagement unilatéral) (6me édition)* Paris: Presses Universitaires de France, 2021, 106.

56 Nicholas, op. cit. (fn. 33), 32.

57 Id., 32.

58 Georges Rouhette 'The Obligatory Force of Contract in French Law' 38, at 40, in Donald Harris and Denis Tallon (editors) *Contract Law Today: Anglo-French Comparisons* Oxford: Clarendon Press, 1989.

59 P.S. Atiyah *The Rise and Fall of Freedom of Contract* Oxford: Clarendon Press, 1979, 406.

60 Pothier (Evans) op. cit., 4, paragraph 4; Pothier (Dupin) op. cit., 5, paragraph 4 ('*le concours des volontés de deux personnes*', which might also be translated as 'the concurrence of the wills of two persons'.)

61 Robert Joseph Pothier (translated by L.S. Cushing) *Treatise on the Contract of Sale by R.J. Pothier* Boston: Charles C. Little and James Brown, 1839, 17, paragraph 31; Pothier, Robert Joseph (M. Dupin: éditeur) *Oeuvres de Pothier: Traité du Contrat de Vente (*Tome deuxième) Paris: Béchet Aîné, Librairie, 1824, pages 13 and 14, paragraph 31.

Pothier's insistence that the essence of a contract derived from the concurrence of the wills of the contracting parties proved to be a significant factor in the thinking of the Drafting Commission when it formulated the articles of the *Code civil* of 1804. This is evident in several dispositions of the Code.[62] The first sentence of former Article 1134, for example, declared that '[a]greements legally formed have the character of law for those who have made them'.[63] This sentence, according to Nicholas, imports the theory by emphasising that a contract is legally binding because the contracting parties have willed this to be the law as between themselves.[64]

Former Article 1165 likewise reflected the theory:

> Contracts have legally binding effect only between the contracting parties; they do not affect third parties, and third parties cannot benefit from them except in the case provided for in Article 1121.[65]

In other words, contracts have the force of law between the contracting parties, and only between the contracting parties, because they have jointly exercised their wills to bring about this legal relationship between them.

Throughout the nineteenth century and during the first part of the twentieth century the theory became so pervasive that it 'was taken for granted as the foundation of contractual doctrine',[66] and it was on the basis of the autonomy of the will that many important contractual principles were subsequently elaborated. Although various other theories have been put forward in the latter half of the twentieth century to explain the foundational basis of contract law, the role of the will of the contracting parties, as Fabre-Magnan has pointed out, still remains of the essence of the contract, and is its most significant criterion.[67]

---

62 Christian Larroumet, Sarah Bros *Droit Civil: Les Obligations: Le Contrat (Tome III: 1re partie: Conditions de formation) (10e édition)* Paris: Economica, 2021, 69.

63 The original French reads as follows: '*Les conventions légalement formées tiennent lieu de loi à ceux qui les ont faites*'. This sentence was taken from Domat, who had declared in his *Lois Civiles* at Book I, Section I, Article 7 as follows: '*Mais toutes les conventions, soit qu'elles ayent (sic), ou n'ayent (sic) point de nom, ont toujours leur effet, & elles obligent à ce qui est convenu*': Domat, op. cit., 66. Strahan has translated this sentence as follows: 'But all covenants, whether they have a peculiar name or not, have always their effect, and oblige the parties to what is agreed upon: Domat (Strahan) Contracts once made, all that has been agreed takes the place of law for those who have made them': Domat (Strahan) op. cit., 162, 163, paragraph VII.

64 Nicholas, op. cit. (fn. 33), 32. Rouhette argues in contrast that the words 'legally formed' indicate that 'the civil law only attaches civil consequences to the agreements which it authorizes, and only on the terms which it determines itself': Rouhette op. cit., 46, 47.

65 The original French reads as follows: *Les conventions n'ont d'effet qu'entre les parties contractantes; elles ne nuisent point au tiers, et elles ne lui profitent que dans le cas prévu par l'article 1121.*

66 Nicholas, op. cit. (fn. 33), 33.

67 Fabre-Magnan, op. cit., 108. For a review of the criticisms directed against the theory of the autonomy of the will, and the various alternative theories put forward, see Fabre Magnon, op. cit. 105–112.

The Simplification of Contractual Liability

In Roman law liability for breach of one or another of the various contract types involved a graded and complicated series of fault categories, from the most serious, *dolus*, to the least serious, *culpa levissima*.[68] One or other of these categories of fault would be variously applicable, depending on the type of contract involved and the nature of the breach. The mediaeval jurists continued to maintain this approach to fault liability, although they were never able to resolve definitively the exact category of fault for which any contracting party in breach would be liable in a specific case.[69] Domat and Pothier also used the graded approach to determine when liability would arise.[70]

When drafting the articles on contractual obligations the Commissioners almost invariably followed the lead of Pothier. But with regard to contractual liability they deliberately chose not to do so. Instead they drafted entirely new provisions. In an address to the Legislative Assembly on 28 January 1804 Commissioner Bigot-Préameneu explained that they had departed from the established approach to contractual liability in order to simplify the law. Bigot-Préameneu noted that in Roman law 'there were different degrees of fault which could be committed in the performance of contracts', and proceeded to enumerate those various degrees of fault.[71] 'This division', Bigot-Préameneu declared, 'is more ingenious than it is useful in practice', and has led to many

68 See pages 20–21 *supra*.

69 James Gordley and Arthur Taylor von Mehren *An Introduction to the Comparative Study of Private Law* Cambridge: Cambridge University Press, 2006, 495.

70 The one category of fault which the medieval jurists did differentiate from that of Roman law was *dolus*, or fraud. Roman law had simply categorised *dolus* as the most serious type of fault, without analysing its nature in a broader context. The medieval and early modern jurists, on the other hand, analysed *dolus* in the context of consent and cause. Cause, as noted above, explains why a contracting party entered into a contract. If that cause was induced by fraud, the party had not given a true consent, because, had he known the truth of the matter, he might not have consented: James Gordley *The Philosophical Origins of Modern Contract Doctrine* Oxford: Clarendon Press, 1991, 88. See also José Vidal *Théorie Générale de la Fraude en Droit Français* Paris: Librairie Dalloz, 1957, 34. Domat and Pothier took the position that although the consent of the innocent party was certainly affected by the other party's fraud, the contract should nevertheless remain a valid contract until the innocent party chose to rescind it: See Domat, op. cit, volume 1, 194, paragraph 249; Pothier (Evans), op. cit., 17, paragraph 29; Pothier (Dupin) op. cit., 20, paragraph 29. This was the position adopted by the drafters of the *Code civil*, as set out in former Articles 1109 and 1117. Former Article 1109: There is no true consent, if consent has only been granted as a result of error, duress or fraud. *(Il n'y a point de consentement valable, si le consentement n'a été donné que par erreur, ou s'il a été extorqué par violence ou surpris par dol.)* Former Article 1117: A contract made in consequence of error, duress or fraud, is not null as of law; it only gives rise to an action in nullity or rescission … (*La convention contractée par erreur, violence ou dol, n'est point nulle de plein droit; elle donne seulement lieu à une action en nullité ou en rescission …*)

71 P.A. Fenet *Recueil Complet des Travaux Préparatoires du Code Civil* (Tome treizième) Osnabrück: Otto Zeller, 1968 (réimpression de l'édition 1827), 229, 230.

complications, which in turn have resulted in much litigation.[72] 'Equity', he declared, 'repudiates such subtle distinctions'.[73]

By virtue of former Article 1101 French contracts were classified into three categories, viz. contracts of giving, contracts of doing and contracts of not doing. Bigot-Préamenau explained that the drafting committee had adopted a single test of liability for all contracts of giving, and a single test for all contracts of doing and not doing. These two tests were set out in former Articles 1137 and 1147, respectively. Former Article 1137 originally read as follows:

> Whether the agreement is for the benefit of one of the parties or for their common benefit, the obligation to take care so that a thing will be preserved, requires the person obligated to use the care of a prudent administrator.
>
> This obligation is more or less extensive for certain contracts whose effects in this regard are explained under the titles that concern them.[74]

Former Article 1147 reads as follows:

> The person who owes a performance shall be ordered to pay damages for non-performance of the obligation or for delay in performing it whenever he fails to establish that non-performance is due to an external cause that cannot be imputed to him provided, moreover, that there is no bad faith on his part.[75]

The introduction of these two articles greatly simplified the rules relating to liability for breach of contract. The test set out in former Article 1137 with regard to contracts of giving was that of the '*bon père de famille*', or 'prudent administrator'. This was simply a literal translation of the Latin phrase *bonus paterfamilias*, i.e. the test by which Roman law determined whether there had

---

72 Id, 230.
73 Id, 230.
74 *L'obligation de veiller à la conservation de la chose, soit que la convention n'ait pour objet que l'utilité de l'une des parties, soit qu'elle ait pour objet leur utilité commune, soumet celui qui en est chargé à y apporter tous les soins d'un bon père de famille.* (On 4 August 2014 the phrase 'the care of a prudent administrator' ('*tous les soins d'un bon père de famille*') was amended to read 'all reasonable care' ('*tous les soins raisonnables*') by virtue of Article 26 of the *Loi no. 2014-873 du 4 août 2014 pour l'égalité entre les femmes et les hommes.*
    Cette obligation est plus ou moins étendue relativement à certains contrats, dont les effets, à cet égard, sont expliqués sous les titres qui les concernent.
75 *Le débiteur est condamné, s'il y a lieu, au payement de dommages et intérêts, soit à raison de l'inexécution de l'obligation, soit à raison du retard dans l'exécution, toutes les fois qu'il ne justifie pas que l'inexécution provient d'une cause étrangère qui ne peut lui être imputée, encore qu'il n'y ait aucune mauvaise foi de sa part.*

been *culpa levis in abstracto.*[76] French jurists subsequently interpreted the test of the *bon père de famille* to be the equivalent of ordinary negligence.[77] The debtor would therefore be at fault if he failed to preserve the thing as would a *bon père de famille.*

From the time of Justinian, fault was an essential element of contractual liability in Roman law. As Roman law developed into the *jus commune* in the mediaeval and early modern periods, the requirement of fault as a necessary element for contractual liability became an axiomatic principle of contract law. The wording of former Article 1137 clearly reflected this, because it declared that the debtor would be at fault if he failed to meet the standard of a *bon père de famille.* However, in the wording of former Article 1147, there was no reference to fault. Former Article 1147 declared that the debtor would be liable whenever he was unable to show that his non-performance had been the result of an 'external cause not imputable to him'. In other words, it appeared that there could be occasions when the debtor would be liable even though he was not at fault. This was completely at odds with the established doctrine of contractual liability. A literal reading of the two articles appeared to indicate that there was a different standard of contractual liability for contracts of giving, on the one hand, and contracts of doing and not doing, on the other.

Throughout the nineteenth century, French jurists 'sloughed over the contradiction, usually by asserting or implying that these standards were always or nearly always the same'.[78] But there clearly was a contradiction between the two articles, and it was only in 1925 that René Demogue was able to provide an interpretation of the two articles which facilitated the reconciliation of their provisions.[79] Demogue noted that contractual obligations could be either obligations of means[80] or obligations of result.[81] An obligation would be one of result when the debtor undertook to achieve a specific end for the creditor, whereas an obligation would be one of means when the debtor undertook only to exercise reasonable care. When an obligation was one of means it came within former Article 1137, whereas when it was one of result it came within former Article 1147. The creditor was required to prove that a breach of an obligation of means had occurred by demonstrating that the debtor had not exercised the due diligence required of a reasonable person in his circumstances. In such cases, the debtor would then have committed a fault. With an obligation of result, on the other hand, the fault of the debtor was presumed when he did not fulfil his obligation, and he would then be liable under former

---

76 See page 21 *supra.*
77 Gordley and von Mehren, op. cit., 499.
78 Id., 499.
79 René Demogue *Traité des Obligations en Général: Source des Obligations* (Tome V) Paris: Librairie Arthur Rousseau, 1925, paragraph 1237, at pages 536–544.
80 *Obligations de moyens.*
81 *Obligations de résultat.*

Article 1147, unless he could show that non-performance had been due to an external cause not imputable to him.[82]

Demogue was thus able to restore the notion of fault for those breaches of contract arising by virtue of former Article 1147, as well as establishing the appropriate standard of liability for those obligations which came within former Article 1137 and those which came within former Article 1147. As a result, former Article 1137 was given a broader interpretation than a literal reading would indicate, and former Article 1147 a narrower one.[83] Although Demogue's interpretation gave rise to some problems, his analysis received near universal approval amongst French jurists, and was accepted in the French courts as the basis for determining liability for contractual breach.[84]

The Reform of the Law of Contract

The centenary of the *Code civil* in 1904 more or less coincided with the coming into force of the German Civil Code (*Bürgerlichesgesetzbuch*) on 1 January 1900, and led in some quarters to unfavourable comparisons of the former with the latter. The contractual provisions of the *Code civil* in particular were thought to be out of date compared to those of the recently enacted German Civil Code.[85] In December 1904 the Minister of Justice responded by setting up a Commission of sixty-one scholars, practitioners and politicians to draft new articles on the Law of Obligations. However, no draft was produced.[86]

A joint Franco–Italian Commission of Jurists did produce a draft of the Law of Obligations in 1927, after ten years of work on the project, but this was never acted upon.[87] When the Second World War ended in 1945 the Minister of Justice set up the *Commission de réforme du Code civil* in June of that year. This Commission worked for a period of some ten years on a draft of a new *Code civil*, but, with regard to the Law of Obligations, its efforts came to nought.[88]

Significant and extensive alterations to the *Code civil* began to occur in the second half of the twentieth century. The great French jurist Jean Carbonnier

---

82 Nicholas, op. cit. (fn. 33), 53.

83 Id., 53.

84 See Nicholas, op. cit. (fn. 33), at page 53, for a discussion of some of the problems which arise as a result of Demogue's interpretation. See also Rowan, op. cit., 225–228.

85 Hélène Boucard 'The Curious Process of Reforming France's Law of Obligations' (2015) 1 *Montesquieu Law Review* 1, 1.

86 Bénédicte Fauvarque-Cosson 'The French Contract Law Reform in a European Context' (2014) *ELTE Law Journal http://eltelawjournal.hu/french-contract-law-reform-european-context/* 1, 2.

87 Guido Alpa 'Réflexions sur le Projet Français de Réforme du Droit des Contrats' (2015) 4 *Revue Internationale de Droit Comparé* 878, 880, 881; Boucard, op. cit., 1.

88 Boucard, op. cit., 1.

(1908–2003) provided the impetus for many of these alterations.[89] Carbonnier was responsible, for example, for the revisions to the law of inheritance, which were adopted into law in 2001.[90] Many other significant revisions to the Code were also made during this period.[91] But what was most striking was the almost complete absence of revision of the law of contractual obligations. In 2004, on the two hundredth anniversary of the *Code civil*, the articles relating to contractual obligations remained almost entirely unchanged from their original wording, apart from some minor amendments here and there.[92] Napoleon had famously predicted the enduring quality of 'his' *Code civil*, while in exile on St. Helena:

> My true glory lies not in having won forty battles: Waterloo takes away the memory of all those victories. But my *Code civil* can never be taken away, it will endure forever.[93]

Some two hundred years later, Napoleon's pronouncement remained manifestly true, at least with regard to the law of contractual obligations. During the bicentennial celebrations, Jacques Mestre, then Dean of the Faculty of Law and Political Science at the Université d'Aix-Marseille, appeared to endorse the notion that the provisions of the Code addressing contractual obligations

89 Between 1964 and 1977 Carbonnier wrote the preliminary reports (*avant-projets*) on the law relating to persons lacking legal capacity (1964, 1968), parental authority (1970), filiation (1972) and divorce (1975). These reports formed the basis for the changes made to the *Code civil* in these areas.

90 In conjunction with Professor Pierre Catala (1930–2012) Carbonnier drew up proposals to reform the law of inheritance, and these proposals were adopted by the French legislature on 3 December 2001. See Jean Carbonnier *Essais sur les Lois* (*2me édition*) Paris: Defrenois Ouvrages 1995.

91 Amongst the reforms were the following: in 2004 a further revision of the law of divorce; in 2005 further revision to the law of filiation; in 2006 a revision of the law of securities, the law of immovable property seizures, and a further revision of the law of successions and gifts; in 2007 the introduction of the law of trusts and the revision of the law relating to the legal protection of adults; and in 2008 the reform of the law of prescription with regard to civil matters. Various other less significant modifications have also been made to the provisions of the Code from time to time, in order to update it. Often these modifications did not involve a rewriting of the original provisions, but rather simply the insertion of additional provisions which addressed those new situations not adequately covered by the original provisions. By 2015 the Code had expanded to 2,534 articles. However, it has become much larger than the number of additional articles would indicate. The original numeration has been preserved, so that many additional provisions have been added as additional subsections of existing articles.

92 In 2005 former Articles 1369-1 to 1369-11 were added to the *Code civil*. These articles were contained in a new Chapter, entitled 'Of Contracts in Electronic Form'.

93 '*Ma vraie gloire n'est pas d'avoir gagné quarante batailles: Waterloo effacera le souvenir de tant de victoires! Ce que rien n'effacera, ce qui vivra éternellement, c'est mon Code civil.*' Jean-François Niort *Homo Civilis, Contribution à l'Histoire du Code civil français (1804–1965)* Presses universitaires d'Aix-Marseille, 2015, no. 526.

did indeed constitute universal principles of Reason, when he declared that they were '*nourri d'intemporalité, voire d'éternité*'.[94]

But in this same two hundred-year period French society had undergone profound social, economic and technological transformations, which had given rise to new types of contractual issues unknown in 1804. The existing articles either did not address these new issues at all, or, if they did, were unable to provide satisfactory solutions. Some method therefore had to be found to adapt the existing articles to these novel circumstances. In the absence of legislative reform, the method most often used involved doctrinal and judicial 'interpretations' of the Code which not infrequently departed significantly from a plain reading.[95] As a result, judicial decisions became in effect a very important source of the law of contract. By 2004 it had become patently obvious that the *Cour de cassation* was actually formulating the law of contract beyond the existing provisions of the Code in many of its judgments.[96]

---

94 'Nourished by timelessness, indeed by eternity'. Quoted in Carole Champalaune *Réforme du droit des contrats: 3 questions à Carole Champalaune* 12 mars 2015 http://www.textes.justice .gouv.fr/dossiers-thematiques-10083/loi-du-...-du-droit-des-contrats-3-questions-a-carole -champalaune-27931.html, 1.

95 For example, see at pages 52–53 *supra* Demogue's interpretation of former Articles 1137 and 1147 as a means of reconciling the requirement of fault in both articles.

96 This is more than a little ironic, given the original intentions of the revolutionaries when the Code was first drafted. The revolutionaries believed that a comprehensive *Code civil* would prevent judges from making law, which they had done under the *ancien régime*. The sale of public offices, including judgeships in the superior courts, had become institutionalised during the reign of François I (1494–1547, reigned from 1515), as a means of augmenting royal revenues. By purchasing a judgeship in a superior court, a commoner would be elevated to the hereditary aristocracy, with all the rights and privileges which this entailed. Purchasing a judgeship thus became one of the most popular means of social advancement. At the commencement of the French Revolution the composition of the superior courts was dominated by judges who were not members of the 'aristocracy of the blood' but who had rather been elevated to this position through the purchase of the office. These *arrivistes* were particularly zealous in ensuring that there was no infringement whatsoever of the rights and privileges of the aristocracy, and they not infrequently rendered dubious judgments to protect those rights and privileges: Albert Goodwin 'A Re-Evaluation of the "Aristocratic Revolt"' 12, 16–18, in James Friguglietti and Emmet Kennedy (editors) *The Shaping of Modern France* Toronto: The MacMillan Company, Collier-MacMillan Canada, Ltd., 1969; Arlette Lebigre *La Justice du Roi* Bruxelles: Editions Complexe, 1995, 58–65; Halpérin, op. cit., 43–45.

The revolutionaries were fiercely determined to eliminate judicial lawmaking, and believed that the introduction of a comprehensive *Code civil* was the means to do so. They even included provisions in the Code which explicitly prohibited judges from making law, such as Articles 4 and 5. Article 4 reads as follows: 'The judge who refuses to render a decision, on the pretext of the silence, obscurity or insufficiency of the law, can be prosecuted for being liable for a denial of justice'. (*Le juge qui refusera de juger, sous prétexte du silence, de l'obscurité ou de l'insuffisance de la loi, pourra être poursuivi comme coupable de déni de justice.*) Article 5 reads as follows: 'It is forbidden for judges to pronounce judgment by way of a general and regulatory disposition with regard to the cases which are submitted to them'. (*Il est défendu aux juges de prononcer par voie de disposition générale et réglementaire sur les causes qui leur sont soumises.*) The combined effect of Articles 4 and 5 requires judges to find a solution to any

The *Code civil* had originally been drafted with the revolutionary ideal of making the law understandable to all French citizens, through the simplicity and clarity of its principles and its wording.[97] But, by the beginning of the twenty-first century, the law of contracts could no longer be said to be easily understandable to the ordinary citizen. The law had instead become a highly specialised and complex subject, which only legally trained experts could know and apply, involving not only the articles of the Code but an extensive overlay of doctrinal and judicial interpretations.[98] As a result, there were increasing demands for a revision of the law. Given the centrality of the law of contracts, it was recognised that a revision of this part of the Code would be the largest and most important ever undertaken, and that it would have far-reaching consequences, not only in and of itself, but also for many other areas of French law.

An important step in this revision was taken in 2003, when a group of thirty-four French academics, under the overall direction of Pierre Catala, Professor Emeritus of the Université Paris II (Panthéon-Assas), embarked on a revision of the entire law of obligations – contractual, quasi-contractual and delictual, as well as the law of prescription. This study became known as the *avant-projet* Catala.[99] The *avant-projet* was completed within three years and was presented to the Ministry of Justice in September 2005.

In his introductory remarks Catala emphasised that although the *avant-projet* would introduce much-needed reforms to the law of obligations, the revised articles would not be a revolutionary departure from the existing law, but would rather be simply an adaptation of that law:

> Our study has shown that numerous solutions in the Napoleonic Code still retain their value after two centuries of application; they will be found either in just the same form as they were cast by our ancestors or re-drafted to suit present day taste better. In this connection, the Reform

---

legal problem from the text of the Code. It should be noted that the *Cour de cassation* always bases its decisions on some article or articles of the Code, and never refers to its previous judgments, thereby maintaining the fiction that it does not make law.

97 Daniel Mainguy '*Le Blog de Daniel Mainguy: La Réforme du Droit des Contrats et des Obligations*' (http://www.daniel-mainguy.fr/article-la-reforme-du-droit-des-contrats-et-des -obligations 15/06/2015, 3. See also Stefan Vogenauer 'The Avant-projet de réforme: An Overview' 3, at 6, in John Cartwright, Stefan Vogenauer and Simon Whittaker (editors) *Reforming the French Law of Obligations* Oxford: Vogenauer and Simon Whittaker (editors) *Reforming the French Law of Obligations* Oxford: Hart Publishing, 2009.

98 Mainguy, op. cit., 3. Amongst the *cahiers de doléance* (grievance submissions) which were drawn up in 1789, a number complained of the complexity of the law, and petitioned for its simplification. One *cahier* in particular complained of the 'baleful erudition of those working in the Court', who would cite 'maxims, jurisprudence, regulations, cases, and the opinions of commentators, including Greeks, Romans, and even the Chinese': Halpérin, op. cit., 48.

99 *Avant-projet* may be translated as 'preliminary draft'. The formal title was *Avant-projet de réforme du droit des obligations et de la prescription*.

Proposals do not propose to break away from the original, but to adjust it.[100]

Catala declared that the new law would maintain the continuity of the existing approach to obligations. The result, unsurprisingly, was that the overall orientation of the *avant-projet* Catala 'remained very faithful to the Code, to its style, to its emblematic rules'.[101] Upon reception of the *avant-projet* Catala, the Ministry of Justice undertook extensive consultations with the legal profession. It received significant feedback from various professional organisations, several of which published critical analyses of the *avant-projet* Catala and made alternative proposals for reform.

In 2006, a second group of academics, under the direction of François Terré, Professor Emeritus of the Université Paris II (Panthéon-Assas), began another revision of the law of obligations. This revision was undertaken in cooperation with the Ministry of Justice and became known as the *avant-projet* Terré. Ultimately three reports were prepared.[102] The first report addressed the law of contracts and was submitted to the Ministry of Justice in December 2008.[103] This report was much less conservative than the *avant-projet* Catala, and 'drew inspiration from all the various existing European and international models'.[104]

In the meantime, the Minister of Justice had announced in September 2007 that the entire law of obligations would be revised, and work began on draft legislation. A first draft of the proposed legislation for the revised law of contract was published in July 2008.[105] This first draft followed the proposals set out in the *avant-projet* Catala in some respects, but in others, as Vogenauer points out, it went 'far beyond the *avant-projet* and display[ed] a much greater willingness to bring the *Code civil* in line with the contract laws

---

100 Pierre Catala (English translation by John Cartwright and Simon Whittaker) *Proposals for Reform of the Law of Obligations and the Law of Prescription* 12, http://www.justice.gouv.fr/art_pix/rapportcatatla0905-anglais.pdf (sic).

101 Fauvarque-Cosson, op. cit., 2. With regard to the revised law of contract, there were 406 draft provisions. 'Of these, 113 remained unchanged and 69 changed only their language, but not their substance; 140 draft articles (34 per cent of the contract law provisions) codified the existing law, normally by restating the case-law of the *Cour de cassation*; and only 84 (21 per cent) were full-blown innovations': Vogenauer, op. cit., 12.

102 F. Terré (dir.) *Pour une réforme du droit des contrats* Dalloz, 2009; F. Terré (dir.) *Pour une réforme du droit de la responsabilité civile* Dalloz, 2011; F. Terré (dir.) *Pour une réforme du régime général des obligations* Dalloz, 2013.

103 Vogenauer, op. cit., 19.

104 The international model contracts relied upon were the Principles of European Contract Law (PECL), the Draft Common Frame of Reference (DCFR), and the Unidroit Principles of International Commercial Contracts: Fauvarque-Cosson, op. cit., 3.

105 Ministère de la Justice *Projet de réforme du droit des contrats* (juillet 2008). http:/www.chairejib.ca/files/sites/38/2010/07/reforme_all.pdf.

of other European jurisdictions and the current international proposals for contract law reform'.[106]

Upon the publication of the proposals for reform of the law of contract, another round of extensive consultations ensued. During this time the Government decided that it would postpone the revision of the law of delictual obligations to a later point in time. On 23 October 2013, the Government issued a second modified version of its *avant-projet,* which addressed not only the law of contracts, but the general regime of obligations and the law of evidence with regard to obligations. The Ministry intended this revised version of the law to replace the existing articles of the *Code civil.* It introduced the new proposals '*par voie d'ordonnance*', i.e. by way of governmental decree, rather than through Parliament. This led to a constitutional challenge by the Senate, which asserted that the Government was not constitutionally empowered to proceed in this manner. The *Conseil constitutionnel* resolved the challenge in the Government's favour, in its decision of 12 February 2015.[107]

Once the *Conseil constitutionnel* had rendered this decision, the Government launched an official consultation process, on 25 February 2015, for the latest version of its revised articles. This revised version was almost an exact replica of the *avant-projet* released by the Government on 23 October 2013. It was officially entitled *Le Projet d'ordonnance portant réforme du droit des contrats, du régime général des obligations et de la preuve des obligations.*[108] The *Projet d'ordonnance* was an 'enabling law', which allowed the Government a period of twelve months to revise the actual *ordonnance,* which then had to be published in its final form as a legally binding governmental decree in the *Journal officiel.*

The definitive version of the new articles was published on 10 February 2016.[109] Although the *Ordonnance* reproduced for the most part the same articles which had appeared in the *Projet d'ordonnance* of 2015, there were some important alterations, and the numeration of the two had changed significantly.[110] The *Ordonnance* declared that the new law would come into effect on 1 October 2016.

---

106 Vogenauer, op. cit., 18.
107 Cons. const., 12 fév. 2015, no. 2015-710.
108 The text of the *Projet d'Ordonnance* can be found at:
        http://www.justice.gouv.fr/publication/j21_projet_ord_reforme_contrats_2015.pdrf.
109 The new law was entitled the *Ordonnance 2016-131 du 10 février 2016 portant réforme des contrats, du régime général et de la preuve des obligations.*
        https://www.legifrance.gouv.fr/2016/10/ordonnance/eli/ordonnance/2016/2/10/JUSC15224666R/j0/texte. Hereafter referred to as the Ordonnance.
110 According to Mercadal, of the 354 articles set out in the *Ordonnance,* approximately 26 per cent were new, 33 per cent modified pre-existing rules either in form or in substance, 15 per cent incorporated interpretative judicial decisions, and 26 per cent maintained the pre-existing articles: Barthélemy Mercadal *Réforme du Droit des Contrats* LeVallois: Editions Francis Lefebvre, 2016, 25.

As the subject matter of the *Ordonnance* came within the constitutional law-making power of Parliament, and had only been temporarily delegated to the Government by virtue of Articles 21 and 38 of the Constitution, the *Ordonnance* as enacted on 1 October 2016 was of regulatory status only, and therefore had to be ratified by Parliament in order to obtain legislative status.[111] Parliament ratified the *Ordonnance* on 20 April 2018 by *Loi* no. 2018-287, which was published in the *Journal officiel* on 21 April 2018.[112] Disagreement between the Senate and the National Assembly concerning some of the provisions in the *Ordonnance* had led to a number of changes to the *Ordonnance*. These changes came about by virtue of an agreement reached on 14 March 2018 by a Joint Committee of the Senate and the National Assembly.[113] The changes were of two types: substantive amendments and interpretative amendments. The substantive amendments became effective only from 1 October 2018, whereas the interpretative amendments were applied retroactively from

---

111 Article 21, paragraph 3 of the Constitution reads as follows: 'He (i.e. the Prime Minister) may, in exceptional cases, deputise for him (i.e. the President) as chairman of a meeting of the Council of Ministers by virtue of an express delegation of powers for a specified agenda': *La Constitution du 4 octobre 1958.*

('*Il peut, à titre exceptionnel, le suppléer pour la présidence d'un conseil des ministres en vertu d'une délégation expresse et pour un ordre du jour déterminé.*')

Article 38 of the Constitution reads as follows: 'In order to implement its programme, the Government may ask Parliament for authorisation, for a limited period, to take measures by Ordinance that are normally the preserve of statute law.

'Ordinances shall be issued by the Council of Ministers, after consultation with the *Conseil d'Etat*. They shall come into force upon publication, but shall lapse in the event of failure to table before Parliament the bill to ratify them by the date set by the Enabling Act. They may only be ratified in explicit terms.

'At the end of the period referred to in the first paragraph hereunder Ordinances may be amended solely by an Act of Parliament in those areas governed by statute law': *La Constitution du 4 octobre 1958.*

('*Le Gouvernement peut, pour l'exécution de son programme, demander au Parlement l'autorisation de prendre par ordonnances, pendant un délai limité, des mesures qui sont normalement du domaine de la loi.*

'*Les ordonnances sont prises en conseil des ministres après avis du Conseil d'Etat. Elles entrent en vigueur dès leur publication mais deviennent caduques si le projet de loi de ratification n'est pas déposé devant le Parlement avant la date fixée par la loi d'habilitation. Elles ne peuvent être ratifiées que de manière expresse.*

'*A l'expiration du délai mentionné au premier alinéa du présent article, les ordonnances ne peuvent plus être modifiées que par la loi dans les matières qui sont du domaine législatif.*')

112 The full title of the Loi was as follows: *Loi no. 2018-287 du 20 avril 2018 ratifiant l'ordonnance no. 2016-131 du 10 février 2016 portant réforme du droit des contrats, du régime général et de la preuve des obligations.*

113 Soulier Avocats 'Reform of French Contract Law – Ratification Law Published on April 21, 2018: General Presentation', 30 May 2018, 1, 2.

http://www.soulier-avocats.com/en/reform-of-french-contract-law-ratification-law-published-on-april-21-2018-general-presentation/.

1 October 2016.[114] When an article which has been amended is cited in this book, the 2018 version will be reproduced, and the text will so indicate.

Some Specific Changes to the Law of Contract

The articles of the *Ordonnance* have been organised in a highly logical and didactic fashion.[115] The revised articles are divided into three chapters, viz. Chapter I – the Source of Obligations, Chapter II – the General Regime of Obligations, and Chapter III – the Proof of an Obligation. Title III of Chapter I focuses on the various types of obligation, separately addressing in each subtitle each different type of obligation. Thus Subtitle I, which is entitled 'The Contract', focuses solely on contractual obligations. It comprises Articles 1101 to 1231–7. Subtitles II and III separately deal with each of the other types of obligations.[116] Chapter II – the General Regime of Obligations – addresses those elements which are equally applicable to all types of obligations. It comprises Articles 1304 to 1352–9. Chapter III sets out the proof required for each type of obligation. It comprises Articles 1353 to 1386-1. Apart from the several drafts which were produced by the Ministry of Justice prior to the publication of the *Ordonnance* and the legislation which authorised the *Ordonnance*, the only other document which provides any indication of the reasoning behind the new provisions is the *Rapport au Président de la République*, which was issued by the Minister of Justice simultaneously with the *Ordonnance*.[117] The *Rapport* will be referred to when necessary in order to explain the reasoning behind the various changes which have been made.

A new definition of the contract is set out in current Article 1101 of Chapter 1. Article 1101 reads as follows:

A contract is a consensus of wills between two or more persons intended to create, modify, transfer or extinguish obligations.[118]

---

114 Id., 2.
115 According to Casu, the new arrangement is 'not only logical, but well nigh intuitive': Gatien Casu 'Le Projet d'Ordonnance Portant Réforme du Droit des Contrats' Deuxième Partie *La Gazette: L'Actualité Juridique et Politique de la Faculté de Droit, Université Lyon III Jean Moulin* `1, 3. At the time Casu made this statement he was referring to the proposed articles in the *Projet d'ordonnance*, but his statement applies equally to the new articles of the *Ordonnance du 10 février 2016*, the arrangement of which replicates that set out in the *Projet d'ordonnance*.
116 Subtitle II is entitled 'Extracontractual Liability' and comprises Articles 1240 to 1245-17; Subtitle III is entitled 'Other Sources of Obligations'. It comprises Articles 1300 to 1303-4.
117 The full title of the *Rapport* is the '*Rapport au Président de la République relative à l'ordonnance no 2016-131 du 10 février 2016 portant réforme du droit des contrats, du régime général et de la preuve des obligations*'. It will hereafter be referred to as the *Rapport*.
118 *Le contrat est un accord de volontés entre deux ou plusieurs personnes destiné à créer, modifier, transmettre ou éteindre des obligations.*

This new definition rectifies a number of problems that were inherent in the previous definition. These problems included the relationship between a contract and an agreement, and the division of contracts into three types, viz. contracts of giving, contracts of doing and contracts of not doing.

The former Article 1101 had defined a contract, *inter alia*, as 'an agreement (*convention*) by which one or more persons bound themselves to one or more other persons, to give, to do or not to do something'.[119] This definition had been inspired by Pothier's definition.[120] Pothier had defined the contract within the wider context of an agreement (*convention*).[121] An agreement involved 'the consent of two or more persons to form some engagement, or to rescind or modify an engagement already made'.[122] A contract was a narrower concept, which Pothier defined as 'an agreement by which two parties reciprocally promise and engage, or one of them singly promises and engages to the other, to give some particular thing, or to do or abstain from doing some particular act'.[123] Thus, according to Pothier, all contracts were agreements, but not all agreements were contracts, as a contract did not encompass those legally binding agreements in which a legal engagement already made was either rescinded or modified. The wording of the former Article 1101 followed very closely the wording in the *Traité des Obligations,* and, consequently, former Article 1101 appeared to reproduce the distinction drawn by Pothier between the wider concept of an agreement and the narrower concept of a contract. Subsequent French doctrinal writing continued to emphasise this distinction, noting that a contract was an agreement, but that not all agreements were contracts.[124]

The problem, however, was that although former Article 1101 appeared to distinguish a contract and an agreement, no other article in the Code defined the two terms or delineated the distinction between them. In fact, the two terms were actually used interchangeably throughout the Code, [125] and in practice, they were treated as synonymous. But if a contract and an agreement were simply synonyms of each other, this would make the phrase in former Article 1101 that 'a contract is an agreement' meaningless, because the phrase would mean no more than that a contract was a contract.

---

119 See page 46 *supra*.
120 See page 45 *supra*.
121 See page 45 *supra*.
122 Pothier (Evans) op. cit., 3, paragraph 3; Pothier (Dupin) op. cit., 4, paragragh 3.
123 Id., 3 and 4, paragraph 3; Id., 4, paragraph 3.
124 See, for example, Fabre-Magnan, op. cit., 185.
125 The term '*convention*' was used repeatedly throughout the former articles. In the section of the Code setting out the General Law of Contract (articles 1101–1369), for example the term '*convention*' appears in the wording of Articles 1110, 1111, 1116, 1117, 1128, 1134, 1135, 1137, 1156, 1161, 1162, 1163, 1165, 1170, 1172, 1182, 1184, 1194, 1226, 1247, 1304, 1305, 1309, 1319 and 1325.

Moreover, although former Article 1101 purported to set out a common definition of a contract, that definition classified contracts into three distinct categories, by noting that when two parties entered into a contract they did so in order 'to give, to do or not to do something'. As a result, all French contracts had to be categorised as being one of these three types. However, this threefold categorisation proved to be incomplete and unsatisfactory. As Fabre-Magnan points out, some contracts, such as the *contrat de location* (contract of renting) or the *prêt à usage* (loan for use), did not fit into the threefold classification of giving, doing or not doing.[126] Some jurists attempted to deal with this problem by adding a fourth category, viz. the contract of giving *à usage*, in order to include such contracts. However, this proposal would have further fragmented the categories of contracts rather than unifying them into a single common concept.

The definition of a contract in the new Article 1101 has resolved these difficulties. Article 1101 now defines a contract as a 'consensus of wills' and avoids all reference to an agreement. The notion of an 'agreement' as a wider concept than a contract has been eliminated, not only from Article 1101, but from all of the articles which now address the general law of contract. As a result, the concept of a contract has been unambiguously widened to embrace all situations in which there is a consensus of wills between two or more persons designed to create, modify, transmit or extinguish obligations.

Moreover, the new definition makes no mention of the three categories of contract, which have been eliminated from the revised articles and consequently no longer comprise an aspect of the new law of contracts. The new definition instead sets out a single definition which applies equally to all types of contract. Whatever the nature of a particular contract, it will now come within the revised definition on the basis of a single and uniform criterion, viz. a consensus of wills.

The elimination of the three categories of contract from the definition has also had the effect of permitting a new and more unified approach to contractual liability. The new definition omits any reference to categories of contract, so that it has become possible to formulate a single definition of contractual liability. Contractual liability is set out in Article 1231-1, which reads as follows:

> The person who owes a performance shall be ordered to pay damages for non-performance of the obligation or for delay in performing it whenever he fails to establish that performance was prevented by *force majeure*.[127]

---

126 Fabre-Magnan, op. cit., 215.
127 *Le débiteur est condamné, s'il y a lieu, au paiement de dommages et intérêts soit à raison de l'inexécution de l'obligation, soit à raison du retard dans l'exécution, s'il ne justifie pas que l'exécution a été empêchée par la force majeure.*

The wording of this article follows very closely the wording of former Article 1147, except that former Article 1147 referred to 'an external cause' (*une cause étrangère*) which could not be imputed to the debtor, whereas the current article more straightforwardly refers to '*force majeure*'. By virtue of Article 1231-1 contractual liability will now arise, whatever the nature of the contract, whenever the debtor cannot prove that his non-performance or late performance was the result of *force majeure*.

Former Article 1147 did not set out an all-embracing standard of liability, as does Article 1231-1, but rather simply set out the standard of liability which would apply to contracts of doing and not doing. As already seen, Demogue classified contracts of doing and not doing as obligations of result.[128] A debtor would be liable when his obligation was one of result when he did not obtain the result, unless he could point to an external cause which prevented him from doing so. Former Article 1147 did not apply to contracts of giving, and the standard of liability for such contracts was set out in former Article 1137. Demogue classified contracts of giving as obligations of means.[129] By virtue of the standard set out in former Article 1137 a debtor was liable when he did not preserve the thing to be delivered according to the care of a *bon père de famille*, or, in its more recent guise, had not exercised 'reasonable care'.

The revised articles, however, do not make any distinction between contracts of doing and not doing, on the one hand, and contracts of giving, on the other. The question then arises as to whether Demogue's classification of obligations into those of means and those of result still pertains in the new regime. Fabre-Magnan asserts that it does, stating that Demogue's analysis remains useful for judges in evaluating the non-performance of the debtor, by making a careful and precise determination of what exactly the debtor contracted to do.[130]

The ongoing utility of Demogue's analysis can be seen in a consideration of current Article 1197. Article 1197 is contained in a small subsection entitled '*Effet translatif*', which may be translated as the 'translative', or 'transferring, effect'.[131] This subsection addresses those contracts which have as their purpose 'the transfer of ownership or some other right'. When this occurs, the

---

128 See page 52 *supra*.

129 See page 52 *supra*.

130 Fabre-Magnan, op. cit., 605. Larroumet, Bros also assert that the distinction between the two types of obligation, even though it does not form a part of the revised articles 0f 2016, still forms part of the positive law: Larroumet, Bros, op. cit., 38.

131 Subsection 2 (*Effet translatif)*' is set out in Chapter IV – 'The Effects of the Contract' (*Les Effets du Contrat*), and within Section I – The Effects of the Contract as Between the Contracting Parties (*Les Effets du Contrat entre les Parties*).

transfer, as stated in the first paragraph of Article 1196, 'arises at the time of the conclusion of the contract'.[132] In other words, it occurs automatically.[133]

The second paragraph of Article 1196 sets out who bears the risk of loss with regard to translative contracts. It reads as follows:

> The transfer of ownership includes the transfer of the risk of loss of the thing. However, the debtor who has an obligation to deliver will assume the risk from the time that he has been put on notice to perform, in conformity with Article 1344-2 and subject to the rules set out in Article 1351-1.[134]

As a result, the debtor of the thing bears an obligation to conserve the thing until the moment of delivery, as declared by Article 1197:

> The obligation to deliver the thing implies the obligation to safeguard it until the time of delivery, by utilising all the care of a reasonable person in doing so.[135]

Article 1197 thus appears to be basically a restatement of former Article 1137.[136] The wording of Article 1197 implies the existence of an obligation of means, so that 'non-performance' as described in Article 1231-1 must be

---

132 *Dans les contrats ayant pour objet l'aliénation de la propriété ou la cession d'un autre droit, le transfert s'opère lors de la conclusion du contrat.*
   Ce transfert peut être différé par la volonté des parties, la nature des choses ou une disposition de la loi.

133 Fabre-Magnan, op. cit., 605.

134 *Le transfert de propriété emporte transfert des risques de la chose. Toutefois le débiteur de l'obligation de délivrer en retrouve la charge à compter de sa mise en demeure, conformément à l'article 1344-2 et sous réserve des règles prévues à l'article 1351-1.*
   Article 1344-2 reads as follows: A notice to deliver a thing passes the risk to the debtor, if the risk has not already passed. (*La mise en demeure de délivrer une chose met les risques à la charge du débiteur, s'ils n'y sont déjà.*) Article 1351-1 reads as follows: When impossibility of performance results in the loss of the thing due, the debtor put on formal notice to perform is nevertheless released if he proves that the loss would likewise have occurred had the obligation been performed.
   He is nevertheless obliged to assign to his creditor the rights and actions attached to the thing.
   (*Lorsque l'impossibilité d'exécuter résulte de la perte de la chose due, le débiteur mis en demeure est néanmoins libéré s'il prouve que la perte se serait pareillement produite si l'obligation avait été exécutée.*
   Il est cependant tenu de céder à son créancier les droits et actions attachés à la chose.)

135 *L'obligation de délivrer la chose emporte obligation de la conserver jusqu'à la délivrance, en y apportant tous les soins d'une personne raisonnable.*

136 The first paragraph of former Article 1137 reads as follows: *L'obligation de veiller à la conservation de la chose, soit que la convention n'ait pour objet que l'utilité de l'une des parties, soit qu'elle ait pour objet leur utilité commune, soumet celui qui en est chargé à y apporter tous les soins raisonnables.* (Whether the agreement is for the benefit of one of the parties or for their

understood, with regard to translative contracts, as a failure to act with reasonable care.

The generalisation of French contract law came about largely through the development of three concepts, viz. consensualism, good faith and cause.[137] These three concepts have all been revisited in the new articles. The concepts of consensualism and good faith have been reaffirmed and enlarged, whereas the concept of cause has been formally eliminated, although many of its specific functions appear to have been retained.

As has already been seen, consent was the primary basis by which a generalised law of contract emerged in French law, and thus became the defining concept of a contract.[138] The requirement of consent was set out in former Article 1108 as the first essential condition of a valid contract.[139] This emphasis on consent as the primordial element for a valid contract remains in the new provisions. Revised Article 1128 reads as follows:

The following are necessary for the validity of a contract:

1. the consent of the parties;
2. their capacity to contract;
3. content which is lawful and certain.[140]

Revised Article 1172 emphasises that in ordinary circumstances it is consent alone which gives rise to a binding contract:

Contracts in principle require only the consent of the parties.

By way of exception, the validity of solemn contracts is subject to the completion of formalities required by the law, and will be of no effect if such formalities are not observed, except where it may be regularised.

Moreover, the law requires the formation of certain contracts to the delivery of a thing.[141]

---

common benefit, the obligation to take care so that a thing will be preserved, requires the person obligated to use all reasonable care.)

137 See pages 42–44 *supra*.
138 See pages 42–43 *supra*.
139 See page 43 *supra*.
140 *Sont nécessaires à la validité d'un contrat: 1. Le consentement des parties; 2. Leur capacité de contracter; 3. Un contenu licite et certain.*
141 *Les contrats sont par principe consensuels.*

   Par exception, la validité des contrats solennels est subordonnée à l'observation de formes déterminées par la loi à défaut de laquelle le contrat est nul, sauf possible régularisation.

   En outre, la loi subordonne la formation de certains contrats à la remise d'une chose.

There was no equivalent article in the former law of contract. The new article emphasises that it is only by way of exception that a contract will not be created by consent alone.[142]

Although the former articles required the element of consent, they nowhere explained what was meant by consent.[143] This gap has been rectified by the wording of the new Article 1101, which declares that a contract is formed by 'the consensus of wills' of the contracting parties. A 'consensus of wills' occurs when the offer of one party and the acceptance of the other are a*d idem*, i.e. when the offer and the acceptance of the contracting parties are at one with each other. In the former articles, the elements of an offer and an acceptance had not been addressed. Their absence meant that the courts were forced to read them into the former articles as an integral part of the concept of consent, and then to develop through decided cases what exactly constituted an offer and an acceptance at law. This hiatus has now been addressed in the revised articles, which set out the essential elements of an offer and an acceptance in Articles 1113 to 1122. These articles represent a distillation of the doctrinal and jurisprudential interpretations of offer and acceptance, derived from the single word 'consent' as set out in former Article 1108.

Good faith was the second element relied upon to generalise the specific Roman law contract types into a single law of contract. Only some of the various Roman law contract types had been *bonae fidei*, i.e. contracts of good faith, whereas others had been *stricti juris*, i.e. contracts of strict performance.[144] The canonists, however, applied the notion of good faith to all types of contracts, and thus further generalised the law of contract.[145] This principle of good faith was incorporated into former Article 1134, which stated in its third sentence that contracts 'must be executed in good faith'.[146]

Good faith as set out in former Article 1134 originally related only to the performance of the contract.[147] However, the French courts increasingly extended the principle to the formation of the contract and to the

---

142 Philippe Dupichot 'Sur le Projet de Réforme du Droit Français des Contrats' *Projet de Réforme du Droit des Contrats: Regards Croisés* 32, 41. Article 1109 defines consensual contracts and those contracts, solemn and real, which derogate from the principle of consensualism. It reads as follows: 'A contract is consensual when it is formed by the simple exchange of consents whatever the manner of expression. A contract is solemn when its formation is subject to formalities determined by the law. A contract is real when its formation is subject to the delivery of a thing'. (*Le contrat est consensual lorsqu'il se forme par le seul échange des consentements quel qu'en soit le mode d'expression. Le contrat est solennel lorsque sa formation est subordonnée à des formalités déterminées par la loi. Le contrat est réel lorsque sa formation est subordonnée à la remise d'une chose.*)

143 Fabre-Magnan, op. cit., 325, 326.

144 See page 20 *supra*.

145 See page 43 *supra*.

146 *Elles doivent être exécutées de bonne foi.* The complete article is reproduced, in English and in French, at page 43, fn. 31 *supra*.

147 Bénabent, op. cit., 46.

precontractual negotiation period.[148] This judicial extension of good faith has been recognised in the new provisions on good faith. Good faith has been elevated into a fundamental contractual principle, which must be observed through the entire life of the contract, beginning in the precontractual negotiating phase. In order to emphasise its importance, it now stands in its own right in current Article 1104, which explicitly declares that good faith is a principle of public order:

> Contracts must be negotiated, concluded and performed in good faith.
>   This provision is one of public order.[149]

The importance placed on the principle of good faith in the new law of contract can be seen in the changes that were made to the final version of the article. The forerunner of current Article 1104, viz. Article 1103 of the *Projet d'ordonnance* (2015), simply declared that contracts 'must be concluded and performed in good faith'.[150] The alteration of the wording from 'concluded and performed' to 'negotiated, concluded and performed', and the addition of the clause declaring that Article 1104 is a provision of public order, strengthen the principle into one of primordial importance.[151] The second sentence of current Article 1102 declares, in this regard, that '[c]ontractual liberty does not permit one to derogate from the rules which touch upon public order'.[152]

Article 1104 does not define good faith.[153] Consequently, it remains incumbent on the courts to determine the circumstances in which there has been a breach of the duty. The absence of a definition has been criticised in some quarters on the basis that the concept is 'vague and inimical to certainty'.[154] But as Bénabent points out, good faith by its very nature is a malleable concept, which must be adapted to each individual case as appropriate.[155] Only by allowing the courts to make a determination on this individualised basis can

---

148 Rowan, op., cit., 35. See also Peter Rosher 'Fears Over French Contract Law Rewrite Largely Overblown, Says Expert Outlaw.Com' *Legal News and Guidance from Pinsent Masons.*
    http://www.outlaw.com/en/articles/2015/may/fears-over-french-contract-law-rewrite -are-largely-overblown-says-expert/.
149 *Les contrats doivent être négociés, formés et exécutés de bonne foi.*
    Cette disposition est d'ordre public.
150 *Les contrats doivent être formés et exécutés de bonne foi.*
151 Current Article 1162 declares that a contract cannot derogate from public order either in its stipulations or in its purpose, whether this is known or not by all the parties. (*Le contrat ne peut déroger à l'ordre public ni par ses stipulations, ni par son but, que ce dernier ait été connu ou non par toutes les parties.*)
152 *La liberté contractuelle ne permet pas de déroger aux règles qui intéressent l'ordre public.*
153 Gael Chantepie et Mathias Latina *La Réforme du Droit des Obligations* Paris: Editions Dalloz, 2016, 94.
154 Rowan, op. cit., 36.
155 Bénabent, op. cit., 268.

the principle 'continue to be applied and developed with the same flexibility that has characterised its evolution to date'.[156]

As indicated above, the duty of good faith now infuses every aspect of a French contract, from the precontractual negotiations, through to the performance of the contract, and extending to its termination. In the precontractual negotiation phase, the duty of good faith limits the parties' freedom of negotiation.[157] In this regard the duty of good faith precludes the parties from engaging in conduct that could mislead the other, from withholding important information from each other, and from terminating the negotiations in a manner which is 'abusive' or 'intolerable'.[158] The duty to negotiate in good faith presupposes that the parties will collaborate with each other in the negotiation process, and that they will act in a way which is 'ethical' and 'loyal'.[159]

Once the contract has been concluded, the parties are then under a duty to perform their contractual obligations in good faith. This means that the parties must conduct themselves in an ethical manner in the performance of the contract.[160] To do so they must be 'loyal', they must cooperate with each other and they must act in a manner which is careful and logical.[161] Loyalty requires that 'the parties perform their obligations faithfully, conscientiously, and diligently'.[162] Cooperation requires the parties to work jointly towards the same end and to 'take account of the interests of the other', particularly when 'there is a relationship of trust or inequality of bargaining power' between them.[163] Acting in a manner which is careful and logical requires the parties to act consistently. 'Conduct that is inconsistent or contradictory', as Rowan notes, 'is regarded as dishonest and incompatible with their relationship'.[164]

Lastly, there is the duty of good faith with regard to the termination of a contract. Although the revised articles do not explicitly refer to such a duty it is highly unlikely that the courts would permit a party to terminate a contract if done in bad faith, given that the courts have intervened to prevent termination in bad faith under the previous regime.[165]

Cause was the third concept used by the canonists to generalise the French law of contracts.[166] Cause could have either an objective or a subjective meaning. The objective meaning arose when applied to the cause of an obligation. In this context, cause simply provided the explanation why a contracting party

---

156 Rowan, op., cit., 36.
157 Id., 36.
158 Id., 37.
159 Id., 37.
160 Id., 38.
161 Bénabent, op. cit., 268.
162 Rowan, op. cit., 38; Bénabent, op. cit., 268.
163 Rowan, op. cit., 38.
164 Id., 41.
165 Id., 41.
166 See pages 43–44 *supra*.

had undertaken a particular obligation, and thus had a somewhat 'mechanical' function. The subjective meaning arose when cause was applied to the contract as a whole, rather than to a specific obligation, and, in this regard, it had a distinctly moralistic edge to it. By resorting to a subjective interpretation a court sought to ascertain why a contracting party had concluded the contract, i.e. what goals that party was pursuing in entering into that particular contract. The courts have made considerable use of the subjective interpretation of cause in recent times, as this enabled them, as with the expanded notion of good faith, to exercise greater supervisory control over matters involving contractual injustice. However, this increased judicial focus on the subjective interpretation of cause led to considerable debate, if not actual confusion, about what exactly the subjective interpretation meant, and what its limits were. This reached the stage, as Dupichot has wryly pointed out, that if someone claimed to understand cause, it was only because it had been badly explained to him.[167]

The drafters of the *Projet d'ordonnance* decided not to include cause in the *Projet*, and this decision has been affirmed in the *Ordonnance du 10 février 2016*.[168] Thus, whereas former Article 1108 laid down four essential conditions for the validity of a contract, including 'a valid cause',[169] current Article 1128 sets out only three essential conditions, viz. consent, capacity and a certain and licit content.

But this third essential condition – a certain and licit content – appears to combine the provisions of former Article 1133, which declared that the 'cause is illicit when it is prohibited by law, or is contrary to public morals or to public policy', with the requirement in former Article 1108 of 'a definite object which forms the subject-matter of the undertaking'.[170] The test of the licitness of the contract is still inherent in the requirements of contractual validity, but that test is now applied to the 'content' of the contract rather than to its cause.

Moreover, although cause has been removed from the conditions essential to the validity of a contract, its influence still pervades the new provisions through the adoption of articles which incorporate the holdings of decided cases.[171] This is so, for example, in the new Article 1162. Article 1162 declares that a 'contract cannot derogate from public order either in its stipulations or

---

167 Dupichot, op. cit., 40.
168 The *Rapport* noted that most foreign legal systems did not include the notion of cause in their law of contract, and that in French contract law cause was poorly defined and covered a multitude of different meanings. Given the difficulty of rendering a precise definition which would include all of its various meanings, as well as the significant criticisms to which it was subject, it was decided that the notion of cause should be replaced by rules which were better defined, and which would thereby enable a judge to arrive at the same results while avoiding the controversies arising from the notion of cause: The *Rapport*, 9.
169 See page 43 *supra* for the wording of former Article 1108.
170 Former Article 1133 reads as follows: *La cause est illicite, quand elle est prohibée par la loi, quand elle est contraire aux bonnes moeurs ou à l'ordre public.*
171 Bruno Dondero *Le blog du professeur Bruno Dondero – le projet d'ordonnance portant réforme du* droit des contrats – 23 fevrier 2015.

in its purpose, whether or not this is known by all the parties'.[172] As Mercadal points out, Article 1162 takes up the role previously performed by former Articles 1108, 1131 and 1133.[173] Former Article 1108 had referred to a 'legal cause' as one of the four essential requirements of a contract, and former Articles 1131 and 1133 had elaborated on this requirement, by prohibiting an 'unlawful cause', or one which was contrary to 'public order', from having any legal effect.[174] The cases which were decided on this basis can thus equally be referred to with regard to Article 1162.[175] However, the beneficial features of cause are now set out explicitly in the legislation, in a manner which is intelligible and foreseeable, rather than being based on unpredictable judicial decisions.[176]

Rebus Sic Stantibus

The Roman jurists had never actually defined the concept of *vis maior*.[177] Instead, they simply referred to specific instances which they considered to come within the ambit of *vis maior*. But there were certain common characteristics in the great majority of these instances, and thus the essential elements of *vis maior* as understood by the Roman jurists can be broadly identified.

Impossibility of performance was one such element. Although initial impossibility of performance involved a mistake rather than *vis maior*, supervening impossibility usually involved the occurrence of an event categorised as *vis maior*. Thus *vis maior* came to be associated with catastrophic events which rendered performance impossible through no fault of the debtor. To qualify as *vis maior* such events also had to be irresistible and unforeseen. This understanding of *vis maior* carried through into the law of the *jus commune*. Grotius, for example, declared in *De Jure belli ac pacis*:

---

http://brunodondero.com/2015/02/26/le-projet-dordonnance-portant-reforme-du -droit-des-contrats/.

172 *Le contrat ne peut déroger à l'ordre public ni par ses stipulations, ni par son but, que ce dernier ait été connu ou non par toutes les parties.*

173 Mercadal, op. cit., 127.

174 Former Article 1131 read as follows: 'An obligation without a cause or with a false cause or with an unlawful cause cannot have any effect'. (*L'obligation sans cause, ou sur une fausse cause, ou sur une cause illicite, ne peut avoir aucun effet.*) Former Article 1133 read as follows: 'A cause is unlawful when it is prohibited by law, and when it is contrary to good morals or to public order'. (*La cause est illicite, quand elle est prohibée par la loi, quand elle est contraire aux bonnes moeurs ou à l'ordre public.*) The reference to 'good morals' was removed from Article 1162, on the basis that it had become obsolete: Fabre-Magnan, op.cit., 480.

175 Mercadal, op. cit., 127.

176 Champalaune, op. cit.
    http://www.textes.justice.gouv.fr/dossiers-thematiques-10083/loi-du-170215-sur-la -simplification-du-droit-des-contrats-3-questions-a-carole-champalaune-27931.html.

177 This reluctance to formulate definitions, as already seen, was characteristic of Roman law, which dealt in specific instances and did not generalise. See pages 11, 23 and 32–33 *supra*.

It is not necessary to speak of impossibilities. It is, in fact, sufficiently evident that no one is bound to do that which is quite impossible.[178]

However, during the medieval period, and primarily as a result of the influence of the canonists, another basis was developed for exempting a debtor from liability for non-performance. This became known as the doctrine of *rebus sic stantibus*. *Rebus sic stantibus* means 'things thus standing' and applied to situations of changed circumstances. By virtue of this principle, a contract would be binding 'only as long and as far as matters remain the same as they were at the time of the conclusion of the contract'.[179] The doctrine was often argued on the basis of an implied condition or term – i.e. the *clausula rebus sic stantibus* – which, it was asserted, must be read into all agreements.

Rebus sic stantibus had not been an aspect of Roman law, although the inspiration for its development can be traced back to observations made by Cicero (106–43 BC). Cicero argued that it was better that a promise not be performed rather than that a crime be committed:

If someone has deposited his sword with you when he was of sound mind, and asks for it back when insane, it would be wrong to return it, and your duty not to return it. Again, if a man who has deposited money with you were to make war on your country, would you return the deposit? I believe not; for you would be acting contrary to the Republic, which ought to be the dearest thing to you. In this way, many things that seem to be honourable by nature become honourable no longer through circumstance: to keep promises, to stand by agreements, and to return deposits become no longer honourable, if what is beneficial changes.[180]

In his *Exposition on the Book of Psalms* St. Augustine (354–430 AD) affirmed Cicero's injunction, in a passage which repeats that injunction almost word for word.[181] Thomas Aquinas (1225–1274) maintained that there were always certain implied conditions which attached to every promise, and that therefore

---

178 Grotius, op. cit., 369 (Book 2, XIII, paragraph 8).
179 Reinhard Zimmermann *The Law of Obligations* Oxford: Oxford University Press, 1996, 579.
180 Cicero (edited by M.T. Griffin and E.M. Atkins) *On Duties* Cambridge: Cambridge University Press, 1991, 137 (Book 3, paragraphs 95 and 96).
181 The passage from St. Augustine reads as follows: '... if, for example, a sword be intrusted to any one, and he promises to return it, when he who intrusted it to him shall demand it: if he chance to require his sword when in a fit of madness, it is clear it must not be returned then, lest he kill either himself or others, until soundness of mind be restored to him. Here then is no duplicity, because he, to whom the sword was intrusted, when he promised that he would return it at the other's demand, did not imagine that he could require it when in a fit of madness': St Augustine *Exposition on the Book of Psalms (Psalm 5, paragraph 7)* Christian Classics Ethereal Library
    www.ccel.org/ccel/schaff/npnf108.toc.html.

'oaths, vows and promises ... are not binding under circumstances under which the promisor did not intend to be bound'.[182] By the middle of the thirteenth century *rebus sic stantibus* had become an integral part of the Canon Law, and was applied by the ecclesiastical courts to vows.[183] The doctrine entered the Civil Law in the fourteenth century, when it was adopted by such prominent jurists as Bartolus de Saxoferrato (1313–1357) and Baldus de Ubaldis (1327–1400).[184] The doctrine flourished in the seventeenth century, in the context of Natural Law.[185] Grotius dealt with the doctrine at various points in his *magnum opus*.[186] By the eighteenth century *rebus sic stantibus* had reached its apogee. Many European jurists at this time espoused the doctrine in one form or another, and it was adopted by a number of European states in the codification of their laws.[187] It formed a part of the *Codex Maximilianeaus bavaricaus civilis* of 1756, and the Prussian General Land Law of 1794, amongst others.[188]

The most notable impact of *rebus sic stantibus*, however, was in the domain of Public International Law. Alberico Gentili (1552–1608) had proposed in his book *De Jure Belli Libri Tres*, published in 1589, that the doctrine be recognised as a principle of International Law.[189] But thereafter the status of *rebus sic stantibus* remained one of the most contentious and problematic aspects of International Law. It was only finally confirmed as a legitimate element of International Law in the twentieth century, by the 1969 *Vienna Convention on the Law of Treaties*.[190]

The Convention had been drafted by the International Law Commission, which is a subsidiary organ of the General Assembly.[191] The Commission acknowledged that 'almost all modern jurists' admit the principle of *rebus sic stantibus*, recognising that treaties might become inapplicable 'through a

---

182 Gordley op. cit., 87, quoting Thomas Aquinas *Summa Theologica,* II–II, q. 88, a. 10; a. 89, a. 9.

183 Robert Feenstra *Fata Iuris Romani* Leyde: Presse Universitaire de Leyde, 1974, 370.

184 Id., 371.

185 Zimmermann, op. cit., 581.

186 In this regard see Andreas Thier 'Legal History' 15, at pages 23, 24, in Ewoud Hondius and Hans Christoph Grigoleit (editors) *Unexpected Circumstances in European Contract Law* Cambridge: Cambridge University Press, 2011.

187 Id., 24–26.

188 Zweigert and Kötz, op. cit., 518, Thier, op. cit., 25–26.

189 Boleslaw Adam Boczek *International Law: A Dictionary* Lanham, Md.: Scarecrow Press, 2005, 9.

190 1155 UNTS 331.

191 The Commission's Report on the final version of the draft articles contains not only the draft articles themselves but also substantial commentaries on the articles. See *Yearbook of the International Law Commission, 1966,* volume II: Draft Articles on the Law of Treaties with Commentaries, 1966 – Text adopted by the International Law Commission at its eighteenth session, in 1966, and submitted to the General Assembly as a part of the Commission's report covering the work of that session (at paragraph 38). (Hereafter *Report of the Commission to the General Assembly.*)

fundamental change of circumstances'.[192] However, it also stressed 'the need to confine the scope of the doctrine within narrow limits and to regulate strictly the conditions under which it may be invoked'.[193]

The Commission then laid down its formulation of the doctrine, in Article 62.[194] The term *rebus sic stantibus* was not used; the article instead refers to a 'fundamental change of circumstances'.[195] Paragraph 1 set out the stringent conditions which were necessary to constitute a fundamental change of circumstances:

> 1. A fundamental change of circumstances which has occurred with regard to those existing at the time of the conclusion of a treaty, and which was not foreseen by the parties, may not be invoked as a ground for terminating or withdrawing from the treaty unless:
>
> a) the existence of those circumstances constituted an essential basis of the consent of the parties to be bound by the treaty; and
> b) the effect of the change is radically to transform the extent of obligations still to be performed under the treaty.

The Commission declared that it 'attached great importance to the strict formulation of these conditions'.[196] It made clear that it had purposely drafted the article in negative form in order 'to emphasize the exceptional character of this ground of termination or withdrawal'.[197] In Paragraph 2 the Commission further restricted the operation of the doctrine by enumerating two situations in which a fundamental change of circumstance could not be raised. Paragraph 3 allows a State signatory to suspend the operation of the treaty on the basis of a fundamental change of circumstance, rather than necessarily terminating it or withdrawing from it.

The Commission also addressed as a separate concept the issue of supervening impossibility of performance. Some members of the Commission were of the opinion that the two concepts of supervening impossibility of performance and fundamental change of circumstances should be combined into a single article, on the basis that it was not always easy to draw a clear distinction between the two concepts.[198] But the Commission came to the conclusion that the two concepts should be kept separate as 'distinct grounds for regarding a treaty as having been terminated', because 'the criteria to be employed in applying the articles were not the same, and to combine them might lead

---

192 *Report of the Commission to the General Assembly*, op. cit., 257.
193 Id., 257.
194 It should be noted that Article 62 appears as draft Article 59 in the Commission's Report.
195 *Report of the Commission to the General Assembly*, op. cit., 258.
196 Id., 259.
197 Id., 259.
198 Id., 256.

to misunderstanding'.[199] Supervening impossibility was set out in Article 61, which reads as follows:

> A party may invoke an impossibility of performing a treaty as a ground for terminating it if the impossibility results from the permanent disappearance or destruction of an object indispensable for the execution of the treaty. If the impossibility is temporary, it may be invoked only as a ground for suspending the operation of the treaty.[200]

In 1973 the International Court of Justice had occasion to consider the meaning of a fundamental change of circumstances in the *Fisheries Jurisdiction case (United Kingdom v Iceland)*.[201] The Court found that a fundamental change in circumstances had not occurred. It declared that in order for a fundamental change in circumstances to arise 'the change of circumstances must have been a fundamental one'.[202] Moreover, for a fundamental change in circumstances to 'give rise to a ground for invoking the termination of a treaty' it was 'necessary that it should have resulted in a radical transformation of the extent of the obligations still to be performed. The change must have increased the burden of the obligations to be executed to the extent of rendering the performance something essentially different from that originally undertaken'.[203]

In 1997 the International Court of Justice again had occasion to consider the issue of a fundamental change of circumstances, in the *Case Concerning the Gabčikovo-Nagymaros Project*.[204] The Court found that there had not been a fundamental change of circumstances. The Court elaborated on its earlier statement to note that '[a] fundamental change of circumstances must have been unforeseen; the existence of the circumstances at the time of the Treaty's conclusion must have constituted an essential basis of the consent of the parties to be bound by the treaty'.[205] The Court then went on to declare that fundamental change of circumstances 'should be applied only in exceptional cases', as the negative and conditional working of Article 62 had been designed to ensure the stability of treaty relations.[206]

---

199 Id., 256.
200 *Report of the Commission to the General Assembly*, op. cit., 255. It should be noted that Article 61 appears as draft Article 58 in the Commission's Report.
201 ICJ Rep. (1973) 3
202 Id., 15, paragraph 37.
203 Id., 17, paragraph 43.
204 ICJ Rep. (1997) 3.
205 Id., 62, paragraph 104.
206 Id., 65, paragraph 104. It should be noted that France is not a signatory to the *Vienna Convention on the Law of Treaties*. At the Conference of Vienna, on 22 May 1969, the French delegation objected to thirteen of the eighty-five proposed articles, and voted against adopting the text. Article 62 was one of the thirteen objectionable articles. The French delegation asserted that Article 62 had been drafted in such a manner as to enable a State party to withdraw from a treaty, or to terminate it, on the basis of a unilateral decision on its

Force Majeure: The Historical Background

Even in its heyday in the seventeenth and eighteenth centuries, the doctrine of *rebus sic stantibus* did not have a significant impact on the development of French contract law. The great French jurist of the sixteenth century, Jacques Cujas (1520–1590), did not even address the topic in his writings.[207] Both Domat and Pothier were content simply to reproduce the traditional Roman law approach to supervening events. In this regard, Domat declared:

> Nobody is bound, in any kind of covenant, to answer for the losses and damages occasioned by accident, such as a thunderbolt, an inundation, a torrent, force, and other events of the like nature...[208]

Domat's use of the word 'accident', which in the original French is *cas fortuit*, was simply a literal translation of the Roman word *casus fortuitus*. Domat did not actually define *cas fortuit* but rather referred to specific instances which would constitute *cas fortuit*. In this, he emulated the Roman jurists.[209]

In his *Traité des Obligations* Pothier addressed the subject of supervening events in a number of passages. He set out the general principle with regard to contracts of giving in paragraph 142, and with regard to contracts of doing and not doing in paragraph 149.[210] Paragraph 142 reads, *inter alia*, as follows:

---

part, whereas general international law declared that such a change must be recognised by the common agreement of the States parties. The French delegation was undoubtedly only too aware that France itself had unilaterally invoked the principle of fundamental change of circumstances when, on 11 March 1966, it had withdrawn its ground and air forces from NATO's integrated command: Olivier Deleau 'Les Positions Françaises à la Conférence de Vienne sur le Droit des Traités' (1969) 15 *Annuaire Français de Droit International* 7, 13. On 7 November 2007 French President Nicholas Sarkosy declared before the United States Congress that France would resume its full role in NATO: 153 Cong. Rec. H13210, 13212.

207 Julie Bédard 'Réflexions sur la Théorie de l'Imprévision en Droit Québécois' (1997) 42 *McGill Law Journal* 761, 769.

208 Domat (Strahan) op. cit., 174, paragraph 190. The original French reads as follows: *Personne n'est tenu dans aucune espèce de conventions, de répondre des pertes, & (sic) des dommages causez (sic) par des cas fortuits, comme sont un coup de foudre, un débordement, un torrent, une violence, & (sic) autres semblables évenements...:* Domat op. cit., 82 (Livre I, Title I, Section III) See also Domat (Strahan) op. cit., at page 206, *Contract of Sale*, Book I, Title, II, Section II, Article XXI, paragraph 286, and page pages 621, 622, 623, *In What Manner Are Formed the Engagements Which Arise from Accidents*, Book II, Title IX, Section I, paragraphs 1596–1600.

209 See page 33 *supra*.

210 There is a discrepancy between the numeration of the paragraphs in the original French version and the English translation of 1806. Whereas in the original French version the paragraph quoted is numbered 149, in the English version it is numbered 148. The English version has inexplicably collapsed paragraphs 148 and 149 of the original into a single paragraph, numbered 148, but then proceeds to number the next paragraph as 150, thereby bringing back into alignment the numeration of the original with the numeration of the translation.

The debtor of specific things, (*d'un corps certain*) is never answerable for accidents, and cases of inevitable necessity, (*cas fortuit et la force majeure, vis divina*) until he is guilty of improper delay; or (according to the law of France, is put on notice to pay – *en demeure de payer,*) at least unless he has subjected himself to the loss arising therefrom by particular agreement; or unless the accident is occasioned by some preceding fault of his own.[211]

Paragraph 149 reads, *inter alia*, as follows:

When a person, who was obliged to do any act, is prevented by accident or force (*quelque cas fortuit et force majeure*) from doing it; and in like manner when a person has been forcibly constrained to do some act which he was obliged not to do, there is no ground for subjecting him to damages ...[212]

The words *force majeure* and *cas fortuit* which Pothier used in the original French text were literal translations of the equivalent Latin words *vis maior* and *casus fortuitus*. Moreover, although Pothier referred to instances both of *force majeure* and *cas fortuit*, he made no distinction as to their effect upon the consequences for the debtor. In both cases, provided that the debtor was not at fault and performance had been rendered impossible, he would not be liable.[213]

Pothier further elaborated on the principle set out in paragraph 142, in several subsequent paragraphs, with regard to the debtor of specific things. In situations where the object of the contract had disappeared, been rendered *hors de commerce* or become lost, the disappearance of the object necessarily rendered the obligation impossible to fulfil, and was therefore extinguished:

Paragraph 613 (649): There cannot be any debt without something being due, which forms the matter and object of the obligation; whence it follows, that if that thing is destroyed, as there is no longer anything to form the matter and object of the obligation there can be no longer

---

211 Pothier (Evans) op. cit., 74, paragraph.142; Pothier (Dupin) op. cit., 73, paragraph 142. In his translation of this passage and paragraph 149 Evans has reproduced in brackets the French and Latin words used by Pothier in the original version. *Vis divina* can be translated as an 'act of God'.

212 Pothier (Evans) op. cit., 76, paragraph 148; Pothier (Dupin) op. cit. 75, paragraph 149.

213 It should be noted that whereas Domat simply emulated the Roman law of *vis maior* by enumerating specific instances of supervening events which would qualify as *force majeure*, Pothier undertook to generalise the concept in a much more doctrinal manner.

any obligation. The extinction of the thing due, therefore, necessarily induces that extinction of the obligation.[214]

Paragraph 614 (650): For the same reason, if the thing which was due, in consequence of something that afterwards occurs, is no longer susceptible of being the matter and object of an obligation, that obligation itself cannot continue. That is the case where the thing which was due can no longer be an article of commerce.[215]

Paragraph 620 (656): There is little difference between a thing being lost, so that it cannot be known where it is, and its having actually ceased to exist. Therefore, if this loss takes place without any fault in the debtor, as when the thing is taken by robbers, the debtor is liberated as much as if the thing had no longer existed, with this difference, that as a thing once destroyed can never be renewed, the debtor is in that case absolutely liberated from his obligation: whereas the thing which is only lost may be recovered, and in this case the debtor is only liberated whilst the loss continues...[216]

Pothier provided an exception to the above articles in paragraph 633 (668), and in so doing summarised the principle itself:

The principle which has been established, that the debtor of a specific thing is discharged from his obligation, when the thing is lost, without any act, default or delay, on his part, is subject to an exception, when he has, by a particular clause in the contract, expressly taken the risk of such loss upon himself.[217]

---

214 Pothier (Evans) op. cit., 384, paragraph 613. Note that at this point the alignment in paragraph numbers between the French original and the English translation has become seriously askew, making it extremely difficult to compare the original to the translation. The primary reason for this is that paragraph 456 of the English translation proceeds to number the next 35 paragraphs as subsections of paragraph 456, which are numbered from 1 to 35, whereas the French original continues to number each of those paragraphs sequentially. As a result paragraph 457 in the English translation corresponds to paragraph 493 in the French original. Various other subsequent errors render the alignment even more askew. The final paragraph in the French original is numbered 932, whereas in the English translation the equivalent passage is numbered 838. The number of the three paragraphs quoted is therefore first indicated as it appears in the English translation and then in brackets in the original French. The French version of the paragraph may be found at Pothier (Dupin) op. cit. 391, 392, paragraph 649.
215 Pothier (Evans) op. cit., 384, paragraph 614; Pothier (Dupin) op. cit., 392, paragraph 650.
216 Pothier (Evans) op. cit., 386, 387, paragraph 620; Pothier (Dupin) op. cit., 394, paragraph 656.
217 Pothier (Evans) op. cit., 392, 393, paragraph 633; Pothier (Dupin) op. cit., 399–401, paragraph 668.

Force majeure would therefore arise, according to Pothier, whenever the object had been destroyed, extinguished or lost, without fault on the part of the debtor, because performance was thereby rendered impossible.

Force Majeure: The Previous Regime

The Drafting Committee addressed the issue of *force majeure* in a number of articles, but primarily in former Articles 1147 and 1148. Although these two articles basically followed the gist of Domat and Pothier's writings, the wording of the two articles was much simplified.

Former Article 1147 has already been discussed, and reproduced above, in the section dealing with the simplification of contractual liability.[218] But as the Article also set out the concept of *force majeure*, it is instructive to reproduce it again at this point:

> The person who owes a performance shall be ordered to pay damages for non-performance of the obligation or for delay in performing it whenever he fails to establish that non-performance is due to an external cause (*une cause étrangère*) that cannot be imputed to him provided, moreover, that there is no bad faith on his part.[219]

Article 1147 declared that the debtor would be liable for damages for non-performance or late performance. Although Article 1147 did not so state, there is no doubt that the Drafting Committee intended the element of fault to be an integral aspect in a finding of liability, because fault had always been an essential element in contractual liability from the *Corpus Iuris* onwards. The debtor, both in Roman law and in the *jus commune*, could only escape liability if he could show that he had not been at fault for non-performance, which would be the case when the non-performance had been the result of some outside supervening event not attributable to him. The Drafting Committee reaffirmed this approach, with the inclusion of the final clause of the article, which declared that the debtor would not be liable for breach in those situations in which the non-performance of the contract was 'due to an external cause' which could not 'be imputed to him'. The 'external cause' which prevented the debtor from performing his contractual obligation was then linked to former Article 1148, which described an 'external cause'. Former Article 1148 reads as follows:

---

218 See pages 51–53 *supra*.
219 *Le débiteur est condamné, s'il y a lieu, au payement de dommages et intérêts, soit à raison de l'inexécution de l'obligation, soit à raison du retard dans l'exécution, toutes les fois qu'il ne justifie pas que l'inexécution provient d'une cause étrangère qui ne peut lui être imputée, encore qu'il n'y ait aucune mauvaise foi de sa part.*

There is no occasion for damages where, in consequence of superior force (*force majeure*) or accident (*cas fortuit*) the debtor has been prevented from conveying or doing that to which he was obliged or has done what he was debarred from doing.[220]

An external cause would therefore occur whenever there had been either *force majeure* or *cas fortuit*. Former Article 1148 referred both to *force majeure* and to *cas fortuit* in a single clause. In paragraphs 142 and 149 (148) Pothier had referred to the two terms on the basis that they were simply two ways of expressing the same principle, so that the consequences for non-performance would be the same whether the supervening event consisted of *force majeure* or *cas fortuit*. The Drafting Committee followed Pothier's lead by including both terms in former Article 1148. Although some French jurists attempted to distinguish *force majeure* from *cas fortuit*, such efforts at differentiation proved unsuccessful in the courts. Consequently, the two terms were treated as though they constituted a single type of occurrence. Reference was ordinarily made only to '*force majeure*'.[221]

Former Article 1302 incorporated the provisions from Pothier's *Traité des Obligations* with regard to the loss of 'a thing certain and determined'. Former Article 1302 reads as follows:

Where a thing certain and determined which is the object of an obligation perishes, may no longer be the subject matter of legal transactions between private individuals, or is lost in such a way that its existence is absolutely unknown, the obligation is extinguished if the thing has perished or has been lost without the fault of the debtor, and before he was under notice of default.

Even where the debtor is under notice of default, if he has not assumed fortuitous events, the obligation is extinguished in the case where the thing would also have perished in the hands of the creditor if it had been delivered to him.

The debtor is obliged to prove the fortuitous event which he alleges.

220 *Il n'y a lieu à aucuns dommages et intérêts lorsque, par suite d'une force majeure ou d'un cas fortuit, le débiteur a été empêché de donner ou de faire ce à quoi il était obligé, ou a fait ce qui lui était interdit.*

221 Nicholas, op. cit. (fn. 33), 202; Jean Carbonnier '*Droit civil: Les Obligations*' (*22e éditio*n) Paris: Presses Universitaires de France, 2000, 312. Both terms were used in some articles, such as Article 1733, but in other articles only one or the other term is used. Thus, in Articles 1929 and 1934 only the term *force majeure* has been used, whereas in former Article 1302 and in Articles 1722 and 1882 only the term *cas fortuit* is used.

In whatever manner a thing which has been stolen may have perished, or been lost, its loss does not excuse the person who took it away from restitution of its price.[222]

Neither *force majeure* nor *cas fortuit* was defined in the Code, so that it fell to the French courts to determine what exactly amounted to *force majeure*. In Roman law, a debtor could only invoke *vis maior* if the supervening event had rendered performance by the debtor impossible.[223] This was also the position of Pothier.[224] However, former Articles 1147 and 1148 did not indicate that impossibility of performance had to be an essential requirement of *force majeure*. Several articles in the *Code civil* did specify that a promise to do that which was initially impossible was void *ab initio*.[225] The reason for this was that there had to be a 'definite object which forms the subject matter of the contract', according to former Article 1108.[226] This requirement could not be satisfied if the object was impossible, thereby preventing the contract from coming into existence.[227] There were also several articles which indicated that *force majeure* would arise when a supervening event had occurred which rendered performance impossible without fault on the part of the debtor.[228] However, it remained unclear whether impossibility was always a necessary aspect of *force majeure*, given the absence of this requirement in former Article 1148.

This led to the contention that *force majeure* was broad enough to encompass not only supervening events which rendered performance impossible but also supervening events which rendered performance more onerous to the debtor. The goal of this particular interpretation of former Article 1148 was to introduce the concept of *rebus sic stantibus* into French contract law. Although *rebus sic stantibus* had not been a part of the French law as articulated by Domat and Pothier, and although it had not been explicitly incorporated

---

222 The original French reads as follows: *Lorsque le corps certain et déterminé qui était l'objet de l'obligation, vient à périr, est mis hors du commerce, ou se perd de manière qu'on en ignore absolument l'existence, l'obligation est éteinte si la chose a péri ou a été perdue sans la faute du débiteur et avant qu'il fût en demeure.*
Lors même que le débiteur est en demeure, et s'il ne s'est pas chargé des cas fortuits, l'obligation est éteinte dans le cas où la chose fût également périe chez le créancier si elle lui eût été livrée.
Le débiteur est tenu de prouver le cas fortuit qu'il allègue.
De quelque manière que la chose volée ait périe ou ait été perdue sa perte ne dispense pas celui qui l'a soustraite, de la restitution du prix.
223 See pages 22 and 33–34 *supra*.
224 See pages 75–78 *supra*.
225 Nicholas op. cit. (fn. 33), 200. See, for examples, former Articles 1108, 1126–1130 and 1172.
226 See page 43 *supra* for the wording of Article 1108.
227 Nicholas, op cit. (fn. 33), 200.
228 See, for example, former Article 1302, and Articles 1601, 1722, 1741, 1788, 1790 and 1867.

into the provisions of the *Code civil*, the concept of *rebus sic stantibus* nevertheless exercised considerable influence on French thinking throughout the nineteenth century. It was referred to in French legal circles as *la théorie de l'imprévision*, i.e. the theory of unforeseen circumstances. Latina defines *imprévision* as 'a generic term which designates a situation in which there has been a disequilibrium in a contract as the result of the occurrence of an event which the parties had not foreseen at the moment when they entered into it'.[229] Those who argued in favour of the termination, or at least the revision, of a contract in such circumstances based their arguments on an interpretation of the 'probable will of the parties'. The contracting parties, it was argued, would have entered into the contract on the basis of an implied condition: viz. that there would be stability in the economic circumstances which were the general context of the contract. In every contract, a tacit clause had to be implied, whereby the price would remain fixed only insofar as the economic situation remained constant. But if the economic situation changed radically, the original price could not be maintained in the changed circumstances.

La théorie de l'imprévision was advanced in a series of cases involving insurance cover in the mid-nineteenth century. There was in France at this time a lottery for conscription, and insurance companies would contract with an insured party to find a substitute should the insured be conscripted.[230] However, in 1843 the number of conscripts called up was raised by law from 80,000 to 140,000.[231] The insurance companies argued that this unforeseen but fundamental change in circumstances radically affected the basis upon which they had calculated their premiums, and they should therefore be released from their contracts due to *imprévision*. In several cases, the lower courts did rescind the contracts by adopting a broad interpretation of *force majeure*. But these decisions were reversed in 1856 by the *Cour de cassation*, which declared that *force majeure* was restricted to instances of absolute impossibility of performance.[232]

However, the debate over *imprévision* did not end with this decision. In 1876 the issue came to a head, in the famous case of the *Syndicat des arrosants de Pélisanne c. de Gallifet e.a.*, otherwise known as the *Canal de Craponne* case.[233] Contracts had been signed in 1560 and 1567, in which it was agreed between the parties that certain farmlands would be irrigated from a canal for a fixed annual sum of money. These contracts remained ongoing for the next

---

229 Mathias Latina *L'imprévision Blog Réforme du droit des obligations (Le blog Dalloz dédié à la réforme des obligations)* 1, 2.
  http://reforme-obligations.dalloz.fr/2015/03/23/limprevision/.
230 Zweigert and Kötz, op. cit., 525.
231 Id, 525.
232 Id., 525, 526. The decision of the *Cour de cassation* may be found at Cass.Civ. 9 jan. 1856, DP 1856.I.35 (*Poissonet et autres c. Barrault et Campagne*).
233 Cass. Civ. 6 mars 1876; S.1876.1.161; D. 1876.1.193, note Giboulot; reproduced in part in Rudden op. cit., 412.

three hundred years, during which time the annual sum of money paid by the landowners remained fixed at the original amount.[234] By the nineteenth century, this sum had become derisory, and the canal owners sought to have the amount paid by the landowners revised on the basis of *imprévision*. The case hinged on the proper interpretation of former Article 1134, which read as follows:

> Agreements lawfully entered into have the force of law for those who have made them. They cannot be revoked except by mutual consent, or for reasons which the law authorises. They must be performed in good faith.[235]

Both the court of first instance and the *Cour d'appel d'Aix* decided that former Article 1134 was qualified, with regard to *contrats successifs*, 'by a power in the courts, when there was no longer an equitable relationship between the payments of one party and the expense of the other, to restore the original balance'.[236] However, the *Cour de cassation* reversed the decisions of the lower courts, declaring that the provisions of Article 1134 were 'general, absolute and applied to all types of contracts, including those of successive performance, and that in no circumstances was it the role of the court, however equitable its decision might appear, to take into consideration the passage of time and the circumstances to modify the contract of the parties and to substitute new clauses for those which were freely accepted by the contracting parties'.[237]

In subsequent cases the *Cour de cassation* reaffirmed that *imprévision* was not a part of *force majeure*. *Force majeure* could only be invoked when performance was absolutely impossible, not when it had simply become more onerous for the debtor. Thus, for example, in the 1925 case of *Delphin e.a., Scté. Des Docks de Plombières c Lugagne* the *Cour de cassation* declared that '*force*

---

234 The contracts were held to be '*contrats successifs*', i.e. contracts of successive performance. Carbonnier defines a *contrat successif* as follows: 'there is ... a *contrat successif* when the obligations of at least one of the contracting parties must be performed by undertakings spread out over time ... A *contrat successif* creates between the parties a truly permanent contractual relationship': Jean Carbonnier *Les Obligations* (Tome 2) Presses Universitaires de France, 2004, 263. Article 1111-1 now defines contracts of successive performance as follows: *Le contrat à exécution successive est celui dont les obligations d'au moins une partie s'exécutent en plusieurs prestations échelonnées dans le temps.* (A contract of successive performance is one of which the obligations of at least one of the parties are performed in a number of acts of performance over a period of time.)

235 *Les conventions légalement formées tiennent lieu de loi à ceux qui les ont faites. Elles ne peuvent être révoquées que de leur consentement mutuel, ou pour les causes que la loi autorise. Elles doivent être exécutées de bonne foi.*

236 Nicholas, op. cit. (fn. 33), 208, 209.

237 Rudden, op. cit., 413.

majeure applies to those events which render performance of the obligation impossible but not to those events which make it more onerous...'.[238]

Moreover, the courts have usually construed *force majeure* in a narrow and restricted manner.[239] Events which have been found to render performance impossible and which therefore constitute *force majeure* have included earthquakes, lightning, storms and floods. Some human actions have also been held to come within the definition, such as riots, pillage, and armed robbery. Certain legal acts, such as orders of the public authority, expropriation, and requisitions have also been held to constitute *force majeure*.[240]

In addition to the requirement that performance be rendered impossible, the decisions of the *Cour de cassation* established three other requirements. An event amounting to *force majeure* had to be external, irresistible and unforeseeable.[241] All three elements had to be present cumulatively.[242] French jurists argued that the three elements derived from the words used in former Articles 1147 and 1148, viz. *'cause étrangère'* which evoked the notion of exteriority; *'force majeure'*, which evoked the notion of irresistibility; and *'cas fortuit'*, which evoked the notion of 'unforeseeability'.[243] This approach became known as the *'formule classique'*, or 'classic formula'.

In 1992 Paul-Henri Antonmattéi published his *Contribution à l'étude de la force majeure*, in which he challenged the notion that *force majeure* necessarily comprised the three components of the *formule classique*. Antonmattéi argued that irresistibility alone was sufficient to give rise to *force majeure*, because it necessarily encompassed the other two elements.[244] Shortly thereafter the *Cour de cassation* affirmed Antonmattéi's thesis, ruling on 1 October 1997 that irresistibility was indeed the only component required to give rise to *force majeure*:

---

238 Id., 431, (Cass. Civ. 17 nov. 1925; DH 1926.35; Gaz. Pal. 1926.1.68 (*Delphin e.a., Scté. Des Docks de Plombières c Lugagne*). However, as Rudden points out, at page 417, French courts 'may in fact discreetly revise contracts, especially where they cannot rescind them because they have been performed'. Pierre Legrand, in his article 'Judicial Revision of Contracts in French Law: A Case Study' (1988) 62 *Tulane Law Review* 963, posits that French courts do indeed revise contracts and examines various situations in which this has occurred. However, at page 1045, Legrand notes 'the steadfast refusal of the courts to revise contracts on the grounds of *imprévision*'.

239 Fabre-Magnan, op. cit., 767.

240 Carbonnier op. cit. (fn. 234), 309. When *force majeure* occurs as a result of an act of law, it is known in French as *'fait du prince'*.

241 Bénabent op. cit., 310.

242 Id., 310.

243 Carbonnier, op. cit. (fn. 234), 308; Bénabent, op. cit., 310. This logical approach of using each of the three key words to define the essential attributes of *force majeure* was certainly not present in the minds of the Drafting Committee when they turned their attention to formulating former Articles 1147 and 1148.

244 Paul-Henri Antonmattei *Contribution à l'Etude de la Force Majeure* Paris; Librairie Générale de Droit et de Jurisprudence, 1992, 63, 64.

The irresistibility of the event is, in and of itself, constitutive of *force majeure*, when foreseeability of that event would not have enabled one to have prevented its consequences, and given that the debtor had taken all measures necessary to prevent the happening of the event.[245]

The *Cour de cassation* reaffirmed the element of irresistibility as the only component required to constitute *force majeure* in a decision rendered on 6 November 2002.[246] In this case, the Court quashed the decision of the court of first instance, which had ruled that there could not be *force majeure* because the onset of illness in an aged person was not an unforeseeable occurrence. The *Cour de cassation* declared that only irresistibility should be considered.

However, during this same period, the *Cour de cassation* also rendered several decisions which continued to take foreseeability into account, albeit not as a separate element in its own right, but rather as a subordinate aspect of irresistibility. In 1994, for example, the Court declared that although irresistibility was, in and of itself, constitutive of *force majeure*, the debtor nevertheless still had to undertake all measures to avoid an occurrence of that event, which foreseeability made necessary. Thus, if the debtor failed to take all such foreseeable measures to prevent the irresistible event, (in this case an armed robbery), he could not then rely on *force majeure*.[247] Similarly, in a case decided in 1998, which involved the collapse of a crane during a cyclone, the Court found that although the event was irresistible, the debtor company had not taken all necessary precautions to protect its crane which foreseeability of the event made necessary, and therefore it could not rely on *force majeure*.[248]

The *Assemblée plénière* eventually sought to clarify the relationship between irresistibility and unforeseeability. This occurred in a decision rendered on 14 April 2006.[249] A purpose-built machine had been ordered by the creditor, so that he might thereby be enabled to undertake certain specialised activities related to his profession. The debtor was the only person capable of constructing a machine of this nature. The debtor was unable to deliver the machine by the agreed date, having become seriously ill with a particularly virulent form of cancer. Instead of informing the creditor of his illness, the debtor proposed to deliver the machine at a later date, to which the creditor agreed. The debtor,

---

245 Cass. Com., 1er oct. 1997, no. 95-12435: JCP G 1998, I, 144, p. 1098, obs. G. Viney.
246 Cass. Civ., 1re, 6 nov. 2002, no. 99-21203: RTD civ. 2003, 301, obs. P. Jourdain; RDC 2003, 59, obs. Ph. Stoffel-Munck.
247 Cass. Civ., 1re, 9 mars 1994, no 91-17459 et 91-17464.
248 Cass. Civ., 2e, 18 mars 1998, no. 95-22014; JCP G 1998, I, 144, p. 1098, obs. G. Viney.
249 Ass. Plén., 14 avril 2006, no. 02-11168; Bull. civ. ass. plén. 2006, no. 5, rapp. Petit, concl. R. de Gouttes; D. 2006, 1577, note P. Jourdain; D. 2006, chron. 566, obs. D. Noguéro, pan., 1933, obs. Ph. Brun et 2645, Obs. B Fauvarque-Cosson; JCP 2006, II, 10087, note P. Grosser; CCC 2006, 152, L. Leveneur; *Defrénois* 2006, 1212, obs. E. Savaux; RTD civ. 2006, 776, obs. P. Jourdain; RDC 2006/4, 1083, obs. Y. –M. Laithier, et 1207, obs. G. Viney; RLDC 2006, no. 2129, note M. Mekki; LPA 6 juil. 2006, 14, note Le Magueresse.

however, knew that he was physically unable to complete construction of the machine by this later date, and in fact he died soon afterwards. At issue was whether in these circumstances *force majeure* could be invoked. The creditor argued that although the fatal nature of the debtor's cancer was irresistible, in the sense that he would inevitably die from it, *force majeure* could not be relied upon, because once the debtor had become aware of his impending demise, he did not then take all steps necessary to mitigate the contractual consequences which foreseeability required.

The *Assemblée plénière* rejected the arguments of the creditor and instead found that the circumstances of this case did indeed give rise to *force majeure*. The Court declared:

> … there can be no occasion for damages when, as a result of *force majeure* or *cas fortuit*, the debtor was prevented from giving or doing that which he was obliged to give or to do, or did that which he was obliged not to do; this will be so when the debtor has been prevented from performing by illness; therefore this event, being unforeseeable at the time of the conclusion of the contract, and given that its consequences were irresistible, constitutes *force majeure*.[250]

As a result of this decision, the *Assemblée plénière* restored the element of unforeseeability as an independent and necessary requirement of *force majeure*. It was now no longer sufficient that the event simply be irresistible; it also had to be unforeseeable.[251] Moreover, the unforeseeability of an event was to be determined at the moment that the contract was concluded. This ruling made it easier for a debtor to plead *force majeure*, because a contracting party would be less likely to foresee the occurrence of an irresistible event upon concluding a contract than during the course of its performance.[252]

Although the *Cour de cassation* clarified the status of unforeseeability as an independent and necessary component of *force majeure* in its *Assemblée plénière* decision of 14 April 2006, it did not discuss whether the third element of the *formule classique*, viz. exteriority, also continued to be an essential element of *force majeure*. From the facts of the case, it could be assumed that exteriority was no longer an essential component, given that the illness of the debtor was not exterior to him. As a result, it remained unclear whether three or only

---

250 Id.
251 This was confirmed in a decision of the *Cour de cassation* on 30 October 2008 (Cass. Civ., 1re, 30 oct. 2008, 07-17134), in which the Court declared that 'only an event having an unforeseeable character, at the time of the conclusion of the contract, and being irresistible in its occurrence, is constitutive of a case of *force majeure*'..
252 Id., 769.

two of the traditional requirements of the *formule classique* were necessary in order to constitute *force majeure*.[253]

Force Majeure: The Current Law

Force majeure is addressed in the new law of contract primarily in three articles, viz. Articles 1218, 1351 and 1351-1. The first paragraph of Article 1218 provides a definition of *force majeure,* and the second paragraph sets out the consequences of *force majeure* when it is either temporary or definitive. Articles 1351 and 1351-1 elaborate on the consequences of *force majeure* when contractual performance has become impossible.

As the former articles did not provide a definition of *force majeure,* Article 1218 fills an important gap in the *Code civil*.[254] Article 1218 reads as follows:

> *Force majeure* arises in a contractual context when an event beyond the control of the debtor, which could not reasonably have been foreseen by him when the contract was entered into, and for which the effects cannot be avoided by appropriate measures, prevents the performance of the debtor's obligation.

If the impediment is temporary, performance of the obligation is suspended unless the delay which results justifies the termination of the contract. If the impediment is permanent the contract is terminated by operation of law and the parties are released from their obligations in line with the conditions set out in Articles 1351 and 1351-1.[255]

The wording of the new definition eliminates all references to the term *cas fortuit*. The terms *force majeure* and *cas fortuit* had been referred to indiscriminately throughout the former articles of the Code. However, the two terms had long been understood to mean exactly the same thing, and therefore only

---

253 In several subsequent cases the *Cour de cassation* declared that the element of exteriority was no longer a necessary element, although in other cases it stated that exteriority was still necessary. Id., 262. See, for example, Cass. Civ. 3e, 2 avril 2003, 01-17724, in which the Court declared that 'a hidden defect cannot be classified as a case of *force majeure*, because *force majeure* necessarily originates from outside the thing leased'.

254 Louis Thibierge 'L'impossibilité d'exécuter' *Blog Réforme du droit des obligations (Le blog Dalloz dédié à la réforme du droit des obligations)* at page 1.
http://reforme-obligations.dalloz.fr/2015/04/28/limpossibilite-dexecuter/.

255 *Il y a force majeure en matière contractuelle lorsqu'un événement échappant au contrôle du débiteur qui ne pouvait être raisonnablement prévu lors de la conclusion du contrat et dont les effets ne peuvent être évités par des mesures appropriées, empêche l'exécution de son obligation par le débiteur.*

Si l'empêchement est temporaire, l'exécution de l'obligation est suspendue à moins que le retard qui en résulterait ne justifie la résolution du contrat. Si l'empêchement est définitive, le contrat est résolu de plein droit et les parties sont libérées de leurs obligations dans les conditions prévues aux articles 1351 et 1351-1.

one term was required. Although the term *cas fortuit* still figures in the wording of the articles which address the specific contracts, the term will no doubt be eliminated when those parts of the Code are revised, so as to accord with the wording of Articles 1218, 1351 and 1351-1.[256]

The new definition also refers to the traditional components of unforeseeability and irresistibility, albeit in a much more nuanced manner. The 14 April 2006 decision of the *Assemblée plénière* had restored unforeseeability as an independent and necessary criterion of *force majeure*, and had further declared that the element of unforeseeability would be determined at the time of the conclusion of the contract. The new definition reaffirms both of these aspects of the *Assemblée plénière*'s 2006 decision. However, the wording of the new Article has refined the element of unforeseeability. The word 'unforeseeability' is not used in the definition; rather the Article refers to 'an event ... which could not have been reasonably foreseen when the contract was entered into...'.[257]

The element of irresistibility is set out in the definition as the second criterion of *force majeure*. It too is expressed in a much more nuanced manner. Irresistibility will arise when an event occurs, 'for which the effects cannot be avoided by appropriate measures...'.[258] The debtor must therefore prove that he took all 'appropriate measures' to avoid the event which occurred, and his actions will be assessed on the basis of whether there were additional 'appropriate measures' which he should have taken.[259]

The wording of the new definition excluded the third element of the *formule classique*, viz. exteriority. The *Rapport* declared categorically:

> The text (of Article 1218) adopts the judicial definition of *force majeure* in contractual matters, abandoning the traditional criterion of exteriority, which had already been abandoned by the *Assemblée plénière* of the *Cour de cassation* in 2006 *(Ass. Plén. 14 avr. 2006, no. 04-18902, no. 04-11168)*.[260]

The majority of French jurists have accepted that exteriority no longer forms an essential aspect of *force majeure*.[261] A more nuanced phrase – 'an event

---

256 See also the wording of Articles 1307-2, 1307-4, 1307-5, 1308 and 1360.

257 '*... un événement ... qui ne pouvait être raisonnablement prévu lors de la conclusion du contrat ...*'.

258 '*... dont les effets ne peuvent être évités par des mesures appropriées ...*'.

259 Fabre-Magnan, op. cit., 772. This wording harks back to those cases in which the *Cour de cassation* declared that there could only be irresistibility when the debtor had done all he could to prevent an event from occurring which was foreseeable, albeit irresistible if it occurred. See page 84 *supra*.

260 The *Rapport*, 19.

261 Fabre-Magnan, however, maintains that the *Cour de cassation* had not abandoned the notion of exteriority, and further that the text of Article 1218 had not abandoned the criterion of

beyond (or literally "escaping") the control of the debtor' – was instead included in the definition.[262] By virtue of this phrase any fact, whether external or internal, which the debtor cannot control, would come within the purview of *force majeure*.[263]

The second paragraph of Article 1218 deals with the effects of *force majeure* on the performance of the debtor. An event amounting to *force majeure* could render performance by the debtor either temporarily impossible or permanently impossible. The original articles of the *Code civil* had not addressed the consequences of *force majeure* when performance was rendered only temporarily impossible. This gap in the Code therefore required the intervention of the *Cour de cassation*. The Court declared in a number of cases that when *force majeure* rendered performance temporarily impossible, the contract would be suspended only for the duration of the event impeding performance. The position adopted by the Court can be seen, for example, in its decision of 22 February 2006:

> *Force majeure* only exonerates the debtor from his obligations for the period of time in which he is prevented from giving or from doing that which he was obliged to give or to do.[264]

The judicial response to *force majeure* of a temporary nature has been encapsulated in the first sentence of paragraph two of current Article 1218. The sentence declares that '[i]f the impediment is temporary, performance of the obligation is suspended...'.[265] This will occur, the sentence goes on to state, 'unless the delay which would result justifies the termination of the contract'.[266] Thus, when the event constituting *force majeure* is temporary, the normal response will be to suspend the debtor's performance for the duration of the event constituting *force majeure*. However, the creditor is at liberty to assert that circumstances do not permit him to await resumption of the debtor's performance, in which case he may seek the termination of the contract from a judge. The judge will then determine whether the *force majeure* in question requires the termination of the contract, or simply its suspension.

Under the previous regime, when the *force majeure* was permanent the debtor was no longer bound by his contractual obligation and the contract

---

exteriority. The requirement of exteriority, in her opinion, has rather simply been drafted in a more sophisticated manner: Fabre-Magnan, op. cit., 770 - 773.

262   ... *un événement échappant au contrôle du débiteur*...

263   Mercadal, op. cit., 201.

264   Cass. Civ., 3e, 22 fév. 2006, no. 05-12032; RTD civ. 2006, 764, obs. J. Mestre et B. Fages; RDC 2006/3, 763, obs. J.B. Seube, et 2006/4, 1087, obs. Y.-M. Laithier. Nine months after a storm the landlord had taken no action to repair the roof, which became the cause of damages suffered by the tenant.

265   *Si l'empêchement est temporaire, l'exécution de l'obligation est suspendue...*

266   ... *à moins que le retard qui en résulterait ne justifie la résolution du contrat.*

automatically came to an end, without the need for any intervention on the part of the court. Both the debtor and the creditor were released from their obligations, the debtor by virtue of *force majeure* and the creditor by virtue of cause. Cause linked the obligation of the debtor to that of the creditor, which meant that when performance by the debtor was obviated by *force majeure*, cause likewise obviated performance by the creditor.[267] The contract was ordinarily considered to have been terminated *ab initio*, so that the parties would be restored to their position prior to the conclusion of the contract. In those situations where this could not occur, the contract was simply terminated from the point at which the *force majeure* had occurred. If a judge was seized of the matter, he had to declare the resolution of the contract.[268]

This same approach has been adopted in current Article 1218. In those instances in which *force majeure* renders non-performance permanent, the contract will automatically come to an end and the contracting parties will be released from their obligations. This will occur 'in line with the conditions set out in Articles 1351 and 1351-1'.[269] Articles 1351 and 1351-1 read as follows:

> Article 1351: Impossibility of performance releases the debtor from his obligations to the extent of that impossibility when it is caused due to an event of *force majeure* and that it is definitive in character, unless the debtor had agreed to bear the risk of the event or has been given prior notice of default.[270]

267 See pages 43–44 and 68–70 *supra* for a discussion of cause. See also page 127 *infra*.
268 Although in the former regime *la doctrine* affirmed that when *force majeure* occurred the contract would be automatically rescinded and both parties released from their obligations by virtue of cause, the usual practice was to resort to former Article 1184 when *force majeure* was raised as a defence. Former Article 1184 provided for the recission of a contract in cases of non-performance by the debtor. When a judge rescinded a contract under former Article 1184 the contract would be declared retrospectively null, and the creditor would be awarded damages, when warranted by the circumstances. Former Article 1184 was originally designed to enable a creditor to proceed against a debtor who had breached his contractual obligations. However, in the 1891 case of *Conjoints Ceccaldi c Albertini*, Cass. Civ., 14 avril 1891, D. 1891.1.329, note Plainiol, Rudden, op. cit., 479, the *Cour de cassation* held that the Article could also be used in cases of *force majeure*. Under former Article 1184 the court possessed a discretion. It could rescind the contract *ab initio* and restore the parties to their original position. But if the *force majeure* had been only partial or temporary in nature, the court could refuse to rescind the contract and instead reduce or vary the creditor's performance in light of the reduced performance of the debtor: Nicholas, op. cit. (fn. 33), 206, 207; William Swadling 'The Judicial Construction of *Force Majeure* Clauses' 3, at 7, in Ewan McKendrick (editor) *Force Majeure and Frustration of Contract* London: Lloyd's of London Press Ltd. 1991. This flexibility has now been expressly built into the wording of current Articles 1218, 1351 and 1351-1.
269 *Si l'empêchement est définitif, le contrat est résolu de plein droit et les parties sont libérées de leurs obligations dans les conditions prévues aux articles 1351 et 1351-1.*
270 *L'impossibilité d'exécuter la prestation libère le débiteur à due concurrence lorsqu'elle procède d'un cas de force majeure et qu'elle est définitive, à moins qu'il n'ait convenu de s'en charger ou qu'il ait été préalablement mis en demeure.*

Article 1351-1: When impossibility of performance results in the loss of the thing due, the debtor put on formal notice to perform is nevertheless released if he proves that the loss would likewise have occurred had the obligation been performed.

He is nevertheless obliged to assign to his creditor the rights and actions attached to the thing.[271]

Article 1351, in conjunction with Article 1218, reproduces the former law by declaring that in those cases in which non-performance is definitive the contract is brought to an end, and the parties released from their obligations. In line with the former law, the contract will presumably be considered to have been terminated *ab initio*, except in those situations where this cannot occur, although the articles do not state this explicitly.

Article 1351-1 addresses translative contracts. Article 1218 indicates that when the loss of the thing occurs as a result of *force majeure*, and the debtor has not accepted the risk nor been put on notice, the debtor will be released from his obligation, and will not be responsible for the loss of the thing. This stands to reason as the title of the thing had already been transferred to the creditor by virtue of current Article 1196.[272] The loss will therefore be borne in such situations by the creditor. In this regard, the new law simply reproduces the former law, as set out in former Article 1302.[273]

Article 1351-1 then goes on to state that in those situations in which the debtor has been put on notice he will nevertheless not bear the loss of the thing if he can prove 'that the loss would likewise have occurred had the obligation been performed'.[274] This wording essentially reproduces the wording of former Article 1302, which stated, *inter alia*:

> Even where the debtor is under notice of default, if he has not assumed fortuitous events, the obligation is extinguished in the case where the thing would also have perished in the hands of the creditor had it been delivered to him.[275]

Thus, when the thing would have been destroyed by *force majeure* at that particular point in time, it makes no difference that the debtor was late in its delivery, because this would not have prevented its ultimate destruction. In

---

271   *Lorsque l'impossibilité d'exécuter résulte de la perte de la chose due, le débiteur mis en demeure est néanmoins libéré s'il prouve que la perte se serait pareillement produite si l'obligation avait été exécutée.*

Il est cependant tenu de céder à son créancier les droits et actions attachés à la chose.

272   See pages 64 *supra* for the complete text of Article 1196.

273   See page 79–80 *supra* for the complete text of Article 1302.

274   ... *que la perte se serait pareillement produite si l'obligation avait été exécutée.*

275   *Lors même que le débiteur est en demeure, et s'il ne s'est pas chargé des cas fortuits, l'obligation est éteinte dans le cas où la chose fût également périe chez le créancier si elle lui eût été livrée.* For the full text of former Article 1302 see page 79–80 *supra*.

such situations, the debtor, both under the former law and under the present law, will not be held liable for its loss.

Under the previous regime *force majeure* operated quite differently when the contractual obligation was one of means rather than one of result. Although the burden of proof lay in both cases with the creditor, the burden was much less onerous when the obligation was one of result rather than one of means. When the alleged fault involved the breach of an obligation of result the creditor had only to prove that the result was not achieved, whereas when the breach was of an obligation of means the creditor had to prove that the debtor failed to take reasonable care (*tous les soins raisonnables*).[276]

Once the creditor had proved that the result was not achieved, it was then incumbent on the debtor to prove that non-performance was the result of *force majeure*. If the debtor could not prove *force majeure* he would be liable, as stated in former Article 1148. The debtor could only escape liability if he could prove that he was unable to take measures to provide against the event.[277] With obligations of result, it was therefore the debtor who carried the burden of proof that there was *force majeure* which would exempt him from liability.

With an obligation of means, on the other hand, it was the creditor who carried the burden, because he had to prove that the debtor did not exercise the 'reasonable care' required of him. This burden of proof required the creditor to demonstrate that a person exercising reasonable care in the same circumstances as the debtor could have made provision against the supervening event which rendered performance impossible.[278] Thus the burden of proof was clearly more onerous for the creditor when the obligation was one of means.

Although the revised articles have removed all reference to contracts of giving, doing and not doing, there is still an ongoing role in the revised law for the categorisation of contractual obligations into those of means and those of result, given the qualitatively different nature of translative contracts. This categorisation will be necessary when proving that non-performance was the result of *force majeure*.

Current article 1231-1 sets out the general test of contractual liability as being either the non-performance, or the late performance, of the debtor's obligation, whenever he cannot demonstrate that non-performance was the

276 Nicholas, op. cit. (fn. 33), 52. The original wording of former Article 1137, as has been seen, was that the debtor had to exercise '*tous les soins d'un bon père de famille*'. That wording was subsequently amended to read '*tous les soins raisonnables*' by virtue of Article 26 of the *Loi no. 2014-873 du 4 août 2014 pour l'égalité entre les femmes et les hommes*.

277 Id, 201. Former Article 1148, it will be remembered, states that the 'debtor is condemned to damages … whenever he does not show that the non-performance is due to an external cause which cannot be imputed to him, even if there is no bad faith on his part'.

278 Nicholas, op. cit. (fn. 33), 201. The original wording of Article 1137 is reproduced at page 51 *supra*.

result of *force majeure* and which is not imputable to him. Demogue's analysis remains useful in the new regime in determining when non-performance arises. Under the new regime, as under the previous regime, non-performance will occur in most situations when the debtor does not produce the result bargained for, unless he can show that non-performance was the result of *force majeure*. The burden is therefore on the debtor, both under the previous regime and under the current regime, to demonstrate that the result was not achieved because of *force majeure*.

Translative contracts, however, derogate from this general principle, both in the former Article 1137 and in the current Article 1197, because in both contexts the debtor's contractual liability arises because of his failure to exercise 'reasonable care' over the thing.[279] This makes the burden of proof more onerous for the creditor, because in these circumstances the creditor must not only prove that the debtor did not act with reasonable care, but also that in exercising reasonable care the debtor should have made provisions against the supervening event which rendered performance impossible. The burden of proof, incumbent on the creditor, has not changed in the revised articles from what it was in the previous articles, and would therefore still need to be analysed on the basis of obligations of means and of result.

Imprévision in Administrative Law

There is a fundamental division in the French legal system between private law, on the one hand, and administrative law, on the other.[280] This division has resulted in two separate court systems, and two discrete bodies of substantive law. Whereas the domain of private law is in general governed by codes such as the *Code civil* and the *Code de commerce*, there is no code which governs administrative law. As a result, the legal rules which have been formulated in administrative law have been developed on an inductive basis from decided cases handed down by the *Conseil d'Etat*. These rules have been worked out by the administrative courts in a manner which can diverge significantly from the approach of the private law courts. This stands to reason, given that the rationale underpinning the orientation of private law and that of administrative law is fundamentally different. In the domain of private law, the role of the law is to treat the two parties equally, whereas in administrative law the public interest is held to outweigh the private interest, and the rules of law are oriented accordingly.

---

279 Former Article 1137 required the debtor to take '*tous les soins raisonnables*' ('all reasonable care') and current Article 1195 requires the debtor to take '*tous les soins d'une personne raisonnable*' (all the care of a reasonable person).

280 See pages 39–40 *supra*.

In 1873 the *Tribunal des conflits* took the opportunity, in the *Blanco* case,[281] to declare explicitly that decisions rendered in the administrative law domain would not be governed by the principles set out in the *Code civil*. Blanco's action was brought against the Prefect of the Department of the Gironde, as representing the State, for damage suffered by his daughter as a result of the conduct of workers employed in the Public Service. Blanco's claim was based on the principles of delictual responsibility as set out in Articles 1382, 1383 and 1384 of the *Code civil*.[282]

The *Tribunal des conflits* held that the principles of the *Code civil* were not applicable when the matter involved the potential liability of the State in such circumstances. In the course of its decision, the *Tribunal des conflits* made the following statement, which has come to characterise the independence and distinctive nature of administrative law:

> ... the responsibility of the State, being neither general nor absolute, is subject to special rules which vary depending on the exigencies of the Public Service and the need to reconcile the rights of the State with the rights of private persons...[283]

In the *Blanco* case the *Tribunal des conflits* declared unequivocally that the decisions of the *Conseil d'Etat* would not be governed by private law principles with respect to matters which fell within its jurisdiction, and that it would act independently of such principles when it saw fit to do so, given the underlying premise of administrative law that the public interest is to outweigh the private interest.

One of the areas in which the *Conseil d'Etat* dramatically departed from the approach traditionally taken by French private law has been with regard to *imprévision*. In a series of cases dating from the latter half of the nineteenth century, the *Conseil d'Etat* recognised the impact of *imprévision* on administrative law contracts.[284] Recognition of *imprévision* as a legitimate consideration was thereafter continuously reaffirmed by the *Conseil d'Etat* throughout the twentieth century.

The most famous case recognising *imprévision* as a legitimate consideration was *Compagnie générale d'éclairage de Bordeaux c. Ville de Bordeaux*, decided in 1916.[285] A contract to provide gas for the purpose of public lighting had

---

281 T. confl., 8 fév. 1873, D. 1873, III, 20. (*Blanco* c. *Le Préfet de la Gironde*) Delictual responsibility in French law is, broadly speaking, the equivalent of tort liability in the Common Law. Articles 1382, 1383 and 1384 set out the basic principles relating to delictual responsibility, and address both intentional tortious acts and negligence within their wording.
282 T. confl., 8 fév. 1873, D. 1873, III, 20. (*Blanco* c. *Le Préfet de la Gironde*).
283 Id.
284 Nicholas, op. cit. (fn. 33), 209.
285 CE 30 mars 1916; S. 1916.3.17, note Hauriou concl. Chardenet; D. 1916.3.25 concl. Chardenet; Rudden, op. cit., 422.

been concluded in 1904 between the City of Bordeaux and the *Compagnie générale d'éclairage de Bordeaux*. The price of the gas was set at a fixed amount for a period of thirty years. Coal was an essential raw material in the production of the gas. With the outbreak of the First World War, the coal-producing areas of France were occupied by the German army, and, as a result, the cost of coal rose precipitously. This had the effect, as the *Conseil d'Etat* observed, of 'completely upsetting the economy of the contract', to the extent that the company found itself unable to ensure the continued production of gas in the changed circumstances.[286] The Court's reference to 'the economy of the contract' was a clear reference to the classic definition of *imprévision*.[287] The *Conseil d'Etat* then declared that the public interest required that the company continue to provide an uninterrupted supply of gas, and noted that this could not be assured if the original terms of the contract were adhered to.[288] It decided that the case should be 'remitted for an assessment of an appropriate indemnity',[289] for the temporary period in which the intervening circumstances had made the production of the gas more onerous.[290]

In making this decision the *Conseil* laid down certain parameters which would govern a finding of *imprévision* in administrative law cases. An administrative judge was not permitted to revise or alter an administrative law contract, but rather simply to award financial compensation to the party who had been disadvantaged by the *imprévision*. A finding of *imprévision* could also be made only if the fundamental change in circumstances was temporary in nature. This was confirmed in the 1932 case of *Compagnie des Tramways de Cherbourg*.[291] In this case the *Conseil d'Etat* declared that if the impossibility of performance became permanent, the matter would then no longer be a case of *imprévision*, but rather one of *force majeure*, which would entitle the party unable to perform to bring the contract to an end.[292] The consequences flowing from *imprévision* and *force majeure* were thus significantly different in administrative law, although, as the Court pointed out in the *Tramways de Cherbourg* case, both required that there be an unforeseen event which was external to the parties.[293]

The fundamental difference in approach between French private law and French administrative law to *imprévision* was originally said to lie in their

---

286 Rudden, op. cit., 427, 428.
287 See page 81 *supra*.
288 Rudden, op. cit., 428.
289 Nicholas, op cit. (fn. 33), 210.
290 Rudden, op. cit, 428.
291 CE, 9 déc. 1932, S. 1933.3.9 (*Compagnie des Tramways de Cherbourg*).
292 Id. In the 1982 case of *Sté Propétrol* (CE, sect, 5, nov. 1982) the *Conseil d'Etat* reasserted that when there was *imprévision* under administrative law the contract remained on foot and the parties still had to perform their contractual obligations once the *imprévision* came to an end.
293 CE, 9 déc. 1932, S. 1933.3.9 (*Compagnie des Tramways de Cherbourg*).

different orientations. Because administrative law recognises the priority of the public interest, the *Conseil d'Etat* could not permit the gas company to fail, because this would have seriously damaged the public interest.[294] In the private law sector, on the other hand, considerations of the public interest do not apply, and the *Cour de cassation* adjudicates between contracting parties on the basis of equality, according to the provisions set out in the *Code civil*.[295] It was therefore thought that *imprévision* could only apply to administrative contracts in which there was an ongoing public interest. However, in 1976, the *Conseil d'Etat* held, in the case of *Département des Hautes Pyrénées*, that *imprévision* would apply to all administrative contracts, whether there was an ongoing public interest or not.[296]

The Introduction of *Imprévision* into Private Law

One of the most noteworthy innovations in the revised contractual provisions has been the introduction of an article which recognises *imprévision* as a legitimate basis for altering the terms of a contract. If there has been one area in which the *Cour de cassation* had 'made proof of an irreproachable consistency', it has been with regard to the theory of *imprévision*.[297] Since 1876, when it brought to an end the debate about the legal status of *imprévision*, the Court has steadfastly refused to recognise *imprévision* as a legitimate basis for undoing a contract. The decision in the *Canal de Craponne* case was based on the wording of former Article 1134, which declared that '[a]greements lawfully entered into have the force of law for those who have made them'.[298] The contract could not therefore be subsequently altered by the intervention of the Court, because former Article 1134 upheld the expressed will of the contracting parties. Their mutual consent to their agreement made that agreement binding law as between them, and this binding law had to be respected by all others, including the courts. The rule laid down by former Article 1134 was 'general and absolute' and it was 'not the place of a court, however equitable it may appear to the judge, to take into consideration the time and the circumstances in order to modify the contract of the parties and to substitute new provisions for those which had been freely agreed to by the contracting

---

294 Fabre-Magnan, op. cit., 621.

295 Nicholas, op. cit. (fn. 33), 210; Zweigert and Kötz, op. cit., 526. In administrative law there was no obstacle in the form of former Article 1134, as there was in private law.

296 CE, 12 mars 1976 (*Département des Hautes Pyrénées Conseil*). In this case the administrative contract had already been terminated when the Court found that *imprévision* would apply. See Fabre-Magnan, op. cit., 556.

297 Latina op. cit., 1, http://reforme-obligations.dalloz.fr/2015/03/23/limprevision/.

298 *Les conventions légalement formées tiennent lieu de loi à ceux qui les ont faites*. See page 43, fn. 31 *supra* for the full text of former Article 1134. This same wording is reproduced in current Article 1103, except that the word *conventions* has been replaced by the word *contrats*.

parties'.[299] The decision was a clear manifestation of the dominance of the theory of the autonomy of the will.[300]

The new law of contract has explicitly reaffirmed the theory of the autonomy of the will in Article 1102:

> Everyone is free to contract, or not to contract, to choose the party with whom he will contract, and to determine the content and the form of the contract, within the limits fixed by the law.
>
> Contractual liberty does not permit one to derogate from the rules which touch upon public order.[301]

As Fabre-Magnon has pointed out, the role of the will of the contracting parties remains of the essence of a contract and is its most significant criterion.[302] But from the latter half of the twentieth century, the notion that the theory of the autonomy of the will represented the foundational basis of contract law has been increasingly challenged, and the dominance of the theory has consequently waned considerably. It has become more and more evident that differences in economic power not infrequently make any real negotiation between contracting parties illusory. When this occurred the resulting contract was referred to as a 'contract of adhesion', because the weaker party was simply forced to adhere to a contract already completely drawn up by the dominant party.[303] In some cases, egregiously unjust conditions were imposed upon the weaker party, which were then defended against judicial intervention by reliance on the theory of the autonomy of the will. In order to undo such contracts the *Cour de cassation* was forced to resort, *inter alia*, to an expansive interpretation of good faith and to the subjective interpretation of cause.[304]

When the then Minister of Justice, Mme Christiane Taubira, launched the official consultation process for the *Projet d'ordonnance* on 25 February 2015, she announced that one of the primary reforming themes of the revised articles would be the protection of the weaker party.[305] The realisation of this theme

---

299 Cass. Civ. 6 mars 1876; S. 1876.1.161; D. 1876.1.193, note Giboulot. (*Syndicat des arrosants de Pélisanne c. de Gallifet e.a.*) Reproduced in part in Rudden op. cit., 412.

300 See pages48–49 *supra*.

301 *Chacun est libre de contracter, ou de ne pas contracter, de choisir son cocontractant et de déterminer le contenu et la forme dans les limites fixées par la loi.*
    La liberté contractuelle ne permet pas de déroger aux règles qui intéressent l'ordre public.

302 Fabre-Magnan, op. cit., 108.

303 Bénabent, op. cit., 43.

304 See page 68–69 *supra*.

305 At the launch of the consultation process on 25 February 2015, Mme Taubira declared that the reform of French contract law would have three primary objectives, viz. to make the law of obligations more readable and more accessible, to reinforce the protection of the weaker party, and to make the law more attractive: *Dépêches JurisClasseur – Actualités* Jeudi 26 Février 2015 – Civil – Réforme du droit des contrats: l'avant-projet soumis à consultation, 1. http://www.web.lexisnexis.fr/depeches-jurisclasseur/depeche.26-02-2015/03.

has been a prominent aspect in the new articles. Thus, under the new law of contract the concept of good faith has been elevated to a position of pre-eminence in Article 1104, and the various judicial interpretations of cause, which had been used to overturn the most extreme situations of contractual abuse, have been transformed into legislative provisions.[306] Various other articles have also been introduced which have no equivalent in the former articles, and which confer a greater degree of explicit protection upon the weaker party. Thus, Article 1110 recognises contracts of adhesion as a legal category, and contrasts such contracts to contracts of free will, i.e. those contracts which have been freely negotiated between the parties.[307] Article 1143 introduces a new concept of economic duress:

> There is also duress when one party, taking advantage of the state of dependence of the other party on him, obtains from him a contractual advantage which the other party would not have granted in the absence of such constraint, and is able to gain an advantage which is manifestly excessive. (2018 version)[308]

These innovations have been designed to protect the weaker party and thereby fulfil the reforming goal of the revision.

But the most significant innovation has undoubtedly been the introduction of a provision designed to protect a contracting party who finds himself in a situation of contractual disequilibrium as a result of *imprévision*. Although *imprévision* was repudiated by the *Cour de cassation* in 1876, it nevertheless remained a much-discussed subject in French legal circles. This debate intensified in recent times as the concept of *imprévision* was introduced into the legal systems of countries of similar stature to that of France. There are now provisions in the civil codes of most European states which provide legal solutions when unforeseen circumstances render the nature of the contract much more onerous for one of the contracting parties.[309] In International Law, as has been

---

306 See pages 68–70 *supra*.

307 Article 1110 (2018 version): *Le contrat de gré à gré est celui dont les stipulations sont librement négociables entre les parties.*

Le contrat d'adhésion est celui qui comporte un ensemble de clauses non négociables, déterminées à l'avance par l'une des parties.

(The contract of free will is one in which the contractual provisions are freely negotiable by the parties.

The contract of adhesion is one that contains a set of non-negotiable clauses determined in advance by one of the parties.)

308 (2018 version) *Il y a également violence lorsqu'une partie, abusant de l'état de dépendance dans lequel se trouve son cocontractant à son égard, obtient de lui un engagement qu'il n'aurait pas souscrit en l'absence d'une telle contrainte et en tire un avantage manifestement excessif.*

309 See Ewoud Hondius and Hans Christoph Grogoleit *Unexpected Circumstances in European Contract Law* Cambridge: Cambridge University Press, 2011, at pages 55–63 (Germany), 70–76 (The Netherlands) and 118–126 (Italy), for a discussion of the relevant provisions.

seen, the concept of a fundamental change of circumstances has been recognised in Article 62 of the 1969 *Vienna Convention of the Law of Treaties.*[310]

Model uniform contract codes drawn up by academics have also recognised *imprévision* as a legitimate aspect of contract law. Of particular note are the Unidroit Principles of International Commercial Contracts,[311] the Principles of European Contract Law,[312] the European Contract Code (otherwise known as the *avant-projet* Gandolfi),[313] and the Draft Common Frame of Reference.[314] Certain common themes run through the model contract codes with regard to *imprévision*, as well as the steps to be taken when it occurs. The Unidroit Principles refer to 'hardship', which arises when an event occurs which 'fundamentally alters the equilibrium of the contract'.[315] The Principles of European Contract Law refer to 'a change in circumstances' in which performance of the contract becomes 'excessively onerous'.[316] The European Contract Code

---

Hondius and Grigolet also examine the state of the law with various other European countries in their book. The *Rapport* noted that France was 'one of the last European countries not to recognise the theory of *imprévision* as a factor moderating the binding force of contracts': 15.

310 See pages 72–74 *supra*. France is not a party to the *Vienna Convention*, and objected, *inter alia*, to the wording of Article 62. See page 74, fn. 206 *supra*.

311 The Unidroit Principles of International Commercial Contracts were first published in 1994, with a second edition in 2004 and a third edition in 2010. They represent a non-binding codification of the general part of international commercial law. The Unidroit Principles can be accessed at:
     www.unidroit.org/english/principles/contracts/principles   2010/integralversionprin cipes2010-e.pdf.

312 In 1989 and 1994 the European Parliament enacted resolutions which expressed the desire to create a common European civil law, beginning with the creation of a common law of contract. The Commission on European Contract Law, which was an independent academic organisation under the direction of Ole Lando, had begun work on such a project in 1982. In 1995 the first part of the Principles of European Contract Law was published. The second part was published in 1999 and the third part in 2002. The Principles of European Contract Law can be accessed at www.trans-lex.org/400200.

313 A first draft of the European Contract Code, otherwise known as the *avant-projet* Gandolfi, was begun in 1995. In 1999 the draft of Book One, entitled 'Contracts in General', was completed in French. The draft of Book One was then published in French in 2001. In 2002 a second revised edition was published in French, German, English, Spanish and Italian. In 2004 a revised 'pocket' edition was published. The European Contract Code can be accessed at www.eurcontracts.eu/site2/docs/EuropeanContr.pdf. Professor Giuseppe Gandolfi of the University of Pavia was the director of the *avant-projet*, hence its name.

314 The Draft Common Frame of Reference (DCFR) was published in 2007. It was the product of a group of European academics who set out to establish model rules as a guide for the member states of the European Union. Its primary focus was originally with regard to a common frame of reference for contract law, although its scope now extends to other areas of private law as well. The DCFR is divided into ten books. Book II addresses contracts and other juridical acts, Book III obligations and corresponding rights, and Book IV rules in relation to specific contracts.

315 Unidroit Principles of International Commercial Contracts, Article 6.2.2.

316 The Principles of European Contract Law, Article 6.111(2).

refers to an 'unforeseen extraordinary event' which has made performance 'excessively onerous'.[317] The Draft Common Frame of Reference refers to 'an exceptional change of circumstances' which would make it 'manifestly unjust to hold the debtor to the obligation'.[318] When such circumstances arise, all four contract codes prescribe that the parties are entitled to renegotiate the contract.[319] If the parties are unable to agree, the matter will then be determined by a judge, either to modify the contract or to terminate it.[320] All four contract codes mandate that throughout the course of these proceedings, the parties must continue to perform their contractual obligations.[321]

In French legal circles, there was much disagreement about whether *imprévision* should be made a part of the revised articles.[322] The extent of this disagreement can be seen in the opposite conclusions reached by the *avant-projet* Catala and the *avant-projet* Terré. The *avant-projet* Catala refused to include a provision addressing *imprévision*, whereas the *avant-projet* Terré did include a provision. This provision appeared as Article 92 of the first volume of the *avant-projet* Terré. It read as follows:

> The contracting parties are required to fulfil their contractual obligations even if their performance has become more onerous. However, the parties must renegotiate the contract with a view to modifying it or terminating it when its performance has become excessively onerous for one of them, pursuant to an unforeseen change of circumstances and provided that the party had not agreed to assume the risk at the conclusion of the contract.
>
> Should the parties be unable to agree after a reasonable period of time, the judge can modify the contract, having regard to the legitimate

317 The European Contract Code, Article 97(1).

318 The Draft Common Frame of Reference, Article 1:110(2), Book III.

319 Unidroit Principles, Article 6.2.3(1); The Principles of European Contract Law, Article 6.111(2); The European Contract Code, Article 97(1), Article 157(3); The Draft Common Frame of Reference, Article 1.110(3)(d).

320 Unidroit Principles, Article 6.2.3(3)(4); The Principles of European Contract Law, Article 6.111(3); The European Contract Code, Article 157(5); The Draft Common Frame of Reference, Article 1.110(2)(a)(b).

321 Unidroit Principles, Article 6.2.1, Article 6.2.3(2); The Principles of European Contract Law, Article 6.111(1); The European Contract Code, Article 97(1); The Draft Common Frame of Reference, Article 1.110, Book III.

322 Even though the *Cour de cassation* would not recognise *imprévision* as a general principle of French law, it was of course entirely permissible for individual contracting parties to include provisions in their contracts which mitigated the consequences of *imprévison,* and this was done in contracts which were professionally drafted as a matter of course. The issue was therefore whether there should be a general provision in the revised articles which would mitigate the consequences of *imprévision* when the parties themselves had not included such a clause. The fact that *imprévision* has been included in the proposed articles is thus likely yet another attempt to fulfil the goal of protecting the weaker party.

expectations of the parties, or terminate the contract at a date and under the conditions which the judge determines.[323]

The first paragraph of Article 92 defines the elements of *imprévision*, and prescribes the process to be followed by the parties when *imprévision* occurs. The second paragraph elaborates on the process of contractual adjustment if the parties cannot agree. Both paragraphs drew heavily upon the criteria set out in the model contract codes with regard to *imprévision*.

The *Cour de cassation*, for its part, declared in its 2007 Report that the Court supported the adoption of provisions dealing with *imprévision*. Responding to the *avant-projet* Catala, the 2007 Report declared as follows:

> The group is unanimously of the opinion … that it is necessary that a reform of the law of obligations extend to the adoption of a genuine theory of *imprévision* capable of playing a role in those circumstances characterised by foreseeability. To rely simply on the principle of good faith would not suffice because it is necessary that the law be formulated with regard to the specific issue of *imprévision* in order better to assure judicial certainty.[324]

A provision addressing *imprévision* was included in the 2008 *avant-projet* of the Ministry of Justice.[325] This provision was only slightly amended in proposed Article 1196 of the 2015 *Projet d'ordonnance*. Proposed Article 1196 ultimately became current Article 1195. It reads as follows:

> If a change of circumstances, unforeseeable at the time of the conclusion of the contract, renders its performance excessively onerous for one party

---

323 F. Terré (dir.) *Pour une réforme du droit des contrats* op. cit., 247. The original French version reads as follows: *Les parties sont tenues de remplir leurs obligations même si l'exécution de celles-ci est devenue plus onéreuse.*

   Cependant, les parties doivent renégocier le contrat en vue de l'adapter ou d'y mettre fin lorsque l'exécution devient excessivement onéreuse pour l'une d'elles par suite d'un changement imprévisible des circonstances et qu'elle n'a pas accepté d'en assumer le risque lors de la conclusion du contrat.

   En l'absence d'accord des parties dans un délai raisonnable, le juge peut adapter le contrat en considération des attentes légitimes des parties ou y mettre fin à la date et aux conditions qu'il fixe.

324 '*A l'unanimité le groupe estime … qu'il est nécessaire qu'une réforme du droit des obligations aille jusqu'à la consécration d'un authentique théorie de l'imprévision susceptible de jouer dans des circonstances caractérisées avec prévision. S'en remettre à la simple application du principe de bonne foi ne serait pas suffisant car il est nécessaire que soit organisé par la loi le champ de l'imprévision de façon à meiux assurer la sécurité juridique*': quoted in Kami Haeri and Mahasti Razavi 'La Prévision dans le contrat, la prévision dans le procès' *Gazette du Palais* mercredi 29, jeudi 30 décembre 2010, 14, at page 15.

325 See Article 136 of the 2008 *avant-projet*.

who had not agreed to assume the risk, this party can request a renegotiation of the contract with the other party. The party must continue to perform his obligations during the renegotiation.

In the event of a refusal or a failure in the renegotiation, the parties can agree to terminate the contract, at a date and under the conditions which they determine, or, when in agreement, they can together request that a judge revise the contract. If they cannot agree after a reasonable period of time, one party can request that a judge revise the contract or terminate it, at a date and under the conditions which the judge determines.[326]

Article 1195 drew its inspiration primarily from the provision on *imprévision* in the *avant-projet* Terré, as well as elements from three of the model contract codes.[327] The first paragraph of Article 1195 mirrors almost word for word the first paragraph of Article 92 of the *avant-projet* Terré, although the order of those words has been significantly rearranged in Article 1195. It should be noted that the first paragraph of Article 1195 does not refer to *imprévision*, but rather utilises the phrase '*un changement de circonstances, imprévisible lors de la conclusion du contrat*', i.e. 'a change of circumstances, unforeseeable at the time of the conclusion of the contract'. This unforeseen change in circumstances must have rendered the contract 'excessively onerous' (*excessivement onéreuse*) for one of the contracting parties.

The phrase 'excessively onerous' is at the heart of Article 1195, because it is this state of affairs which defines the contemporary concept of *imprévision*. The phrase 'excessively onerous' was utilized in Article 92 of the *avant-projet Terré* and replicates the language used in Article 6.111(2) of the Principles of European Contract Law and Article 97.1 of the European Contract Code.[328]

Use of the phrase 'excessively onerous' indicates that performance of the contract by the affected party is still possible. This is confirmed by the final sentence in the first paragraph, which states that the affected party 'must continue to perform his obligations' during any renegotiation which takes

---

326 *Si un changement de circonstances, imprévisible lors de la conclusion du contrat rend l'exécution excessivement onéreuse pour une partie qui n'avait pas accepté d'en assumer le risque, celle-ci peut demander une renégociation du contrat à son cocontractant. Elle continue à exécuter ses obligations durant la renégociation.*

En cas de refus ou d'échec de la renégociation, les parties peuvent convenir de la résolution du contrat, à la date et aux conditions qu'elles déterminent, ou demander d'un commun accord au juge de procéder à son adaptation. A défaut d'accord dans un délai raisonnable, le juge peut, à la demande d'une partie, réviser le contrat ou y mettre fin, à la date et aux conditions qu'il fixe.

327 As Fauvarque – Cosson points out, the 2008 *avant-projet* drew upon the provisions of three of the four model contract codes, viz. The Unidroit Principles of International Commercial Contracts, the Principles of European Contract Law and the Draft Common Frame of Reference: Fauvarque-Cosson, op. cit., 3.

328 See page 98–99 *supra*.

place.[329] This phraseology emphasises the essential difference between *force majeure* and *imprévision*.

In the mid-nineteenth century, as seen above, there had been a concerted effort to introduce *imprévision* into French contract law, on the basis that *force majeure* was wide enough to include *imprévision*, given the similarities between the two concepts.[330] Both concepts involve the unforeseen occurrence of an external and irresistible event which radically alters the nature of the agreement, through no fault of the debtor. These similarities convinced a number of lower courts to extend *force majeure* to include *imprévision*. But in the *Canal de Craponne* case, the *Cour de cassation* emphatically rejected the notion that *force majeure* could be extended to include *imprévision*.[331]

Had *imprévision* been included in the concept of *force majeure*, on the basis of an implied term, this would have fundamentally undermined the essential attributes of *force majeure*. Since Roman times *force majeure* had been understood as an event which had rendered performance impossible, without fault on the part of the debtor, and which thereby terminated the contract. There could be no liability in such circumstances because there had been no fault on the part of the debtor.

This is very different from an unforeseen event which renders performance more onerous, or even excessively more onerous. In such circumstances, the contract has not been brought to an end by the intervention of the unforeseen circumstances, because the debtor is still capable of performing his obligation. The question then is whether the debtor should still be bound by his contract, having freely agreed to its terms, and should therefore bear the consequences of the change in circumstances in a contractual situation which is still ongoing.

The essential difference between *force majeure* and *imprévision* is that there cannot be performance in situations of *force majeure*, because performance has become impossible, and therefore that contract is necessarily at an end, whereas in situations of *imprévision* performance is still possible, and therefore the contract remains ongoing. This fundamental difference between *force majeure* and *imprévision* mitigates against the two concepts being merged into a single all-embracing concept, requiring instead that they be kept separate and distinct. This is precisely what had been done in the *Vienna Convention on the Law of Treaties*,[332] as well as in the model contract codes.[333] It is also precisely what occurred in the *Projet d'ordonnance*, which has now become the current law. Thus *force majeure* retains its traditional attributes in current

329   This sentence reflects the wording of Article 6.2.1 of the Unidroit Principles, which declares as follows: 'Where the performance of a contract becomes more onerous for one of the parties, that party is nevertheless bound to perform it obligations subject to the following provisions on hardship'.

330   See pages 80–81 *supra*.

331   See pages 81–82 *supra*.

332   See pages 72–74 *supra*.

333   See pages 98–99 *supra*.

Articles 1218, 1351 and 1351-1, whereas the newly introduced concept of *imprévision* is dealt with as a separate concept in Article 1195.

Although the *Cour de cassation* under the previous regime had steadfastly refused to permit alterations to a contract by reason of *imprévision*, this did not preclude contracting parties from writing into their contracts *force majeure* clauses which enabled them to revise the terms in the event of *imprévision*. Such clauses were entirely permissible by virtue of the principle of contractual freedom. Given this freedom, recourse to Article 1195 will only be possible when there is no clause already within the contract which addresses the issue of *imprévision*.[334]

Recourse to Article 1195 will also not be possible if the contract is aleatory, or, even if it is not, when the debtor has nevertheless assumed the risk.[335] Moreover, recourse to Article 1195 will depend on the time at which the contract was concluded.[336] If the change in circumstances was not foreseen at the moment of entering into the contract, but afterwords did become foreseeable, the fact that it was unforeseeable at the time the contract was concluded will be the decisive factor in allowing the affected party to have recourse to the article.[337]

The second paragraph of Article 1195 sets out the procedure to be followed by a party disadvantaged by *imprévision*. It too draws its inspiration from the common approach to *imprévision* set out in Article 92 of the *avant-projet* Terré and the model contract codes. That common approach prescribes that should the contracting parties not be able to negotiate an adjustment to their contract, the issue will then be determined by a judge, who will either modify the contract or terminate it. This is the approach adopted in Article 1195. But although modelled on the *avant-projet* Terré and the model contract codes,

---

334   Mercadal, op. cit., 169. Clauses which exclude the application of Article 1195 are now routinely inserted into commercial contracts.

335   Both an aleatory contract and a commutative contract are defined in Article 1108, in contradistinction to each other. Article 1108 reads as follows: 'A contract is commutative where each of the parties undertakes to provide a benefit to the other which is regarded as the equivalent of what he receives. It is aleatory where the parties agree that the effects of the contract – both as regards its resulting benefits and losses – shall depend on an uncertain event'. (*'Le contrat est commutatif lorsque chancune des parties s'engage à procurer à l'autre un avantage qui est regardé comme l'équivalent de celui qu'il reçoit. Il est aléatoire lorsque les parties acceptent de faire dépendre les effets du contrat, quant aux avantages et aux pertes qui en résulteront, d'un événement incertain'.*) Article 1197 specifically declares that the debtor must not have assumed the risk (... *pour une partie qui n'avait pas accepté d'en assumer le risque...*).

336   Casu, op. cit. (deuxième partie), 3.

337   Article 1195 specifies that *imprévision* is to be determined from the moment of the conclusion of the contract. In this regard, the determination of *imprévision* is the same as the determination of *force majeure*, which, according to Article 1218, is also to be determined from the moment of the conclusion of the contract. See page 87 *supra*.

the procedure set out in Article 1195 is much more detailed and elaborate than the procedure set out in those instruments.

Article 1195 requires the party affected by the change in circumstances to request a renegotiation of the contract with the other party. Should the other party either refuse to renegotiate or should renegotiations take place but fail, the parties can then agree either to terminate the contract, upon agreed conditions or to request that a judge revise the contract.

However, should the parties fail to agree on either alternative, then one of them can unilaterally request that a judge revise or terminate the contract, at a date and under conditions which the judge sees fit. Article 1195 has thus introduced into French contract law the possibility that a contract may now be altered and imposed upon a contracting party without his consent.[338] In this regard, Article 1195 constitutes a fundamental break from the law as it previously existed. Under the former regime, a judge could not intervene to rewrite or terminate a contract, by virtue of the theory of the autonomy of the will.[339] But Article 1195 now empowers him to do so.

Nevertheless, the primary aim of Article 1195 is actually to resolve problems arising from *imprévision* through the mutual consent of the contracting parties themselves.[340] Article 1195 was drafted so as to uphold, as far as possible, the mutual will of the contracting parties as the fundamental basis for resolving the problem. Thus the party affected by *imprévision* must continue to perform his obligations under the contract throughout the proceedings, and the parties must themselves first attempt to renegotiate the terms of the contract. Even if they cannot successfully renegotiate a revised contract, they are then required, by mutual agreement, either to terminate the contract, which at this point will only be possible if they can agree on the terms of its termination, or to agree to maintain the contract on foot in a revised form, on terms determined by a judge. The article has thus been drafted to encourage the parties to resolve their problem through a mutual agreement of one sort or another, i.e. either to terminate the contract on terms agreed to by the parties or to maintain the contract in a revised form, on terms determined by a judge. In either case termination or revision can only occur through the mutual agreement of the contracting parties.

It is only when all of the above-mentioned measures have failed that one of the parties may unilaterally request that the contract be either revised or terminated by a judge. In other words, intervention by a judge without the mutual agreement of the contracting parties is reserved until the very final stage in the proceedings, when the parties cannot agree on anything. The judge will then decide how to proceed and will impose such conditions upon the parties as he sees fit.

338 Mercadal, op. cit., 167.
339 See pages 48–49 *supra*.
340 Casu, op. cit., (deuxième partie) 3.

Although the second stage of the procedure still involves the agreement of the parties, it is unusual in that it requires the contracting parties, apart from terminating the contract on agreed terms, to accept the revised terms of the contract as determined by a judge, even though at the time of their agreement to do so, they will not know what those revised terms are. It is highly unlikely, as Fabre-Magnan points out, that contracting parties would agree to such an open-ended contract binding upon them.[341]

The third stage in the proceedings is even more draconian. At this point in the proceedings, when no agreement whatsoever has been reached between the parties, unilateral action can be taken by one of the parties which will be binding on both of them, so that the recalcitrant party may find himself bound by a revised contract which he did not want to continue in, and on terms which he did not agree to, or will find a contract which he did want to main-tain terminated and on terms to which he did not agree. In other words, the final stage of Article 1195 enables a judge to impose upon a contracting party terms to which he has not consented.[342] Whereas stage two permits a contract-ing party to agree to abide by the revised terms of his contract as determined by the judge, stage three removes even this limited and attenuated agreement, so that a recalcitrant party by stage three may have a revised contract imposed upon him without his consent.

It may be that stage two and stage three, with their increasingly coercive characteristics, have been designed to encourage contracting parties to freely renegotiate their contract at stage one, knowing that if they do not do so, that their freedom to negotiate revised terms will be increasingly taken away from them, until at stage three a revised contract may very well be imposed upon them without their consent and indeed against their will. The *Rapport* notes that the risk of having their contract either terminated or revised by the judge should encourage the contracting parties to negotiate.[343]

However, the wording of the Article, and the procedure set out therein, may actually give rise to problems which, from the outset, inhibit a success-ful renegotiation between the parties. At stage one, the parties are legally obliged to renegotiate the terms of the contract when one of them asserts that he is now subject to an excessively onerous obligation by virtue of *imprévi-sion*.[344] This means that at the initial stage, the affected party can unilaterally determine that performance of his obligations under the contract has become 'excessively onerous' and invoke Article 1195 to require the renegotiation of its terms, which the other party is then legally obliged to undertake. But

---

341 Fabre-Magnan, op. cit., 623, 624.
342 Mercadal, op. cit., 167.
343 The *Rapport* 16.
344 This assertion by the affected party, as well as the subsequent negotiations between them, must be made in good faith, as required by Article 1104: *Les contrats doivent être négociés, formés et exécutés de bonne foi. Cette disposition est d'ordre public.* (Contracts must be negoti-ated, concluded and performed in good faith. This provision is one of public order.)

how does the affected party determine that performance of his obligation has become 'excessively onerous'? There are no guidelines or directions in the Article as to the meaning of 'excessively onerous', and the affected party can obtain no assistance from a judge because there can be no recourse to a judge until later in the process, when renegotiation at the initial stage has not been successful.[345] The party who has benefitted from the change in circumstances may in good faith have a completely different view about the extent to which performance of the affected party's obligations has become more onerous. Given that contracts which are professionally drawn up will already address the possibility of *imprévision* through the inclusion of hardship clauses, it can be assumed that Article 1195 has been designed to protect those who do not draw up their contracts on a professional basis and are therefore not aware that they should include contractual provisions addressing *imprévision*. But those who are not thus aware are much less likely to know what would constitute performance which has become 'excessively onerous'. Yet by virtue of the wording of Article 1195 such relatively uninformed persons are unilaterally entitled to assert that their contractual obligation has become 'excessively onerous' and thereby force a renegotiation of the contract.

If the party who has benefitted from the change in circumstances is of the opinion that performance of the other party's obligation has not become 'excessively onerous', but merely more onerous, then he will of course not want to renegotiate away his benefit, so that failure of the renegotiation process will be assured, as would failure to come to an agreement to submit the matter to a judge, or to terminate the contract.[346] If all attempts at renegotiation fail, the affected party can then unilaterally request that a judge revise or terminate the contract. It is thus only at this third stage that the debtor may learn that performance of his obligation is actually not 'excessively onerous'.

---

345 When the then Minister of Justice, Mme Christiane Taubira, launched the *Projet d'ordonnance* on 25 February 2015, she referred specifically to the introduction of provisions in the new law of contract which would allow the parties to renegotiate their contract when *imprévision* had occurred. An example of *imprévision* was given. *Imprévision* would arise if a major international crisis, which had been unforeseen, occurred which made it impossible for a company to provide a certain product at the price agreed upon in the contract, except by selling at a loss and thereby putting the company in danger of survival: *Réformer le droit des contrats, Présentation en Conseil des ministres le 25 février 2015, Lancement d'une grande consultation* www.justice.gouv.fr/publication/j21dp_projet_ord_reforme_contrats_2015.pdf The example appears to be simply an adaptation of the Administrative Law case of *Compagnie générale d'éclairage de Bordeaux c. Ville de Bordeaux*, CE, 30 mars 1916; S. 1916.3.17, note Hauriou concl. Chardenet; D. 1916.3.25 concl. Chardenet; Rudden, op. cit., 422: see page 93 *supra*. This example does little to elucidate the meaning of 'excessively onerous'. Does the example provide the benchmark of what constitutes 'excessively onerous', so that a company must be on the verge of bankruptcy before it can be said that its obligations have become 'excessively onerous', or does the example simply provide the most extreme instance of an obligation which has become 'excessively onerous'? If the latter, what less extreme instances will nevertheless still constitute an obligation which has become 'excessively onerous'?

346 Latina, op. cit., 3.

On the other hand, it is also only at this stage that the party who has benefitted may learn that the obligation of the other party has indeed become 'excessively onerous' and have a revised contract imposed upon him against his will.

In order to avoid these problems, the *Chambre de Commerce et d'Industrie (Paris Ile-de-France)* suggested during the consultation period that a clause be added to Article 1195 to the effect that the judge readjust the contract 'with regard to the usages, market practices and legitimate expectations of the parties'.[347] This clause was not included in Article 1195. Its inclusion would have provided an appropriate test for a *bona fide* claim by one of the parties that performance of his obligation had been rendered 'excessively onerous' through *imprévision*, as well as the framework within which any renegotiation to adjust the terms of the contract would take place.

One of the very few decisions, to date, in which Article 1195 has been successfully invoked was rendered by the *Tribunal de commerce de Paris* on 14 December 2022.[348] In this case, a company had entered into a contract with another company to supply ceramic tiles, which the second company would then resell to clients. The contract had been concluded prior to the outbreak of the Russo–Ukrainian War. As a result of the war, the costs of energy, primary materials and transportation for the supplier increased exponentially, to the extent that it became impossible for the supplier to fulfil its obligations under the terms originally agreed upon. The supplier sought to renegotiate the contract, but the parties were unable to reach an agreement. The supplier then invoked the theory of *imprévision* before the *Tribunal de commerce de Paris*, requesting that the Tribunal intervene to revise the terms of the contract, as authorised by Article 1195.

The Tribunal found that the conditions necessary to establish *imprévision* had been satisfied. It noted in particular the extraordinary rise in the cost of energy.[349] It further noted that the supplier had not agreed to assume the financial risk resulting from unforeseen and external circumstances, and that neither party had been in a position to take into account the exceptional rise in prices which had occurred.[350] Given that the parties were unable to agree on the terms of a revised contract, nor to terminate it, Article 1195 empowered the judge, in the last resort, and at the request of one party only, to 'revise the

---

347 '*... en considération des usages, des pratiques du marché et des attentes légitimes des parties*': Yves Fouchet Projet d'ordonnance portant réforme du droit des contrats: Réponse de la CCI Paris Ile-de-France à la consultation ouverte par la Chancellerie, Rapport présenté par Yves Fouchet et adopté le 7 mai 2015, 19.

    http://www.cci-paris-idf.fr/.../reforme-droit-des-contrats-fou1505.pdf.

348 TJ, Paris, 14 déc. 2022, no. 2022033136.

349 The price of gas had increased by 316 percent: T. com. Paris, 14 déc. 2022, no. 2022033136.

350 Marine Hardy et Jean-Baptiste Olivo '*Est-il possible de renégocier son contrat si le prix de l'énergie est devenu trop onéreux?*'

    https://www.village-justice.com/articles/est-possible-renegocier-son-contrat-prix -energie-est-devenu-trop-onereux, 45236.html.

contract or terminate it, at a date and under the conditions which the judge determines'.[351] The Tribunal decided not to accede to the supplier's request to revise the terms of the contract, on the basis that the supplier had not provided the Tribunal with the financial particulars necessary to enable it to calculate a modification to the terms of the contract. However, it did decide to terminate the contract.[352]

As Lorant et al. point out, the guidelines set out in this case are clear: a contracting party who seeks a judicial revision of the contract by invoking *imprévision* must demonstrate that the change of circumstances is of extraordinary consequence to the performance of the contract, and that precise and detailed particulars of the revision sought must be presented by the applicant to the Court. It is only when these two conditions are satisfied that the Court may impose a judicial revision on the parties. Otherwise, the Court is only entitled to terminate the contract.[353]

It should be noted that there are significant differences between *imprévision* in administrative law and *imprévision* as set out in Article 1195. *Imprévision* in administrative law is a matter of public policy, and therefore the contracting parties cannot exclude it from their contract, whereas they can do so under Article 1195, as this is a suppletive article.[354] Moreover, an administrative law judge is not empowered to revise a contract or to alter its contractual provisions upon the occurrence of *imprévision*, but rather only to award financial compensation to the disadvantaged party. By virtue of Article 1195, on the other hand, a judge may both revise and terminate a contract, and may modify or delay performance by the debtor. Article 1195 also enables the contracting parties to limit the powers of the judge by themselves contractually assuming the risk of *imprévision*, or by choosing to renegotiate amicably the terms of the contract. The differing approaches of private law and of administrative law to the concept of *imprévision* clearly reflect the different orientations of the two parts of the law, viz. that private law seeks to treat the contracting parties equally, whereas administrative law gives greater emphasis to the public interest.

---

351 *A défaut d'accord dans un délai raisonnable, le juge peut, à la demande d'une partie, réviser le contrat ou y mettre fin, à la date et aux conditions qu'il fixe.*

352 Philippe Lorant, Arnaud Raynouard et Adélie Grimaldi (Deloitte. Société d'Avocats) '*Théorie de l'imprévision: que retenir de l'application de l'article 1195 du Code civil par le Tribunal de commerce de Paris?*' 13 février 2023, 1.

     https://blog.avocats.deloitte.fr/theorie-de-limprevision-que-retenir-de-lapplication-de -larticle-1195-du-code-civil-par-le-tribunal-de-commerce-de-paris.

353 Id., 2.

354 See page 162–163 *infra* regarding suppletive articles.

The Impact of COVID-19

In December 2019 a hitherto unknown coronavirus, COVID-19, suddenly erupted in Wuhan, China. The virus proved to be extremely contagious and spread rapidly throughout the world, resulting in death in many cases. On 30 January 2020, the World Health Organisation declared COVID-19 to be a public health emergency of international concern, and on 11 March 2020, it declared COVID-19 a pandemic.[355] COVID-19 has had a catastrophic impact throughout the world. Hundreds of millions of people have caught the virus and many millions have died. COVID-19 has become the most deadly pandemic since the Spanish flu of 1918–1919.[356] It has caused devastating social and economic disruption worldwide, resulting in the largest global recession since the Great Depression.

The virus first made its appearance in France on 24 January 2020, when a case was confirmed in Bordeaux. It spread rapidly throughout France, in successive waves, causing many people to fall ill, and many to die. In order to slow the spread of the virus, the government imposed three strict lockdowns at various points during 2020 and 2021.[357] It also put in place regional restrictions and curfews, closed non-essential businesses, and made compulsory the wearing of facemasks and the possession of a health pass. The devastating impact of the pandemic, as well as the extreme measures taken to control its spread, caused widespread and far-reaching difficulties to many businesses and commercial enterprises, including the closure of factories and workplaces, the disruption of supply chains, limitations on the free movement of personnel, labour shortages, and severely weakened consumer demand.[358]

French courts traditionally have not been receptive to the argument that a pandemic, or an epidemic, constitutes *force majeure*. Epidemic diseases which have not been accepted as *force majeure* include SARS,[359] Dengue fever,[360] H1N1,[361] Ebola[362] and the Chikungunya virus.[363] In each case, the courts held that the conditions required to constitute *force majeure* had not been satisfied. However, the exceptional nature of the COVID-19 crisis led to an early

---

355 'A pandemic is the worldwide spread of a new disease. An epidemic, on the other hand, is when many more cases of a health condition occur than expected in a certain region, but it does not spread further': www.healthdirect.gov.au.

356 An estimated 50 million people died, worldwide, as a result of the Spanish flu: www.cdc.gov.

357 These three lockdowns occurred from 17 March to 10 May 2020, 30 October to 1 December 2020 and 26 February to 2 May 2021, respectively.

358 Duncan Fairgrieve and Nicole Langlois 'Frustration and Hardship in Commercial Contracts: A Comparative Law Perspective' (2020) *Jersey and Guernsey Law Review* 142, 143.

359 CA, Paris, 29 juin 2006, no. 04/09052.

360 CA, Nancy, 22 novembre 2010, no. 09/00003.

361 CA, Besançon, 8 janvier 2014, no. 12/02291.

362 CA, Paris, 29 mars 2016, no. 15/05607.

363 CA, Basse-Terre, 1 déc. 2018, no. 17/00739; CA, Saint Denis de la Réunion, 29 déc. 2009, no. 08/02114.

judicial response which reversed this trend. On 12 March 2020, the Colmar Court of Appeal recognised COVID-19 as an instance of *force majeure*, in a case involving an immigration matter.[364] An asylum seeker held in administrative detention failed to appear before the Court because he had come into contact with a person likely to have been infected with the virus. There would be a risk of contagion were the asylum seeker to attend the hearing. The Court held that the applicant's absence was justified on the basis that 'these exceptional circumstances, which led to the absence of Mr. Victor G. from today's hearing, constitute a *force majeure* event, being external, unforeseeable and irresistible ...'.[365]

The French government also quickly signalled that it would consider the pandemic, at least in the domain of public law, as an instance of *force majeure*. On 28 February 2020, the then Minister of the Economy and Finance, Bruno Le Maire, announced that, due to the exceptional nature of the crisis, COVID-19 satisfied all the conditions of *force majeure*.[366] As a result 'contracting parties should recognise that difficulties encountered by their co-contractors are attributable to *force majeure*' and 'companies with public procurement contracts should not be penalised in the event of late performance'.[367]

This initial response by the government was then followed up by far-reaching legislative action. On 23 March 2020, the French Parliament adopted a law authorising the government to enact *ordonnances* to deal with the pandemic. The government declared a 'state of public health emergency' (*un état d'urgence sanitaire*) on 24 March 2020, and then proceeded, on 25 March 2020, to enact twenty-seven *ordonnances* dealing with COVID-19.[368] These *ordonnances* were designed to alleviate the impact of the pandemic itself, as well

---

364 CA, Colmar, 12 mars 2020, no. 20/01098.

365 Id. The Court of Appeal then confirmed this holding in a number of subsequent decisions, relating to the safety of its personnel: See CA, Colmar, 16 mars 2020, no. 20/01142 and no. 20/01143 and 23 mars 2020, no. 20/01206 and no. 20/01207.

366 Déclaration de M. Bruno Le Maire, ministre de l'économie et des finances, sur l'impact économique de l'épidémie de COVID-19 et les mesures de soutien en faveur des entreprises, à Paris le 28 février 2020:

vie-publique.fr/discours/273763-bruno-le-maire-28022020-cronavirus.

The statement of Le Maire in the original French reads as follows: '*L'Etat considère le coronavirus comme un cas de force majeure pour les entreprises. Ce qui veut dire que pour tous les marchés publics de l'Etat, si jamais il y a un retard de livraison de la part des PME (petites et moyennes entreprises) ou des entreprises, nous n'appliquerons pas de pénalités, car nous considérons le coronavirus comme un cas de force majeure*'.

367 Id. Because Le Maire referred to 'companies with public procurement contracts' his statement should be understood as limiting the recognition of COVID-19 as *force majeure* to public law only.

368 The state of public health emergency was originally for a period of two months, i.e. it was to come to an end on 24 May 2020. However, it was extended to 24 July 2021. A second state of public health emergency was declared on 15 October 2020. The state of public health emergency was lifted on 1 June 2021, and a four month transition period was then put in place.

as the measures taken by the government to combat it. Of particular note was *Ordonnance n° 2020–306*, which addressed the consequences that COVID-19 could have on contractual performance.[369] Article 6 of the *Ordonnance* declared that its provisions applied both to private law and to administrative law. Article 4 conferred on debtors a statutory postponement of their contractual obligations. Under Article 4 late performance penalties (*astreintes*), penalty clauses (*clauses pénales*), termination clauses (*clauses résolutoires*) and forfeiture clauses (*clauses prévoyant une déchéance*) were 'deemed not to have come into force or effect' for a prescribed period of time. Contractual deadlines for the termination of contracts were also extended for a prescribed period of time, by virtue of Article 5. Article 5 provided for the extension of contractual deadlines for the termination of contracts for a prescribed period. *Ordonnance n° 2020–306* was originally scheduled to come to an end after a two-month period, but was extended several times.

Ordonnance n° 2020-306 did not expressly identify COVID-19 as an instance of *force majeure*, but its effect was 'to create a situation analogous to temporary *force majeure*'.[370] The benefit for debtors in not explicitly identifying COVID-19 as an instance of *force majeure* was that they were not required to provide legal proof that temporary *force majeure* had actually occurred. The rationale behind this scheme was to prevent a surge in lawsuits which might otherwise overwhelm the courts and to encourage contracting parties to settle their outstanding contractual obligations in some alternative and non-judicial manner. But the postponements in contractual performance set out in *Ordonnance n° 2020–306* were only temporary in nature. This meant that all outstanding obligations for payment still eventually had to be paid according to the terms of the contract.[371] Contractual matters involving non-performance or delay in performance not resolved at the termination of the statutory period of postponement therefore ultimately had to be resolved by recourse to the law of contract.

It is important to note at this point that *force majeure* is not a matter of public policy, and its provisions may thus be replaced by a *force majeure* clause.[372] Many contracts do in fact contain a *force majeure* clause of one

---

369 Ordonnance no. 2020-306 du 25 mars 2020 relative à la prorogation des délais échus pendant la période d'urgence sanitaire et à l'adoption des procédures pendant cette même période (as amended by the ordonnance no. 2020-427 of 15 April 2020).
  https://www.legifrance.gouv.fr.

370 Catherine Pédamon and Radosveta Vassileva 'Contractual Performance in COVID-19 Times: Does Anglo-French Legal History Repeat Itself?' (2021) 29 *European Review of Private Law* 3, 20. See pages 87–88 *supra* for a discussion of temporary *force majeure*.

371 Pédamon and Vassileva, op. cit., 21.

372 In this regard see current Article 1102: 'Everyone is free to contract or not to contract, to choose the person with whom to contract, and to determine the content and the form of the contract, within the limits imposed by legislation. Contractual freedom does not allow derogation from rules which are an expression of public policy'. (*Chacun est libre de contracter ou de ne pas contracter, de choisir son cocontractant et de déterminer le contenu et la forme du*

sort or another.[373] Although this book does not extend to the consideration of *force majeure* clauses, such clauses, in the context of COVID-19, have assumed a crucial role in the way contracting parties attempt to work out their obligations under their contract. The interpretation of the wording of a *force majeure* clause will almost certainly be the determinative factor in ascertaining the extent of a party's contractual obligations, and whether or not that party can successfully modify or escape his obligations.[374]

Should a contract affected by COVID-19 not contain an applicable *force majeure* clause, the contract will then be governed by the general law. This became particularly critical with regard to commercial leases. The crippling impact of COVID-19, and the far-reaching and forceful governmental measures taken to combat it, led to the closure of a large number of commercial rental properties, prompting the tenants of those properties in many cases to unilaterally withhold rental payments and to assert that they were not obliged to pay rent during the periods of lockdown.[375] This in turn prompted the landlords of those properties to sue their tenants for the unpaid rent. A large number of cases came before the courts of first instance and of appeal to determine whether the tenants were obliged to do so, and the courts rendered a variety of conflicting judgments.

Commercial tenants put forward four legal arguments in their defence. The first was that of *force majeure*. Revised Article 1218 requires the debtor to prove that the event in question was beyond his control, that it was unforeseeable when the contract was entered into and that the effects of the supervening event could not be avoided by appropriate measures.[376] Commercial

---

contrat. *Dans les limites fixées par la loi. La liberté contractuelle ne permet pas de déroger aux règles qui intéressent l'ordre public.*)

373 A *force majeure* clause is a clause which provides for the adjustment or termination of the contract when certain specified events affecting the performance or outcome of the contract occur.

374 This was the issue in the case of *EDF (Electricité de France) and Total Direct Energie*, decided by the Paris Court of Appeal on 28 July 2020: CA, Paris, 28 juillet 2020, no. 20/06689. The decision of the Paris Court of Appeal was affirmed by the Cour de cassation on 11 May 2022: Cass. Com., 11 mai 2022, no. 20-20.622 (*EDF (Electricité de France) and Total Direct Energie*).

375 Gide Loyrette Nouel 'Covid-19 and commercial rents: the French Supreme Court rules in favour of lessors in the frame of three Court decisions dated 30 June 2022' (19 July 2022), 1.

   https://www.gide.com/en/news/covid-19-and-commercial-rents-the-french-supreme
   -court-rules-in-favour-of-lessors-in-the-frame.

376 These requirements are set out in the first paragraph of revised Article 1218, which reads as follows: 'In contractual matters there is *force majeure* where an event beyond the control of the debtor, which could not have been foreseen at the time of the conclusion of the contract and whose effects could not be avoided by appropriate measures, prevents performance of his obligation by the debtor'. (*Il y a force majeure en matière contractuelle lorsqu'un événement échappant au contrôle du débiteur, qui ne pouvait être raisonnablement prévu lors de la conclusion du contrat et dont les effets ne peuvent être évités par des mesures appropriées empêche*

tenants contended that these requirements were amply satisfied with regard to COVID-19 and the measures adopted by the government. The precipitous fall in commercial activities and the losses thereby sustained were directly linked to the public health crisis, making it impossible for commercial tenants to pay their rent.[377] It was argued that the rent due should therefore be suspended for the duration of the government lockdowns, as set out in the second paragraph of revised Article 1218.[378]

The problem with this argument, however, was that the courts had continuously held that *force majeure* could not be raised as a defence with regard to obligations involving financial payments. Such obligations are considered to be generic in nature and are therefore always capable of performance.[379] In other words, the financial difficulties of a debtor cannot constitute *force majeure*.[380] This had been confirmed by the *Cour de cassation* in 2014, when it declared that 'the debtor of a contractual obligation of an unpaid sum of money cannot exonerate himself from this obligation by invoking *force majeure*'.[381] Nevertheless, arguments based on *force majeure* were still put forward by commercial tenants.

---

l'exécution de son obligation par le débiteur.) See pages 85–89 *supra* for a detailed discussion of revised Article 1218.

377 Arnaud Boix 'Bail Commercial et loyers Covid: la Cour de cassation a tranché dans l'intérêt des bailleurs' (11 juillet 2022), 1.
     https://www.village-justice.com/articles/bail-commercial-loyers-covid-juin-2022-cour-cassation-vient-trancher-dans,43129.html.

378 The second paragraph of revised Article 1218 reads as follows: 'If the prevention is temporary, performance of the obligation is suspended unless the delay which results justifies termination of the contract. If the prevention is permanent, the contract is terminated by operation of law and the parties are discharged from their obligations under the conditions provided by articles 1351 and 1351-1'. (*Si l'empêchement est temporaire, l'exécution de l'obligation est suspendue à moins que le retard qui en résulterait ne justifie la résolution du contrat. Si l'empêchement est définitif, le contrat test résolu de plein droit et les parties sont libérées de leurs obligations dans les conditions prévues aux articles 1351 et 1351-1.*)

379 See pages 119 and 130–132 *infra* for a discussion of *force majeure* and obligations of a generic nature. French law has inherited this approach to generic goods from Roman law. See page 31 *supra* in this regard.

380 Bénabent, op. cit., 311.

381 '... *le débiteur d'une obligation contractuelle de somme d'argent inexécutée ne peut s'exonérer de cette obligation en invoquant un cas de force majeure*'. Cass. Com., 16 sept. 2014, no. 13-20306; RTD civ. 2014, 890, obs. H. Barbier; D. 2014, 2217, note J. François; RDC 2015/1, 27, obs. O. Deshayes. This would mean, as Deckert noted, that even though COVID-19 could be characterised as a *force majeure* event, it could not exonerate those debtors whose contractual obligations involved the payment of a sum of money. *Force majeure* could only be raised as a defence to the non-performance of contractual obligations that do not involve a payment obligation: Katrin Deckert 'Le droit des contrats en général et la force majeure en particulier à l'épreuve de la crise de la Covid-19' (12 avril 2021) https://www.cciparis-idf.fr.

The second argument put forward by commercial tenants was based on Article 1722. Article 1722 applies a special rule of *force majeure* to leased premises. It reads as follows:

> If, during the term of the lease, the leased thing is destroyed in its entirety by a fortuitous event, the lease is terminated by operation of law; if it is destroyed only in part, the tenant may, depending on the circumstances, request either a reduction in the price or the termination of the lease itself. In either case, there is no need for any compensation.[382]

The argument was that Article 1722 entitled the tenants to a reduction in their rent. The state of public health emergency was a 'fortuitous event' which had resulted in the 'partial loss' of the premises, as those premises could not be operated for the purpose rented. Given that the *Cour de cassation* had held, in a decision rendered in 2018, that Article 1722 would not be limited to loss that was material in nature, but would also extend to loss that was economic or judicial in nature,[383] commercial tenants submitted that this interpretation should equally apply in the circumstances of their case.

The courts of first instance and of appeal provided widely varying interpretations of Article 1722. Two examples will suffice to illustrate the differing judicial approaches. In a decision rendered on 6 May 2021, the Versailles Court of Appeal rejected the argument of the partial loss of the rented premises.[384] The Court noted that the premises had not been 'destroyed' either in whole or in part and that the inability of the tenant to use the premises was the result of the economic use to which the premises had been put rather than the premises themselves. Moreover, the tenant's inability to use the premises was limited in time, which was a factor unrelated to Article 1722.[385]

On the other hand, in a decision rendered on 16 December 2021,[386] the Douai Court of Appeal held that the partial loss of the rented premises 'was not restricted to the case of a material loss of the thing and extended to the

---

382 *Si, pendant la durée du bail, la chose louée est détruite en totalité par cas fortuit, le bail est résilié de plein droit; si elle n'est détruite qu'en partie, le preneur peut, suivent les circonstances, demander ou une diminution du prix, ou la résiliation même du bail. Dans l'un et l'autre cas, il n'y a lieu a aucun dédommagement.* Cf. the Roman law approach at page 29 *supra*, and the position expressed by Domat, at pages 153–154 *infra*.

383 Cass. Civ., 3e, 8 mars 2018, no. 17-11.439. See also Jean-Marc Peyron 'La destruction partielle d'un immeuble devenu impropre à la destination du bail entraîne la résiliation de plein droit du bail' (14 juin 2018).

   lexplicite.fr/la-destruction-dun-immeuble-devenu-impropre-a-la-destination-prevue-au-bail.

384 CA, Versailles, 6 mai 2021, no. 19/08848.

385 Id. See also Pascal Jacquot – Dalloz-Actualité (Edition du 22 septembre 2022) 'Covid et Perte de la Chose Louée: Premier Arrêt au Fond', 25 mai 2021.

   https;//www.dalloz-actualite.fr.

386 CA, Douai, 16 déc. 2021, no. 21/03259.

judicial loss in those cases where, as a result of circumstances, the tenant finds himself in a situation in which it is impossible to enjoy the thing or to utilise it in conformity with its purpose, particularly when this arises as a consequence of laws or regulations, or as a result of an administrative decision'.[387] The decisions of the two Courts of Appeal thus flatly contradicted each other.

A third argument put forward by commercial tenants involved Article 1719. Article 1719 reads as follows:

A lessor is bound, by the nature of the contract, and without need of any particular stipulation:

1. To deliver the thing leased to the lessee and, where the main dwelling of the latter is concerned, a decent lodging. When the premises leased as a dwelling are not fit for that use, the lessor may not assert the nullity of the lease nor its cancellation to demand eviction of the occupant;
2. To maintain that thing in order so that it can serve the use for which it has been let;
3. To secure to the lessee a peaceful enjoyment for the duration of the lease;
4. To secure also the permanence and quality of plantings.[388]

This argument was based on '*l'exception d'inexécution*', otherwise known in English as the defence of non-performance. Prior to the 2016 revision *l'exception d'inexécution* had not been set out in the *Code civil*, but had nevertheless been recognised as a legitimate defence in judicial decisions. *L'exception d'inexécution* entitles a party to a synallagmatic contract to withhold performance of his contractual obligations, either in whole or in part, when the other contracting party has not performed his obligations.[389] The defence does not entitle the party raising it to disregard or abandon his obligations; it merely

---

387 '... *n'est pas restreinte au cas de perte matérielle de la chose et s'étend à la perte juridique dans les cas où, par suite des circonstances, le preneur se trouve dans l'impossibilité de jouir de la chose, ou d'en faire un usage conforme à sa destination, notamment à la suite de dispositions légales ou réglementaires ou d'une décision administrative*'.

388 *Le bailleur est obligé, par la nature de contrat, et sans qu'il soit besoin d'aucune stipulation particulière:*

    1. De délivrer au preneur la chose louée, et s'il s'agit de son habitation principale, un logement décent. Lorsque des locaux loués à usage d'habitation sont impropres à cet usage, le bailleur ne peut se prévaloir de la nullité du bail ou de sa résiliation pour demander l'expulsion de l'occupant.

    2. D'entretenir cette chose en état de servir à l'usage pour lequel elle a été louée;

    3. D'en faire jouir paisiblement le preneur pendant la durée du bail;

    4. D'assurer également la permanence et la qualité des plantations.

389 The defence of *l'exception d'inexécution* is derived from the medieval Roman law defence of *exceptio non adimpleti contractus* (exception of a non-performed contract): Nicholas, op. cit. (fn. 33), 213.

entitles him to suspend those obligations. Since the 2016 revision, *l'exception d'inexécution* has been explicitly set out in revised Articles 1217 and 1219. Article 1217 reads as follows:

> A party towards whom an undertaking has not been performed or has been performed imperfectly may:
>
> • refuse to perform or to suspend his own obligations:
> • seek enforced performance in kind of the undertaking;
> • obtain a reduction in price;
> • provoke the termination of the contract;
> • claim reparation of the non-performance of the contract;
>
> Sanctions which are not incompatible may be combined; damages may always be added to any of the others.
>
> (2018 version)[390]

Article 1219 reads as follows:

> A party may refuse to perform his obligation, even where it is enforceable, if the other party does not perform his own and if this non-performance is sufficiently serious.[391]

The argument based on Article 1719 was that, as a result of the governmental lockdowns, landlords of rental properties were unable to fulfil their obligation to 'deliver' the premises for the commercial purposes for which they had been leased, because no commerce could be conducted during the periods of lockdown. The premises were consequently not 'fit for that use', as required by Article 1719. The failure of landlords to perform their part of the contract entitled the tenants, by virtue of Articles 1217 and 1219, to raise the defence of *l'exception d'inexécution* and so to withhold their rent during the periods of lockdown.

This argument had been rejected by the District Court of Paris, in a decision rendered on 25 February 2021.[392] The Court declared that Article 1719

---

390 (2018 version) *La partie envers laquelle l'engagement n'a pas été exécuté, ou l'été imparfaite-ment, peut;*
  • *refuser d'exécuter ou suspendre 'exécution de sa propre obligation;*
  • *poursuivre l'exécution forcée en nature de l'obligation;*
  • *obtenir une réduction du prix;*
  • *provoquer la résolution du contrat;*
  • *demander réparation des conséquences de l'inexécution.*
    Les sanctions qui ne sont pas incompatibles peuvent être cumulées; des dommages et intérêts peuvent toujours s'y ajouter.
391 *Une partie peut refuser d'exécuter son obligation, alors même que celle-ci est exigible, si l'autre n'exécute pas la sienne et si cette inexécution est suffisamment grave.*
392 TJ, Paris, 25 fév. 2021, no. 18/02353.

'did not require the landlord to guarantee to the tenant the foot-traffic of the leased premises and the stability of the legal framework in which his business is carried on'.[393] Commercial tenants nevertheless continued to assert this interpretation of Article 1719.

A fourth argument put forward by commercial tenants was based on the principle of good faith, as set out in revised Article 1104. According to revised Article 1104, good faith is a principle of public order and requires that contracts be negotiated, concluded and performed in good faith.[394] In certain cases, this requirement of good faith may impose upon the parties a modification of the manner in which their contractual obligations are performed.[395] Commercial tenants relied on Article 1104 to argue that their landlords were acting in bad faith by demanding the payment of rent under the original terms of the lease, without taking into account the altered conditions wrought by the government lockdowns.[396] They asserted that in the circumstances the principle of good faith required a modification of their rental payments.

The courts necessarily had to determine on a case-by-case basis whether landlords and tenants had acted in good faith in the circumstances. In this regard, they examined the conduct of individual landlords and tenants, with particular focus on the extent to which each of the two parties was open to renegotiating an adaptation of the financial terms of the lease during the periods of government lockdowns.[397]

This individualised approach inevitably led to a wide diversity of findings. Two cases will suffice to illustrate the diverse holdings which could ensue. In a decision rendered on 10 July 2020,[398] the District Court of Paris found that the tenant had to pay the full amount of the rent and tenant's charges owed, because the tenant had 'never requested the easing of his obligation over a clearly determined period', thereby breaching his duty of good faith, whereas the landlord had acted in good faith 'by not demanding the immediate payment of the rent and tenant's charges due according to the terms of the lease, and had proposed an alternative arrangement'.[399]

---

393 '*Cet article n'a pas pour effet d'obliger le bailleur à garantir au preneur la chalandise des lieux loués et la stabilité du cadre normatif, dans lequel s'exerce son activité*': Tribunal judiciaire de Paris, 25 février 2021, no. 8/02353.

394 *Les contrats doivent être négociés, formés et exécutés de bonne foi.*
   Cette disposition est d'ordre public.

395 Boix, op. cit., 3.

396 Id., 3.

397 Gide Loyrette Nouel, op. cit., 2, 3.

398 TJ, Paris, 10 juil. 2020, no. RG 20/04516.

399 '*Il ressort de ces éléments que le bailleur n'a pas exigé le paiement immédiat du loyer et des charges dans les conditions prévues au contrat mais a proposé un aménagement, et que le preneur n'a jamais formalisé de demande claire de remise totale ou partielle des loyers et/ou charges dus, ni sollicité d'aménagement de se obligations sur une période bien détérminée*'. Tribunal judiciaire de Paris, 10 juillet 2020, no. RG 20/04516.

On the other hand, in a decision rendered on 31 May 2021,[400] the District Court of Paris granted the tenant an eighteen-month extension on the rent owed. The court observed that 'taking into account the circumstances of this case, which demonstrate a real effort on the part of the tenant to maintain his business, the regulations currently in place and the situation of the company, the good faith of the tenant must be recognised, whereas the termination of the lease would entail very serious economic consequences'.[401]

The numerous decisions rendered by the courts of first instance and of appeal with respect to these legal questions were so diverse, and so much at odds with each other, that the matters in question could only be definitively resolved by recourse to the *Cour de cassation*. The *Cour de cassation* chose three 'pilot' appeals (*trois pourvois pilotes*), from amongst the thirty that were then before the Court, in order to declare the law with regard to the above four matters.[402] The Court took into account a note from the Ministry of the Economy, Finance and Recovery (*Ministère de l'économie, des finances et de la relance*) on the impact of the lockdowns on commercial rents.[403] The note indicated that approximately 45 percent of retail premises were closed during the health crisis, that the total amount of rent and charges was estimated at more than three billion euros, and that these businesses had been able to benefit from three aid mechanisms (*fonds de solidarité, l'aide aux coûts fixes et l'aide loyers*) as well as other support measures.[404]

The *Cour de cassation* handed down its decisions on the three pilot appeals on 30 June 2022.[405] The three decisions collectively addressed each of the four issues raised above. The Court rejected all four arguments that the tenants had put forward and held that the obligation to pay rent had neither been suspended nor nullified by the government lockdowns.[406]

The Court addressed the issue of *force majeure*, as set out in Article 1218, by noting that a tenant who was prevented from enjoying the rented premises pursuant to the terms of the lease was actually the creditor of the benefit of which he had been deprived.[407] The tenant could not therefore invoke *force majeure* in order to suspend the payment of the rent, as *force majeure*

---

400 TJ, Paris, 31 mai 2021, no. 21/50515.
401 '*Compte tenu des circonstances de la cause qui démontrent un réel effort du locataire pour la continuation de son commerce, des règlements effectués et de la situation du la société MABIL-LON 2009, la bonne fois du preneur doit être reconnue tandis que la résiliation du bail entraînerait de très lourdes conséquences économiques*'. TJ, Paris, 31 mai 2021, no. 21/50515.
402 Gide Loyrette Nouel, op. cit. 4; Boix, op cit., 1.
403 Osborne Clarke 'Covid 19 lockdowns & commercial rents' (4 July 2022)
     https://www.osborneclarke.com/insights/covid-19-lockdowns-commercial-rents.
404 Id.; Gide Loyrette Nouel, op. cit., 4; Lacoste et al, op. cit. 2.
405 Cass. Civ., 3e, 30 juin 2022, no. 21/19.889; Cass. Civ., 3e, 30 juin 2022, no. 21/20.127; Cass. Civ., 30 juin 2022, no. 21/20.190.
406 Gide Loyrette Nouel, op. cit., 2.
407 Margot Lacoste et Christophe Sciot-Siegrist 'Baux commerciaux et état d'urgence sanitaire: commentaire des arrêts de la Cour de cassation du 30 juin 2022' (5 juillet 2022), 2.

is a defence available only to debtors.[408] In this regard, the Court declared as follows:

> It derives from Article 1218 of the *Code civil* that the creditor who has been unable to benefit from the counterpart to which he was entitled cannot obtain the cancellation of the contract or the suspension of his obligation by relying on *force majeure*.[409]

The *Cour de cassation* had already made exactly this same ruling in a case decided in 2020.[410] In the 2020 case, a couple had entered into an accommodation agreement with an agency operating thermal baths. The couple were unable to enjoy the full vacation period because the husband suddenly fell ill and had to be hospitalised. His illness was not reasonably foreseeable and could not have been avoided by appropriate measures. The couple sought the termination of the contract and an indemnity from the company on the basis of *force majeure*. Their claim was rejected by the *Cour de cassation*, which noted that 'the creditor who has not been able to enjoy the contractual benefit which was his right cannot obtain the termination of the contract by invoking *force majeure*'.[411]

In addition, the *Cour de cassation* also rejected the argument of the commercial tenants concerning *force majeure* by noting that there was nothing preventing the tenants from fulfilling their obligation to pay the rent due. The Court thereby reaffirmed its decision of 16 September 2014,[412] in which it declared that the payment of a sum of money cannot be 'impossible' in the context of Article 1218 of the *Code civil*.[413]

The *Cour de cassation* then turned to the issues raised by Article 1722. Whereas the Court dealt with the issue of *force majeure* in one decision only, it addressed the issues raised by Article 1722 in all three decisions. Commercial tenants maintained that by virtue of Article 1722, they had been deprived of the premises for the purpose for which they had been rented during the

---

https://www.lemondedudroit.fr/decryptages/82579-baux-commerciaux-..e-sanitaire
-commentaire-arrets-courdecassation-30-juin-2022.html.

408 Fabre-Magnan, op. cit., 773.

409 '*Il résulte de l'article 1218 du code civil que le créancier qui n'a pu profiter de la contrepartie à laquelle il avait droit ne peut obtenir la résolution du contrat ou la suspension de son obligation en invoquant la force majeure*': Cass. Civ., 30 juin 2022, no. 21/20.190.

410 Cass. Civ., 1re, 25 nov. 2020, no 19/21060.

411 '*... le créancier qui n'a pu profiter de la prestation à laquelle il avait droit ne peut obtenir la résolution du contrat en invoquant la force majeure*': Cour de cassation, 25 novembre 2020, no 19/21060.

412 Cass. Com., 16 sept. 2014, no. 13-20306; RTD civ. 2014, 890, obs. H. Barbier; D. 2014, 2217, note J. François; RDC 2015/1, 27, obs. O. Deshayes. See page 112 *supra*.

413 '*... étant rappelé que le preneur reconnaît qu'il n'était pas dans l'impossibilité d'exécuter son obligation de payer le loyer ...*': Cass. Civ., 30 juin 2022, no. 21/20.190.

periods of lockdown, so that they were therefore entitled to a reduction of their rent.[414] The Court, however, gave short shrift to this argument:

> The effect of this general and temporary measure, with no direct link to the contractually defined intended use of the leased premises, cannot therefore be deemed equivalent to the loss of the thing, within the meaning of Article 1722 of the *Code civil.*[415]

Government lockdowns, occasioned by a public health crisis, which had the effect of preventing the public from frequenting commercial premises, could not, in the Court's opinion, be considered 'a loss of the leased thing' within the meaning of Article 1722. This was because the lockdowns were temporary and general in nature, with the single objective of preserving public health, and were without direct link with the contractual purpose of the rented premises.[416]

The *Cour de cassation* also dismissed the arguments based on Article 1719. Any failure to deliver the premises according to their intended purpose was due solely to the actions taken by the government; consequently, the landlord had not failed in his obligation to deliver the premises in conformity with the stated purpose.[417] Further on in its judgment, the Court dismissed both the argument based on Article 1719 and that based on Article 1722 in the same sentence:

> The effect of this general and temporary measure, with no direct link to the contractually defined intended use of the leased premises, cannot

---

414 As seen above, the Court had already held, in a previous case, that loss, within the meaning of Article 1722, could involve economic or judicial loss as well as material loss. See page 113 *supra.*

415 '*L'effet de cette mesure générale et temporaire, sans lien direct avec la destination contractuelle du local loué, ne peut donc être assimilé à la perte de la chose, au sens de l'article 1722 du code civil*': Cour de cassation, 30 juin 2022, no. 21/20.190. The same wording is reproduced in the judgment of the Cour de cassation: Cass. Civ., 3e, 30 juin 2022, no. 21/19.889. Similar. albeit expanded, wording was used in the judgment of the Cour de cassation at Cass. Civ., 3e, 30 juin 2022, no. 21/20.127. The wording used in no. 21/20.127 is reproduced at page 120 *infra.*

416 Lacoste et al., op. cit., 2.

417 The actual wording of the Court was as follows: '*Ayant relevé que les locaux loués avaient été mis à disposition de la locataire qui admettait que l'impossibilité d'exploiter, qu'elle alléguait, était le seul fait du législateur, la cour d'appel en a exactement déduit que la mesure générale de police administrative portant interdiction de recevoir du public n'était pas constitutive d'une inexécution de l'obligation de délivrance*': Cass. Civ., 30 juin 2022, no. 21/20.190. In coming to its conclusion the Court did no more than to confirm its decision of 2018 (Cass. Civ., 3e, 22 mars 2018, no. 17-17194) in which it had ruled that the impossibility to deliver pursuant to the prohibition by the public authorities cannot be imputed to the landlord. This interpretation of Article 1722 was confirmed by the Cour de cassation in its decision of 23 November 2021: Cass. Civ., 3e, 23 nov. 2021, no. 21/21.867.

be imputed, on the one hand, to the landlords, so that they cannot be reproached for a lack of their obligation of delivery, and on the other hand, deemed equivalent to the loss of the thing, within the meaning of Article 1722 of the *Code civil*.[418]

Therefore the tenants of commercial premises could not rely on the defence of *l'exception d'inexécution* to suspend payment of their rent, pursuant to Articles 1217 and 1219.

Finally, the *Cour de cassation* addressed the issue of good faith, as set out in Article 1104, in one of its decisions.[419] The tenant in this case alleged that the landlord had not acted in good faith. Three weeks after the end of the lockdown, the landlord had served the tenant with an enforcement measure, seeking payment of the full amount of the rent which had accrued during the closure of the premises, without having first made any attempt at renegotiation of the contract, in order to adapt it to the changed circumstances, apart from a proposal to postpone one month's rent.[420] The *Cour de cassation* rejected the tenant's claim, and found that the landlord had acted in good faith. The Court approved the decision of the Court of Appeal which, after having found that the lessor had proposed, in vain, to defer payment of the rent for April 2020, 'deduced, in its absolute discretion to find the facts, that [the landlord] had taken the exceptional circumstances into account and therefore showed her good faith'.[421]

As a result of these three decisions the *Cour de cassation* definitively rejected the arguments of commercial tenants, based on Articles 1218, 1719 and 1722, that their rent should be either suspended or nullified during the periods of government lockdown. Those articles, according to the *Cour de cassation*, could not be interpreted in a manner to justify the non-payment of rent, and the tenants were therefore contractually obligated to do so.

The *Cour de cassation* was unable to deal in the same definitive manner with good faith. This was because good faith is a matter which must be determined on a case-by-case basis. Consequently, there will no doubt be cases in which it is found that landlords have not complied with their obligation to act in good faith. However, given the finding of the Court that an offer to postpone the rent for a period of one month was sufficient to demonstrate the good faith

---

418 'L'effet de cette mesure générale et temporaire, sans lien direct avec la destination contractuelle du local loué, ne peut être, d'une part, imputable aux bailleurs, de sorte qu'il ne peut leur être reproché un manquement à leur obligation de délivrance, d'autre part, assimilé à la perte de la chose au sens de l'article 1722 du code civil': Cass. Civ., 3e, 30 juin 2022, no. 21/20.127.

419 Cass. Civ., 30 juin 2022, no. 21/20.190.

420 Id.; See also Gide Loyrette Nouel, op cit. 6.

421 'Ayant constaté que la bailleresse avait vainement proposé de différer le règlement du loyer d'avril 2020, la cour d'appel, qui n'était pas tenue de suivre la locataire dans le détail de son argumentation, en a souverainement déduit que la bailleresse avait tenu compte des circonstances exceptionnelles et ainsi manifesté sa bonne foi': Cass. Civ., 30 juin 2022, no. 21/20.190.

of the landlord, the Court may very well be signalling that it will be relatively easy for landlords to demonstrate their compliance with the duty to perform the lease in good faith.[422]

The one area which remains unresolved with regard to commercial leases is whether the impact of COVID-19 and the government responses entitle tenants to seek redress on the basis of *imprévision*, as set out in Article 1195. In this regard conflicting decisions by lower courts have made for uncertainty. For example, in a decision rendered on 12 December 2019[423] (and thus prior to the outbreak of COVID-19), the Versailles Court of Appeal declared that *imprévision* did not apply to commercial leases. This was so because

> the legal framework governing commercial leases contains numerous special provisions concerning the revision of the lease agreement (three year revision, index-linked escalator clause), there is no need to apply the general provisions of the aforementioned article 1195, and they are to be excluded in favour of the special rules contained in the legal framework governing commercial leases.[424]

On the other hand, the District Court of Paris, in a decision rendered on 22 June 2022, rejected this holding, declaring on the contrary that 'no legal disposition excludes the application of this mechanism of contractual revision with regard to commercial leases'.[425] The Court then went ahead and considered whether there had been *imprévision* in the circumstances of the case. The Court held that the onset of the pandemic did constitute an unforeseen change in circumstances, but found that the effect of this unforeseen change had not thereby made performance of the tenant's obligations under the lease 'excessively onerous', as required by Article 1195.[426]

There is, however, some doubt about whether '*imprévision*' can actually occur in the context of a commercial lease, as the obligation to pay rent cannot be made 'excessively onerous' to perform.[427] But the resolution of this matter must await a decision of the *Cour de cassation*.

---

422 Gide Loyrette Nouel, op. cit., 8.
423 CA, Versailles, 12 déc. 2019, no. 18/07183.
424 '*Dès lors que le statut des baux commerciaux prévoit de nombreuses dispositions spéciales relatives à la révision du contrat de bail (révision triennale, clause d'indexation) il n'y a pas lieu de faire application des dispositions générales de l'article 1195 précité, ces dernières devant être écartées au profit des règles spéciales du statut des baux commerciaux*': CA, Versailles, 12 déc. 2019, no. 18/07183.
425 TJ, Paris, 22 juin 2022, no. 20/08161. See also Louis Thibierge 'Quel champ d'application pour l'article 1195 du Code civil?' (12 septembre 2022) lagbd.org/Quel_champ_d_applica tion_pour_l'article_1195_du_Code_civil
426 TJ, Paris, 22 juin 2022, no. 20/08161.
427 Gide, Loyrette Nouel, op. cit., 7; Thibierge, op cit. For a detailed discussion of the term 'excessively onerous' see pages 100–107 *supra*. As a point of comparison, the financial difficulties of the debtor cannot be raised as a defence of *force majeure* under Article 1218.

In spite of the ongoing uncertainty surrounding Article 1195, the *Cour de cassation* has decisively clarified the law with regard to the payment of rent for commercial tenancies. Although the Court's rejection of the arguments submitted by commercial tenants regarding the loss of the leased thing (Article 1722) and the landlord's obligation to deliver (Article 1719) apply only to commercial leases, there is no reason why the findings of the Court should not equally apply to civil leases and professional leases.[428]

With regard to *force majeure* (Article 1218) the application of the Court's findings will be even wider. In its decision of 30 June 2022,[429] the Court reaffirmed that a creditor cannot invoke *force majeure, as* this is a defence available only to debtors, and that the debtor of a money obligation cannot rely on *force majeure*, as a money debt is always capable of being performed. These limiting factors will apply in all situations involving *force majeure*. Only those debtors whose contractual performance does not involve the payment of a money debt will be entitled to raise the defence of *force majeure*.

But even in those situations in which *force majeure* can be raised, such as the non-performance of a contractual obligation which is not monetary in character, the nature of the pandemic makes it difficult to satisfy the three essential conditions of *force majeure*. In order to successfully invoke *force majeure*, the debtor must show that the event was beyond his control, that it was unforeseeable when the contract was entered into, and that the effects of the supervening event could not be avoided by appropriate measures.

There is little doubt that COVID-19 satisfies the first condition. The pandemic, as well as the measures taken by the government, clearly put the matter beyond the control of the debtor. But the two remaining conditions may be more difficult to satisfy. The issue with the second condition concerns the time at which the pandemic became foreseeable. If the debtor was aware of COVID-19 before he concluded the contract, he cannot then plead *force majeure*. Fixing the date at which the pandemic became reasonably foreseeable by the debtor thus becomes crucial. But fixing the date is complicated by the fluid and mutating nature of the virus, by its unpredictable and incremental spread throughout the world, and by the varying responses of the government in combatting it.

The outer limits regarding unforeseeability present no problem – those contracts concluded before December 2019 will clearly come within the ambit of unforeseeability, and those contracts concluded after the declaration of the state of a public health emergency will clearly not. However, there is a considerable area of uncertainty between these two points. When exactly should the

---

428 Gide Loyrette Nouel, op. cit., 8. As Gide Loyrette Nouel point out, 'for residential leases the question appears generally moot since tenants were forced to stay at home, unless one were to consider the hypothesis of a tenant "stuck" abroad due to the pandemic and the banning of flights, and who was unable to use his home': Id., 10.

429 Cass. Civ., 30 juin 2022, no. 21/20.190.

date of reasonable foreseeability be fixed? Should it be on 4 March 2020, which was the official confirmation that there was an epidemic in France? Or should it be on 16 March 2020, when the first lockdown in France was declared? Or should it be on 23 March 2020, when the public health emergency law was enacted?[430] Perhaps the date should actually be much earlier; sometime in December 2019, for example, when the virus was first identified in Wuhan, China, or 30 January 2020, when the World Health Organisation declared COVID-19 to be a public health emergency of international concern. Fixing the actual date that the pandemic became reasonably foreseeable is indispensable in determining which contracts concluded or renewed in February and March 2020 will be entitled to raise the defence of *force majeure*.

The third condition may also be difficult to satisfy. A debtor must prove that there were no alternative ways for him to fulfil his contractual obligations and that performance had truly been rendered impossible as a result of the virus. But the changing nature of COVID-19, with its successive variants and their differing degrees of contagiousness and morbidity, in conjunction with a consideration of the increasingly effective protection of vaccinations, are complicating factors in attempting to determine whether COVID-19 does indeed satisfy the criterion of irresistibility. If the debtor has fallen seriously ill as a result of COVID-19 this will almost certainly constitute an instance of irresistibility, as will his failure to perform as a result of government lockdowns.[431] But by virtue of the variable nature of the pandemic, and the ever-changing responses of the government, there will inevitably be a grey area in which there is much uncertainty about whether this criterion has been fulfilled.[432]

Another complicating factor relates to the temporal aspect of the pandemic. The second paragraph of Article 1218 notes that the impact of *force majeure* on the debtor's performance may be either temporary or permanent in its effect. The Article declares that when the *force majeure* is temporary, the debtor will only be relieved of his performance for the duration of the delay, and must then once again perform when the *force majeure* is no longer in effect.[433] However, Article 1218 also specifies that should the delay become too long, the creditor is entitled to bring the contract to an end. Although

---

430 Pédamon and Vassileva, op. cit., 24.

431 Id., 25.

432 It should be noted that of the Colmar Court of Appeal, in its decision of 12 March 2020, considered whether there were any alternative 'appropriate means' for the applicant to appear before the court, and concluded that there were not, given that the detention centre did not possess the equipment necessary for the applicant to appear by means of a videoconference: CA, Colmar, 12 mars 2020, no. 20/01098.

433 The second paragraph of Article 1218 reads as follows: 'If the impediment is temporary, performance of the obligation is suspended unless the delay which results justifies the termination of the contract. If the impediment is permanent the contract is terminated by operation of law and the parties are released from their obligations in line with the conditions set out in Articles 1351 and 1351-1'. (*Si l'empêchement est temporaire, l'exécution de l'obligation est suspendue à moins que le retard qui en résulterait ne justifie la résolution du contrat. Si*

the pandemic will in some cases result in permanent non-performance by the debtor, in others, it will have only a temporary effect. However, given the changing and mutating nature of the virus and the variable effect that it has on individuals, the likely duration of the delay may become problematic, leading to uncertainty about whether the delay will be temporary or permanent in nature, and if temporary, for how long.

Each contractual debtor purportedly affected by *force majeure* will of course need to be assessed on the particular facts of the case. However, the multiple problems outlined above lead to the conclusion that the doctrine of *force majeure* may actually not be 'best placed to adequately address the challenges of performance resulting from the COVID-19 pandemic'.[434] If this is indeed so, resorting to the doctrine of *imprévision*, as set out in Article 1195, might be a better way of dealing with the issues raised by COVID-19. Article 1195, as seen above, has been invoked with regard to the payment of rent for commercial leases, albeit with conflicting decisions by the lower courts on its applicability.

There are, however, a number of problems that arise with regard to Article 1195. First, there is relatively limited access to Article 1195. The doctrine of *imprévision* only became a part of the *Code civil* on 1 October 2016, and therefore only applies to contracts concluded after this date. Contracts concluded before 1 October 2016 will continue to be governed by the contract law of the previous regime, i.e. when *imprévision* was not a recognised aspect of the law. Moreover, Article 1195 requires that there be 'a change of circumstances, unforeseen at the time of the conclusion of the contract'.[435] The necessity of establishing unforeseeability at the time of the conclusion of the contract raises the same issues as have already been discussed with regard to *force majeure*, viz. how and when to determine the date that the pandemic became foreseeable.[436]

Article 1195 also requires that a debtor who invokes Article 1195 'must continue to perform his obligations during the negotiations'.[437] This means that a debtor cannot obtain immediate relief from his contractual obligations. In addition, the requirement that performance has become 'excessively onerous' ('*excessivement onéreuse*') has not yet been judicially defined.[438] Consequently,

---

l'empêchement est définitif, le contrat est résolu de plein droit et les parties sont libérées de leurs obligations dans les conditions prévues aux articles 1351 et 1351-1.)

434 Pédamon and Vassileva, op. cit., 26.

435 '... *un changement de circonstances, imprévisible lors de la conclusion du contrat...*'.

436 See page 123–124 *supra*.

437 '*Elle continue à exécuter ses obligations durant la renégociation*'.

438 Jean Sébastien Borghetti 'Non-Performance and Change of Circumstances under French Law' 509, at 519, in Ewould Hondius, Marta Santos Silva, Andrea Nicolussi, Pablo Salvador Coderch, Christiane Windehorst and Fryderyk Zoll (editors) *Coronavirus and the Law in Europe* Cambridge: Intersentia, 2020; Fairgrieve and Langlois, op. cit., 150. In its decision of 14 December 2022 the Tribunal de commerce de Paris declared that *imprévi-*

undertaking an action on the basis of Article 1195 remains unsettled and risky. The debtor may allege that his performance has become 'excessively onerous' only to find out that this is not so.[439]

Article 1195 also sets out a long and unpredictable process of renegotiation between the parties.[440] Although this might turn out to the advantage of the debtor should the parties be able to renegotiate the terms of their contract, it may well be that they are unable to do so,[441] in which case Article 1195 empowers a judge in the final resort to impose a revised contract on them. To avoid this outcome, it is usual for contracting parties, as Borghetti points out, to circumvent Article 1195 with a *force majeure* clause of their own. A typical *force majeure* clause will take matters involving *imprévision* into consideration, but will keep the resolution of the matter within the control of the parties, rather than surrendering it to the discretion of a judge.[442] As a result, there have been very few instances of parties resorting to Article 1195 in order to resolve their contractual problems.

COVID-19 has wrought enormous havoc on French society as a whole, and in particular on contractual relationships. But the doctrines of *force majeure* and of *imprévision* both seem to offer only limited possibilities of recourse for parties who seek to mitigate or discharge their contractual obligations as a result of the impact of the virus.

---

sion would occur when there was 'a fluctuation of an extraordinary character' ('*le caractère extraordinaire de la fluctuation*') after the conclusion of the contract: T. com., Paris, 14 dc. 2022, no. 2022033136. A rise of 316 percent in the price of gas after the conclusion of the contract was held to be of an 'extraordinary character', i.e. that it was 'excessively onerous' ('*excessivement onéreuse*'): Lorant et al., op. cit., 2. See pages 106–107 *supra* for a discussion of this case.

439 See pages 106–107 *supra*.

440 See pages 103–107 *supra*.

441 This is precisely what happened in the case involving Article 1195 decided by the District Court of Paris: TJ, Paris, 22 juin 2022, no. 20/08161. The tenant entered into negotiations with the landlord under the negotiating procedure set out in Article 1195, but the parties were unable to reach a renegotiation of the lease. The Court noted that 'as a result of the terms of Article 1195 of the *Code civil* the obligatory force of the contract remained in effect during the entire period of negotiations between the parties. The [tenant] could not therefore unilaterally excuse himself from paying the rent and charges due to [the landlord] on the ground that the latter did not provide the desired response to his request to adapt the two leases' (*En outre, il résulte des termes précités de l'article 1195 du code civil que la force obligatoire du contrat est maintenue pendant toute la période des négociations conduites par les parties. La [...] ne pouvait donc se dispenser unilatéralement de payer le loyer et les charges dues à la [...] au motif que cette dernière n'avait pas apporté la réponse espérée de sa demande d'adaptation des deux baux*): TJ, Paris, 22 juin 2022, no. 20/08161.

442 Borghetti, op. cit., 519.

The Risk of Loss

The consequences of *force majeure* for the creditor will depend on whether the contract was unilateral or bilateral. In both types of contract, when *force majeure* occurs, the debtor is released from his obligation to perform. With unilateral contracts, this simply means that the creditor does not receive the benefit under the contract which would otherwise have been due to him.[443] With regard to bilateral contracts, the issue which arises once the debtor has been released from his obligation is whether the debtor can still demand performance from the creditor. Under the former law of contract, this was dealt with by the concept of cause. Cause, as has been seen above, was an essential element for valid contracts in the former law of contract. It was by virtue of cause that the obligations of the contracting parties were rendered interdependent, as each contractual obligation was the cause of the other. As a result, when the debtor was released from his contractual obligation the creditor was also released from his contractual obligations. The debtor therefore was unable to claim counter-performance from the creditor, and if the creditor had already performed in whole or in part, the debtor had to make restitution.[444] Consequently, the risk of loss fell upon the debtor, because the counter-performance which he expected under the terms of the contract and which could still be provided to him by the creditor would not now occur.[445] This was known by its Latin appellation of *res perit debitori*, i.e. the thing perishes at the risk of the debtor.

There was no provision in the former articles which indicated that the rule of *res perit debitori* was the general principle for allocating loss in the event of *force majeure*. Throughout the *Code civil* there were only scattered references, set out in the articles relating to the specific contracts, which indicated who bears the loss.[446] But although there was no article which established the rule as a general principle, this flowed logically from the interdependence

---

443 Larroumet, Bros, op. cit., 762.
444 Nicholas, op. cit. (fn. 33), 205.
445 Larroumet, Bros, op. cit., 763, 764.
446 These references, because they are set out in the articles relating to the specific contracts, have remained in effect, even though the general law of contract has now been revised. Thus, for example, Article 1722 releases the renter from future payments when the thing rented has been destroyed by *force majeure*. Article 1722 reads as follows: If, during the rental period, the thing rented is destroyed in whole by accident, the rent is cancelled by force of law; if it is only destroyed in part, the renter can, according to the circumstances, request either a diminution of the price, or the cancellation of the rental agreement. In either case, there is no occasion for damages. (*Si, pendant la durée du bail, la chose louée est détruite en totalité par cas fortuit, le bail est résilié de plein droit; si elle n'est détruite qu'en partie, le preneur peut, suivant les circonstances, demander ou une diminution du prix, ou la résiliation même du bail. Dans l'un et l'autre cas, il n'y a lieu à aucun dédommagement.*) As seen above, Article 1722 figured prominently in the debate about whether commercial rent was payable during COVID-19. See pages 114–115 and 119–121 *supra*.

of contractual obligations effected by cause, and French courts consequently generalised the rule in their decisions.

The general rule of *res perit debitori* continues to apply in the current articles. However, under the current articles, cause has been deleted as an essential criterion of a valid contract. Therefore cause can no longer be the basis for maintaining that the obligations of the contracting parties are interdependent. However, the second paragraph of Article 1218 specifically states that when the non-performance of the debtor's obligation becomes definitive through *force majeure*, the contract is automatically terminated, and both parties are released from their obligations.[447] Article 1218 states that this is subject to the provisions of 1351 and 1351-1. Article 1351 reiterates that the debtor is released from his obligation upon the occurrence of *force majeure* when he meets the requirements set out in the articles.[448] It will be the debtor who bears any loss – *res perit debitori* – because Article 1218 specified that both parties had been released from their obligations. Therefore, under the wording of the new provisions, the debtor cannot require performance from the creditor who is, like the debtor, released from his obligations by virtue of the intervention of *force majeure*.

Under the former law of contract the general rule of *res perit debitori* did not apply when the contract was one which related to the transfer of a thing, as occurs with contracts of sale and contracts of exchange.[449] If the rule *res perit debitori* were to apply in such cases, and the thing to be transferred to the creditor was destroyed by *force majeure* while still in the possession of the debtor, it would be the debtor who would bear the loss, and the creditor would not be obliged to pay the cost of the thing.[450] However, this was not the approach of French law.

In French law, by virtue of former Article 1138, ownership in the thing was transferred from the moment of the conclusion of the contract, by the exchange of consent of the contracting parties:

> The obligation to deliver the thing is perfected by the simple consent of the contracting parties.

It makes the creditor the owner and puts the thing at his risk from the moment when it should have been delivered, even if delivery has not been made, unless the debtor is not in a position to deliver, in which case the thing remains at the risk of the debtor.[451]

---

447 See page 89 *supra*.
448 See pages 89–90 *supra*.
449 Fabre-Magnan, op. cit., 775.
450 Id., 775.
451 *L'obligation de livrer la chose est parfaite par le seul consentement des parties contractantes. Elle rend le créancier propriétaire et met la chose à ses risques dès l'instant où elle a dû être livrée, encore que la tradition n'en ait point été faite, à moins que le débiteur ne soit en demeure de la livrer; auquel cas la chose reste aux risques de ce dernier.*

Once consent was given, the thing became at that moment the property of the person who had acquired it, even if the thing had not yet been delivered when *force majeure* intervened and caused the thing to perish.[452] In such cases, the rule *res perit debitori* was replaced by another rule, viz. the rule '*res perit domino*', i.e. that the thing perished at the expense of its owner, i.e. the creditor.[453] The rationale for this was that the debtor, by transferring ownership to the creditor, had thereby fulfilled his primary obligation under the contract, and the creditor was then the owner who would be held to pay the price agreed upon.[454]

This is also the case under the current régime. With translative contracts, Article 1196 declares that when there is 'alienation of the ownership or some other real right, the transfer of ownership takes place at the moment the contract is concluded'.[455] Article 1196 thus reiterates the same consequence as set out in former Article 1138, to the effect that if *force majeure* subsequently occurs, it will be the owner, i.e. the creditor, who will bear the loss: *res perit domino*. This is explicitly stated in the first sentence of the third paragraph of Article 1196:

The transfer of ownership includes the transfer of the risk to the thing.[456]

The rule of *res perit domino*, however, will not apply when the debtor has been put on notice to deliver the thing, as set out in Article 1344-2.[457] Having been put on notice will make the debtor liable for any risks associated with the thing.

Under the former articles, the rule of *res perit domino* applied only to the transfer of specific goods. Roman law did not recognise that *vis maior* could relieve a debtor of liability when the contract was one which involved generic goods.[458] This was also the approach of Pothier:

The extinction of obligations by the extinction of the thing due, cannot take place with regard to obligations of a sum of money, a certain quantity of corn, or wine, or to obligations of an indeterminate thing,

---

452 Fabre-Magnan, op. cit., 776.
453 Bénabent, op. cit, 317.
454 Fabre-Magnan, op. cit., 776.
455 *Dans les contrats ayant pour objet l'aliénation de la propriété ou d'un autre droit, le transfert s'opère lors de la conclusion du contrat.*
456 *Le transfert de propriété emporte transfert des risques de la chose.*
457 'However, the debtor who has an obligation to deliver will be liable for the risk of loss from the time that he has been put on notice, in conformity with the provisions of Article 1344-2 and subject to the rules set out in Article 1351-1'. (*Toutefois le débiteur de l'obligation de délivrer en retrouve la charge à compter de sa mise en demeure, conformément à l'article 1344-2 et sous réserve des règles prévues à l'article 1351-1.*) The complete texts of Articles 1344-2 and 1351-1 are reproduced, respectively, at pages 64, fn. 134 *and 89, supra.*
458 See page 31 *supra.*

as a cow or horse, not specifying any cow or horse in particular. There cannot be in this case any extinction of the thing due, as there can be no extinction of what is indeterminate.[459]

Pothier's approach was adopted by the Drafting Committee and written into the *Code civil*. The first paragraph of former Article 1302 declared that it was only with regard to specific goods, i.e. a 'certain and determined thing', that *force majeure* applied:

> When a thing certain and determined, which was the object of the obligation, has perished, is put out of commerce, or is lost in a way in which one can absolutely ignore its existence, the obligation is extinguished if the thing has perished or has been lost without the fault of the debtor and before he was required to deliver.[460]

As a result, former Article 1138 could apply only to goods which had been specifically designated. It did not apply when the contract was one which involved generic goods. In such cases, the transfer of ownership of things which were generic occurred only when the generic goods were actually delivered to the purchaser, or when they were designated, in which case former Article 1138 then did apply.[461] If generic goods were not designated, the contract was considered to be one of doing, i.e. of delivering the generic goods, rather than one of giving. Thus, if generic goods were destroyed by a supervening event which would otherwise have constituted *force majeure*, the debtor would not be able to plead *force majeure* and would not be relieved of his contractual obligation. In such cases, the debtor was always presumed to be able to procure the generic goods on the market.[462]

Generic goods are not specifically addressed in the new regime. There is no wording in the current articles which is the equivalent of the wording of the former Article 1302, referring to the perishing of 'a thing certain and determined, which is the object of the contract'.[463] Moreover, the classifica-

---

459 Pothier (Evans) op. cit., 387, 388, paragraph 622; Pothier (Dupin) op. cit., 395, 396, paragraph 658.
460 *Lorsque le corps certain et déterminé qui était l'objet de l'obligation vient à périr, est mis hors du commerce, ou se perd de manière qu'on en ignore absolument l'existence, l'obligation est éteinte si la chose a péri ou a été perdue sans la faute du débiteur et avant qu'il fût en demeure.*
461 G. Hubrecht *Droit Civil* (15e édition) Paris: Sirey, 1993, 89.
462 Carbonnier, op. cit. (fn.221), 309. Generic goods, which include debts of money, were addressed by the *Cour de cassation* in Cass. Com., 16 sept. 2014, no. 13-20306; RTD civ. 2014, 890, obs. H. Barbier; D. 2014, 2217, note J. François; RDC 2015/1, 27, obs. O. Deshayes. The debtor, having fallen gravely ill, argued that he was exonerated from paying a debt of money to the creditor on the basis of *force majeure*. The Court, however, found that the debtor of a contractual obligation to pay a sum of money could not be exonerated from this obligation on the basis of *force majeure*.
463 '... *le corps certain et déterminé qui était l'objet de l'obligation*...'.

tion of French contracts into giving and doing has been abolished, so that no distinction can now be made between contracts of giving, i.e. of transferring title to specific goods, on the one hand, and contracts of doing, i.e. of delivering generic goods, on the other, as occurred under the former regime.

However, the wording of the second paragraph of current Article 1218 and Article 1351 preserves the practice of differentiating between specified goods and generic goods which occurred in the previous regime, albeit in a different manner. These two articles have already been previously reproduced, but bear repeating at this point. The second paragraph of Article 1218 reads as follows:

> If the event which prevents performance is temporary, performance of the obligation is suspended, unless the delay which would result justifies the termination of the contract. If the event which prevents performance is definitive, the contract is terminated automatically and the parties are released from their obligations under the conditions set out in Articles 1351 and 1351-1.[464]

Article 1351 reads as follows:

> The impossibility of performing the contractual undertaking discharges the debtor where it results from an event of *force majeure* and is definitive, unless he had agreed to bear the risk of the event or he had previously been given notice to perform.[465]

The wording of these two articles would ordinarily exclude generic goods from the protection of *force majeure*. This is because in the event of the destruction of generic goods by what would otherwise be *force majeure* the debtor is not thereby rendered incapable of remedying his non-performance (Article 1218), nor does performance become impossible (Article 1351). In such cases, the debtor will still be able to procure the equivalent generic goods on the market.[466] The debtor may decide to designate the generic goods as

---

464 *Si l'empêchement est temporaire, l'exécution de l'obligation est suspendue à moins que le retard qui en résulterait ne justifie la résolution du contrat. Si l'empêchement est définitif, le contrat est résolu de plein droit et les parties sont libérées de leurs obligations dans les conditions prévues aux articles 1351 et 1351-1.*

465 *L'impossibilité d'exécuter la prestation libère le débiteur à due concurrence lorsqu'elle procède d'un cas de force majeure et qu'elle est définitive, à moins qu'il n'ait convenu de s'en charger ou qu'il ait été préalablement mis en demeure.*

466 This interpretation of Articles 1218 and 1351 is supported by Marc Mignot 'Commentaire Article par Article de l'Ordonnance du 10 février 2016 portant réforme du droit des contrats, du régime général et la preuve des obligations (VI)' *Petites Affiches*, No. 67, 04/04/2016, 5. Mignot asserts that the distinction between generic goods and specific goods must subsist under the new regime because one of the conditions of *force majeure*, viz. the impossibility to perform, cannot be satisfied with regard to generic goods. See also Fabre-Magnan, op. cit. 767, 768.

specified goods. Should the debtor do so, their destruction without fault on his part would enable him to claim the benefit of *force majeure*, because once specified the destruction of the designated goods makes it impossible for the debtor to perform.

The introduction of *imprévision* into the current law of contract as a basis for either altering or terminating a contract may also give rise to loss by one or other of the contracting parties. When the party claims under Article 1195 that performance of his obligation has become 'excessively onerous' as the result of an unforeseen event, and so initiates the process to obtain relief, he must nevertheless continue to perform his obligation throughout the period of sorting out whether that obligation has truly become 'excessively onerous' and what consequences should result. The issue then becomes whether the debtor can be relieved of the excessive amount he paid in the interim period once a new arrangement has been agreed to by the parties, or, if they cannot agree, when the matter has been decided by a judge. The party who has benefitted from the change in circumstances is unlikely to agree to a change which will deprive him of his advantage. In the case of *force majeure*, when an event renders performance by the debtor impossible, both contracting parties are relieved of their obligations, and to the extent that there has been partial performance by either party, that performance must be reimbursed. When there has been a loss, the rules of Article 1351 (*res perit debitori*) and Article 1351-1 (*res perit domino*) determine which of the two parties bears that loss.

But unlike *force majeure*, there are no set rules for determining how any loss resulting from *imprévision* will be determined, nor who will bear that loss. Articles 1352 to 1352-9 of the new provisions set out the rules relating to restitution. However, those rules do not apply to contracts subject to Article 1195. In such cases, a judge seized of the matter is at complete liberty to revise or terminate the contract as he sees fit, by virtue of the wording of the Article:

> Upon the failure to agree after a reasonable delay, the judge can, at the request of one of the parties, revise the contract or bring it to an end, at the date and under the conditions which he determines.[467]

If the parties can neither agree to submit the contract to a judge for his readjustment, nor agree to a termination of the contract, so that in these circumstances one of the parties may unilaterally seek readjustment of the contract, or termination of the contract, on what basis does the judge do so? The article seems to leave all of these questions first to the pure agreement of the parties themselves in a new round of negotiations, and then, if those negotiations cannot result in either a readjustment of the contract or the termination of the contract, at the pure discretion of the judge. But, as Stoffel-Munck points out,

---

467   *A défaut d'accord dans un délai raisonnable, le juge peut, à la demande d'une partie, réviser le contrat ou y mettre fin, à la date et aux conditions qu'il fixe.*

the readjustment of a contract by a judge is not a role for which he is particularly suited or equipped:

> To judge is to render to each what is his due according to justice; the mastery of the law guided by a sense of equity will suffice in this regard. But to fix the terms of a contract into the future requires the expertise of a man of business. The judge is here out of his element, particularly in those cases in which knowledge of a technical nature is required, which the judge does not possess.[468]

The effects of *imprévision* will often be asymmetrical, in the sense that the change in circumstances will render the contract excessively onerous for one party without this change affecting the other party. In these circumstances the unaffected party will seek to keep the contract on foot rather than renegotiate a concession.[469] But should the parties be unable to renegotiate the contract, a judge, who may be ill-equipped to make a decision of this nature, is then entitled to rule that the unaffected party must lose his benefit and remain in the contract under conditions imposed on him by the judge for the duration of the contract, when it may not be in that party's economic interest to do so.

Summary

French law was derived, to a very large degree, from Roman law. It developed primarily in an academic context, in the faculties of the medieval and early modern universities. The law of contracts had been a very important and innovative part of Roman law, and consequently French jurists focused considerable attention on this aspect of the law. The academic orientation of French jurists ensured that the French law of contract, although based upon the Roman law of contracts, evolved over time into something radically different from its Roman law antecedents. Roman law, and the Roman law of contract types, were essentially pragmatic in nature, responding to specific legal problems as and when they arose, and never rising to a level of generalisation. Roman jurists had thus concentrated on the process of conceptualisation, which involved the ongoing refinement of each individual part of their legal system, and of their specific contract types, without ever drawing conclusions about any common elements which might link them to each other. French legal scholars, on the other hand, concentrated on the processes of generalisation and systematisation. As a result, over the course of several centuries French academics converted the discrete Roman law contract types into a uniform and generalised law of contract. The

---

468 Philippe Stoffel-Munck 'La Réforme en Pratique: La Résiliation pour Imprévision' (2015) *AJ Contrats d'Affaires* 262, 264.
469 Id., 264.

jus commune that emerged was a rationally coherent system of general rules and abstract legal principles, unlike its Roman law forebear.

During the Middle Ages, the academic process of generalisation was facilitated by the influence of the canonists, who shaped many of the principal features of French contractual obligations. It was the canonists who insisted that all agreements were legally enforceable, whatever the nature of the contract, and by so doing thereby introduced the fundamental notion that all contracts would be valid solely on the basis of consent. The canonists also contributed in large measure to the distinctly moral tone which characterises French contract law to this day.

The academic emphasis on reason led to the conclusion that legal principles and rules were universal and could be rationally deduced by the right use of human reason. It also contributed to the process of systematisation by maintaining that these universal principles and rules could be set out in a comprehensive legal code. This comprehensive legal code found expression in the creation of the *Code civil* in 1804. The processes of generalisation and systematisation in the formulation of the Code led to the simplification of the complicated Roman law categories of liability, which were reduced during the process of codification to two categories, as set out in former Articles 1137 and 1147.

The articles of the *Code* which addressed contractual obligations remained virtually unchanged for over two hundred years. In 2016 these articles were at length revised and updated by the *Ordonnance 2016-131 du février 2016 portant réforme des contrats, du régime général et de la preuve des obligations.* Many of the traditional elements which characterised French contract law remained in place after the revision, although, amongst other things, the quintessentially French concept of cause was formally abolished, and an article addressing the contentious concept of *imprévision* was introduced. Moreover, contractual liability was further simplified, by being reduced from two categories to one, as set out in current Article 1231-1.

French law inherited from Roman law the notion that a debtor could only be liable when he was at fault. Thus the concept of *force majeure*, like that of *vis maior*, is the antithesis of fault. But in other respects, *force majeure* was completely unlike *vis maior*. *Vis maior* had been simply a disparate collection of individual instances, reflecting the practical nature of Roman law and the pragmatic law of its specific contract types. But in transforming *vis maior* into *force majeure*, French jurists created an abstract and theoretical concept, initially defining *force majeure* by criteria drawn by way of exegesis from the provisions of the *Code civil* and then, since the revision of 2016, by Article 1218. The articles which address *force majeure*, both in the former and the current regimes, are set out in a manner which logically connects them with other related contractual matters to create a rational and interlocking whole. This reflects the academic and theoretical orientation of French law.

French law had also followed Roman law in maintaining that contractual performance had to have been rendered impossible, without fault on the part of the debtor, in order to qualify as *force majeure*. There had been no concept of *imprévision* in the Roman law of contracts and, until 2016, this remained true in French private law.[470] A change in circumstances making performance more onerous therefore would not qualify to terminate or revise a contract.

But this state of affairs was dramatically reversed in the revision of 2016, with the introduction of Article 1195. Article 1195 provides potential relief to a debtor who claims to have suffered an unforeseeable change in circumstances which has rendered performance 'excessively onerous'. French contract law, as has been seen above, is characterised by a distinct moral tone. This moral aspect was certainly a factor in the introduction of Article 1195, as the then Minister of Justice Mme. Taubira indicated on 25 February 2015, when she announced that one of the primary reforming themes of the revised articles was the protection of the weaker party. The introduction of Article 1195 in the revised articles affected some of the most fundamental elements of French private contract law, such as the theory of the autonomy of the will, with its concomitant prohibition on judicial intervention into the terms of the contract.

Although the introduction of a provision addressing *imprévision* was a radical departure from traditional French law, the new articles on *force majeure* basically reproduced the pre-existing approach to *force majeure* in the previous regime. Moreover, the French propensity for systematisation has ensured that revised Articles 1218, 1351 and 1351-1, dealing with *force majeure*, have been kept completely separate and distinct from Article 1195, so that entirely different consequences ensue from a finding of *force majeure* and one of *imprévision*.

---

470 See pages 92–95 *supra* with regard to the approach of French administrative law.

3   English Law

'There's a divinity that shapes our ends, Rough-hew them how we will'.*
William Shakespeare

The Historical Development of English Law

English law was largely uninfluenced by Roman law and developed quite separately from the legal systems of continental Europe. It therefore evolved into a unique and idiosyncratic legal system. Two separate and distinct legal systems were thus engendered in Europe, one based on Roman law and the other not. These two systems developed historically in significantly different ways; as a result English law 'differs fundamentally from the continental system'.[1] The origins of the English legal system can be traced back to the twelfth century. During the reign of Henry II, three Royal Courts were established between 1154 and 1189 AD, each with jurisdiction over a specific subject matter.[2] These three Courts were collectively known as the Royal Courts of Westminster.

The Royal Courts operated by way of the writ system. When a litigant sought to appear in one of the Royal Courts he first had to obtain a writ from the Chancellor's office. The writ set out the facts of the case as provided by the plaintiff and commanded the defendant to appear before the Royal Court in order to answer the charge brought against him.

---

* Shakespeare, William *Hamlet* Urbana, Illinois: Project Gutenberg. Retrieved August 18, 2024 from www.gutenberg.org.ebooks:19033.

1 RC van Caenegem *An Historical Introduction to Private Law* Cambridge: Cambridge University Press, 1988, 3.

2 The Court of King's Bench exercised jurisdiction over serious criminal matters, the Court of Exchequer over royal taxes and the Court of Common Pleas over legal matters between private litigants, with particular emphasis on property matters. It should be noted that throughout the Middle Ages the Royal Courts did not exercise an exclusive jurisdiction throughout England. English feudal lords possessed the right of 'seigneurial authority', by which they had the right, *inter alia*, to exercise legal jurisdiction over their vassals. As a result the baronial and manorial courts of the feudal lords provided another avenue for legal redress. There were also in existence the Ecclesiastical Courts, the Courts of the Shires, Hundreds and Counties and the Courts of the Law Merchant, among others: K.M. Teeven *A History of the Anglo-American Common Law of Contract* New York: Greenwood Press, 1990, 2–4.

DOI: 10.4324/9781003533450-4

Initially the writs were drawn up in an *ad hoc* manner, simply setting out the nature of the plaintiff's plea. However, over time the writs became standardised. This occurred because the same types of cases frequently arose, with the result that a writ drawn up in a previous case could be used again in a subsequent case without change.[3] By the end of the thirteenth century the number and wording of the writs had become fixed, and thereafter it became necessary, if a plaintiff were to appear before one of the Royal Courts, to ascertain first whether the particular facts of his case could be brought within the standardised wording of one of the writs listed in the Register of Writs. Each writ set out a particular form of action, briefly describing the type of dispute and setting out the procedure and method of trial for its resolution. These procedures differed from writ to writ, depending on the nature of the dispute in question.

In the twelfth century the English legal system was considered to be the most advanced European legal system then in existence. It was primarily for this reason that it successfully resisted the influence of Roman law, which was otherwise so enthusiastically received throughout Western Europe. By the twelfth century the writ system was firmly established in England, well before Roman law had even begun to be taught in the continental law faculties. There was consequently no need to upgrade the English legal system, unlike in continental Europe.[4]

The writ system operated well throughout the twelfth and thirteenth centuries. But by the fourteenth century problems were arising which could not be addressed by the existing writs or which did not adequately do justice to the plaintiff's claim. This led over time to the establishment of a separate court, known as the Court of Chancery. The Court of Chancery intervened to provide legal recourse where none existed within the writ system. It also provided additional remedies when those set out in the writs did not satisfy the needs of the plaintiff. This supplementary and alternative system of law, administered in a separate court, came to be known as 'Equity', in which established equitable principles and rules were developed. As a result, the English system of law was comprised of two parts, viz. the Common Law rules, as embodied in the writ system and administered by the Royal Courts of Westminster, and the equitable principles and rules developed in the Court of Chancery. Recourse to the Common Law was the normal procedure, and a plaintiff would ordinarily seek to have his case resolved within the framework of the Common Law. It was only if the matter at hand could not be addressed by the Common Law, or if the remedy provided for in the applicable writ did not do justice to the claim of the plaintiff, that the plaintiff would then have recourse to Equity.

---

3 K. Zweigert and H. Kötz *An Introduction to Comparative Law* (third revised edition, translated by Tony Weir) Oxford: Clarendon Press, 1998, 184.
4 RC van Caenegem *Judges, Legislators and Professors* Cambridge: Cambridge University Press 1987, 114; A.W.B. Simpson *Invitation to Law* Oxford: Basil Blackwell Ltd. 1988, 66, 67.

Unlike French law, there was no pre-existing source of authority in English law where the rules of law could be found. Instead the judge, working within the framework of the writ system, had to decide himself whether a particular case came within the ambit of the chosen writ.[5] The judge's decision on these matters was recorded in his written judgment. In order to ensure consistency and to treat like alike, it became the practice of judges to apply the same findings in the cases before them as had been used in like previous cases. Initially this case law was understood to constitute simply the accumulation of judicial wisdom, and was thought to be persuasive rather than binding in nature. But by the nineteenth century the doctrine of *stare decisis* had become an integral part of the law, so that decided cases were considered to be binding, and lower court judges were bound to follow the decisions of superior court judges.

Major reforms to the legal system took place in the nineteenth century. In 1832 the number of writs was greatly reduced,[6] and in 1852 the writ system was abolished completely.[7] Thereafter, a plaintiff commenced an action simply by way of a general writ of summons, setting out therein his cause of action. Moreover, a plaintiff could now join several different causes of action in the same writ. This had not previously been possible under the writ system. Between 1873 and 1875 the three *Judicature Acts* were enacted.[8] By virtue of these Acts, the Royal Courts of Westminster and the Court of Chancery were abolished, and a new Supreme Court of Judicature was created, consisting of the High Court of Justice and the Court of Appeal. The judges of this new Court were empowered to apply both the rules of the Common Law and those of Equity in a single hearing.

Another important change in the English legal system involved the growth of legislation as an important source of law. The decided cases, whether from the Common Law or from Chancery, had traditionally formed the greatest part of the rules of law in the English legal system. Parliament could of course enact legislation, and when it did so the rule of parliamentary supremacy ensured that any such law would supersede any case law at variance with the statute law. But there were relatively few parliamentary enactments prior to the nineteenth century. This state of affairs changed in the nineteenth century, with Parliament enacting an ever increasing amount of legislation, so that by the beginning of the twentieth century legislation had become a very important additional source of law. However, a considerable part of English law remains judge made law to this day, including most of the law of contract.

---

5 H. Patrick Glenn *Legal Traditions of the World* (fifth edition) Oxford: Oxford University Press, 2014, 240.

6 *Uniformity of Process Act 1832*, 2 & 3 Will IV, c 39; *Real Property Limitation Act 1833*, 3 & 4 Will IV, c 27, s 36.

7 *Common Law Procedure Act 1852*, 15 & 16 Vict. c 76, ss 2, 3, 41.

8 *Supreme Court of Judicature Act* (1873) 36 & 37 Vict c 125; *Supreme Court of Judicature (Commencement) Act* (1874) 37 & 38 Vict c 83; *Supreme Court of Judicature Act* (1875) 38 & 39 Vict c. 77.

'The role of the judge', when making law, 'is simply to decide the particular case before him. His power to develop the law is limited to relevant points of law which arise in the case ...'.[9]

French law deals with matters involving the legal responsibility of the executive by means of a separate body of substantive rules of law which are administered in a separate court system, and which are governed by a different rationale to that which applies in private law.[10] There is, in other words, a structural dichotomy in French law between private law and public law, and this dichotomy constitutes the most important division in the French legal system. This dichotomy does not exist in English law. Legal issues involving the public authorities are dealt with in the same courts as private law matters, and are resolved by the same legal principles. There is thus no counterpart in English law to the special and different provisions of French administrative law with regard, for example, to contracts. In the Common Law the same law applies to all contracts, both private and public.[11] Contracts between private individuals and the State will be subject to the same principles as those that govern contracts between private individuals.[12]

The Development of Contract Law

Prior to the nineteenth century the law of contract remained relatively undeveloped in England and was generally considered to be simply an adjunct to property law.[13] The first book on the subject, Powell's *Essay upon the Law of Contracts and Agreements*, was only published in 1790, and amounted to little more than a treatise which addressed land transactions and marriage

---

9 John Cartwright *Contract Law: An Introduction to the English Law of Contract for the Civil Lawyer* Oxford: Hart Publishing, 2023, 39.

10 See pages 39–40 *supra*.

11 Bernard Rudden *A Sourcebook on French Law* (third edition) Oxford: Clarendon Press, 1991, 141, 142. See *Davy v Spelthorne* (1983) 3 All ER 278 and *Roy v Kensington and Chelsea and Westminster Family Practitioner Committee* (1992) 1 All ER 705.

12 However, the procedure to be followed in an English court will differ depending on whether the matter before the court is public or private in nature, i.e. 'depending on whether the purpose of the case is to enforce the public duties of a State agency or State body, or the private rights of a citizen': Peter de Cruz *Comparative Law in a Changing World* (third edition) London: Routledge-Cavendish 2007, 105. The primary remedy to be pursued in a public law matter will be an application for judicial review. Judicial review empowers the Court reviewing the decision of an administrative tribunal simply to rule on the legality of the tribunal's decision; the Court is not entitled to substitute its own judgment for that of the tribunal. Should the Court find that the tribunal has acted illegally in some way it must remit the matter to the tribunal for a rehearing.

13 A.W.B. Simpson 'Historical Introduction' 1, 13 in M.P. Furmston *Cheshire, Fifoot and Furmston's Law of Contract* (sixteenth edition) Oxford: Oxford University Press, 2012. See also Morton J. Horowitz 'The Historical Foundations of Modern Contract Law' (1974) 87 *Harvard Law Review* 917, 920; and Barry Nicholas 'Rules and Terms – Civil Law and Common Law' (1974) 48 *Tulane Law Review* 946, 946–947.

settlements.[14] Peter Carey declared in 1845 that the law of contracts was 'almost totally without cultivation'.[15]

There was actually no 'law of contract' in the Common Law prior to the nineteenth century. Instead, there was rather a 'law of contracts', in that contractual arrangements were governed by specific writs depending on their particular nature. There was the writ of covenant, whereby a party solemnly bound himself by way of seal. There was the writ of debt, whereby a party could sue another for the payment of a liquidated sum due, or a specific quantity of fungible goods. There was the writ of detinue, whereby a party could sue another for wrongfully detaining goods which belonged to another.[16] There was also the writ of *assumpsit*, which by the nineteenth century had become the most common writ in use for contractual arrangements.[17] *Assumpsit* could be used in a variety of situations, the most common of which was the bringing of suit for breach of promise when the defendant either did not perform or when he performed in a manner which did not comply with his undertaking.[18]

Prior to the Industrial Revolution England was a predominantly rural and agricultural country, and the greatest part of the country's wealth consisted of land held by the aristocracy and gentry.[19] The law of real property was consequently the most developed and sophisticated part of the law. The law of real property had evolved from feudal principles, which had been adapted and modernised over the course of centuries.[20] The focus on real property law reflected the pragmatic orientation of English judges and practitioners in shaping the law to respond to the actual societal conditions of rural and agricultural communities dominated by a landowning class. Because contracts did not play an important role in such a society, the law of contract remained undeveloped.

This was very different from the law of France, where the law of contract became a very important part of the law from an early stage. Although England and France were both essentially feudal and post-feudal societies in the medieval and early modern eras, they differed with regard to the importance given to the law of contract. The explanation for the focus on contract law in France

---

14 P.S. Atiyah *The Rise and Fall of the Freedom of Contract* Oxford; Clarendon Press, 1979, 360.

15 Peter Stafford Carey 'A Course of Lectures on the Law of Contract: Lecture I' (1845) 4 *The Law Times*, 563, 563.

16 As the result of a sale, for example, in which the buyer paid for the goods, but the seller then refused to deliver them. Detinue has become a tort in contemporary law.

17 'Assumpsit' is a Latin word which means 'he has undertaken'. Equity also plays a role in the law of contracts, albeit a relatively small one. The equitable remedies of specific performance and injunction are available in contractual disputes, at the discretion of the judge.

18 The existence in the Common Law of a law of contracts, rather than a law of contract, was a point of similarity which the English legal system shared with Roman law. But whereas the law of contracts in Roman law was an extremely important and sophisticated part of the legal system, it remained in England a minor and undeveloped part.

19 Atiyah, op. cit., 12, 24.

20 van Caenegem, op. cit. (fn. 4), 114.

lies in the fact that French law developed to a large degree from Roman law, and this development occurred primarily in an academic context. The Roman foundation of the developing French law was in many respects excitingly 'new and foreign', which was part of its appeal to legal scholars.[21] This was especially true of the Roman law of contracts which, as the most important and innovative part of Roman law, exerted a particular fascination in university circles. Consequently, the law of contractual obligations formed an important part of the evolving French law.

In England, by way of contrast, the law developed independently of Roman law, in the hands of pragmatic judges and practitioners, who were themselves a part of the landowning class. They focused on developing a law which was in practical harmony with the actual functioning of society and, in particular, with the importance of land as the most significant measure of wealth. Real property law thus became the most developed and sophisticated part of the law. Contract law, on the other hand, was generally unimportant in any practical sense and was therefore neglected. The English concentration on real property law and the neglect of contract law reflect the general character of English law, which is one of pragmatism. The law evolves in step with the actual developments of society, and a judge will formulate a rule of law only insofar as this is necessary to resolve the dispute before him.

However, the onset of the Industrial Revolution in the nineteenth century compelled a radical new approach to the traditional focus on real property law and the neglect of contract law. Over the course of some one hundred years the Industrial Revolution completely transformed the nature of British society.[22] During this time British society went from being essentially rural and agricultural in nature to being urban and industrialised. The magnitude of the transformation can be seen in some comparative statistics. In 1770 total manufacturing in the United Kingdom was valued at £30 million; by 1871 this had increased to £348 million. In 1801 the population was some 10.6 million people; by 1861 it had grown to 21.2 million. Between 1801 and 1861 the gross national product of the United Kingdom increased from £10.7 million to £668.0 million, and by 1870 British export trade was more than four times greater than that of the United States, and was larger than the combined export trade of France, Germany and Italy.[23] With the explosion in commercial activity generated by the Industrial Revolution, the law of contract necessarily became vitally important, and 'by the mid-nineteenth century a unified contract law had replaced the fragmented forms of action'.[24]

---

21 Id., 114.
22 The Industrial Revolution can be dated from approximately 1770 to approximately 1870.
23 R. Danzig '*Hadley v Baxendale*: A Study in the Industrialisation of the Law' (1975) 4 *Journal of Legal Studies* 249, 259; Atiyah, op. cit., 224.
24 Warren Swain 'Contract as Promise: The Role of Promising in the Law of Contract. An Historical Account' (2013) 17 *Edinburgh Law Review* 1, 7.

English law, as seen above, was traditionally judge-made law, i.e. a 'law of the case', with the Rule of Precedent ensuring that consistency and justice were maintained from case to case.[25] However, as English society became more and more transformed as a result of the Industrial Revolution, judges increasingly found that they could not rely on precedents, either because there was no precedent which addressed the radically different types of problem now before them, or because the precedents which did exist were no longer relevant in the radically changed social and commercial circumstances. This was particularly true in the law of contract. Rather than attempting to adapt old Common Law precedents to the new situations where they simply did not apply and could shed no relevant assistance, English judges and practitioners began instead to look for guidance and direction to legal sources outside the strict parameters of the traditional Common Law.[26] The most influential 'outside' source to which English judges and practitioners had reference turned out to be the works of Robert Joseph Pothier, and in particular his *Traité des Obligations*.

The Influence of Robert Pothier

Pothier's *Traité des Obligations* was published in 1764. By 1781 Sir William Jones was enthusiastically recommending Pothier to English lawyers, exhorting them in his *Essay on Bailments* to 'read him again and again'.[27] Jones praised Pothier for his 'luminous method, apposite examples, and clear manly style, in which nothing is redundant, nothing deficient...'.[28] Jones was so impressed by Pothier that he considered it his foremost duty to ensure that English judges and practitioners became familiar with his writings:

> ... if my undissembled fondness for the study of jurisprudence were never to produce any greater benefit to the public, than barely the introduction of Pothier to the acquaintance of my countrymen, I should think that I had in some measure discharged the debt, which every man, according to lord Coke, owes to his profession.[29]

25 See page 138 *supra*.
26 In this regard consider the statement of Lord Mansfield CJ, in *Johnson v Spiller* (1784) 3 Doug. 371, 373; 99 ER 702, 703: '... as the usages of society alter, the law must adapt itself to the various situations of mankind'.
27 William Jones *An Essay on the Law of Bailments* London: J. Nichols, 1781, 29; reprinted New York and London: Garland Publishing Inc., 1978.
28 Id., 29.
29 Id., 29, 30.

By the end of the eighteenth century, a small but influential circle of English judges and authors had come to know and esteem Pothier's works.[30] This circle, however, necessarily remained small, because it was limited to those who were fluent in French.

In 1806, the English barrister David William Evans produced an English translation of Pothier's *Traité des Obligations*, accompanied by his own observations on the application of Pothier's treatise to English law. Evans' work was entitled *A Treatise on the Law of Obligations, or Contracts*, and comprised two volumes. The first volume consisted of Pothier's *Traité des Obligations*, translated into English. The second volume consisted of the work of Evans himself, in which he applied certain principles propounded by Pothier to the Common Law, as well as translations of selections from the works of the eighteenth-century French Chancellor d'Aguesseau.[31]

With the publication of Evans' translation, Pothier quickly became very well-known in English legal circles, and his writings were soon considered to be of the highest authority.[32] English judges throughout the nineteenth century attested repeatedly to the regard in which they held Pothier and the impact which his writings had on their decisions. A small sampling of such statements will illustrate Pothier's influence at this time. In the case of *Cox v Troy*, for example, Best J. penned these effusive comments:

> But the authority of Pothier is expressly in point. That is as high as can be had, next to the decision of a Court of Justice in this country. It is extremely well known that he is a writer of acknowledged character; his writings have been constantly referred to by the Courts, and he is spoken of with great praise by Sir William Jones in his Law of Bailments...[33]

Best J. concluded this panegyric by declaring that 'there could not be a better guide than Pothier on this subject'.[34] In similar vein, Lord Campbell acknowledged in *Hall v Wright* the 'high authority of Pothier', declaring that he was 'one of the most celebrated of modern jurists'.[35] Fry J. likewise affirmed the high authority of Pothier in *Smith v Westcroft*:

> Now, it appears to me that on the general question I cannot try the case more favourably than by applying the principles laid down by Pothier.[36]

---

30 Bernard Rudden 'Pothier et la *Common Law*' 91, 93 in Joël Monéger, Jean-Louis Sourioux et Aline Terrasson de Fougères (éditeurs) *Robert-Joseph Pothier, d'hier à aujourd'hui* Paris: Economica 2001.

31 Id., 93.

32 Atiyah, op. cit., 399.

33 (1822) 5 B & Ald. 474, 480, 481; 106 ER 1264, 1266.

34 Id., 481; 1266.

35 (1858) El. Bl. & El. 746, 760; 120 ER 688, 694.

36 (1878) 9 Ch. D. 223, 229, 230.

Academic writers were no less effusive. Sir John Byles, in his book *A Treatise on the Law of Bills of Exchange*, which was first published in 1829, declared as follows:

> In France this subject has been briefly but luminously treated, first by Dupuy de la Serra, in a little book entitled '*L'Art des Lettres de Change*', and afterwards by Pothier, whose work, as well as his other performances, and in particular the *Traité des Obligations,* evinces a profound acquaintance with the principles of jurisprudence, and extraordinary acumen and sagacity in their application; the result of the laborious exercise of his talents on the Roman law. There cannot be a greater proof of the surpassing merit of his works, than that, after the lapse of more than half a century, and stupendous revolution in all the institutions of his country, many parts of his writings have been incorporated, word for word, in the new Code of France. The *Traité du Contrat de Change* is often cited in the English Courts of Law.[37]

Samuel Warren, in his book *A Popular and Practical Introduction to Law Studies*, published in 1835, referred to the 'great treatise' of Pothier on the Law of Contracts, which he 'strenuously recommended to the student's attention'.[38]

Pothier's influence on English law extended into many different areas. His greatest influence, however, was on the development of the English law of contract. The great appeal of Pothier to English judges and practitioners lay in the fact that his *Traité des Obligations* set out in simple and straightforward language general contractual principles which did not yet then exist in the Common Law, and which English judges were seeking in order to develop further the contract law of their own legal system. Pothier's purpose in writing the *Traité des Obligations* had been to set out the general and universal principles of contract law. As a proponent of Natural Law, Pothier had no doubt that such general and universal principles did in fact exist, and this belief also figured in the minds of many of his English admirers. Jones, for example, noted that the 'greatest portion' of Pothier's works constituted 'law at Westminster as well as at Orleans'.[39]

---

37 Sir John Barnard Byles 'The Preface to the First Edition' at xiv and xv, in *A Treatise on the Law of Bills of Exchange* (12th edition) London: H. Sweet, 1876.

38 Samuel Warren *A Popular and Practical Introduction to Law Studies* London: A. Maxwell, 1835, 336.

39 Jones, op. cit., 29. Charles G. Addison, whose *Treatise on the Law of Contracts* was first published in 1847, similarly maintained that the principles of contract law were universal: 'The law of contract may justly be said to be a universal law and adapted to all times and races, and all places and circumstances, being founded upon those great and fundamental principles of right and wrong deduced from natural reason which are immutable and eternal': Charles G. Addison 'Extract from the Preface of the First Edition' vi, in *A Treatise on the Law of Con-*

By 1865 Pothier had been cited in English cases more than four hundred times either by counsel or the judge.[40] There are in addition numerous cases where it is apparent that the court was drawing on Pothier's work even though he was not directly cited in the judgment. In *Adams v Linsell*, for example, no mention is made of Pothier, but his guiding presence shimmers throughout '*en eminence grise*'.[41] The development of the classical English law of contract in the nineteenth century was thus paradoxically influenced by a Frenchman writing in the eighteenth century.

The Nature of the English Contract

In spite of the considerable influence which Pothier exercised on the development of the English law of contract, English contract law did not come to replicate French contract law, and, in fact, the two laws of contract are significantly different from each other.[42] The explanation for this seeming discrepancy is that when a legal principle or rule is borrowed from one legal system and transplanted into another the transplant is radically transformed by the system into which it has been transplanted. This is particularly true when a legal concept is borrowed from the Civil Law, and transplanted into the Common Law, which is so fundamentally different from the Civil Law. The borrowed concept, when it becomes integrated into the receiving legal system, is 'understood differently by the host culture and is therefore invested with a culture-specific meaning at variance with the earlier one'.[43] When transplanted

---

tracts (second edition) (volume 1) London: W. Benning and Co. Law Booksellers, 1849. In the Preface Addison also praised 'the elaborate and elegant works of Pothier': Id., vii. See also Nicholas, op. cit. (fn. 13), 947.

40 Rudden, op. cit. (fn. 30), 97. The *Traité des Obligations* was the most cited work, but reference was made to almost all of the treatises at one point or another.

41 (1818) 1 B. & A. 681; 106 ER 250.

42 Pothier's influence was particularly strong in four areas, viz. the development of the doctrine of offer and acceptance, the development of the notion of mistake, the development of the doctrine of frustration and the development of the measure of damages: JM Perillo 'Robert J Pothier's Influence on the Common Law of Contract' (2005) 11 *Texas Wesleyan Law Rev.* 267; W Barnes '*Hadley v Baxendale* and Other Common Law Borrowings from the Civil Law' (2005) 11 *Texas Wesleyan L Rev* 627.

In *Solle v Butcher* (1950) 1 KB 671, at 691–692, Lord Denning L.J. cast doubt on the ongoing validity of Pothier as a source of English contract law: '… the doctrine of French law as enunciated by Pothier is no part of English law'. Lord Denning M.R. subsequently emphatically rejected Pothier as a source of English contract law with regard to the identity of the other contracting party, in the case of *Lewis v Averay* (1972) 1 QB 198, at 206: 'It has sometimes been said that if a party makes a mistake as to the identity of the person with whom he is contracting there is no contract, or, if there is a contract, it is a nullity and void, so that no property can pass under it. This has been supported by a reference to the French jurist Pothier; but I have said before, and I repeat now, his statement is no part of English law'.

43 Pierre Legrand 'The Impossibility of Legal Transplants' (1997) 4 *Maastricht Journal of European and Comparative Law* 111, 117.

into a new legal system a legal concept thus becomes an integral part of that legal system, and operates in conformity with the nature and structure of that system.

This process of transformation was clearly at work with the borrowed concepts of Pothier. The writings of Pothier constitute juristic law. As a jurist, Pothier produced a canonical body of law which was 'conceptualized, systematic and clear, with institutions sharply distinguished from one another'.[44] His oft-quoted *Traité des Obligations*, for example, was organised into a rationally coherent system of general rules and abstract concepts, which were linked together into a unified whole by overarching and interconnected legal principles.

It was from this juristic writing that English judges and practitioners turned in order to obtain contractual principles and rules which were lacking in their own law of contract. But in doing so they proceeded in a typically Common Law manner, by selectively taking a principle or rule out of its canonical context and adopting it into case law as the means of resolving the specific problem at hand. The borrowed concept was thereby transformed into an integral part of the Common Law, operating in conformity with the nature and structure of the Common Law. In the Civil Law, the principle or rule constitutes an abstract concept which forms part of a seamless and logically interconnected theoretical order. In the Common Law, on the other hand, the concept becomes separated from its wider context and is utilised piecemeal to resolve a specific problem. In the Common Law context, the concept is absorbed into a judicial decision and becomes intrinsically connected to that particular case.

As Legrand points out, judge-made law does not actually consist of 'rules' in the orthodox sense of the term:

> To represent the common law as a set of rules is to inflict an 'alien conception' on it. Judicial decisions may, in time, produce what appears like a set of rules; yet 'the rules of judge-made law are never authentically promulgated as rules, but are left to be inferred from cases'. Specifically, nowhere can an authoritative repository of the 'rules' ever be found. The 'rules' are, therefore, no more than renditions by later judges of patterns which they perceive as having emerged from discrete and particularistic judicial interventions.[45]

As a result a principle or rule borrowed from the Civil Law becomes mutated by its introduction into the Common Law and loses its original significance as an abstract and binding legal formulation. It becomes simply a part of a

---

44 Alan Watson 'Roman Law and English Law: Two Patterns of Legal Development' (1990) 36 *Loyola Law Review* 247, 268.

45 Pierre Legrand 'European Legal Systems Are Not Converging' (1996) 45 *International and Comparative Law Quarterly* 52, 67, 68.

judge-made decision which may, in subsequent cases, be 'subject to legitimate change by judges in the course of their application'.[46] Thus, although there certainly were significant borrowings from Pothier which became a part of the English law of contract, those borrowings from French contract law became thoroughly anglicised in the process of integration into the Common Law.

French contract law, as seen above, was derived almost entirely from Roman law and was formulated in an academic context, with a significant moral input from the canonists during the Middle Ages. The doctrine of consensualism provided the basis of contract formation, so that both onerous agreements and gratuitous undertakings were legally binding, provided that the parties had freely consented.[47] Consequently French contract law 'has a general and abstract character and applies to any kind of agreement'.[48] The moral aspects of French contract law ensure that it places a premium on evaluating the behaviour of the contracting parties as well as addressing any inequalities which may exist between them.[49]

This is in marked contrast to the English law of contract. The nature and structure of English contract law has been formulated primarily in the context of the Industrial Revolution. As a result, English contract law has been shaped largely by commercial transactions. As Harris and Tallon point out, commercial transactions have been 'treated by the judges as the paradigm of contract'.[50] In this context economic considerations were paramount, and the focus of the law was on 'the exchange of economic value achieved by the contract'.[51] Contracts in English law were generally understood to be essentially 'bargains' between the contracting parties.

The economic orientation of the English contract finds expression in two of its most important characteristics, viz. the requirement of consideration and the absence of a general principle of good faith. Whereas French contracts are formed by the simple consent of the parties, an English contract is legally enforceable only when something of value has been given in exchange for the other party's promise.[52] 'The doctrine in its classical sense', as noted by McMeel, 'requires an element of reciprocity before a promise is legally

---

46 Id., 68.

47 Martin Vrankin *Western Legal Traditions* Sydney: The Federation Press, 2015, 106.

48 Donald Harris and Denis Tallon 'Conclusion' 379, 386 in Donald Harris and Denis Tallon (editors) *Contract Law Today: Anglo-French Comparisons* Oxford: Clarendon Press, 1989.

49 Id., 385, 386.

50 Id., 386.

51 Id., 386.

52 '... as a general rule only a promise supported by consideration will be enforceable at common law': *The Pioneer Container* (1994) 2 All ER 250, per Lord Goff of Chievelely, at pages 255, 256.

recognised. There must be some requested or stipulated counter-promise or counter-performance for a promise to be enforced'.[53]

The origins of consideration are uncertain. It has been argued in some quarters that consideration is an indigenous product of English law, and in others that it is an adaptation of the French concept of *cause*.[54] Whatever its origins, by the sixteenth-century consideration had developed into 'the vital element which caused parol promises to be legally binding'.[55] The House of Lords unanimously confirmed this understanding of consideration in the 1778 case of *Rann v Hughes*.[56] The judgment of the Court was delivered by Skynner CB. The Court noted that there was no difference in English law between parol and written contracts, and then declared that an action in *assumpsit* 'could only be founded on a parol promise if it was supported by consideration':[57]

> It is undoubtedly true that every man is by the law of nature, bound to fulfil his engagements. It is equally true that the law of this country supplies no means, nor affords any remedy, to compel the performance of an agreement made without sufficient consideration, such agreement is *nudum pactum, ex quo non oritur actio*, and whatsoever may be the sense of this maxim in the civil law, it is in the last mentioned sense only that it is to be understood in our law.[58]

The decision in *Rann v Hughes* encapsulates the ethos of the Industrial Revolution. Common Law contracts were understood to be essentially commercial transactions. Consequently, a binding force was attached to contracts 'on account of the fact that they were instruments necessary in business; a promise made in contract was sanctioned ... when it was part of a bargain, and in this case only'.[59]

Another very important difference between the English and French laws of contract involves the concept of good faith. The approach of the two laws to good faith also demonstrates very clearly the moral character of French contract law in contrast to the economic character of English contract law.

---

53 Gerard McMeel 'Pillans v Van Mierop (1765)' 23, at 26, in Charles Mitchell and Paul Mitchell (editors) *Landmark Cases in the Law of Contract* Oxford and Portland: Hart Publishing, 2008.

54 David Ibbetson *Historical Introduction* 1, at 10, in M.P. Furmston *Cheshire, Fifoot and Furmston's Law of Contract* (seventeenth edition) Oxford: Oxford University Press, 2017.

55 Sir John Baker *An Introduction to English Legal History* (fifth edition) Oxford: Oxford University Press, 2019, 374. In *Golding's Case*, decided in 1586, the Court declared as follows: 'In every action upon the case upon a promise there are three things considerable, consideration, promise and breach of promise': (1586) 2 Leon 71; 74 ER 367.

56 (1778) 4 Bro. P.C.27; 7 Term Rep. 350n; 2 ER 18.

57 Baker, op. cit., 374–375.

58 (1778) 4 Bros. P.C. 27; 7 Term Rep 350n; 2 ER 18. The Latin phrase means 'a gratuitous promise engenders no legal action'.

59 René David *English Law and French Law* London: Stevens & Sons, 1980, 103.

In French law, the concept of good faith had been introduced into the law of contract in the Middle Ages by the canonists.[60] It thereafter played an important role in French contract law. It was incorporated into the *Code civil* in former Article 1134, which declared that contracts 'must be performed in good faith'.[61] Although former Article 1134 required a contracting party to exercise good faith only in the performance of the contract, judicial decisions extended the exercise of good faith to the pre-negotiation stage and to the formation of the contract. These judicial extensions of good faith were then incorporated into current Article 1104 in the 2016 revision. Good faith was declared in the current Article 1104 to be a principle of public order, so that the principle is now recognised as one of primordial importance.[62]

The English approach to good faith has been markedly different. In stark contrast to French contract law, there is no general requirement in English contract law that a contract be performed in good faith. Cartwright emphasises the extent of this absence in a striking passage:

> In saying that there is no duty of good faith ... we are saying that there is no duty to negotiate a contract in good faith; nor any general duty to perform the contract in good faith, nor to renegotiate in good faith in the event of a significant change in circumstances affecting the balance of the contract; nor any general duty on parties to exercise in good faith their rights arising under the contract.[63]

This wholesale absence of a duty of good faith reflects the context in which English contract law developed in the nineteenth century. As contracts were conceived of as bargains, 'the parties were regarded as "self-interested" individuals, best placed to enter into whatever "bargains" they considered would benefit them'.[64] No general doctrine of good faith developed. Instead, a rigorous principle of *caveat emptor* became a part of English contract law in the nineteenth century.[65] One of the earliest cases in which *caveat emptor* applied was the 1811 case of *Baglehole v Walters*.[66] The defendant sold a ship 'with all faults as they now lie'. The plaintiff purchased the ship and discovered that there was significant damage to the floor-timbers, making it unseaworthy. Lord Ellenborough found for the defendant:

---

60 See page 43 *supra*.
61 *Elles doivent être exécutées de bonne foi.*
62 Article 1104 reads as follows: *Les contrats doivent être négociés, formés et exécutés de bonne foi. Cette disposition est d'ordre public.* (Contracts must be negotiated, concluded and performed in good faith. This provision is one of public order.)
63 Cartwright, op. cit., 66.
64 Vrankin, op. cit., 108.
65 'Buyer beware'.
66 (1811) 3 Camp. 154, 170 ER 1388.

If a ship is sold with all faults, the seller is not liable to an action in respect of latent defects which he knew of without disclosing at the time of the sale, unless he used some artifice to conceal them from the purchaser. The very object of introducing such a stipulation is to put the purchaser on his guard, and to throw upon him the burthen of examining all faults, both secret and apparent ... It would be most inconvenient and unjust, if men could not, by using the strongest terms which language affords, obviate disputes concerning the quality of the goods which they sell. In a contract such as this, I think there is no fraud, unless the seller, by positive means, renders it impossible for the purchaser to detect latent defects ...[67]

Lord Ellenborough drew a clear distinction between active deception and passive deception on the part of the seller. Liability would arise only if the seller had engaged in active deception. Otherwise *caveat emptor*.

The principle of *caveat emptor* was emphatically endorsed in the 1871 decision of *Smith v Hughes*.[68] The buyer wanted to purchase old oats, and so indicated to the seller. The oats which the seller was offering for sale were not old oats, but the seller did not disclose this fact to the buyer, who had the opportunity to examine the oats himself. The seller knew that the buyer thought that the oats were old, but did nothing either to encourage or to disabuse him of his mistaken belief. The Court held that the seller was not liable. Cockburn CJ set out the principle in the following passage:

The question is whether, under such circumstances, the passive acquiescence of the seller in the self-deception of the buyer will entitle the latter to avoid the contract. I am of the opinion that it will not ... I take the true rule to be that where a specific article is offered for sale, without express warrant, or without circumstances from which the law will imply a warranty ... and the buyer has full opportunity of inspecting and forming his own judgment, the rule *caveat emptor* applies.[69]

This ruling by Cockburn CJ emphatically established the principle that there was no general obligation on the part of a contracting party to reveal information which was known to him but not to the other party, even though that

---

67 Id., 156, 1339.
68 (1871) LR 6 QB 597.
69 Id., 603. The same issue arose again several years later in the case of *Ward v Hobbes* (1878) 4 App. Cas. 13 (HL). This case involved the sale of pigs by auction. The pigs were sold 'with all faults'. The seller was aware that the pigs were infected with typhoid, but the purchaser was not. All but one of the pigs died, but not before infecting other pigs belonging to the plaintiff, which also died. The court of first instance held against the plaintiff, as did the House of Lords.

knowledge would affect the other party's decision whether or not to enter into the contract.[70]

The principle of *caveat emptor*, like consideration, was emblematic of the ethos of the age. As Nicholas notes, it 'expresses the philosophy of a free-enterprise society where the parties are bargaining on equal terms and each does indeed have "full opportunity of ... forming his own judgment"'.[71] A duty to negotiate in good faith 'would be inconsistent with the nature of the relationship which the law attributes to the parties'.[72]

Since its heyday in the nineteenth century, the principle of *caveat emptor* has been mitigated in a number of significant ways. There have, for example, been numerous statutory provisions which require that information of one kind or another be provided. Prominent among these provisions is the Sale of Goods Act 1979, which replaced the original Sale of Goods Act 1893.[73] The Sale of Goods Act requires that the title, description, quality and reasonable fitness of goods be included as implied terms in certain contracts for the sale of goods.[74] There are also legislative provisions which have incorporated the principle of good faith in order to give effect to European Union law. An example is the Unfair Terms in Consumer Contract Regulations 1999, which incorporates a requirement of good faith in conformity with an EU directive. In addition, there are certain contracts which by their nature have been held to embody the principle of good faith. Contracts *uberrimae fidei*, i.e. contracts of insurance, fall into this category.[75] So too do contracts of employment, contracts of partnership and contracts involving a fiduciary relationship. But although the principle has been mitigated in various specific ways, no general principle of good faith yet exists in contemporary English contract law. This is so not only in the negotiation of a contract, but also in its performance. This is the consequence of the importance attached by the courts to certainty in commercial transactions, dating from the Industrial Revolution. 'The contract', as Cartwright notes, 'is what the parties agreed, and ... the courts will not allow a

---

70 Barry Nicholas 'The Obligation to Disclose Information – The English Report' 166, at 169, in Donald Harris and Denis Tallon (editors) *Contract Law Today: Anglo-French Comparisons* Oxford: Clarendon Press,

71 Id., 169.

72 Cartwright, op. cit., 68, 69. In this regard see the comments of Lord Ackner in *Walford v Miles*. '... the concept of a duty to carry on negotiations in good faith is inherently repugnant to the adversarial position of the parties when carrying on negotiations': (1992) 2 AC 128, 138 (HL).

73 *Sale of Goods Act* 1893, 56 & 57 Vict., c.71; *Sale of Goods Act*, 1979, c. 54.

74 See subsections 12, 13, 14(2) and 14(3) of the *Sale of Goods Act*. These guarantees had previously been declared by the courts to be implied terms in contracts of sale. See the discussion on implied terms at pages 158–161 *infra*.

75 *Uberrima fides*, or *uberrimae fidei* in its genitive form, means 'utmost good faith'.

general principle, or an implied term, of "good faith" to undermine the terms expressly agreed by the parties'.[76]

In 1988, Bingham LJ, in the case of *Interfoto Picture Library Ltd v Stiletto Visual Programmes Ltd.*, contrasted the approach of Civil Law jurisdictions to that of the Common Law:

> In many civil law systems and perhaps in most legal systems outside the common law world, the law of obligations recognises and enforces an overriding principle that in making and carrying out contracts parties should act in good faith...

> English law has, characteristically, committed itself to no such overriding principle but has developed piecemeal solutions in response to demonstrated problems of unfairness.[77]

There was an attempt by Leggett J., in the 2013 case of *Yam Seng PTE Ltd v International Trade Corporation Ltd.*, to introduce good faith as a general principle into English contract law.[78] But this was not to be. In the 2016 case of *MSC Mediterranean Shipping Company S.A. v Cottonex Anstalt*[79] the Court of Appeal reaffirmed the traditional position that there is no general principle of good faith in English contract law. Bick-Moore LJ took the opportunity to reject the proposition regarding good faith put forward by Leggett J. in *Yam Seng*. Bick-Moore LJ observed that the 'recognition of a general duty of good faith would be a significant step in the development of our law of contract with potentially far-reaching consequences'.[80] He indicated that he was not in favour of such a step, and declared that 'the better course is for the law to develop along established lines than to encourage judges to look for what the judge called in this case "some general organising principle" drawn from cases of disparate kinds'.[81] Bick-Moore LJ then warned that there would be 'a real danger that if a general principle of good faith were established it would be invoked as often to undermine as to support the terms in which the parties have reached agreement'.[82] This decision by the Court of Appeal forcefully reasserts the traditional approach of not recognising a general principle

---

76 Cartwright, op. cit. 70. See in this regard *MSC Mediterranean Shipping Co SA v Cottonex Anstalt* (2016) EWCA Civ. 789, at page 152 *infra*.

77 (1989) QB 433, 439 (CA); (1988) 1 All ER 348, 353 (CA). Bingham LJ described the principle of good faith as 'playing fair', 'coming clean' or 'putting one's cards face upwards on the table', and defined good faith as 'in essence a principle of fair and open dealing': Id., 439; Id., 352.

78 (2013) EWHC 111. See in particular paragraphs 119 to 153 of Leggett J.'s judgment.

79 (2016) EWCA Civ 789.

80 Id., paragraph 45.

81 Id., paragraph 45.

82 Id., paragraph 45.

of good faith in contract law. As a result English contract law continues to be radically different from its French counterpart in this important particular. [83]

Absolute Liability for Contractual Non-Performance

Yet another extremely important difference between English contract law, on the one hand, and French contract law, on the other, was the principle in English contract law of absolute liability, which does not exist in French law. French law predicates liability for contractual non-performance upon fault.[84] This, however, is not so in the Common Law. Contractual obligations in the Common Law were traditionally thought to be absolute. This means that liability will arise whenever the defendant does not perform his contractual obligations, whether or not he has been at fault. The plaintiff need only prove that the defendant did not perform. Given that contractual liability is absolute, neither initial impossibility nor supervening impossibility are factors which would necessarily render a contract void. As Nicholas points out, in the Common Law there is 'nothing inconceivable in a promise of the impossible or a promise to deliver a thing which does not exist'.[85]

The principle of absolute liability was established in 1647 in the case of *Paradine v Jane*.[86] The case arose as a result of events which occurred during the English Civil War. Paradine was the owner of premises in Oxford, which he had rented to Jane under a twenty-one year lease. During the civil war, Oxford became the centre of the Royalist forces. Jane was ejected from the premises, which then became the Royalist headquarters. Paradine subsequently sued Jane by writ of debt for three years of unpaid rent. In his defence, Jane submitted that he had been forcibly dispossessed, and argued that he should not be required to pay that portion of the rent which accrued when he had not been in possession. In his pleading, Jane declared as follows:

> ... that a certain German prince, by name Prince Rupert, an alien born, enemy to the King and kingdom, had invaded the realm with an hostile army of men; and with the same force did enter upon the defendant's possession, and him expelled, and held out of possession from the 19 of July 18 Car. till the Feast of the Annunciation, 21 Car...[87]

---

83 See pages 43 and 66–68 *supra* for a discussion of the French law of good faith.
84 See pages 50–53 *supra*.
85 Barry Nicholas *The French Law of Contract* (second edition) Oxford: Clarendon Press, 1992, 116.
86 (1647) Aleyn 26, Style 47, 82 ER 519, 897.
87 (1647) Aleyn 26, 26–27; Style 47, 47; 82 ER 519, 519; 82 ER 897, 897. Prince Rupert (1619–1682) was indeed a 'German prince', but he was hardly an 'enemy of the king'. He was in fact the nephew of Charles I, being the son of Elizabeth of Bohemia, who was the sister of Charles. In addition to being a German prince Rupert was also an English lord, as Charles had made him the Earl of Holdernesse and the Duke of Cumberland. During the civil war Rupert

Jane was not seeking relief on the basis that the 'German prince' and his 'hostile army' had prevented him from performing his contractual obligation, as is sometimes mistakenly asserted. He was not arguing that performance of his contractual obligation had been rendered impossible by virtue of the supervening event, but rather that the supervening event had made performance by the landlord impossible, so that he had been unable to enjoy the use and benefit of the land. Jane was putting forward the proposition that he should not be obliged to comply with his obligation when he had been deprived of the counter-performance by the other contracting party through a supervening event.[88]

In attempting to convince the Court that Jane was not liable for the arrears of rent, Jane's counsel apparently made reference to the Civil Law in his submissions. This is evident in the case report set out in Styles, which notes as follows:

> Also by the law of reason it seems that defendant in our case ought not to be charged with the rent, because he could not enjoy that that was let to him, and it was no fault of his own that he could not, and the civil-law, and canon-law, and moral authors do confirm this…[89]

One can only speculate what specific references Jane's counsel might have actually made to the Court. He may possibly have referred to the Roman law rule with regard to the allocation of risk in rental situations, i.e. the rule of *res perit locutoris*, which specified that in the circumstances in which Jane found himself the risk of loss would be borne by the lessor.[90] He may also have referred to contemporary French law, which affirmed the Roman law rule:

---

was the commander of the Royalist cavalry. When the Royalist forces were eventually defeated, the king became a prisoner of the parliamentarians. Rupert surrendered to the parliamentary forces and was banished from England. Hence the pleading in *Paradine v Jane* that Rupert was an 'enemy to the king'. Charles was executed for high treason in 1649 and a Commonwealth established. The monarchy was restored in 1660, and the son of Charles I became king as Charles II, at which time Rupert returned to England. He was the commander of the English navy during the Second and Third Anglo–Dutch Wars (1665–1667 and 1672–1674, respectively) and became the first Governor of the Hudson's Bay Company. The Hudson's Bay Company laid claim to great swathes of territory surrounding Hudson's Bay, extending into what is now western Canada. These territories were known as Prince Rupert's Land. Rupert died peacefully on 29 November 1682: Frank Kitson *Prince Rupert: Portrait of a Soldier* London: Constable, 1994; Frank Kitson *Prince Rupert: Admiral and General at Sea* London: Constable, 1998.

88 Cliona Kelly '*Paradine v. Jane*: A Doctrine of Absolute Contractual Liability?' (2004) 12 *Irish Student Law Review* 64, 66.

89 Style, 47, 48; 82 ER 519, 520.

90 I.3.24.4. See page 29 *supra*. He may also have dwelt on the intervention of a 'hostile army', which in Roman law also relieved the debtor of liability. See, in this regard the following passage from the Digest: 'If the force of a catastrophic storm befalls him, should the lessor be held responsible to the lessee for anything? Servius says that the owner should be responsible

If the tenant is turned out by the act of the prince, by a superior force, or by some other accident; or if the land or tenement is destroyed by an inundation, by an earthquake, or other event; the lessor, who was bound to give the land or tenement, cannot demand any rent for it, and will be obliged to restore so much of it as he has received; but without any other damages; for no man is to be accountable for accidents.[91]

Had the circumstances of *Paradine v Jane* occurred in France, Jane clearly would not have had to pay the arrears in rent. In the French law of this period, the doctrine of cause made contractual obligations interdependent, so that the obligation of one party was the cause of the other party's obligation.[92] Thus, should one party be unable to fulfil his contractual obligations through no fault of his own as a result of a supervening event, this necessarily relieved the other contracting party of his obligations.

Submissions based on the Civil Law, however, did not convince the Court of King's Bench. Rolle J. set out the obligations of a contracting party in a passage which has come to be the touchstone for absolute contractual liability in the Common Law:

Where the law creates a duty or a charge, and the party is disabled to perform it without any default in him and hath no remedy over, there the law will excuse him. As in the case of waste, if a house be destroyed by tempest or by enemies the lessee is excused ... when the party by his own contract creates a duty or charge upon himself, he is bound to make it good if he may, notwithstanding any accident by inevitable necessity, because he might have provided against it by his contract. And therefore if a lessee covenant to repair a house, though it be burnt by lightning or thrown down by enemies, yet he ought to repair it.[93]

This passage identifies two types of situation and establishes that in the event of a supervening event, the consequences for the contracting parties will depend on which situation was involved. In the first situation, a party will be released from his contractual obligation when he is prevented from performance by a subsequently enacted law. But a party will not be released from his

---

to his tenant farmer for all force against which resistance is impossible, as, for example, that of rivers, jackdaws, and starlings, and if some similar event occurs, or if there is an enemy invasion': D.19.2.15.2 (Ulpian). See also D.13.6.18 (Gaius).

91 Jean Domat *The Civil Law in Its Natural Order* (translated by William Strahan) volume 1, Boston: Charles C. Little and James Brown, 1850; reissued by Fred B. Rothman & Co., Littleton, Colorado: 1980, 265, paragraph 485. The expression 'act of the prince' is a literal translation of the French expression '*fait du prince*', which might more appropriately be translated as 'acts of government'.

92 See pages 89 and 127 *supra*.

93 (1647) Aleyn 27, 27; 82 ER 897, 897.

contractual obligation upon the intervention of some supervening event when he has freely contracted that obligation. The reason for the difference in the two situations, Rolle J. declared, was that in the second situation the defendant could have inserted a clause into the contract which would have exempted him from liability, should such an event occur. The Court noted that Jane's obligation to pay rent was one which he himself had agreed to. He had not included any exempting clause. He was therefore obliged to fulfil his obligation, even though he was unable to benefit from the counter-performance of the landlord:

> Now the rent is a duty created by the parties upon the reservation, and had there been a covenant to pay it, there had been no question but the lessee must have made it good, notwithstanding the interruption by enemies, for the law would not protect him beyond his own agreement...[94]

The law, as Rolle J. emphasised, would not protect a contracting party beyond the terms to which he himself had freely agreed. The decision of the Court was held in subsequent cases to apply to all contracts, whatever the writ by which they were governed. Moreover, no relief was available at Equity. In 1667 the Chancellor declared in *Maynard v Moseley* that 'Chancery mends no man's bargain'.[95]

Paradine v Jane did not actually address the issue of whether a defendant would be released from his contractual obligation when a supervening event had rendered his performance impossible, but rather whether a defendant would still be obliged to perform his obligation when the supervening event in question had rendered performance of the counter-performance impossible. Nevertheless, *Paradine v Jane* came to stand for the principle of absolute contractual liability, by which a contracting party would be liable even when some supervening event had rendered performance of his obligation impossible, unless he had made provision against such an eventuality in the contract.

This interpretation of *Paradine v Jane* has been affirmed in many subsequent cases. In 1706, for example, Holt CJ declared in *Thornborow v Whitacre* that 'when a man will for a valuable consideration undertake to do an impossible thing, though it cannot be performed, yet he shall answer in damages'.[96] The rule was again emphatically asserted by Lord Ellenborough, in the 1809 decision of *Atkinson v Ritchie*:

> Their relative claim upon, and duties in respect of, each other are conclusively fixed and determined by the terms of their own written contract.

94 (1647) Aleyn 27, 27–28; 82 ER 897, 897–898.
95 (1667) 3 Swan 655; 36 ER 1009, 1011.
96 (1706) 2 LD. Rayn. 1164, at 1165.

No exception which is not contained in the contract itself, can be engrafted upon it by implication, as an excuse for its non-performance. [97]

No less emphatic was the declaration of Lord Campbell some fifty years later, in the 1859 case of *Brown v Royal Insurance Co*:

There was nothing unlawful in this contract, and if it is impossible for the defendants to perform it, they must pay for that impossibility.[98]

The principle of absolute contractual liability was reaffirmed throughout the nineteenth century in a myriad of judgments.[99] It remains the foundational premise of contemporary English contract law. The 1987 case of *Eurico SpA v Philip Brokers (The Epaphus)* is a good illustration. In this case Donaldson MR declared as follows:

My starting point is that parties to any contract are free to agree upon any terms which they consider appropriate, including a term requiring one of the parties to do the impossible, although it would be highly unusual for parties knowingly so to agree. If they do so agree and if, as is inevitable, he fails to perform, he will be liable in damages.[100]

The court might very well have referred to the judgment of Lord Kenyon in the 1801 case of *Blight v Page*, when he declared that '[i]f a man undertakes what he cannot perform, he shall answer for it to the person with whom he undertakes'.[101]

The explanation for the ready acceptance of the absolute contract into English law, as Nicholas notes, lies in the fact that the primary remedy for breach of contract, derived from the forms of action, is an award of damages. Justice Holmes had famously declared in his magisterial book *The Common Law* that '(t)he only universal consequence of a legally binding promise is, that the law makes the promisor pay damages if the promised event does not come to pass'.[102] Nicholas contends that Holmes was actually doing no more

---

97 (1809) 10 East 530; 103 ER 877, 878.

98 (1859) 1 El. & El. 853, 859; 120 ER 1131, 1133.

99 See, for example, *Hadley v Clarke* (1799) 8 TR 259, 101 ER 1377; *Blight v Page* (1801) 3 Bos & Pul 295n, 127 ER 163; *Touteng v Hubbard* (1802) 3 Bos & Pul 292, at 300, 127 ER 161, at 166; *Sjoerds v Luscombe* (1812) 16 East 201, 104 ER 1065, at 1067; *Medeiros v Hill* (1832) 8 Bing 231, 131 ER 390 *Spence v Chodwick* (1847) 10 QB 517, 116 ER 877; *Hall v Wright* (1858) E, B & E 765; 29 LJQB 43; 120 ER 695, (1843–60) All ER 734; and *Kearon v Pearson* (1861) 7 H & N 386, 158 ER 523.

100 (1987) 2 Lloyd's Rep. 215, 218.

101 (1801) 3 Bos & Pul 295n, 127 ER 163.

102 O.W. Holmes Jr. *The Common Law* (1881) Project Gutenberg https://www.gutenberg.org 301.

in this statement than explicitly stating what had already long been implicitly understood in the Common Law: viz. that 'what a defendant had promised was not simply to perform, but either to perform or, in the alternative, to pay damages; and the payment of damages is never impossible'.[103] The Common Law principle that contractual liability is absolute unless otherwise qualified is one of the most distinguishing aspects of English contract law, and has no parallel in either Roman or French law, which are based on the premise *impossibilium nulla obligatio*.[104]

The Will Theory

As already seen above, the theory of the autonomy of the will dominated the French law of contract during the nineteenth century.[105] This same theory equally dominated English contract law. In England it was known as 'the will theory'.

The notion that a contract arises from the will of the parties and that it is their joint will which creates the legal obligation between them was almost certainly introduced into English law by Pothier.[106] The will theory 'gained ground fast when the translation of Pothier's book first appeared', and there is no doubt that Pothier's book was 'one of the most important sources' in introducing the will theory into English contract law.[107] This can be seen from the following passage in Evans:

> As every contract derives its effect from the intention of the parties, that intention, as expressed, or inferred, must be the ground of every decision respecting its operation and extent, and the grand object of consideration in every question with regard to its construction.[108]

By the mid-nineteenth century, the will theory had become the universally accepted basis for explaining and justifying the legally binding nature of contracts. The will theory dominated the legal sphere because it facilitated the 'new commercial and industrial order' ushered in by the Industrial Revolution, and reflected the prevailing political, economic and social ethos of liberalism and *laissez-faire*.[109] Cohen aptly describes the will theory as an integral part of the spirit of the age:

103 Nicholas, op. cit. (fn. 13), 96.
104 'There is no obligation to do the impossible'.
105 See pages 48–49 *supra*.
106 See page 48 *supra*.
107 Atiyah, op. cit., 406
108 William David Evans *A Treatise on the Law of Obligations, or Contracts (An Appendix to Pothier on Obligations)*, Volume 2, Philadelphia: Robert H. Small, 1853, Appendix V, 30, 31.
109 D.W. Greig and J.L.R. Davis *The Law of Contract* Sydney: The Law Book Company Limited, 1987, 22.

Contractualism in the law, that is, the view that in an ideally desirable system of law all obligations would arise only out of the will of the individual contracting freely, rests not only on the will theory of contract but also on the political doctrine that all restraint is evil and that government is best which governs least. This in turn is connected with the classic economic optimism that there is a sort of pre-established harmony between the good of all and the pursuit by each of his own selfish economic gain.[110]

The influence of the will theory can be seen in numerous cases from this period.[111] The principle was perhaps best stated by Kindersley V.C. in the 1869 case of *Haynes v Haynes*:

When both parties will the same thing, and each communicates his will to the other, with a mutual agreement to carry it into effect, then an engagement or contract between the two is constituted.[112]

The will theory was extremely important in shaping classical contract law, and its influence was 'to be found in every corner of contract law'.[113] Given the primacy of the will theory, the function of the Court was reduced to that of determining the implications of what the parties had already chosen to do, as set out in their contract. The Court could have no independent function in the context of this doctrine.[114] The will theory has proved to be a most tenacious idea. As Atiyah points out, 'the modern lawyer, accustomed as he is to the many derogations from freedom of contract, still takes it for granted that contractual obligations are created by the will or the intention of the parties'.[115]

The Implied Term

The origins of the implied term are obscure and it is uncertain when exactly the concept first made its appearance in English law.[116] In the nineteenth century, English judges increasingly made use of the implied term in order to introduce terms which they considered normal or usual into particular types

---

110 Morris R. Cohen 'The Basis of Contract' (1933) 46 *Harvard Law Review* 553, 558.
111 See, for example, *Dickenson v Dodds* (1876) Ch.D. 463, at 473, and *Cundy v Lindsay* (1878) 3 A.C. 459, at 465.
112 (1869) 1 Dr. &. Sm. 426; 433; 62 ER 442, 445.
113 Atiyah, op. cit., 408.
114 Id., 408.
115 Id., 406.
116 Richard Austin-Baker 'Implied Terms in English Contract Law' (Chapter 10) 225 in Larry A. DiMatteo, Qi Zhou, Severine Saintier and Keith Rowley (editors) *Commercial Contract Law: Transatlantic Perspectives* Cambridge University Press, 2013.

of contracts.[117] Resort to the implied term was purportedly meant simply to complete the ordinary incidents of the contract as they would have been understood by the parties. But in reality, given the radically changing legal and social context in which contracts were then being formulated, the implied term could actually be used by English judges as another means of importing elements of continental mercantile law or civil law.[118]

Implied terms were used in a wide variety of contexts and for a wide variety of purposes. Contracts of sale provided one of the most fertile grounds for their development, and are amongst the earliest examples of their application. The original position in a contract of sale, both with regard to title and quality or description of goods, had been *caveat emptor*, i.e. buyer beware. The buyer had to protect himself against defects in title or quality by obtaining an express warranty from the seller. He could then sue the seller in tort for deceit, if default occurred. Otherwise, he had no remedy. The introduction of implied terms into contracts of sale in the nineteenth century gradually enlarged the buyer's right to sue in the absence of an express warranty.[119]

English courts had recognised from an early period that custom and usage would properly comprise implied terms in contracts involving commercial transactions. But in *Hutton v Warren*,[120] decided in 1836, Parke B. noted that implied terms of custom and usage were not restricted to such contracts:

> It has long been settled that in commercial transactions extrinsic evidence of custom and usage is admissible to annex incidents to written contracts in matters with respect to which they are silent. The same rules have also been applied to contracts in other transactions of life in which known usages have been established and prevailed; and this has been done upon the principle of presumption that, in such transactions, the

---

117 Ibbetson, op. cit. (fn. 54), 17.

118 Id., 17.

119 Thus, in 1815 the court held in *Laing v Fidgeon* that there was an implied term that goods had to be of merchantable quality whenever there was a sale by description: (1815) 6 Taunt. 108, 109; 128 ER 974, 974. Similarly in *Jones v Bright*, decided in 1829, the court held that there was an implied term that goods sold for a particular purpose shall be fit for that particular purpose: (1829) 5 Bing 533, 546; 130 ER 1167, 1173. See also *Okell v Smith* (1815) 1 Stark 107; 171 ER 416; *Bluett v Osborne* (1816) 1 Stark 384; 171 ER 504. In 1864, guarantee of title to a chattel was declared in *Eichholz v Bannister* to be an implied term in all contracts of sale: (1864) 144 ER 284. See also *Morley v Attenborough* (1849) 3 Ex 500; 154 ER 943. By way of contrast, guarantee of title had long been an integral part of French law with regard to the sale of chattels: Domat (Strahan) op. cit., 230 (book I, title II, section X, paragraph III); Robert Joseph Pothier (M. Dupin: éditeur) *Oeuvres de Pothier: Traité du Contrat de Vente* (Tome deuxième) Paris: Béchet Aîné, Librairie, 1824, 20, paragraph 42; 38, paragraph 83. Article 1603 of the *Code civil* requires the seller to furnish a good title to the goods he sells: 'The seller has two primary obligations, viz. that of delivering and that of warranting the thing that he is selling' (*Il a deux obligations principales, celle de délivrer et celle de garantir la chose qu'il vend.*)

120 (1836) 1 M & W 466; 150 ER 517.

parties did not mean to express in writing the whole of the contract by which they intended to be bound, but to contract with reference to those known usages.[121]

The courts also had resort to the implied term in order to quarantine contracts of personal service from the rule of strict liability for non-performance. All contracts for personal services were held to contain an implied term that a contracting party would not be liable for non-performance if he became unable to perform his personal obligation, either because he had died or had become otherwise incapacitated. In *Hall v Wright*[122] Pollock CB described this use of the implied term as follows:

> Now it must be conceded on all hands that there are contracts to which the law implies exceptions and conditions which are not expressed. All contracts for personal services which can be performed only during the lifetime of the party contracting are subject to the implied condition that he shall be alive to perform them: and should he die, his executor is not liable to an action for the breach of contract occasioned by his death. So a contract by an author to write a book within a reasonable time, or by a painter to paint a picture within a reasonable time, would in my judgment be deemed subject to the condition that, if the author became insane or the painter paralytic, and so incapable of performing the contract by the act of God, he would not be liable personally in damages any more than his executors would be if he had been prevented by death.[123]

Eventually, the courts formulated a sufficient number of implied terms for various types of contract, such as leasing, agency, partnership, insurance and employment, that there could be said to be a set of rules which governed each type of contract whenever certain common types of problems arose. Each of these specific types of contract came to have its own particular 'laws', which would be applied by the courts in the event that the parties had not contracted out of them, which they were normally entitled to do in most circumstances.[124]

The development of implied terms in English contract law might appear to be completely at variance with the tenets of the will theory, whereby a contract came into existence through the mutual intention of the contracting parties, with its terms formulated solely upon the expression of their joint wills. However, the courts were able to reconcile the introduction of implied terms with the will theory by maintaining that the implied term, albeit unexpressed,

---

121 Id., 475; 521.
122 (1859) El. Bl. & El. 765; 120 ER 695.
123 Id., 793, 794; 706. See also the comments of Branwell B. at page 778; 700.
124 Austin-Baker, op. cit., 230; Andrew Frazer 'The Employee's Contractual Duty of Fidelity' (2015) 131 *Law Quarterly Review* 53, 57, 58.

did no more than recognise the joint will of the parties, and actually gave effect to their mutual intention.[125] This meant that an implied term could never contradict or even vary the express terms of the contracting parties, and the implied term had to be so clear and obvious that its content would be acknowledged by the parties as that which would go without saying.[126]

The implied term has no counterpart in French law. French contract law instead employs what are known as *lois impératives* and *lois supplétives*. These two terms can be translated as 'mandatory rules' and 'supplementary rules', respectively. As has been seen, when the Roman law of specific contract types was generalised into a uniform law of contract, this did not mean that the particular rules relating to the specific contract types thereby disappeared.[127] On the contrary, the developing Civil Law not only retained but actually further developed the specific, or nominate, contracts. The nominate contracts were regulated by the general law of contract, but their particular incidents were also specifically addressed in separate sections of the *Code*. Thus, for example, there is a separate section on the contract of sale, which comprises Articles 1582–1701. This is true of all the nominate contracts, each of which has a separate section in the *Code*, in which the particular incidents of that specific type of contract are addressed.[128]

The articles which address the incidents of a particular nominate contract comprise the *lois impératives* and *lois supplétives*. The advantage of having such articles is that they are pre-existing rules of law.[129] They do not have to be implied into a contract, as occurs in the Common Law. In fact, a French judge is not permitted to imply terms into a contract.[130] The *lois impératives* constitute those provisions which address the public interest, and which therefore must form part of every contract. Contracting parties cannot exclude or derogate from these provisions by way of contractual agreement. The *lois supplétives*, on the other hand, constitute provisions which fill in the gaps in a contract, according to its normal and particular incidents, and which will therefore apply unless the parties have expressed an intention to contract otherwise. Although there are a small number of articles which are specifically designated as being either *lois impératives* or *lois supplétives*, it is for the most

---

125 Sir David Hughes Parry *The Sanctity of Contracts in English Law* London: Stevens & Sons Limited, 1959, Reprinted London: Sweet & Maxwell; Littleton, Colorado: Fred B Rothman & Co., 1986, 43.

126 Id., 43. See in this regard *Reigate v Union Manufacturing Co.* (1918) 1 KB 592, per Scrutton L.J., at 605.

127 See pages 46–47 *supra*.

128 See pages 201–202 *infra* for an example of the special provisions relating to contracts of renting.

129 Nicholas, op. cit. (fn. 85), 33. See also Richard Austin-Baker *Implied Terms in English Contract Law* Cheltenham and Northampton Mass: Edward Elgar, 2011, 3.

130 Nicholas, op. cit. (fn. 85), 34. Attempts by litigants to ascertain the 'probable will' of the parties, in order to introduce *imprévision* as a part of *force majeure*, were firmly rejected by the French courts in the nineteenth century. See pages 80–83 *supra*.

part up to the courts to determine whether a particular article constitutes a *loi impérative* or a *loi supplétive*. Most of the articles in the *Code civil* which deal with contractual matters are *lois supplétives*.[131]

The Origins of the Doctrine of Frustration

Given the doctrine of strict liability for non-performance in English contract law, it was not possible that there could be anything comparable in the Common Law to *vis maior* or *force majeure*. Apart from the very limited exception of personal contracts, liability for non-performance was absolute. In order to avoid liability a contracting party always had to provide an explicit exemption clause in his contract. If he did not do so, he would be required to bear the consequences of non-performance.

During the nineteenth century, as has been seen, the range and application of the implied term was continuously expanded by the courts. The notion that the implied term might be used to mitigate the rule of absolute liability for non-performance was vigorously canvassed in 1859 in the case of *Hall v Wright*.[132] This case involved a claim for breach of promise of marriage. The defendant argued that after making the promise and before the breach, he had begun to suffer from a disease which caused 'bleeding from the lungs', and which consequently had made him 'incapable of marriage without great danger to his life, and therefore unfit for the married state'.[133] The case was appealed from the Court of Queen's Bench, which found in favour of the defendant, to the Exchequer Court, which decided in the plaintiff's favour, by a margin of four to three. The four majority judges, viz. Willes J., Crowder J., Martin B. and Williams J., applied the rule in *Paradine v Jane*. In their opinion the contract of marriage meant simply the ceremony of marriage. The contract was unconditional and therefore the defendant was liable for its breach. Willes J. declared as follows:

> The contract in this case is stated by the plaintiff in the declaration, and admitted by the defendant in his pleas, to have been in terms an unconditional one: and it is guess work, not construction, to read it as conditional. Its performance is not impossible; and it is not enough to shew, in answer to an action upon a contract, that its performance is inconvenient or may be dangerous. The delicacy of health, as alleged as an excuse, is the man's misfortune, not to be visited, beyond what is inevitable, upon the woman. If either party is to have the option of breaking off the

131 René David *Le Droit Français* (Tome 1) Paris: R. Pichon et R Durand-Auzias, 1960, 15; Nicholas, op. cit. (fn. 85), 33.
132 (1858) El. Bl. & El. 741, 120 ER 688. (Court of Queen's Bench); (1859) El. Bl. & El. 765; 120 ER 695 (Exchequer Court).
133 (1858) El. Bl. & El. 741, 120 ER 688 (Court of Queen's Bench).

match, it ought to be the woman. The Court have no right to say what is best for her.[134]

The three dissenting judges, Pollock C.B., Bramwell B. and Watson B., considered the contract of marriage not simply as a contract obliging the parties to undertake the ceremony of marriage, but rather as a contract initiating the commencement of a new state of being, viz. the state of being married. If a man could not exist in such a state because of some serious danger to his health then he must be excused from being obliged to undertake the ceremony. On this basis, the dissenting judges were of the opinion that the rule in *Paradine v Jane* must be mitigated by the introduction of an implied term. The judgment of Bramwell B. cogently set out the position of the dissenting judges. Bramwell B. began by acknowledging that 'the excuse for not performing the contract must be found in the terms of the contract itself'.[135] He noted that such a term was not contained in the contract in question and then continued as follows:

> ... as there is no reason why such term should be in his particular contract unless it is in all such contracts, the question is reduced to this: Is it a term in an ordinary agreement to marry that, if the man from bodily disease cannot marry without danger to his life, and is unfit for marriage from the cause mentioned at the time appointed, he shall be excused marrying then? The plea assumes it is. I think it is. Of course I admit that parties might stipulate otherwise, but, if they do not, I think they are implied terms of the ordinary contract.[136]

The majority had been able to bring the circumstances of this case within the rule of *Paradine v Jane* only by adopting an extremely narrow interpretation of what was meant by the promise to marry. By restricting the promise to marry to the ceremony of marriage they were able to escape having to take into account the consequences which would flow from such a union, and whether in such circumstances an implied term would be warranted. Their failure to address this issue clearly angered Pollock CB, who did not mince his words in rebuking the decision of the majority:

> I think, if the man can say with truth "By the visitation of Providence I am not capable of marriage," he cannot be called upon to marry: and I think this is an implied condition in all agreements to marry. I think that a view of the law which puts a contract of marriage on the same footing

---

134 (1859) El. Bl. & El. 765, 785, 786; 120 ER 695, 703.
135 Id., 777, Id., 700.
136 Id., 777, Id., 700.

as a bargain for a horse, or a bale of goods, is not in accordance with the general feelings of mankind, and is supported by no authority.[137]

Pollock C.B., however, was in the minority. There would be no mitigation of the doctrine of absolute liability in this case.

But the opportunity to mitigate came up again in 1863 in the case of *Taylor v Caldwell*.[138] This case was decided by the redoubtable Blackburn J., as he then was.[139] There is little doubt that the reasoning of the three dissenting judges in *Hall v Wright* inspired Blackburn J. to adopt the implied term as the means by which to mitigate the doctrine of absolute performance, and thereby to introduce a concept analogous to *force majeure*.

The defendants in *Taylor v Caldwell* had granted the plaintiffs a licence to use a music hall on certain specified dates, so that the plaintiffs could put on a series of concerts. However, before the plaintiffs were able to stage any of the concerts, the hall was accidentally destroyed by fire. The plaintiffs then sued the defendants on the basis that the defendants were in breach of their contractual obligation to provide a hall and were therefore liable to the plaintiffs for the expenses the plaintiffs had incurred in advertising the proposed concerts. Counsel for the plaintiffs specifically referred to the rule in *Paradine v Jane* to assert that the 'destruction of the premises by fire will not exonerate the defendants from performing their part of the agreement'.[140]

Blackburn J. began his judgment by reaffirming the traditional rule as set out in *Paradine v Jane*:

... where there is a positive contract to do a thing, not in itself unlawful, the contractor must perform it or pay damages for not doing it, although

---

137 Id., 795; Id., 706.
138 (1863) 3 B & S 826; 122 ER 309.
139 Colin Blackburn, Baron Blackburn (1813–1896) was one of the outstanding judges of the nineteenth century, who delivered many decisions of the highest importance. Blackburn was born in Scotland, and educated at Edinburgh Academy, Eton and Trinity College, Cambridge. He was called to the Bar in 1838. He was appointed a puisne judge to the Court of Queen's Bench in 1859. He soon proved to be one of the most able judges on the Bench, and was promoted to the Court of Appeal in 1876, at which time he was made a Lord of Appeal in Ordinary and a life peer, as Baron Blackburn of Killearn. Apart from *Taylor v Caldwell*, Blackburn J. gave the leading judgments in the following cases: *Tweedle v Atkinson* (1861) 1 B&S 393; 121 ER 721; *Rylands v Fletcher* (1868) UKHL 1; *Smith v Hughes* (1871) LR 6 QB 597); *Harris v Nickerson* (1873) LR 8 QB 286; *R v Negus* (1873) LR 2 CP 34; *Ashbury Railway Carriage and Iron Co Ltd v Riche* (1875) LR 7 HL 653; *Poussard v Spiers and Pond* (1876) 1 QBD 410; *Brogden v Metropolitan Railway Company* (1876–1877) 2 AC 439; *Erlanger v New Sombrero Phosphate Co* (1878) 3 App Cas 1218; *Speight v Gaunt* (1883–1884) LR 9 App Cas 1; *Foakes v Beer* (1884) 9 App Cas 605.
140 (1863) 3 B&S 826, 830; 122 ER 309, 311.

in consequence of unforeseen accidents, the performance of his contract
has become unexpectedly burthensome or even impossible.[141]

However, Blackburn J. then sought to find a way to limit the rule. Resorting
to a comparative analysis Blackburn J. recognised that the facts before him fell
within the ambit of *vis maior* in Roman law and *force majeure* in French law.
The defendant, through no fault of his own, had been unable to perform his
obligation as a result of a supervening event which had resulted in the physical
destruction of the subject matter. In such circumstances, under both Roman
law and French law, the debtor would be discharged from his contractual obligation. Blackburn J. referred specifically to two passages from the Digest and
to passages from Pothier's works in order to illustrate how this was so.

The two passages quoted from the Digest note that a debtor would not
be liable on a *stipulatio* or a legacy for not transferring property, viz. a slave
named Stichus, if the slave died through no fault of the contracting party
before the date of delivery. Blackburn J. cited these passages in the original
Latin.[142] The English translations are as follows:

If Stichus has been promised to be given on a certain date and dies
before that date, the promisor is not liable.[143]

If by reason of a legacy or as a result of a stipulation you owe me a certain
man, you will not be liable to me after his death, except where it was
your fault that you did not give him to me when he was still alive. This
happens if you either failed to give him when requested or killed him.[144]

Blackburn J. then referred to several passages from Pothier to the same
effect.[145] Blackburn J. relied mainly on a passage from Pothier's *Traité des*

---

141 Id., 833; Id., 312.

142 (1863) 3 B&S 826, 834; 122 ER 309, 312, 313.

143 D.45.1.33 (Pomponius).

144 D.45.1.23 (Pomponius). Buckland points out that the references by Blackburn J. to a *stipulatio* were wholly inapposite, because a *stipulatio* was a *stricti iuris* unilateral contract, and
thus 'had nothing to do' with the bilateral contract of hire which was under consideration.
Buckland also notes that Blackburn J. made reference to Pothier's *Traité du Contrat de
Vente*, and points out that 'sale is not hire': W.W. Buckland '*Casus* and Frustration in Roman
and Common Law' (1933) 46 *Harvard Law Review* 1281, 1288.

145 Blackburn J. was very familiar with the works of Pothier, as he had 'made copious references'
both from the *Traité des Obligations* and from the *Traité du Contrat de Vente* 'in his work
of sale'. As Simpson points out, Blackburn J. had 'some years earlier in his work on the contract of sale ... employed the same reasoning in the slightly different context of risk in sale':
A.W.B. Simpson 'Innovation in Nineteenth Century Contract Law' 171, at 195, in A.W.B.
Simpson *Legal Theory and Legal History* London: The Hambleton Press, 1987, citing Blackburn C. *A Treatise on the Effect of the Contract of Sale on the Legal Rights of Property and
Possession in Goods, Wares and Merchandise* (1845) London, 172 *et seq*. Blackburn J. referred
to his own book at page 314 of *Taylor v Caldwell*.

Obligations, which he incorporated into his judgment more or less *verbatim*. He also referred to several passages from Pothier's *Traité du Contrat de Vente*, although he did not reproduce those passages in full as he did the first passage from the *Traité des Obligations*.[146] Blackburn J.'s reference to the passage from the *Traité des Obligations* reads as follows:

> ... the principle in the Civil law is adopted as applicable to every obligation of which the subject is a certain thing. The general subject is treated of by Pothier, who in his *Traité des obligations*, partie 3, chap. 6, art. 3, § 668 states the result to be that the debtor *corporis certi* is freed from his obligation when the thing has perished, neither by his act, nor his neglect, and before he is in default, unless by some stipulation he has taken on himself the risk of the particular misfortune which has occurred.[147]

In the original passage, Pothier refers to a '*corps certain*'.[148] Evans translates this as a 'specific thing'. Blackburn J. refers to a 'certain thing'[149] and also uses

---

146 Blackburn J. cites the relevant passages as follows: Pothier *Traité du Contrat de Vente* (see part. 4, § 307, etc; and part. 2, ch. 1, sect 1, art. 4, § 1). These passages may be found, respectively, in M. Dupin (éditeur) *Oeuvres de Pothier Tome Deuxèime Traité du Contrat de Vente* Paris: Béchet Aîné, 1824, at pages 137–141 (paragraph 307 and particularly paragraph 308) and pages 24 and 25, paragraphs 56–58.

147 (1863) 3 B&S 826, 834, 835; 122 ER 309, 313. The original passage from Pothier reads as follows: '*Le principe, que nous avons établi, que le débiteur d'un corps certain est libéré de son obligation, lorsque la chose due est périe sans son fait et sans sa faute, et avant qu'il ait été mis en demeure, reçoit exception dans le cas auquel le débiteur se serait, par une clause particulière du contrat, chargé du risque des cas fortuits*': Robert Joseph Pothier (M. Dupin: éditeur) *Oeuvres de Pothier: Traité des Obligations* Paris: Pichon-Bechet, Successeur de Bechet Aîné, Librairie, 1827, 399–401, paragraph 668. The passage, as translated by Evans, reads as follows: 'The principle which has been established, that the debtor of a specific thing is discharged from his obligation, when the thing is lost, without any act, default or delay, on his part, is subject to an exception, when he has, by a particular clause in the contract, expressly taken the risk of such loss upon himself': Robert Joseph Pothier (translated by William David Evans) *A Treatise on the Law of Obligations, or Contracts* (volume 1) Philadelphia: Robert H. Small, 1826, 392, 393, paragraph 633.

148 Paragraph 668 was the inspiration for the first paragraph of former Article 1302 of the *Code civil*, which reproduces very nearly the words used by Pothier in paragraph 668 and also summarises his observations in paragraphs 649, 650 and 656. See pages 75–77 *supra*. Former Article 1302 reads as follows: *Lorsque le corps certain et déterminé qui était l'objet de l'obligation, vient à périr, est mis hors du commerce, ou se perd de manière qu'on en ignore absolument l'existence, l'obligation est éteinte si la chose a péri ou a été perdue sans la faute du débiteur et avant qu'il fût en demeure.* (When a certain and determined thing which was the object of the obligation, has perished, is put out of commerce, or is lost in a way in which one can absolutely ignore its existence, the obligation is extinguished if the thing has perished or has been lost without the fault of the debtor and before he was required to deliver.)

149 (1863) 3 B & S 826, 834; 122 ER 309, 313.

the Latin phrase 'a debtor *corporis certi*', i.e. a debtor of a specific, tangible thing.[150]

Blackburn J. noted that 'the Civil Law is not of itself authority in an English Court', but then went on to declare that it nevertheless 'affords great assistance in investigating the principles on which the law is grounded'.[151] As the facts of this case seemed to fall within the context of *vis maior* and *force majeure*, Blackburn J. sought to import the same principles into the Common Law. There were, however, serious obstacles in doing so.

In order to escape liability for contractual non-performance a debtor in both Roman law and French law had to prove that the non-performance had occurred without fault on his part. But in the Common Law fault was not a consideration. By virtue of the rule in *Paradine v Jane* liability for non-performance would arise even if there had been no fault on the part of the party who had failed to perform.[152] Moreover, in French law, when the object of the contract has been destroyed or has otherwise disappeared without fault on the part of the debtor, the contract cannot thereafter continue to exist, because one of its essential requirements, viz. the object, has disappeared.[153] But in the Common Law, there can be a valid contract, and the defendant can be liable for its non-performance, even when the subject matter of the contract is not in existence, because the Common Law, unlike the Civil Law, does not require an object, to be actionable.[154]

Blackburn J. overcame these difficulties by eliding the fundamental differences between the legal systems through the device of the implied term. He connected the case before him to the concepts of *vis maior* and *force majeure* by stating that in the Civil Law a release from the contract is always 'implied in every obligation of the class which they call *obligatio de certo corpore*',[155] and then by declaring that 'the same condition of the continued existence of the thing is implied by English law'.[156] By emphasising the common element of a necessary implication in both legal systems Blackburn J. was able to utilise the Common Law device of an implied term in order to mitigate the rule of absolute contractual liability in those circumstances when the specified subject matter of a contract had been destroyed through no fault of the defendant:

---

150 Id., 835; 313.

151 Id., 835; 313. See the comments of Tindell CJ in *Acton v Blundell* (1843) 12 M & W 324, 353; 152 ER 1223, 1234, reproduced at page 7, fn. 26 *supra*, and page 257 *infra*.

152 Blackburn J. made note of the exceptions to this rule, which involved contracts of personal service and bailments where the bailed goods had perished without fault on the part of the bailee. See (1863) 3 B & S 826, 835, 836, 838, 839; 122 ER 309, 313, 314.

153 See former Article 1108, at page 43 *supra*, which required that a valid contract have an object, and current Article 1128, at page 65 *supra*, which requires that a valid contract contain content which is lawful and certain.

154 For an illustration of this point see the Australian case of *McRae v The Commonwealth Disposals Commission* (1951) 84 CLR 377.

155 (1863) 3 B&S 826, 834; 122 ER 312.

156 Id., 835; 313.

... where, from the nature of the contract, it appears that the parties must from the beginning have known that it could not be fulfilled unless when the time for the fulfilment of the contract arrived some particular specified thing continued to exist, so that, when entering into the contract, they must have contemplated such continuing existence as the foundation of what was to be done; there, in the absence of any express or implied warranty that the thing shall exist, the contract is not to be construed as a positive contract, but as subject to an implied condition that the parties shall be excused in case, before breach, performance becomes impossible from the perishing of the thing without default of the contractor.[157]

Blackburn J. then found that there was such an implied term in the contract between the plaintiffs and defendants:

In the present case, looking at the whole contract, we find that the parties contracted on the basis of the continued existence of the Music Hall at the time when the concerts were to be given; that being essential to their performance.[158]

Blackburn J. justified this new use of the implied term by reference to the will theory, then so much in vogue both in England and in France.[159] The implied term which Blackburn J. relied upon was, in his opinion, actually a term which expressed the mutual intention of the parties themselves:

There seems little doubt that this implication tends to further the great object of making the legal construction of such an agreement such as to fulfil the intention of those who entered into the contract.[160]

By linking the Roman and French concepts of *vis maior* and *force majeure* to the Common Law by means of the purportedly common element of a necessary implication in all three legal systems, Blackburn J. was able to introduce a concept into English contract law which was ostensibly analogous to *vis maior*

---

157 Id., 833, 834; 312.
158 Id., 839; 314.
159 See pages 48–49 and 158–159 *supra*.
160 (1863) 3 B&S 826, 834; 122 ER 312. But Blackburn J. flatly contradicted himself by having earlier in his judgment declared as follows: 'The parties when framing this agreement evidently had not present to their minds the possibility of such a disaster, and have made no express stipulation with reference to it, so that the answer to the question must depend on the general rules of law applicable to such a contract': (1863) 3 B&S 826, 833; 122 ER 312. As Simpson wryly notes, Blackburn J.'s new doctrine 'represents a curiously complex blend of common and civil law development, linked, inevitably, to the central doctrine of *consensus* by fiction': Simpson op. cit. (fn. 145), 197.

and *force majeure*. As a result, a contract in English law could now be set aside when the subject matter of that contract concerned a specific person or thing, and that person or thing had perished as the result of a supervening event not attributable to the defendant.[161] However, in emphasising that there was an implied term in Roman and French law Blackburn J. could be said to have been resorting to a subtle sleight of hand.

The implied term actually does not exist in either Roman or French law. In Roman and French law *vis maior* and *force majeure* do not arise as the result of a court construing an intention, but are rather the result of the application of rules of law which must be applied to contracts when their conditions have been satisfied.[162] The former Article 1147, for example, was a *loi impérative*. By virtue of this article, when the performance of a contractual obligation becomes impossible as a result of *force majeure* the debtor must be freed from that obligation. This is a mandatory rule of French contract law. There is no issue of the court having to find whether or not there was an implied term in the contract in question.[163] This is likewise the case with the revised articles. Current Articles 1218, 1351 and 1351-1 are mandatory rules.[164]

The essential difference between Roman and French law, on the one hand, and English law, on the other – which Blackburn J. chose to ignore – is that whereas Roman and French law apply a rule in situations involving the destruction of the object through a supervening event not attributable to the debtor, English law construes an intention on the part of the contracting parties in the same circumstances.[165] The concept which Blackburn J. introduced into English contract law did, however, replicate the principles of *vis maior* and *force majeure* by requiring that performance be rendered physically impossible, either through the physical destruction of the subject matter of the contract, or through death or impairment in a personal contract, without fault on the part of the defendant, in order for the defendant to escape liability for non-performance.

But it was not simply the defendant whom Blackburn J. relieved of liability by virtue of the supervening event. Blackburn J. stated that both parties were to be excused from their obligations from the time that the supervening event took place:

---

161 R.G. McElroy and Glanville Williams 'The Coronation Cases – I' (1941) 4 *The Modern Law Review* 241, 242.

162 D.J. Ibbetson *A Historical Introduction to the Law of Obligations* Oxford: Oxford University Press, 1999, 224.

163 David, op. cit. (fn. 131), 15.

164 See page 86 *supra* for the text of Article 1218 and page 89–90 *supra* for the texts of Articles 1351 and 1351-1.

165 Ibbetson, op. cit. (fn. 162), 224.

... the parties shall be excused in case, before breach, performance becomes impossible from the perishing of the thing without default of the contractor.[166]

This point was emphasised again further on in the judgment when Blackburn J. declared that 'both parties are excused'.[167] By finding that the supervening event equally 'excused both parties' Blackburn J. departed significantly from the concepts of *vis maior* and *force majeure* upon which he was purporting to rely. In Roman and French law *vis maior* and *force majeure* exonerate the debtor from liability, and are thus 'related to the obligation of one party'.[168] *Vis maior* and *force majeure* act as a defence which a debtor can raise when his performance has become impossible through no fault of his own.[169] By ruling that the supervening event excused both parties, Blackburn J. formulated a very different response to supervening events, by which the contract as a whole was terminated automatically for both parties, from the moment of the supervening event.[170]

The reason underlying this ruling by Blackburn J. was to ensure that the losses which the parties incurred as a result of the supervening event would be allocated more or less equally between them, rather than requiring one of them to bear all of the losses, as would have occurred had the doctrine in *Paradine v Jane* applied.[171] In most ordinary contracts one party undertakes a non-monetary performance, for which the other party pays a sum of money. By virtue of the ruling in *Taylor v Caldwell* each of the two contracting parties bore a risk, which Treitel labels as the 'performance risk' and the 'payment

---

166 (1863) 3 B&S 826, 834; 122 ER 309, 312.

167 Id., 840; 315.

168 Nicholas, op. cit. (fn. 13), 955.

169 In Roman law, as Buckland points out, 'there was no question of an implied agreement deducible from the circumstances'. *Vis maior*, or *casus* as Buckland refers to it, having rendered performance impossible, 'released the party whose performance was impossible and entitled the other, on grounds of *bona fides*, to recover anything he had paid for the performance which had become impossible': Buckland, op. cit., 1288.

   In French law *force majeure* released the debtor from the performance of his obligation, and cause, under the former regime, released the creditor from his counter-performance. Under the current regime, cause has been removed as an essential criterion of a valid contract. Therefore cause can no longer be the basis for maintaining that the obligations of the contracting parties are interdependent. However, the second paragraph of Article 1218 specifically states that when the non-performance of the debtor's obligation becomes definitive through *force majeure*, the contract is automatically terminated, and both parties are released from their obligations. See page 89 *supra*.

170 Nicholas, op. cit. (fn. 13), 955.

171 As Lord Wright observed in *Joseph Constantine SS Line Ltd. v Imperial Smelting Corpn Ltd.* (1941) 2 All ER 165, at 185: '... the results of holding a man to the absolute terms of a contract would often be so unjust, that from early times, as the example of Blackburn J. in *Taylor v Caldwell* show, the courts set themselves to avoid these results whenever justice seemed to require it'.

risk'.[172] The 'performance risk' was borne by the party providing the payment, and the 'payment risk' by the party providing the performance. When the performance was rendered impossible by the supervening event, the party providing payment, who bore the 'performance risk', could no longer receive the performance nor was he entitled to damages for non-performance, and the party providing the performance, who bore the 'payment risk', was no longer entitled to receive the payment agreed upon.[173] As Treitel points out, '(t)he statement in *Taylor v Caldwell* that "both parties are excused" has the effect that each party bears one of these two risks'.[174] The rationale underpinning Blackburn J's formulation was thus to provide a more equitable result for the parties.[175]

The Doctrine Expanded

The issue of impossibility of performance arose again in 1874 in the case of *Jackson v Union Marine Insurance Co. Ltd*.[176] In *Taylor v Caldwell* impossibility of performance relieved the defendant of liability because the subject matter of the contract had been physically destroyed without fault on the part of the defendant. But in *Jackson v Union Marine Insurance Co. Ltd* the question was whether this new doctrine could be extended to circumstances purportedly giving rise to impossibility in a commercial context, when there had been no physical destruction of the subject matter.

The plaintiff was a shipowner who had contracted to supply the charterers with a ship to transport iron rails from Newport to San Francisco. The charterparty specified that the shipowner was to send a ship 'with all possible dispatch' from Liverpool to Newport.[177] The reference to 'all possible dispatch' was the only clause in the charterparty which referred to a timeframe within which the terms of the contract were to be performed. The contract also declared that the shipowner was not to be held liable for dangers and accidents of navigation. The plaintiff took out insurance with the defendant's insurance company on the chartered freight for the voyage. While on route from Liverpool to Newport, the ship ran aground in Caernarvon Bay and was seriously damaged. The repairs required to render the ship seaworthy took some six months to complete, after which it would then have been possible for the ship to proceed to Newport. In the meantime, the charterers sought to conclude alternative arrangements with the shipowner to supply them with another ship. This the shipowner refused to do, and further refused to release the charterers from the

---

172 Sir Guenter Treitel *Frustration and Force Majeure* (third edition) London: Sweet & Maxwell, 2014, 44, 45.
173 Id., 45.
174 Id., 45.
175 See the comments of Lord Bingham in this regard at page 254, fn. 9 *infra*.
176 (1874) LR 10 CP 125.
177 Id., 142.

contract. The charterers then abandoned the charterparty and proceeded to charter another ship.

The plaintiff claimed insurance from the defendant for a total loss on the chartered freight. The defendant disputed the plaintiff's insurance claim on the basis that the charterers were still bound by the charterparty and were therefore liable for failing to load the ship when it would have eventually arrived at Newport. If this were the case, the insurers would not be liable for the insurance claim.

The Exchequer Chamber found that the charterers were not bound by the charterparty and were therefore not liable for failing to load the ship. Bramwell B. wrote the judgment for the majority. He framed his decision on the basis of impossibility of performance, noting that 'the jury have found that the voyage the parties contemplated had become impossible' and then proceeding to justify the jury's finding in his judgment.[178] Bramwell B. held that there was an implied term in the charterparty that the ship be supplied to the charterers within a reasonable period of time, and that this had not occurred:

> The question turns on the construction and effect of the charter. By it the vessel is to sail to Newport with all possible dispatch, perils of the seas excepted. It is said this constitutes the only agreement as to time, and, provided all possible dispatch is used, it matters not when she arrives at Newport. I am of a different opinion. If this charterparty be read as a charter for a definite voyage or adventure, then it follows that there is necessarily an implied condition that the ship shall arrive at Newport in time for it.[179]

The existence or non-existence of the express phrase 'with all possible dispatch' did not affect the existence of the implied term for arriving at a reasonable time:

> The same result is arrived at by what is the same argument differently put. Where no time is named for the doing of anything, the law attaches a reasonable time. Now, let us suppose this charterparty had said nothing about arriving with all possible dispatch. In that case, had the ship not arrived at Newport in a reasonable time, owing to the default of the shipowner, the charterers would have had a right of action against the owner, and would have had a right to withdraw from the contract .... The charterers would be discharged, because the implied condition to arrive in a reasonable time was not performed. Now, let us suppose the charter contains, as here, that the ship shall arrive with all possible dispatch, – I ask again, is that so inconsistent with or repugnant to a further

178 Id., 141.
179 Id., 142, 143.

condition that at all events she shall arrive within a reasonable time or is that so needless a condition that it is not to be implied: I say certainly not. I must repeat the foregoing reasoning. Let us suppose them both expressed, and it will be seen they are not inconsistent nor needless. Thus, I will use all possible dispatch to get the ship to Newport, but at all events she shall arrive in a reasonable time for the adventure contemplated. I hold, therefore, that the implied condition of a reasonable time exists in this charter.[180]

The running aground of the ship, and the delay of six months required for its repair, had resulted in the frustration of the adventure, thereby making performance impossible.[181]

In his judgment, Bramwell B. made reference to *Taylor v Caldwell*:

But, not arriving in time for the voyage contemplated, but at such a time that it is frustrated, is not only a breach of contract, but discharges the charterer. And so it should, though he has such an excuse that no action lies. *Taylor v Caldwell* is a strong authority in the same direction.[182]

The reference to *Taylor v Caldwell* is interesting because Bramwell B declared that it was 'a strong authority' for his decision, yet he made no effort to explain how the decision in *Taylor v Caldwell* applied to the circumstances of this case. Blackburn J. had relied heavily on Roman and French law in order to justify his decision in *Taylor v Caldwell*. But Branwell B. made no reference whatsoever either to Roman or to French law. Although Blackburn J. was one of the judges in *Jackson v Union Marine Insurance Co Ltd*, he was content simply to concur with Bramwell B., without adding any remarks of his own in order to explain how *Taylor v Caldwell* was a 'strong authority' for the decision in this case.

Blackburn J. had declared in *Taylor v Caldwell* that there would be an implied term relieving a contracting party of liability when 'a specified thing' which constituted 'the foundation' of the contract had been destroyed without fault on the part of the contracting party.[183] But unlike *Taylor v Caldwell*, the facts of *Jackson v Union Marine Insurance Col Ltd* did not involve any physical destruction of the essential subject matter of the contract. This fundamental difference between the two cases was emphasised by Cleasby B. in his dissenting judgment:

---

180 Id., 143, 144.
181 Bramwell B.'s actual words were as follows: '... the voyage in question, the adventure, should be accomplished and not frustrated'. (1874) LR 10 CP 125, 146.
182 Id., 148.
183 *Taylor v Caldwell* (1863) 3 B&S 826, 833, 834; 122 ER 309, 312.

No doubt when the existence of a particular person or thing, or state of things, can be regarded as the very foundation of a particular transaction, it may be implied that, if the foundation fails, the transaction which is founded upon it ceases to be effectual. But, in this subject I would beg to refer to the clear and comprehensive judgment of my Brother Blackburn in *Taylor v Caldwell*.[184]

Cleasby B. seemed to be challenging Blackburn J. to explain how the principles he enunciated in *Taylor v Caldwell* could be said to apply in this situation, when there had been no physical destruction of the essential subject matter and where, according to the express terms of the contract, performance could still occur. Blackburn J., however, did not rise to the challenge.

Vis maior and *force majeure* of course do not arise only when the essential subject matter of the contract has been physically destroyed by virtue of some unforeseen supervening event, without fault on the part of the debtor. The essential element of both *vis maior* and *force majeure* does not lie in the physical destruction of the essential subject matter of the contract, although this will very often occur, but rather in the fact that contractual performance by the debtor, whatever that may involve, has been rendered impossible by some unforeseen supervening event, without fault on his part. [185]

In *Taylor v Caldwell* Blackburn J. had only introduced into English contract law that aspect of *vis maior* and *force majeure* which involved the physical destruction of the essential subject matter of the contract, thereby making contractual performance impossible. But in *Jackson v Union Marine Insurance Co. Ltd* the principle was extended to include a situation of commercial impossibility, based on the implied term that time was of the essence. It also did not involve any physical destruction of the subject matter of the contract. This was clearly an extension of the principle, although not acknowledged as such by Bramwell B. Bramwell B. did, however, continue to adhere to the ratio in *Taylor v Caldwell* that performance must be rendered impossible in order for the doctrine to apply. In this, he restricted the ambit of the doctrine to the limitations set out in both *vis maior* and *force majeure*, which Blackburn J. had relied upon in arriving at his decision.

In *Taylor v Caldwell* Blackburn J. had narrowed the scope of absolute contractual liability, as laid down in *Paradine v Jane*, by finding that there would necessarily be an implied term between the contracting parties which relieved them of contractual liability in the event that the subject matter of the contract had been physically destroyed by an unforeseen supervening event, without fault on the part of either party. The Exchequer Chamber in *Jackson v Union Marine Insurance Co Ltd* further narrowed the scope of absolute contractual

---

184 (1874) LR 10 CP 125, 141.
185 See pages 22–23 *supra,* regarding Roman law, and pages 75–80, 82 and 86 *supra,* regarding French law.

liability by finding that an implied term also necessarily arose in situations involving commercial impossibility, even though the subject matter had not been destroyed by an unforeseen supervening event.[186] Both cases were decided on the basis that performance had become impossible, and, in this regard, they corresponded to the Roman and French doctrines of *vis maior* and *force majeure*. But both cases differed radically from *vis maior* and *force majeure* by relying on an implied term in order to relieve the defaulting party of liability. As seen above, no implied term arises in the context of Roman and French law, because *vis maior* and *force majeure* constitute mandatory rules of law.

The Doctrine Further Expanded

Throughout the nineteenth century, the French courts had grappled with the issue of whether *force majeure* should apply only on the basis of the impossibility of performance, or whether it might also be applied on the basis of a radical change of circumstances.[187] This issue was not ultimately resolved until 1876, by the decision of the *Cour de cassation* in the *Canal de Craponne* case. As seen above, the *Cour de cassation* decided that *force majeure* could only apply when performance had become impossible, but not when it had simply become more onerous.[188] In 1903 this same issue came to be played out in the English context, in a series of cases collectively known as the 'coronation cases'. These cases arose as a result of the postponement of the coronation of Edward VII, due to the sudden illness which overtook the king several

---

186 Cleasby B. was of the opinion that the doctrine of an implied term should apply only to situations which involved the physical destruction of the essential subject matter of the contract, and that in all other circumstances the doctrine of absolute contractual liability should continue to apply: 'Now, according to the law of England, if a person engages absolutely to do something, the fact of its becoming impossible or attended with penalties, is in general no answer: *Paradine v Jane*, so often referred to, and many subsequent cases. ... the rule is founded upon the presumption that, where the engagement is absolute, the party takes upon himself the risk of being able to perform the contract' (1874) LR 10 CP 125, 139.

187 See pages 80–83 *supra*.

188 See pages 81–82 *supra*. This decision, as seen above, has now been overturned by the introduction of Article 1195 in the Ordonnance du 10 février 2016. Article 1195 recognises that a fundamental change in circumstance can be grounds for seeking the revision or termination of a contract, when it has made the debtor's performance 'excessively onerous'. See pages 100–103 *supra*.

days before his coronation.[189] The most significant of these cases was *Krell v Henry*.[190]

In *Krell v Henry* the defendant Henry had rented a room overlooking the route of the coronation procession for £75, for the two days on which it was to take place, in order to view the procession. The written contract consisted of two letters between the defendant and the plaintiff's solicitors, in which the defendant paid a deposit of £25, and promised to pay the balance on 24 June 1902, i.e. two days before the coronation was to take place. The purpose for which the rooms had been rented was not stated in the terms of the contract. In this regard *Krell v Henry* was 'unique among the coronation cases'.[191]

On the morning of 24 June, it was announced that the coronation would not take place as planned, and the defendant refused to pay the balance due under the contract. The plaintiff thereupon sued, arguing that the terms of the contract as agreed upon by the parties were still quite capable of being performed. The defendant argued that there was an implied term in the contract, viz. that the room had been rented on those particular days for the sole purpose of viewing the coronation procession. Although it was still physically possible to occupy the room, the underlying basis upon which the contract had been concluded had been radically changed into something fundamentally different, as a result of the king's illness.

The Court of Appeal affirmed the submission of the defendant. Vaughan Williams L.J. wrote the judgment of the Court. He conceived the primary issue before the Court in terms of a comparative analysis, as indicated in the first sentence of his judgment:

> The real question in this case is the extent of the application in English law of the principle of the Roman law which has been adopted and acted on in many English decisions, and notably in the case of *Taylor v Caldwell*.[192]

Vaughan Williams L.J. acknowledged that as a result of the decision in *Taylor v Caldwell* 'it is clear that the principle of the Roman law has been introduced into the English law'.[193] The issue before him in this case was to determine

---

189 On 10 December 1901 an announcement appeared in *The Times*, stating that the coronation of King Edward VII would take place on 26 and 27 June 1902. Many contracts were then entered into, for the purpose obtaining an advantageous position to view the proceedings. On 24 June the King fell ill with a form of appendicitis, which necessitated him being operated upon, and which resulted in the postponement of the coronation ceremonies: Treitel, op. cit., 313, 314.

190 (1903) 2 KB 740 (CA).

191 Treitel, op. cit., 317.

192 (1903) 2 KB 740, 747, 748.

193 Id., 748.

'how far this principle extends'.[194] He noted that 'the principle of the Roman law' applied with regard to '*obligationes de certo corpore*' i.e. that 'a particular specific thing continued to exist',[195] as had been the case in *Taylor v Caldwell*.[196] But he then queried whether the developing principle of frustration in English law was necessarily limited to those instances in which the object of the contract had been destroyed, as was the case in Roman and French law. Vaughan Williams L.J. did not think so:

> I do not think that the principle of the civil law as introduced into the English law is limited to cases in which the event causing the impossibility of performance is the destruction or non-existence of some thing which is the subject-matter of the contract or of some condition or state of things expressly specified as a condition of it.[197]

Then, in a radical departure from Roman and French law, he declared that '[w]hatever may have been the limits of Roman law', English law would recognise that frustration could be invoked not only when performance of the contract had become impossible by the destruction of the thing which was the subject-matter of the contract, but also when there had been a fundamental change in circumstances:

> … English law applies the principle not only to cases where the performance of the contract becomes impossible by the cessation of existence of the thing which is the subject matter of the contract, but also to cases where the event which renders the contract incapable of performance is the cessation or non-existence of an express condition or state of things, going to the root of the contract, and essential to its performance.[198]

The reference in this passage to a 'state of things, going to the root of the contract and essential to its performance' was also described by Vaughan Williams L.J. as 'the substance of the contract'.[199] The 'substance of the contract', Vaughan Williams L.J. declared, would be ascertained by determining whether the 'substantial contract needs for its foundation the assumption of the existence of a particular state of things'.[200] If it does, then the 'non-existence of the state of things assumed by both contracting parties as the foundation of the contract' will give rise to frustration and 'there will be no

194 Id., 748.
195 Id., 748.
196 See pages 165–172 *supra*.
197 (1903) 2 KB 740, 749.
198 Id., 748.
199 Id., 749.
200 Id., 749.

breach of the contract'.[201] Moreover, the 'substance of the contract' need not necessarily be ascertained from the terms of the contract itself, but could rather be determined 'from necessary inferences drawn from the surrounding circumstances'.[202]

As a result of the decision in *Krell v Henry* the doctrine of frustration was significantly and qualitatively differentiated from the concepts of *vis maior* and *force majeure*. Vaughan Williams L.J. explicitly acknowledged this in rendering his decision.[203] In Roman law, the texts referring to *vis maior* or *casus* almost invariably referred to instances in which performance had become actually impossible. This was also true of *force majeure* in French private law, which at that time permitted termination of the contract only when performance had become impossible, through no fault of the debtor. But, as Buckland and McNair point out, once the decision in *Krell v Henry* had been rendered, there was 'no direct point of comparison with Roman law, because frustration not amounting to actual impossibility is little represented in the texts' of the *Corpus Iuris*.[204] Thus, even though the Roman and French concepts of *vis maior* and *force majeure* had originally provided the inspiration for the development of frustration, the English doctrine would not be constrained in its development by the limitations set out in those concepts, as a result of the decision in *Krell v Henry*.

---

201 Id., 749.
202 Id., 748.
203 Id., 748.
204 W.W. Buckland and Arnold D. McNair *Roman Law and Common Law: A Comparison in Outline* (second edition, revised by F.H. Lawson) Cambridge: Cambridge University Press, 1965 (first published in 1936), 245. However, Lord Shaw of Dumfermlane, a Scottish judge of the House of Lords, declared in the case of *Horlock v Beal* (1916) AC 486, 513 that the 'wider application of the principle' given by Vaughan Williams LJ was in fact 'not unknown to Roman jurists and was approved'. This appears to be a reference to the principle of *rebus sic stantibus*, although Lord Shaw did not mention the principle by name. In support of this assertion, Lord Shaw referred to several passages from the Digest, involving, *inter alia*, the sale of land which had become *extra commercium* because a body had been buried therein, and to the sale of a slave who had been manumitted. But these passages would seem to illustrate the consequences of mistake rather than that of *rebus sic stantibus* (see page 22 *supra*).

    Cicero had certainly discussed the possibility of *rebus sic stantibus* in his philosophical writings (see page 71 *supra*), but Lord Shaw did not refer to Cicero in his judgment. Moreover, as Kelly pointed out, as a court advocate and politician, Cicero 'dealt in the ordinary law of murder, outrage, partnership, etc. without more than a very rare reference to a higher law...': J.M. Kelly *A Short History of Western Legal Theory* Oxford: Clarendon Press, 1992, 59. Nicholas notes that Roman jurists differentiated between the law, on the one hand, and philosophical musings, on the other: 'Certainly the jurists, as men of culture and education, must have been acquainted with current philosophical ideas, and yet, severely practical as they were in their attitude to law, they may well in their writings have ignored the philosopher's *ius naturale* or *ius gentium* as mere speculation': Barry Nicholas *An Introduction to Roman Law* Oxford: Clarendon Press, 1962, 56. See also H.F. Jolowicz 'Academic Elements in Roman Law' (1932) 48 *Law Quarterly Review* 171, 179.

The doctrine of frustration could therefore be invoked when 'the contract becomes impossible of performance by reason of the non-existence of the state of things assumed by both contracting parties as the foundation of the contract'.[205] This meant that it now became possible to invoke frustration in situations in which the contract was still quite capable of physical and commercial performance, but in which the surrounding circumstances of that contract had become altered in some significant way. In *Krell v Henry* Vaughan Williams L.J. seemed to be endorsing a variation of the doctrine of *clausula rebus sic stantibus*, although he did not say so in so many words.[206]

The Doctrine Narrowed

Blackburn J. had relied on Roman and French law in initially formulating the doctrine of frustration in order to limit the new doctrine to the destruction or disappearance of the *corpus certum*, i.e. the very subject matter of the contract.[207] This limitation on the doctrine of absolute contractual liability was both objectively predictable in advance and was objectively applicable upon occurrence. An implied term between the contracting parties would naturally be assumed to have been in existence whenever there had been supervening impossibility of performance as a result of the destruction or disappearance of the *corpus certum*.

The decision in *Krell v Henry* had the effect of greatly expanding the element of subjectivity into the doctrine. When performance of the contract itself was still eminently possible, what criteria should be used in order to determine when a fundamental change of circumstances had occurred, which would give rise to frustration? Vaughan Williams L.J. attempted to formulate that criteria by declaring that 'the cessation or non-existence' of the existing 'state of things' had to be 'essential to the performance of the contract'.[208] But this did not mean 'essential to the performance of the contract' in the sense that the terms of the contract itself were no longer physically or commercially capable of performance, but rather that circumstances surrounding the defendant's performance which were 'essential' were now no longer in existence. But by what criteria would the surrounding circumstances be judged to be 'essential'

---

205 (1903) 2 KB 740, 749.

206 It should be recalled that by virtue of the doctrine of *clausula rebus sic stantibus* a clause is implied into the contract whereby it will remain binding 'only as long and as far as matters remain the same as they were at the time of the conclusion of the contract': Zimmermann, op. cit., 579. The idea of implied conditions had been repudiated by David Hume: 'Hume, in his *Enquiry into Principles of Morals* (1751) Sect. III, Part II, treats the objective approach to intention in the law as well–established law, and suggests that giving effect of "secret reservations" was a "Jesuitical" or Catholic notion'. Quoted in Atiyah, op. cit., 407, fn. 21.

207 This was one of the two circumstances in which *vis maior* and *force majeure* would arise in Roman and French law, respectively. The other circumstance was when the performance of the contract had otherwise become impossible, without fault on the part of the debtor.

208 (1903) 2 KB 740, 748.

to the performance of the contract, to the extent that those circumstances amounted to an implied term between the parties? Vaughan Williams L.J. declared that any such implied term had to be 'assumed by both parties as the foundation of the contract',[209] and 'as going to the root of the contract'.[210] But the language he employed was of its very nature imprecise and capable of different interpretations with regard to the 'essentialness' of the changed circumstances.

The decision in *Krell v Henry* created considerable unease, because its inherently subjective test was thought by many to undermine the certainty of contract. As Treitel has pointed out, the fear was that a contracting party might attempt to invoke frustration, and thereby be relieved of his contractual obligations, simply 'because a supervening change of circumstances had turned the contract, for that party, into a very bad bargain'.[211]

McCardie J. addressed this issue in the 1918 case of *Blackburn Bobbin Co v Allenby*:

> The perils of the rule may appear in later years. If it be extended too far, it may tend to sap the foundations of contract law as they now exist. It is, I venture to say, of the utmost importance to a commercial nation that vendors should be held to their business contracts. When a change of circumstance is to absolve from liability, provision to that effect should be inserted in the bargain.[212]

McCardie J. declared that the rule in *Krell v Henry* 'should not be unduly extended. It is only in exceptional cases that it can be safely applied'.[213]

In the 1923 House of Lords decision of *Larringa & Co. v Société Franco-Americaine des Phosphates de Medulla*[214] Viscount Findlay also cast doubt on the rule in *Krell v Henry*:

> I share the doubts which have been expressed (see *Pollock on Contracts* (8th ed.), p. 439, and the following pages) as to the extension of this

---

209 Id., 749.
210 Id., 748.
211 Treitel, op. cit., 53.
212 (1918) 1 KB 540, 552. McCardie J.'s decision was affirmed by the Court of Appeal: (1918) 2 KB 467 (CA). The problem which McCardie J. adverted to had been foreseen by the majority judges of the Exchequer Court in *Hall v Wright*. Martin B., for example, had expressed the same view as McCardie J.: 'I think it very much better to adhere to the rule than to create an ordinary exception for which, no doubt, plausible reasons may be given. To admit exceptions of this kind utterly destroys the certainty of the law, and in my opinion is inconvenient': (1859) El. Bl. & El. 765, 789; 120 ER 695, 704. See also the comments of Cleasby B. in his dissenting judgment in *Jackson v Union Marine Insurance Co Ltd.* (1874) LR 10 CP 125, at 132.
213 (1918) 1 KB 540, 551.
214 (1923) LJKB 455; (1923) 14 Ll. L. Rep. 457.

doctrine to such cases as *Krell v Henry* and the other cases known as the Coronation cases. In each case the question must be what was the basis on which the contract proceeded. It may be that the parties contracted in the expectation that the particular event would happen, each taking his chance, but that the actual happening of the event was not made the basis of the contract.[215]

His Lordship then went on to affirm the position taken by McCardie J in *Blackburn Bobbin Co v Allen*:

> I wish to add that I entirely agree with the observations made by McCardie J., as to the dangers attending any undue extension of the doctrine of frustration as a defence to actions of contract. The doctrine is perfectly sound and thoroughly established, but care is very necessary in its application to particular cases.[216]

Lord Wright, giving judgment for the Privy Council in the 1935 case of *Maritime National Fish Limited v Ocean Trawlers, Limited*,[217] made reference to Viscount Findlay's criticism of *Krell v Henry*, noting that Viscount Findlay had questioned 'the correctness of that decision'.[218] Lord Wright himself declared that the rule in *Krell v Henry* was 'certainly not one to be extended'.[219] In spite of these negative assessments, *Krell v Henry* has remained an integral part of the doctrine of frustration. However, its holding has been construed very narrowly in subsequent cases. This 'reflects the importance which the English courts have come, in the interests of commercial certainty, to attach to the principle of sanctity of contract'.[220]

The decision of the House of Lords in 1956, in the landmark case of *Davis Contractors Ltd. v Fareham UDC*, provides a very good example of this restrictive approach.[221] The facts in *Davis Contractors* were as follows. A contract had been concluded between the appellant contractors and the respondent urban district council, whereby the contractors had agreed to build seventy-eight houses for the Council for the fixed price of £94,424, and to do so within a period of eight months. Due to a shortage of skilled labour and building materials, which occurred as a result of unexpected circumstances and without

---

215 Id., 459; Id., 460.
216 Id., 459, 460; Id., 460.
217 (1935) AC 524.
218 Id., 528.
219 Id., 529. The holding in *Krell v Henry* was also severely criticised in the Australian case of *Scanlan's New Neon Limited v Tooheys Limited* (1943) 67 CLR 169, by Latham CJ, at pages 188–194. In his extensive analysis of *Krell v Henry* Latham CJ referred to many critical English decisions.
220 Treitel, op. cit., 55.
221 (1956) AC 696; (1956) 2 All ER 145.

the fault of either party, the contractors took twenty-two months to complete the project, at a cost of £115,233. The contractors sought to obtain payment in excess of the £94,424 agreed to in the contract, and argued that the contract had been frustrated by the unforeseen shortages, thereby terminating it and entitling the contractors to claim a greater sum on the basis of a *quantum meruit.*

The House of Lords unanimously rejected the argument of the contractors. The unexpected shortages did not amount to frustration. Lord Reid made the following observations:

> In a contract of this kind the contractor undertakes to do the work for a definite sum and he takes the risk of the cost being greater or less than he expected. … It may be that the delay could be of a character so different from anything contemplated that the contract was at an end, but in this case, in my opinion, the most that could be said is that the delay was greater in degree than was to be expected. It was not caused by any new and unforeseeable factor or event: the job proved to be more onerous but it never became a job of a different kind from that contemplated in the contract.[222]

Lord Radcliffe, after declaring that '[f]rustration is not to be lightly invoked as the dissolvent of a contract',[223] then proceeded to articulate his 'radically different' test, which would prove to be so central in the subsequent development of the doctrine of frustration:

> … frustration occurs whenever the law recognizes that without default of either party a contractual obligation has become incapable of being performed because the circumstances in which performance is called for would render it a thing radically different from that which was undertaken by the contract. *Non haec in foedera veni.* It was not this that I promised to do.[224]

He then continued as follows:

---

222 Id., 724; Id., 155, 156.
223 Id., 727; Id., 159.
224 Id., 729, 160. The Latin phrase might be thought to be a quote from the *Digest* or the *Institutes*. But as Sir John Megaw notes, in a letter to *The Times*, 20 December 1980, the phrase was actually taken from Virgil's epic poem, the *Aeneid*, at Book 4, lines 338 and 339. The phrase 'forms part of Aeneas' shabby excuses for his planned desertion of Queen Dido': Furmston, op. cit., 776, fn. 23. The passage from the *Aeneid* reads as follows: '*Neque ego hanc abscondere furto speravi (ne finge) fugam, nec coniugis umquam pretendi taedas aut haec in foedera veni*'. ('Neither did I hope to hide this flight by trickery (do not imagine), nor did I ever hold forth the torches of a husband or come into these agreements'.)

... it is not hardship or inconvenience or material loss itself which calls the principle of frustration into play. There must be as well such a change in the significance of the obligation that the thing undertaken would, if performed, be a different thing from that contracted for.

I am bound to say that, if this is the law, the appellants' case seems to me a long way from a case of frustration.[225]

Davis Contractors represents the paradigm example of an 'imprudent bargain'.[226] The unexpected shortage of skilled labour and materials, as McKendrick points out, certainly resulted in hardship for the contractors, but it did not constitute a radical change in the nature of the obligation, and thus did not qualify as frustration.[227]

Subsequent cases have continuously confirmed this narrow interpretation of the doctrine.[228] In 2007, in the Court of Appeal decision of *Edwinton Commercial Corporation v Tsavliris Russ, The Sea Angel*, for example, Rix L.J. emphasised the narrow application of the doctrine, finding in the circumstances of the case that there had not been frustration:

... the test of 'radically different' is important: it tells us that the doctrine is not to be lightly invoked; that mere incidence of expense or delay or onerousness is not sufficient; and that there has to be as it were a break in identity between the contract as provided for and contemplated and its performance in the new circumstances.[229]

These decisions confirm that a contract cannot be frustrated unless the supervening event has rendered the change in circumstances into something which is either impossible, or which is 'different in kind' or 'radically different'. The Courts have thereby ensured that a contracting party cannot rely on *Krell v*

---

225 (1956) AC 696, 729; (1956) 2 All ER 145. 160. This very point had been made four years earlier in *British Movietonews Ld. v London and District Cinemas Ld* ((1952) AC 166, by Viscount Simon, at page 185: 'The parties to an executory contract are often faced, in the course of carrying it out, with a turn of events which they did not at all anticipate – a wholly abnormal rise or fall in prices, a sudden depreciation of currency, an unexpected obstacle to execution, or the like. Yet this does not in itself affect the bargain they have made'.

226 Ewan McKendrick 'Frustration and Force Majeure – Their Relationship and a Comparative Assessment' 27, 37 in Ewan McKendrick (editor) *Force Majeure and Frustration of Contract* London: Lloyd's of London Press Ltd., 1991.

227 Id., 37.

228 See, for example, *Tsakiroglou & Co Ltd v Noblee and Thorl GmbH* (1962) AC 93(HL), at 115, per Viscount Simonds L.C.; *Pioneer Shipping Ltd. v BTP Tioxide Ltd; The Nema* (1982) AC 724 (HL), at 752, per Roskill LJ; *Paal Wilson & Co A/S v Partenreederei Hannah Blumenthal; The Hannah Blumenthal* (1983) 1 All ER 34 (HL), at 44, 45, per Brandon LJ; *J Lauritzen A/S v Wijsmuller BV (The Super Servant Two)* (1990) 1 Lloyd's Rep 1 (CA), at 8, per Bingham LJ.

229 (2007) 2 All ER Comm. 634, 664, 665.

Henry to invoke the doctrine of frustration simply on the basis that performance has become more onerous than he had anticipated at the time that he entered into the contract.[230]

Although *Krell v Henry* has never been overruled, it has in a sense been 'quarantined'. In his judgment, Vaughn Williams L.J. had declared that 'the use of the rooms was let and taken for the purpose of seeing the Royal procession'.[231] Further on in his judgment, he stated that 'it is the coronation procession and the relative position of the rooms which is the basis of the contract as much for the lessor as the hirer'.[232] These two phrases have been interpreted as meaning that the contracting parties had shared a common purpose which underpinned their contract, and that this common purpose had been frustrated.[233]

Krell v Henry has thus given rise to the *rara avis* of 'frustration of common purpose', of which it has become the classic example. Frustration of common purpose occurs when 'the common purpose for which the contract was entered into can no longer be carried out because of some supervening event'.[234] But frustration of common purpose will occur only in extremely rare cases.[235] This is primarily because parties do not normally contract on the basis of a common purpose, but rather almost invariably do so as counterparties, whose purposes are contrasting and divergent.[236] In this regard, *Krell v Henry* was highly unusual. As McKendrick notes, *Krell v Henry* is 'a very narrow decision', and it is clear that its 'scope will not be extended'.[237]

---

230 McKendrick, op. cit. (fn. 226), 38.

231 (1903) 2 KB 740, 750.

232 Id., 751. Romer L.J. only reluctantly concurred with Vaughan Williams L.J.'s judgment. Romer L.J. cast some doubt on whether the parties had not actually considered the possibility that the procession might not, for some reasons or other, take place on the day in question. If that were so, then in Romer L.J.'s opinion, the risk should be borne by the defendant Henry. Id., 755. Sterling L.J. 'entirely agreed' with the judgment of Vaughan Williams L.J.: Id., 755.

233 'The point of the contract', as Marcus Smith J. observed, 'was the purchase and sale of a room with a view: the view never came to pass': *Canary Wharf (BP4) T1 Limited v European Medicines Agency* (2019) EWCH 335 (Ch), paragraph 38.

234 Ewan McKendrick *Contract Law* (fourteenth edition) London: Red Globe Press, 2021, 297.

235 Id., 297.

236 Frustration of common purpose is also qualitatively different from other instances of frustration. In a typical contract, one party agrees to supply goods or services, and the other party agrees to pay a sum of money for those goods or services. A supervening event which results in frustration will normally occur in such arrangements because performance by the supplier of the goods or services has been rendered either impossible or has been transformed into something 'radically different'. It is therefore usually the supplier who seeks to be discharged from the contract in such circumstances. But in cases of frustration of common purpose it is normally the recipient of the goods or services who seeks the discharge of the contract. This is 'because the supplier's performance is no longer of any use to the recipient for the purpose for which both parties had intended it to be used': Treitel, op. cit., 307.

237 McKendrick, op. cit. (fn. 234), 298. In this regard see, for example, the comments of Newey J. in *North Shore Ventures Ltd v Anstead Holdings Inc.* (2010) EWHC 1485 (Ch), paragraph

Frustration and Leases

English law developed to a very large degree as the result of two factors, viz. the writ system and judicial lawmaking.[238] It thus developed in a fragmented, incremental and pragmatic manner. Unlike French law, it was neither systematic nor logically interconnected in structure, and, consequently, it has not infrequently produced legal anomalies. One of those anomalies is the lease.

The writ system and the incremental nature of judicial lawmaking were both important factors in the creation and development of the lease. In medieval England property was classified as being either real or personal; land and buildings were real property, chattels were personal property. Real property devolved to the first son by virtue of the rule of primogeniture; personal property, on the other hand, devolved into three parts: one part to the widow, one part to the children and one part to the Church.[239] In the event of a legal dispute involving property the choice of writ was contingent on the nature of the property. Certain remedies were available only in cases involving real property.

The Common Law first began to provide tenants with legal protection in the thirteenth century. At first, the legal interest of a tenant was considered to be simply a contractual one, which entitled the tenant, in the event of a breach of his tenancy agreement, to sue for damages based on trespass. A tenant who had been dispossessed of his leasehold interest was unable to recover possession, as the writ which restored possession – the writ of *novel disseisin* – was available only to those who had been dispossessed of real property, and a leasehold interest was not considered to be real property.[240]

Over time the law gradually accorded a greater measure of legal protection to the tenant. In 1235 a new writ – *quare ejecit infra terminum* – enabled a tenant to recover possession of his rented premises. But the writ limited the tenant's right to take action only against his landlord and the landlord's successors in title. The writ could not be used against third parties.[241] The writ of *trespass de ejection firmae*, which became available in the late fifteenth century, removed this limitation and thereby enabled the tenant to recover possession

---

310; All ER Rep (Comm) 2011) 81, at 151: 'Subsequent cases have, moreover, warned that frustration in general, and *Krell v Henry* in particular, should not be extended. In *Maritime National Fish Ltd v Ocean Trawlers Ltd* (1935) AC 524 at 529, (1935) All ER Rep 86 at 89, Lord Wright, giving the judgment of the Privy Council, said that *Krell v Henry* was 'certainly not one to be extended'. In *J Lauritzen AS v Wijsmuller BV*, The *Super Servant Two* (1990) 1 Lloyd's Rep 1 at 8, Bingham L.J. said: 'Since the effect of frustration is to kill the contract and discharge the parties from further liability under it, the doctrine is not to be lightly invoked, must be kept within very narrow limits and ought not to be extended…'.

238 See pages 136–138 *supra.*

239 Harold Potter *An Historical Introduction to English Law and its Institutions* (second edition) London: Sweet & Maxwell, Limited, 1943, 481.

240 Anthony P. Moore, Scott Grattan and Lynden Griggs *Real Property Law* (sixth edition) Sydney: Thomson Reuters (Professional) Australia Limited, 2016, 661.

241 Id., 662.

against third parties.[242] The fact that the tenant could now exercise a right of possession against all and sundry meant that he came to be regarded as having an interest in land, as well as having a contractual interest. But a tenant still could not avail himself of the real property actions, and so the tenant's proprietary interest was bizarrely classified as an interest in personal property, known as a 'chattel real'.[243]

A lease therefore created both a contractual bond between the landlord and tenant and a proprietary interest for the tenant.[244] With the emergence of the doctrine of frustration, the question arose as to whether frustration could apply to the contractual bond between the landlord and tenant, given the proprietary interest of the tenant.

In the 1916 case of *London and Northern Estates Company v Schlesinger*,[245] the Court held that frustration did not apply to a residential lease. The plaintiff had let residential premises to the defendant, an Austrian subject, for a term of years, shortly before the outbreak of the First World War. When the war began the defendant became an enemy alien, and by virtue of an Order in Council was prohibited from residing within certain specified areas, which included the premises he had leased. The plaintiff sued for rent payable subsequent to the Order, and the defendant argued that the lease had been terminated upon the issuance of the Order. The defendant maintained that the foundation of the contract had been destroyed, as he was no longer permitted to reside in the rented premises. The Court held that frustration did not arise in these circumstances. Lush J. focused on the dual character of the lease:

> It is not correct to speak of this tenancy agreement as a contract and nothing more. A term of years was created by it and vested in the appellant, and I can see no reason for saying that because this Order disqualified him from personally residing in the flat it affected the chattel interest which was vested in him by virtue of the agreement. In my opinion it remains vested in him still.[246]

This same conclusion obtained in the 1920 case of *Whitehall Court Ltd v Ettlinger*.[247] A lessee was deprived of possession of rented premises during the First World War by military authorities, pursuant to powers granted under the Defence of the Realm Regulations. The military remained in possession of the premises until the expiration of the lease. The landlord sought payment of

---

242 Id., 662.
243 Id., 662.
244 'The forms of action we have buried, but they still rule us from their graves': Frederick W. Maitland *The Forms of Action at Common Law* Cambridge: At the University Press, 1936, Lecture 1.
245 (1916) 1 KB 20.
246 Id., 24.
247 (1920) 1 KB 680.

rent. The lessee argued, *inter alia*, that the lease had been terminated by reason of frustration. The Court, however, held that the agreement had not been frustrated. It reaffirmed the words of Lush J. in *London and Northern Estates Company v Schlesinger*,[248] and concluded by noting that '[t]he agreement here is not only a contract. It also creates an estate by demise for a term of years. Therefore I think that the plaintiffs are entitled to recover their rent'.[249]

The House of Lords had occasion to consider the matter in 1922 in the case of *Matthey v Curling*.[250] The facts of this case were very similar to those of *London and Northern Estates Company v Schlesinger* and *Whitehall Court Ltd v Ettlinger*. During the term of a residential lease, the military authorities took possession of the premises under the Defence of the Realm Regulations, and remained in possession until after the expiration of the lease. The landlord sought payment of rent and damages for breach of covenants of the leasehold agreement. The lessee argued, *inter alia*, that the lease had been terminated as a result of frustration. This argument was rejected in the Court of Appeal by both Bankes L.J. and Younger L.J., who relied primarily on the ruling of Lush J. *supra*.[251] But Atkin L.J., in dissent, disagreed with his colleagues that frustration could never apply to a lease:

> I will, however, add it does not appear to me conclusive against the application of a lease of the doctrine of frustration that the lease, in addition to containing contractual terms, grants a term of years. Seeing that the instrument as a rule expressly provides for the lease being determined at the option of the lessor upon the happening of certain specified events, I see no logical absurdity in implying a term that it shall be determined absolutely on the happening of other events – namely, those which in an ordinary contract work a frustration.[252]

On appeal to the House of Lords the decision of the Court of Appeal was confirmed. Only Lord Atkinson referred explicitly to the question of whether frustration could apply to a lease, stating that he thought that the case of *Whitehall Court v Ettlinger* had been rightly decided.[253] Lord Buckmaster did not explicitly refer to frustration, but did express doubt as to whether there had in fact been any impossibility at all in this case.[254] The other three law lords did not express separate opinions.

The issue of whether a lease could be terminated by frustration arose again in the 1945 case of *Cricklewood Property and Investment Trust Ltd v Leighton's*

---

248 Id., 686, 687.
249 Id., 687.
250 (1922) 2 AC 180.
251 (1922) 2 AC 180, at 185, 186 (per Bankes LJ), and 210 (per Younger LJ).
252 Id., 199, 200.
253 Id., 237.
254 Id., 230.

Investment Trust Ltd.[255] In 1936 the lessees entered into a building lease for a term of 99 years. The Second World War began in 1939 before any of the buildings had been constructed, and government war restrictions made it impossible for the lessees to construct the buildings agreed upon in the lease. The plaintiffs commenced an action for payment of rent, and the defendants countered, *inter alia*, that the lease had been frustrated by virtue of the government restrictions. At first instance, Asquith J. rejected the defendant's argument out of hand:

> It is not disputed that the doctrine of frustration has no application to an ordinary lease; *Matthey v Curling; London and Northern Estates v Schlesinger*; and *Whitehall Court, Ld. v Ettlinger*; nor has it any application to the lease of a furnished house, as was decided recently by Birkett J in *Swift v MacBean*. The *ratio decidendi* of these decisions is plain. A contract may be frustrated, but a demise is more than a contract. It is a conveyance of an estate in land or a chattel real. It transfers proprietary as well as personal rights. This seems to me just as true of a building lease as of any other kind of lease.[256]

The Court of Appeal confirmed the decision of Asquith J. MacKinnon L.J. declared that the doctrine of frustration 'has never been applied to a demise of real property. Indeed, there is authority that it cannot be so applied'.[257]

The House of Lords upheld the decision of the Court of Appeal, unanimously finding that frustration did not apply, as the suspension in building occasioned by the government restrictions was not, in the words of Viscount Simon L.C., 'so fundamental as to destroy the basis of the agreement'.[258] When the government restrictions were imposed the lease still had ninety years to run, and thus the restriction on performance could only be for a relatively short period of time in relation to the total term of the lease.[259]

However, on the issue of whether frustration could ever apply to terminate a lease the House of Lords was evenly divided. Lord Russell and Lord Goddard L.C.J. held that it could not apply, whereas Viscount Simon L.C. and Lord Wright held that in some circumstances it could. Lord Porter did not express an opinion on the matter. Viscount Simon L.C. argued that to declare that frustration could not apply to a lease because it created a proprietary interest in the lessee was a circular one: 'if we assume that frustration can only arise in cases where there is a contract and nothing else, the conclusion of course

---

255 (1945) AC 221; (1945) 1 All ER 252.
256 *Leightons Investment Trust, Limited v Cricklewood Property and Investment Trust, Limited* (1943) 1 KB 493, 495.
257 Id., 496.
258 *Cricklewood Property and Investment Trust Ltd v Leighton's Investment Trust Ltd.* (1945) AC 221, 228; (1945) 1 All ER 252, 255.
259 Id, 231, 232; Id., 257 (per Viscount Simon L.C., with whom all of the law lords agreed).

follows that frustration cannot arise in the case of a lease'. He conceded that frustration would not normally arise in a lease in which the primary purpose was to grant the lessee the right to use the land as he liked during the term of the lease, but contrasted this with a lease for the purpose of building, which he thought much more likely to be subject to the doctrine of frustration. He quoted the dissenting passage of Lord Atkin from *Matthey v Curling, supra,* and declared that that passage exactly expressed his view.[260]

Lord Wright noted that the contractual element of a lease entitled either party to determine the lease upon the breach of its terms, and that this would consequently bring to an end the lessee's proprietary interest. Lord Wright set out various examples illustrating when this would occur. He then continued as follows:

> These results all flow from the general nature of the contract as under-stood in English law and its application to particular conditions of fact. I do not find that they depend on the circumstance that the lease involves a tenure and creates an estate in land. If the contract is avoided or dis-solved, as it may be by either party, under the express terms of the lease, the estate in land falls with it. I do not see why this may not be also true if the lease were dissolved by operation of law.[261]

Although there were no reported cases in which frustration had been applied to a lease, Lord Wright did not think that this would preclude the application of the doctrine. Although frustration would not normally apply to a lease, Lord Wright observed that the doctrine was 'modern and flexible and not subject to being constricted by an arbitrary formula'.[262] He therefore declared that he would not be 'prepared to state as a universal principle that it can in no circumstances be applied to a lease'.[263]

Lord Russell, on the other hand, was adamant that frustration could not apply to a lease. A lease agreement was 'much more than a contract' because 'it creates and vests in the lessee an estate or interest in the land'.[264] This dis-tinction between a contract and a lease prevented frustration from applying to a lease:

> When a contract is frustrated it is because what is called the 'venture' or 'undertaking' in which the parties have contracted to engage can no longer be carried out. The court in such circumstances declares the con-tract to be, or treats it as being, no longer binding on the parties. That

260 (1945) AC 221, 229, 230; (1945) 1 All ER 252, 256.
261 Id., 240; Id., 262.
262 Id., 241; Id., 263.
263 Id., 241; Id, 263.
264 Id., 233; Id., 258.

is an end of the matter. But when a lease is in question, and has been granted by one to another, it is the lease which is the 'venture' or 'undertaking' upon which the parties have embarked. The contractual obligations thereunder of each party are merely obligations which are incidental to the relationship of landlord and tenant created by the demise, and which necessarily vary with the character and duration of the particular lease ... I know of no power in the court to declare a lease to be at an end except upon finding that some event has occurred on the happening of which the lease terminates by reason of some express provision in the document. In such a case the term ends not because the court exercises a power to terminate it, but because in the events which have happened the lease operates only as a demise for the shorter period.[265]

Lord Goddard L.C.J. similarly emphasised the proprietary element of the lease:

Now whatever be the true ground on which the doctrine is based it is certain that it applies only where the foundation of the contract is destroyed so that performance or further performance is no longer possible. In the case of a lease the foundation of the agreement in my opinion is that the landlord parts with his interest in the demised property for a term of years, which thereupon becomes vested in the tenant, in return for a rent. So long as the interest remains in the tenant there is no frustration though particular use may be prevented.[266]

Given that Lord Porter did not express an opinion on the matter, the issue remained an open question.

It was only in 1980, with the decision of *National Carriers Ltd v Panalpina (Northern) Ltd.*,[267] that the House of Lords rendered a definitive judgment on the matter. The defendants in this case had rented a warehouse for the commercial storage of their goods, for a period of ten years. Vehicles could access the warehouse only by means of a single street, which was closed by the local authority in order to demolish a derelict building opposite the warehouse. The road closure continued for a period of twenty months. During this time the defendants were unable to make use of the warehouse. The plaintiffs sued for recovery of unpaid rent, and the defendants argued that the lease had been frustrated by the road closure. The House of Lords found that frustration could not apply in the circumstances of the case, as the length of time in which there had been no access to the warehouse was relatively minor in relation to the term of the lease, and, consequently, the defendants had failed to raise a triable issue. But the House of Lords took the opportunity to resolve the

---

265 Id., 234; Id., 258.
266 Id., 245; Id., 265.
267 (1981) AC 675; (1981) 1 All ER 161.

question of whether frustration could in fact apply to leases. A majority of the judges decided that the doctrine of frustration could indeed apply, although it was emphasised that this would occur only in exceptional circumstances. Each of the five judges rendered a separate judgment.

The judgment of Lord Wilberforce may be taken as representative of the opinion of the Court.[268] Lord Wilberforce acknowledged that in many, if not most, cases the frustration of a lease could not occur, 'because the tenant will have that which he bargained for, namely, the leasehold estate'.[269] But he then continued by stating that there might be cases where this was not so:

> A man may desire possession and use of land or buildings for, and only for, some purpose in view and mutually contemplated. Why is it an answer, when he claims that this purpose is 'frustrated', to say that he has an estate if that estate is unusable and unsaleable: in such a case the lease, or the conferring of an estate, is a subsidiary means to an end, not an aim or end of itself.[270]

In this regard Lord Wilberforce quoted with approval the 1971 decision of the Supreme Court of Canada, in the case of *Highway Properties Ltd. v Kelly, Douglas & Co. Ltd*:

> It is no longer sensible to pretend that a commercial lease, such as the one before this court, is simply a conveyance and not also a contract. It is equally untenable to persist in denying resort to the full armoury of remedies ordinarily available to redress repudiation of covenants, merely because the covenants may be associated with an estate in land.[271]

Lord Wilberforce concluded by holding that 'the doctrine of frustration is capable of application to leases of land', although he prefaced this statement by noting, as did the other judges, that such cases would be rare.[272]

The decisive argument, as Furmston notes, 'was the essential unity of the law of contract and the belief that no type of contract should as a matter of law

---

268 See pages 222 and 225 *infra* for further analysis of the judgments in the case.
269 Id., 694; Id., 171.
270 Id., 694, 695; Id., 171. See also the statement of Lord Simon of Glaisdale at page 705; 178: 'I can for myself see nothing about the fact of creation of an estate or interest in land which repels the doctrine of frustration. It cannot be that land, being relatively indestructible, is different from other subject matter of agreement: that would perhaps make a lease so much the less likely to be frustrated in fact, but would not constitute inherent repugnance to the doctrine. In any case, we are concerned with legal interests in the land rather than the land itself'.
271 (1971) 17 DLR (3d) 710, 721 (per Laskin J.), quoted by Lord Wilberforce at page 696; 172.
272 (1981) AC 675, 697; (1981) 1 All ER 161, 173.

be excluded from the doctrine'.[273] Lord Russell alone of the judges expressed some hesitation about the extension of frustration to leases, although he indicated that he 'was prepared to accept that the termination of a lease may be involved in the frustration of a commercial adventure when, as merely incidental to the overall commercial adventure, and a subordinate factor, a lease has been granted'.[274] Given the statements of the other judges that the application of frustration would be rare when the primary purpose of the lease was the creation of an interest in land, it may very well be that the statement of Lord Russell reflects the real extension of the doctrine to leases, i.e. that it now actually applies basically to a lease whose primary purpose is commercial and in which the creation of an interest in land is 'merely incidental'.

The 'real extension' of the doctrine was put to the test in the case of *Canary Wharf (BP4) T1 Limited* v *European Medicines Agency*,[275] decided in 2019 by the High Court judge Sir Marcus Smith. An Agreement to Lease and a Construction Management Agreement had been signed on 5 August 2011 between a British company, Canary Wharf, as landlord, and a European Union regulatory body, the European Medicines Agency (hereafter EMA), as tenant. The Agreements committed the parties to enter into a Lease, which was signed on 21 October 2014. The leased premises, at 30 Churchill Place, Canary Wharf, London, were to serve as the European Union headquarters of the EMA. The premises possessed a 'bespoke' character, as they 'were purpose built to the EMA's specifications'.[276] The lease ran for a period of twenty-five years and did not include any break clauses.[277]

The United Kingdom voted on 23 June 2016 to withdraw from the European Union. On 29 March 2017, the British government invoked Article 50 of the Lisbon Treaty, under which the United Kingdom began the formal process of withdrawing from the European Union.[278] In response, the European Union announced that it was relocating its EMA headquarters from London to Amsterdam.[279] The EMA informed Canary Wharf that when the United Kingdom withdrew from the European Union the EMA would consider the lease to have been terminated by frustration, thereby releasing it from its obligations as tenant. Canary Wharf then sought a declaration from the

---

273 Michael Furmston *Cheshire, Fifoot, & Furmston's Law of Contract* (17th edition) Oxford: Oxford University Press, 2017, 728. In this regard see in particular the comments of Lord Simon at page 701; 161 and Lord Roskill at pages 712–714; 184–185.

274 (1981) AC 675, 707; (1981) 1 All ER 161, 181.

275 (2019) EWHC 335 (Ch).

276 Id., paragraph 61.

277 A break clause is a term in a commercial lease that permits a landlord or tenant to terminate the lease part way through the term.

278 'Any member state may decide to withdraw from the union in accordance with its own constitutional requirements': *Lisbon Treaty*, 13 December 2007 (OJ C 306, 17.12.2007).

279 Regulation (EU) 2018/1718 of the European Parliament and of the Council of 14 November 2018, amending Regulation (EC) 726/2004 as regards the location of the seat of the European Medicines Agency (2018) *Official Journal of the European Union* L291/3.

High Court to the effect that neither the withdrawal of the United Kingdom from the European Union, nor the relocation of the EMA outside the United Kingdom, would result in the frustration of the lease, and that the EMA would therefore continue to be bound by its obligations under the lease.[280]

The EMA argued that Brexit was an unforeseen event which would frustrate the lease on two grounds, viz. supervening illegality and frustration of common purpose.[281] The primary argument put forward by the EMA was that frustration had occurred by supervening illegality. Frustration by supervening illegality occurs when there is a change in the law which makes contractual performance unlawful. Most cases have involved wartime situations in which contractual performance has become illegal because the law prohibits the contracting party from trading with the enemy.[282] In the case at hand, it was argued that the supervening illegality would arise because the legal consequences of the withdrawal of the United Kingdom from the European Union would make it unlawful for the EMA, as a matter of European Union law, to pay rent to Canary Wharf pursuant to the lease, or otherwise to deal with immovable property outside the European Union.[283] Five grounds were put forward in this regard, viz.:

1. that once the United Kingdom had left the European Union, the EMA would lose the privileges and immunities granted to it under Protocol 7 of the *Treaty of the European Union* and the *Treaty on the Functioning of the European Union*, which were necessary to its proper functioning and independence;
2. that after the withdrawal of the United Kingdom, the EMA would not be able, as a matter of law, to be lawfully located in the premises;
3. that the EMA would not be able, as a matter of law, to make profitable use of the premises;
4. that the EMA would have no power to meet its obligations under the lease, including the obligation to pay rent;
5. that if the EMA had to continue paying rent under the lease while also paying to rent premises elsewhere, such a double payment of rent would seriously impair the EMA's capacity, effectiveness and independence.[284]

The EMA also argued, in the alternative, that the withdrawal of the United Kingdom from the European Union would result in the frustration of the

---

280 (2019) EWHC 335 (Ch), paragraph 4.
281 Id., paragraph 34. See page 185 *supra* for a discussion of frustration of common purpose.
282 In this regard see *Zinc Corporation Limited v Hirsch* (1916) 1 KB 541, 556; *Fibrosa Spolka Akcyjna v Fairbairn Lawson Combe Barbour, Limited* (1943) AC 32, 40; *Denny, Mott & Dickson Ltd v James B. Fraser & Co. Ltd* (1944) AC 265, 272.
283 (2019) EWHC 335, (Ch), paragraphs 10 and 96.
284 Précis of Id., paragraph 7.

common purpose of the lease.[285] This common purpose was purportedly to be found in the mutual contemplation of the parties that the headquarters of the EMA would be permanently based in London for the next twenty-five years. Given that this would not now occur the common purpose of the lease failed.

Canary Wharf denied that the lease had been frustrated. It disputed many of the specific points put forward by the EMA under its five grounds and also argued more broadly that neither the withdrawal of the United Kingdom from the European Union nor the relocation of the headquarters of the EMA away from London could amount to a frustrating event.[286] Canary Wharf further argued that there had not been a common purpose. On the contrary, the parties had each bargained solely with regard to their own separate interests.

In his judgment, Smith J. held that the lease would not be frustrated, either by supervening illegality or by frustration of common purpose.[287] Smith J. began by reviewing the juridical bases for frustration,[288] and fixed upon the test set out by Lord Radcliffe in *Davis Contractors Ltd v Farnham*[289] as having 'stood the test of time'.[290] Lord Radcliffe emphasised that the supervening event had to render performance of the contract into something radically different from what the parties had agreed to:

> … frustration occurs whenever the law recognises that without default of either party a contractual obligation has become incapable of being performed because the circumstances in which performance is called for would render it a thing radically different from that which was undertaken by the contract. *Non haec in foedera veni*. It was not this that I promised to do.[291]

Smith J. concluded that, following *National Carriers Ltd v Panalpina (Northern) Ltd,*[292] the 'prevailing wisdom' was that the test laid down by Lord Radcliffe 'best encapsulates the essence of the doctrine of frustration'.[293] Frustration would therefore arise '[o]nly if the supervening event renders the

---

285 Id., paragraph 34.
286 Id., paragraph 8.
287 (2019) EWHC 335 (Ch), paragraph 258.
288 Id., paragraphs 26 and 27. See also pages 211–229 *infra* for a discussion of the juridical bases of frustration.
289 (1956) 1 AC 696.
290 (2019) EWHC 335 (Ch), paragraph 22.
291 (1956) 1 AC 696, 729, quoted by Smith J at paragraph 22. See pages 182–184 *supra* for a detailed discussion of the *Davis Contractors* case. See also pages 219–222 and 224–227 *infra*.
292 (1981) 1 AC 675. See pages 191–193 *supra* for a discussion of the *Panalpina* case.
293 (2019) EWHC 335 (Ch), paragraph 27. Smith J. quoted from the judgments of Lord Simon and Lord Roskill, from the *Panalpina* case, at paragraphs 23, and 26(5), respectively, in arriving at his conclusion.

performance of the bargain "radically different", when compared to the considerations in play at the conclusion of the contract'.[294]

Smith J. then addressed the issue of supervening illegality. After reviewing the constitution of the EMA and the relevant European Union law,[295] as well as the provisions of the Lease,[296] Smith J. came to the conclusion that the EMA would not lack legal capacity to dispose of, or otherwise deal with, the premises after the withdrawal of the United Kingdom from the European Union.[297] Although he acknowledged that the privileges and immunities of the EMA would be 'materially and adversely affected' by the withdrawal of the United Kingdom,[298] he held that this would not affect the legal capacity of the EMA to deal with immovable property.[299] Smith J. based this finding on Article 71 of the 2004 Regulation of the European Parliament and of the Council of 31 March 2004:

> The [EMA] shall have legal personality. In all Member States it shall enjoy the most extensive legal capacity accorded to legal persons under their laws. It may in particular acquire or dispose of movable and immovable property and may be a party to legal proceedings.[300]

The EMA had contended that Article 71 was 'inward looking', i.e. that it conferred no powers on the EMA outside the territory of the European Union.[301] But after reviewing the provisions of the *Treaty on European Union* and of the *Treaty on the Functioning of the European Union,* as well as a number of decisions of the Court of Justice of the European Union, Smith J. held that this was not so; the EMA did in fact have capacity to act extra-territorially, including the capacity to acquire or dispose of movable and immovable property.[302] This meant that the EMA was capable of assigning or subletting the premises under the Lease,[303] and further that it was obliged to continue paying rent under the Lease.[304]

Smith J. also rejected the contention of the EMA that the European Union did not have the capacity to designate the headquarters of the EMA outside the territory of the Member States of the European Union. After briefly disposing

---

294 (2019) EWHC 335 (Ch), paragraph 27.
295 Id., paragraphs 62–91.
296 Id., paragraphs 92–95.
297 Id., paragraphs 96–165.
298 Id., paragraphs 130–139.
299 Id., paragraphs 140–160.
300 Id., paragraphs 65, 141.
301 Id., paragraph 145.
302 Id., paragraph 145(3). See *Treaty on European Union,* 13 December 2007 (OJ C 202, 7.6.2016) and *Treaty on the Functioning of the European Union,* 13 December 2007 (OJ C 202, 7.6.2016).
303 (2019) EWHC 335 (Ch), paragraph 145(5).
304 Id., paragraph 159.

of arguments relating to customary international law, Smith J. focussed on Article 341 of the *Treaty on the Functioning of the European Union*:

> The seat of the institutions of the Union shall be determined by common accord of the governments of the Member States.[305]

Although it would be politically inexpedient to do so, this Article nevertheless did permit the European Union to locate the headquarters of its agencies outside the territory of the European Union, if that was the 'common accord' of the member States:

> By Article 341 ... the EMA's headquarters (or seat) will be where the institutions of the Union determine 'by common accord of the governments of the Member States'. This is, therefore, an inter-Governmental decision. The EMA's case requires me to read into Article 341 TFEU an implied limitation on the power of the governments of the Member States to select by common accord headquarters outside the territories of the Member States of the European Union. I do not consider that such an implied limitation can appropriately be drawn.[306]

Smith J. then went on to observe that even if the EMA did lack legal capacity under European Union law, this would not qualify as frustration by supervening illegality under English law.[307] In this regard Smith J. noted that although English law took account of the legal capacity of a foreign entity when entering into a contract within the English jurisdiction,[308] it did not take account of any subsequent illegality which might arise under foreign law once the entity had entered into an English contract:

> This is a case where the supervening illegality arises under a foreign law that is not the applicable law. Generally speaking, the validity and enforceability of a contract governed by English law is not as a general rule affected by the question whether the contract would be regarded as valid or whether its performance would be lawful according to the law of another country. The English law of frustration discounts illegality arising under a foreign law ...[309]

---

305 Article 341, *Treaty on the Functioning of the European Union*, 13 December 2007 (OJ C 202, 7.6.2016). Reproduced at paragraph 87 of the judgment.
306 (2019) EWHC 335 (Ch), paragraph 156.
307 Id., paragraphs 166–208.
308 Id., paragraph 177.
309 Id., paragraph 187.

In support of this proposition, Smith J. referred to the case of *Goldman Sachs International v Novo Banco SA*,[310] in which Lord Sumption declared:

> ... the discharge or modification of a contractual liability is treated in English law as being governed only by its proper law, so that measures taken under another law, such as that of a contracting party's domicile, are normally disregarded: *Adams* v *National Bank of Greece SA* (1961) AC 255.[311]

English law would therefore remain applicable even if European Union law rendered the EMA legally incapable, which Smith J. had already found was not so.

Smith J. then considered the possibility that he might be wrong on the above points. But even if this were so, this was a case of self-induced frustration.[312] The 'legal effects of the United Kingdom's withdrawal from the European Union', Smith J. found, 'could have been, but were not, ameliorated by the European Union'.[313] This was so because 'the 2018 Regulation could have gone further in making arrangements for the EMA's departure from London, but did not do so.[314] The Lease was therefore not frustrated because what frustration there might be was self-induced by the failure of the EU to take appropriate action.[315]

Smith J. next addressed the issue of frustration of common purpose. The EMA contended that the common purpose of the parties was to be found in the mutual contemplation of the parties that the headquarters of the EMA would be permanently based in London for the next twenty-five years. Given that this would not now occur the common purpose of the lease failed. Smith J. 'rejected this aspect of the [EMA's] case, finding that there was no such

---

310 (2018) UKSC 34.

311 Id., paragraph 12

312 Smith J. described self-induced frustration as 'simply a reference to post-contractual events and actions which indicate that certain options – that might have ameliorated the frustrating event – have been closed off by the acts or omissions of the party claiming frustration': (2019) EWHC 335 (Ch), paragraph 206.

313 Id., paragraph 208(3).

314 Id., paragraph 206(4).

315 Id., paragraph 207. McKendrick criticises this aspect of the judgment as follows: 'To require the EU in such circumstances to explore all options, including a possible run-off period during which the EMA would continue to occupy premises it otherwise lacked the capacity to occupy, sets the bar for invoking frustration at such a high level that it becomes almost impossible to envisage the doctrine being invoked successfully in practice'. However, McKendrick then acknowledges that this point was not material to the final outcome of the case, 'given the clear conclusion that the EU had the capacity to designate the seat of the EMA outside the EU and the EMA itself had the capacity to hold or deal with immovable property outside the territory of the EU': Ewan McKendrick 'Brexit, Uncertainty and the Doctrine of Frustration' (2019) 34 *Journal of International Banking Law and Regulation* 199, 203.

common purpose'.[316] Smith J. focused first on the parties' expectations as to risk, and in this regard considered the issue of foreseeability.[317] He found that when the Agreement to Lease and the Management Construction Agreement were signed on 5 August 2011, the withdrawal of the United Kingdom from the European Union was foreseeable only as 'a theoretical possibility'.[318] As such neither party '[could] be criticised for failing to take it into account',[319] so that 'withdrawal of the United Kingdom from the European Union was not relevantly foreseeable when the Agreements were entered into'.[320] But Smith J. also found that it was foreseeable over the twenty-five year term of the lease 'that there might be some development that would require the EMA involuntarily to have to leave the Premises due to circumstances beyond its control'.[321] He noted that the lease contained provisions, which enabled the EMA to assign and sublet the premises.[322] These provisions were 'long and extremely carefully worded'.[323] They were a clear indication that the EMA had understood that at some point in time in the future it might be required to move its headquarters from London to another location. This, in combination with the length of the term, and the absence of a break clause, demonstrated that the EMA had 'assumed the risk of change over a 25-year period'.[324]

Smith J. also considered the 'bespoke' nature of the premises. He found that there was no common purpose between the parties which would give rise to frustration. Although the parties evinced a common purpose to the limited extent that the EMA was attracted to the premises because 'they could be "sculpted" in such a way to suit the EMA', and Canary Wharf 'saw this as a relevant factor attracting the EMA to be the key-stone tenant', this 'common purpose never amounted to a mutual contemplation that one of the purposes of the Lease was to provide a permanent headquarters for the EMA for the next twenty-five years and that if that could not be achieved, the common purpose of the Lease had failed'.[325] Smith J. noted that the parties conducted

---

316 Jamie Sutherland 'Leases, Brexit and Frustration' (2019) 23 *Landlord & Tenant Review* 191, 192.

317 Smith J. had earlier noted that whereas a common purpose of the parties does not have to be contractual (in the sense that it does not have to be a term of the contract, express or implied), it must be assessed as at the time of contracting, by reference to the mutual intentions of the parties, objectively': (2019) EWHC 335 (Ch), paragraph 41(1).

318 Id., paragraph 215.

319 Id., paragraph 212.

320 Id., paragraph 216. Smith J. had earlier noted that whereas a common purpose of the parties does not have to be contractual (in the sense that it does not have to be a term of the contract, express or implied), it must be assessed as at the time of contracting, by reference to the mutual intentions of the parties, objectively': (2019) EWHC 335 (Ch), paragraph 41(1).

321 (2019) EWHC 335 (Ch), paragraph 226.

322 Id., paragraph 218(1).

323 Id., paragraph 218(1).

324 Id., paragraph 224.

325 Id., paragraph 217.

negotiations in their own commercial interests. He came to the conclusion that '[o]utside the terms of the Lease, the parties' purposes were not common, but divergent':[326]

> In this case I find no common purpose beyond the purpose to be derived from a construction of the Lease. This is not a case like *Krell v Henry* where the parties had a common purpose going beyond their agreement, which was thwarted. The parties approached the Agreements as counterparties, and they bargained hard – if amicably – to get what they wanted.[327]

In summary, Smith J. noted that the present case did not 'come close to a case of frustration of common purpose',[328] and that the 'EMA cannot say this is not what it bargained for'.[329] Smith J. concluded his judgment by declaring that 'the Lease will not be frustrated on the withdrawal of the United Kingdom from the European Union. This is neither a case of frustration by supervening illegality nor one of frustration of common purpose', and the 'EMA therefore remains obliged to perform its obligations under the Lease'.[330]

As McKendrick points out:

> The decision may be said to affirm the importance of certainty in English contract law, at least in the sense that the court confirmed that the doctrine of frustration operates within very narrow confines and that it will not be used by the courts as an instrument to rescue a party from entry into a transaction which, with the benefit of hindsight, can be seen to have been improvident.[331]

This is particularly true with regard to leases. Although *National Carriers Ltd v Panalpina (Northern) Ltd.*[332] recognised that the doctrine of frustration could in fact apply to leases, the fact 'that a lease creates a legal estate in land'. necessarily means that 'there is much about the proprietary nature of leases (and the benefits which leases can confer on third parties, besides the original landlord and tenant) which makes frustration particularly difficult to

---

326 Id., paragraph 245.
327 Id., paragraph 244.
328 Id., paragraph 247.
329 Id., paragraph 248.
330 Id., paragraph 258. Permission was granted to the EMA to appeal the decision of Smith J. to the Court of Appeal, but the appeal was withdrawn in July 2019 when the EMA found a subtenant for the premises.
331 McKendrick op. cit. (fn. 315), 199.
332 (1981) AC 675; (1981) 1 All ER 161. See pages 191–193 *supra* for a discussion of this case.

establish'.[333] Consequently, although the doctrine now applies to leases, it will, as Lord Hailsham LC noted in *Panalpina*, nevertheless 'hardly ever' do so.[334]

The issue of the dual character of a lease in English law has no counterpart in French law. A lease in French law is classified simply as a specific contract and does not contain any proprietary interest resembling the English lease-hold estate. The *Cour de cassation* ruled in 1861 that leases, however long their duration, do not create a dismemberment of the proprietary right of the lessor.[335]

Title VIII of the *Code civil* sets out, in Articles 1708 to 1831, the specific rules which govern the contract of lease. Article 1709 defines the elements of a lease: viz. that it consists of an obligation to provide a thing during a certain period of time in exchange for a payment.[336] Article 1713 provides that any movable or immovable may be leased.[337] Article 1719, paragraph 3 states that the landlord must grant peaceful enjoyment to the tenant.[338] The *Cour de cassation* has declared that this obligation is absolute, unless prevented by *force majeure*.[339]

As a specific contract, the lease is subject to the general principles of *force majeure* and, in addition, to a number of specific rules set out in the section governing leases. Four articles explicitly address *force majeure*. These articles are Articles 1722, 1730, 1733 and 1755.[340] Article 1722 declares that if the thing leased is totally destroyed by *force majeure* during the term of the lease, the lease is automatically terminated. If it is only partly destroyed, the tenant may ask for a revision of the price or termination of the contract. Damages cannot be awarded in such cases.[341] Article 1730 states that when an inventory

---

333 Sutherland, op. cit., 194.

334 (1981) AC 675, 692; (1981) 1 All ER 161, 169.

335 Req., 6 mars 1861, 417 (*Syndicat Vollot c Chaussergues du Bord*).

336 *Le louage des choses est un contrat par lequel l'une des parties s'oblige à faire jouir l'autre d'une chose pendant un certain temps et moyennant un certain prix que celle-ci s'oblige à lui payer.*

337 *On peut louer toutes sortes de biens meubles ou immeubles.*

338 *Le bailleur est obligé, par la nature du contrat, et sans qu'il soit besoin d'aucune stipulation particulière:*
    3) d'en faire jouir paisiblement le preneur pendant la durée du bail.

339 Cass. 3e Civ., 9 octobre 1974, 73-11.721.

340 See pages 114–115 and 119–121 *supra* for a discussion of Article 1722 in the context of COVID-19.

341 *Si pendant la durée du bail, la chose louée est détruite en totalité par cas fortuit, le bail est résilié de plein droit; si elle n'est détruite qu'en partie, le preneur peut, suivant les circonstances, demander ou une diminution du prix, ou la résiliation même du bail. Dans l'une et l'autre cas, il n'y a lieu à aucun dédommagement.* The *Cour de cassation* has declared that this article is not of 'ordre public', and therefore parties to a contract of lease may adapt the contract. See Cass. Civ., 3e, 17 déc. 2015, no. 14-25.523. The original French of Article 1722 actually refers to *cas fortuit*, rather than *force majeure*, as occurs in the English text. But as seen at page 86 *supra*, *cas fortuit* and *force majeure* are considered to mean the same thing. Reference to *cas fortuit* has now been removed from the revised articles on contractual obligations and will eventually be completely eliminated from the *Code civil* as it is progressively revised.

of fixtures has been made between the parties, the tenant must give back the object of the lease in the same state, according to the inventory, unless it was destroyed or damaged by decay or *force majeure*.[342] Article 1733 states that the tenant is liable for a fire which damages the movable or immovable thing unless he proves that the fire occurred as a result of *force majeure*.[343] Article 1755 provides that with regard to a residential lease, no repairs deemed as incumbent upon a tenant may be charged to the tenant if the repair is due to decay or *force majeure*.[344]

In addition to the provisions of Article 1755, residential leases are also governed by a separate law, viz. *Loi no 89-462 du 6 juillet 1989*.[345] Article 2, paragraph 1 of this Act declares that all of the articles of the Act are of '*ordre public*', which means that no residential lease contract may derogate from them.[346] Article 7 refers to *force majeure* in subsections (c) and (d). Article 7(c) states that the tenant is liable for damages or destruction of the rented housing unless he proves that it was due, *inter alia*, to *force majeure*.[347] Article 7(d) declares in the first sentence that no repairs deemed as incumbent upon the tenant may be charged to the tenant if the repairs are due, *inter alia*, to *force majeure*.[348] Although Article 7(d) seems at first glance simply to repeat Article 1755 of the *Code civil*, there is an important difference that Article 1755 permits contracting parties to depart from its provisions, whereas this is not possible with Article 7(d), as it is classified as of '*ordre public*', by virtue of Article 2(1) of the Act.

---

342 *S'il a été fait un état des lieux entre le bailleur et le preneur, celui-ci doit rendre la chose telle qu'il l'a reçue, suivant cet état, excepté ce qui a péri ou a été dégradé par vétusté ou force majeure.*

343 *Il répond de l'incendie, à moins qu'il prouve:*
   Que l'incendie est arrivé par cas fortuit ou force majeure, ou par vice de construction.
   Ou le feu a été communiqué par une maison voisine.

344 *Aucune des réparations réputées locatives n'est à la charge des locataires quand elles ne sont occasionnées que par vétusté ou force majeure.* The *Cour de cassation* has declared that Article 1755 does not apply if the parties have stipulated otherwise in the contract. See Cass. Civ., 3e, 14 déc. 1988, no. 87-12.636. This ruling is echoed by the above-mentioned Cass. Civ., 3e, 17 déc. 2015, no. 14-25.523.

345 The full title of the Act is *Loi no. 89-462 du 6 juillet 1989 tendant à améliorer les rapports locatifs et portant modification de la loi no. 86-1290 du 23 décembre 1986.*

346 *Les dispositions du présent titre sont d'ordre public.*

347 *Le locataire est obligé:*
   c) De répondre aux dégradations et pertes qui surviennent pendant la durée du contrat dans les locaux dont il a la jouissance exclusive, à moins qu'il ne prouve qu'elles ont eu lieu par cas de force majeure, par la faute du bailleur ou par le fait d'un tiers qu'il n'a pas introduit dans le logement.

348 *Le locataire est obligé:*
   d) De prendre à sa charge l'entretien courant du logement, des équipements mentionnés au contrat et les menues réparations ainsi que l'ensemble des réparations locatives définies par décret en Conseil d'Etat, sauf si elles sont occasionées par vétusté, malfaçon, vice de construction, cas fortuit ou force majeure.

Frustration and COVID-19

The first two cases of COVID-19 came to light in the United Kingdom on 31 January 2020. The virus spread rapidly throughout the population. In response, the government introduced a national lockdown on 23 March 2020.[349] This remained in effect until June 2020, when the lockdown was lifted and various regional restrictions were imposed. However, an upsurge in cases led to the reimposition of a second national lockdown on 5 November 2020. This remained in effect until December 2020. A third national lockdown was imposed in January 2021 and remained in effect until 8 March 2021. Thereafter a phased exit from lockdown was introduced. There are currently no restrictions in place in England.

COVID-19, and the governmental responses to it, had more or less the same devastating impact on English society, and on English commercial enterprises, as occurred in France.[350] There have, for example, been the same widespread problems with regard to contractual performance. The British government reacted by implementing a series of legislative provisions relating to the virus.[351] These provisions, however, were largely regulatory in nature, and did not involve any significant changes to the law of contract.[352] As a result, the problems of contractual non-performance were left to the judiciary

---

349 On 7 April 2020 the British Institute of International and Comparative Law called for 'a breathing space' in commercial contract disputes arising from the COVID-19 pandemic, and proceeded to examine the private law response to the pandemic, as well as drafting a set of proposed practical guidelines on how companies could manage legal disputes responsibly: British Institute of International and Comparative Law *'Breathing Space – Concept Notes on the Effect of the Pandemic on Commercial Contracts'*, 1.

    https://www.biicl.org/projects'breathing-space-concept-notes-on-the-effect-of-the-pandemic-on-commercial-contracts?cookiesset=1&ts=1713781018.

350 The impact of COVID-19 on French society, and on French businesses and commercial enterprises, has been discussed at pages 109–126 *supra.*

351 See, for example, the *Coronavirus Act* 2020 c. 7, enacted on 25 March 2020. The Act can be accessed at the following site: https://www.legislation.gov.uk/ukpga/2020/7/contents.

    For a detailed review of the measures taken by the government to combat the wide ranging and deleterious effects of the pandemic on British society see Hugh Beale and Christian Twigg-Flesner 'ÇOVID-19 and English Contract Law' 461 et. seq., in Ewould Hondius, Marta Santos Silva, Andrea Nicolussi, Pablo Salvador Coderch, Christiane Windehorst and Fryderyk Zoll (editors) *Coronavirus and the Law in Europe* Cambridge: Intersentia, 2020, and Catherine Mitchell 'What Does Covid-19 Teach Us About English Contract Law?' *Cambridge Core* (Published online by Cambridge University Press) 8 February 2024, 1 et seq.

    https://www.cambridge.org/core/journals/legal-studies/article/what-does-covid19 -teach-us-about-english-contract-law/700EE330C37F60F6C37F60CF0707B07 B7EEBF9E8.

352 Beale and Twigg-Flesner, op. cit., 462, 477. Coronavirus provisions frequently extended enforcement proceedings, but did not relieve a contracting party of his obligation to perform under the terms of the contract. Section 82 of the *Coronavirus Act*, for example, suspends a landlord's right of re-entry or 'forfeiture' for business tenancy for the 'relevant period', but does not relieve the tenant from payment of rent due under the tenancy agreement.

to resolve, in those situations where the parties themselves could not come to an amicable renegotiation of their contract.

The starting point in resolving such problems was to determine whether the contract in question contained a *force majeure* clause.[353] Most professionally drawn commercial clauses do contain such a clause. The issue would then be 'the precise scope of such a clause', which would be 'a matter of construction in each case'.[354] In the absence of a *force majeure* clause, or should the *force majeure* clause be held not to apply, the general law of contract, i.e. the doctrine of frustration, would be applicable.[355]

COVID-19, however, has given rise to contractual problems that the doctrine of frustration is not particularly well adapted to address.[356] The doctrine of frustration is extremely narrow in scope, requiring either that performance be rendered impossible, or that the nature of the contract be radically changed into something fundamentally different. A supervening event amounting to frustration terminates the contract at the moment of the supervening event, and occurs by operation of law. The court cannot intervene to modify or adapt the contract in such circumstances. Consequently, contractual obligations will be either entirely discharged, should frustration be found to have occurred, or, should it not, they will remain enforceable in their original form.[357] This 'all or nothing' approach means that, unlike French law, there is almost no scope to address a situation of partial or temporary frustration. Whereas Article 1218 of the *Code civil* provides for temporary *force majeure*, in which the debtor may obtain a suspension of his contractual obligations for the duration of the *force majeure*,[358] there is no equivalent provision in the English doctrine of frustration. This has long been the accepted position.[359] Peel sets this out very emphatically:

> These rules (re partial frustration in civil law jurisdictions) have no direct counterpart in English law, under which, in cases of partial impossibility the contract is either frustrated or remains in force. There is no such

---

353 See page 7 *supra* for a definition of a *force majeure* clause. *Force majeure* clauses are not dealt with in this book..

354 Duncan Fairgrieve and Nicole Langlois 'Frustration and Hardship in Commercial Contracts: A Comparative Law Perspective' (2020) *Jersey and Guernsey Law Review* 142, 164.

355 It should be noted that English courts take a strict approach to the construction of *force majeure* clauses.

356 Catherine Pédamon and Radosveta Vassileva 'Contractual Performance in COVID-19 Times: Does Anglo-French Legal History Repeat Itself?' (2021) 29 *European Review of Private Law* 3, 34.

357 Beale and Twigg-Flesner, op. cit., 471.

358 See pages 88 *supra*.

359 See, for example, *Mount v Oldham Corp.* (1973) QB 309.

concept as partial or temporary frustration on account of partial or temporary impossibility.[360]

But the problems generated by COVID-19 were, in many cases, temporary in nature. Given the absence of any concept of partial or temporary frustration, such problems could not be addressed by the doctrine of frustration. This has been underscored in the decisions concerning COVID-19 that have come before the courts involving commercial leases. As in France, many commercial leases were adversely affected by COVID-19, and this led 'tenants to look for ways to mitigate their rental liabilities'.[361] Recourse to the doctrine of frustration, however, would not benefit many commercial tenants. This is because, when frustration occurs, it necessarily brings the contract between the parties to an end.[362] As Tanney points out, this means that:

> from a tenant's viewpoint frustration is a nuclear option: it eliminates the tenant's rental liability, but at the price of ending the lease in its entirely. A plea of frustration is therefore unattractive to tenants seeking to pay less rent while the pandemic continues, whilst wishing to retain their leases for hoped-for better times ahead.[363]

In *Bank of New York Mellon (International) Ltd. v Cine-UK Ltd and other cases*,[364] the issue was whether tenants of commercial premises remained liable to pay their rent notwithstanding that they had been subject to the enforced closure of, or inability to trade from, their premises.[365] The tenants argued, *inter alia*, that the doctrine of frustration should be interpreted in a manner which would allow a temporary suspension. This was rejected by Master Dagnall, who reaffirmed that temporary frustration was not a part of the doctrine:

> … there is no such thing as a 'temporary frustration', effectively suspending the contract for a period of time, in law. Both Treitel and the case-law, in particular my initial citations from *Panalpina*, make clear that frustration has the effect of discharging the contract and ending it. That is one reason why such a 'radical difference' has to exist. Frustration does not suspend the contract, rather it terminates it and so that it does not subsequently revive. What the Tenants are seeking to do is to introduce

360 Edwin Peel *Frustration and Force Majeure* (fourth edition) London: Thomson Reuters, trading as Sweet & Maxwell, 2022, 198, 199. See also Beale and Twigg-Flesner, op. cit., 466–468.
361 Anthony Tanney 'Leases and the Doctrine of Frustration' (2021) 25 *L. & T. Review* 59, 59.
362 Cartwright, op. cit. 273.
363 Tanney, op. cit., 59.
364 (2021) EWHC 1013 (QB).
365 Id., paragraph 1.

one possible version of the flexibility that Lord Simon said would require statute. There is no case-law as to general 'temporary frustration'.[366]

The same conclusion was reached by Mr. Justice Foxton, in *London Trocadero (2015) LLP v Picturehouse Cinemas Limited and others.*[367] This case involved a claim for unpaid rent for premises operating as a cinema. Due to government lockdowns, the premises could not be so used. The defendants argued that they were not liable for the rental payments which had arisen when the premises could not be used as a cinema, on the basis, *inter alia*, that there had been a partial failure of consideration.[368] The defendants acknowledged that the lease had not come to an end as a result of frustration, and that the landlord was not in breach of the terms of the lease. Mr. Justice Foxton rejected the submission of the defendants:

> Allowing failure of basis as a self-standing concept to provide a defence to a contractual claim would be tantamount to extending the doctrine of frustration so as to allow obligations under a contract to be suspended as a result of what might be termed temporary or partial frustration. There is of course no such principle as the law currently stands. It is clear that frustration brings a contract to an end and discharges the parties from all of their future obligations. Indeed, the possibility of temporary frustration was a significant issue in the Cine-UK case decided by Master Dagnall and was rejected by him. It is perhaps telling that the Defendants in this case do not put forward partial or temporary frustration as a defence.[369]

The above two decisions were then appealed to the Court of Appeal, and were heard together in the case of *Bank of New York Mellon (International) Ltd v Cine-UK Ltd; London Trocadero (2015) LLP v Picturehouse Cinemas Ltd and others.*[370] The appellants argued that they should be relieved from paying rent during the periods in which it was unlawful to operate a cinema as a result of COVID-19, and presented a number of arguments to this end, all of which were rejected by the Court of Appeal. Interestingly, the doctrine of frustration

---

366 Id., paragraph 211(a).
367 (2021) EWHC 2591 (Ch).
368 Id., paragraph 56. Failure of consideration, as Mr. Justice Foxton points out, is now more commonly referred to as 'failure of basis'.
369 (2021) EWHC 2591 (Ch), paragraph 168. See also *Salam Air SAOC v Latam Airlines Group SA* (2020) EWHC 2414 (Comm) and *Wilmington Trust SP Services (Dublin) Ltd v Spicejet Ltd* (2021) EWHC 1117 (Comm). Both cases involved the leasing of aircraft. The defendants in both cases argued, *inter alia*, that they were not liable for non-payment of rent as a result of frustration. However, this submission failed in both cases, largely on the basis of the 'hell or highwater' clauses contained in their lease agreements.
370 (2022) EWCA Civ. 1021.

was not one of the arguments put forward by the appellants. Its absence clearly demonstrated that the appellants had accepted as definitive the findings of the two judges at first instance that there could be no temporary or partial frustration which would relieve them of their rental liabilities.

An additional problem pertains to the role of foreseeability. Foreseeability, as seen above, is an essential attribute of the French law of *force majeure*, as set out in Article 1218.[371] However, foreseeability in the French context is limited to the debtor, as *force majeure* operates as a defence for the debtor's contractual non-performance. In the English context, on the other hand, a supervening event which qualifies as frustration entitles either contracting party to discharge the contract. As a result, foreseeability is a relevant factor with regard to both parties, rather than simply a factor for the debtor, as occurs in French contract law. This makes the issue of foreseeability more complex in the English context. It must be determined whether one party foresaw the supervening event, whether both parties foresaw it, or whether neither party foresaw it. To further complicate matters, a supervening event may be foreseeable, although not actually foreseen, by one, both or neither of the contracting parties. This makes foreseeability, as Smith J. noted, 'something of a slippery concept that needs careful handling'.[372]

The issue of foreseeability will not be a concern when neither party foresaw the supervening event. It does become a matter of concern when one party foresaw the possibility of the supervening event and the other did not. When this occurs, 'the normal inference will be that that risk is taken by the former party'.[373] This was the holding of the Court in the 1931 case of *Walton Harvey Ltd v Walker & Homfrays Ltd*.[374] The contract was not frustrated in this case because the defendants knew, and the plaintiffs did not, of the risk of compulsory acquisition of the property. The defendants could have provided against the risk, but did not.[375]

---

371 See page 87 *supra*.
372 *Canary Wharf (BP4) T1 Limited v European Medicines Agency* (2019) EWHC 335 (Ch), paragraph 213.
373 Peel, op. cit., 484.
374 (1931) 1 Ch. 274.
375 A contract had been signed between the plaintiff advertising agency and the defendant hotel owners, whereby the defendants agreed to allow an advertising sign to be placed on the roof of their hotel for a period of seven years. However, the hotel was compulsorily purchased and demolished by the Local Authority before the expiry of the seven year term. The plaintiff sued for breach of contract and the defendants responded by asserting that the contract had been frustrated. The Court held that the contract had not been frustrated, on the basis that the defendants knew that the Local Authority was interested in purchasing the hotel and that this could very well occur during the seven year term of the contract. The defendants should therefore have made provision for such an eventuality in their contract, and were liable in damages for breach of contract.

Frustration is said to be excluded when the supervening event was foreseen by both parties.[376] In this regard, Lord Brandon declared, in the case of *The Hannah Blumenthal*,[377] that to bring about frustration there must be 'some outside event or extraneous change of situation not foreseen or provided for by the parties at the time of contracting'.[378] Lord Denning, however, had previously cast doubt on this proposition, in the case of *Ocean Tramp Tankers Corp v VO Sovracht (The 'Eugenia')*:[379]

> It has frequently been said that the doctrine of frustration only applies when the new situation is 'unforeseen' or 'unexpected' or 'uncontemplated', as if that were an essential feature. But it is not so. The only thing that is essential is that the parties should have made no provision for it in their contract. The only relevance of it being 'unforeseen' is this: if the parties did not foresee anything of the kind happening, you can readily infer they have made no provision for it: whereas, if they did foresee it, you would expect them to make provision for it. But cases have occurred where the parties have foreseen the danger ahead, and yet made no provision for it in the contract. Such was the case in the Spanish Civil War when a ship was let on charter to the republican government. The purpose was to evacuate refugees. The parties foresaw that she might be seized by the nationalists. But they made no provisions for it in their contract. Yet, when she was seized, the contract was frustrated.[380]

Lord Denning concluded that in such circumstances there was still 'room for the doctrine to apply if it be a proper case for it'.[381]

When the supervening event was foreseeable by both parties, but not actually foreseen by them, the court must then determine whether one or the other of the parties should be considered to have assumed the risk of the supervening event, as a matter of the construction of the contract.[382] Should the court find that one of the parties has assumed the risk, this will exclude the possibility of frustration.[383]

---

376 This is because 'the court will generally construe the contract as providing implicitly for the risk of occurrence of the event': Fairgrieve and Langlois, op. cit., 155.

377 *Paal Wilson & Co. A/S v Partenreederei Hannah Blumenthal (The Hannah Blumenthal)* (1983) 1 AC 854.

378 Id., 909.

379 (1964) 2 QB 226.

380 Id., 289. The case Lord Denning was referring to was *WJ Tatem Ltd v Gamboa* (1939) 1 KB 132. Consider also the statement of Rix LJ in *Edwinton Commercial Corporation v Tsavliris Russ (Worldwide Salvage & Towage) Ltd (The "Sea Angel")* (2007) EWCA Civ 547, at paragraph 99: 'It is certainly true however, that a contract may be frustrated even though the supervening event was foreseeable or contemplated'.

381 (1964) 2 QB 226, 289.

382 Fairgrieve and Langlois, op. cit., 155, 156

383 Id., 156.

Given these complications and uncertainties, the precise role of foreseeability within the doctrine of frustration is problematic. This was in all likelihood one of the reasons which prompted Smith J. to put forward a very nuanced approach to foreseeability in *Canary Wharf (BP4) T1 Limited v European Medicines Agency*.[384] Smith J. declared that foreseeability was no more than a factor to be taken into account when considering whether frustration had arisen:

> The foreseeability of the frustrating event is relevant only insofar as it informs the parties' knowledge, expectations, assumptions and contemplations, in particular as to risk. If a future event is sufficiently foreseeable that it should have informed the manner in which the parties framed their agreement (particularly so far as the risk allocation provisions were concerned), then (to put it no higher than this) a court will be inclined to consider that the parties will have framed their agreement taking this factor into account. Foreseeability is, thus, no more than a factor to be taken into account. There will, no doubt, be many cases where something can be foreseen as a theoretical possibility, but where neither party can be criticised for failing to take it into account.[385]

In spite of the uncertainties surrounding foreseeability, it is a crucial factor when determining whether contracts have been frustrated as a result of COVID-19. But problems arise in attempting to take it into account. There is first the question as to what exactly might have been foreseeable. A major epidemic had long been anticipated in certain scientific quarters, and public warnings had been issued of its imminent arrival, to those who were listening. In retrospect, SARS, MERS and Ebola all seem to have been 'early warnings of a more profound health crisis'.[386] But as Smith J. observed, 'something can be foreseen as a theoretical possibility, but where neither party can be criticised for failing to take it into account'.[387]

Focus must therefore be not on the possible future outbreak of some undefined epidemic disease, but rather on the actual emergence and impact of COVID-19. The relevant question is to determine at what point in time the outbreak of COVID-19 became 'sufficiently foreseeable that it should have informed the manner in which the parties framed their agreement'.[388] But as

---

384 (2019) EWHC 335 (Ch).
385 Id., paragraph 211.
386 Catherine MacMillan 'Covid-19 and the Problem of Frustrated Contracts' (2021) 32 *King's Law Journal* 60, 65.
387 (2019) EWHC 335 (Ch), paragraph 211.
388 Id., paragraph 211. This question was addressed by Deputy ICC Judge Curl KC, in the case of *Bridger and Co Ltd v Specialist Lending Ltd (t/a Duologi)* (2023) EWHC 2562. Dismissing arguments based on frustration arising from COVID-19 he declared as follows, at paragraph 35: 'Covid was plainly in contemplation in August and September 2020. Anyone

already seen in the discussion of COVID-19 in the French context, fixing the date of such foreseeability is problematic.[389] COVID-19 first made its appearance in Wuhan, China, in December 2019. There could not therefore have been foreseeability with regard to contracts made prior to December 2019. On the other hand, when the Prime Minister told the public on 23 March 2020 to stay at home, it would be difficult, if not impossible, to assert at this point that the pandemic was an unforeseen supervening event.[390] There is, however, an uncertain middle ground, in which it may not be clear when the impact of the virus was foreseeable and when it should have been taken into account in allocating risk.

An additional complicating factor is whether the foreseeability of COVID-19 requires the impact of the pandemic to have been actually foreseen by one or both parties, or whether it need only be reasonably foreseeable. As Twiggs-Flesner points out, to proceed on the basis that the pandemic was not foreseen sets the bar lower than proceeding on the basis that the pandemic was not reasonably foreseeable.[391] When a party asserts that frustration has occurred, it will be much easier to do so on the basis that the supervening event was not foreseen, even though it may have been reasonably foreseeable.[392] Proceeding on the basis that the supervening event was not reasonably foreseeable requires a higher evidentiary burden of proof. It would also require a determination of what exactly was reasonably foreseeable.[393] Should foreseeability simply involve a knowledge of the existence and spread of the virus, or should it go to a knowing assessment of the gravity of its impact. These two aspects of foreseeability will not necessarily be known at the same point in time.

Foreseeability is a matter which is complex and not delineated in a definitive manner. How the various approaches to foreseeability play out with regard to claims that COVID-19 is a frustrating event remains to be seen, and must be determined in the light of the individual facts of each particular case.

To conclude, it is evident, at least from the small number of cases that have been decided thus far, that the English courts are unwilling to contemplate any change to the strict approach to the doctrine of frustration, in order to address what might very well be no more than 'a once-in-a-generation occurrence'.[394]

---

assuming a commercial liability at around that time would certainly have factored Covid into their reckoning. On any view, Covid was baked into the commercial scene and every other kind of scene by late summer 2020'.

389 See pages 123–124 *supra*.

390 MacMillan, op cit., 65.

391 Christian Twiggs-Flesner 'A Comparative Perspective on Commercial Contracts and the Impact of Covid-19 – Change of Circumstances, *Force Majeure*, or What? in Katharina Pistor *Law in the Time of COVID-19* (2020) (https://scholarship.law.columbia.edu.books/240) 155, 161.

392 Id., 162.

393 Id., 162.

394 Mitchell, op. cit., 61. See also Beale and Twigg-Flesner, op. cit., 488, 489.

Instead, the courts have opted to maintain the traditional English contract values of stability, certainty and sanctity of contract. In *Bank of New York Mellon (International) Ltd v Cine-UK Ltd; London Trocadero (2015 LLP v Picturehouse Cinemas Ltd and others,* the Chancellor Sir Julian Flaux was explicit in this regard, declaring that the coronavirus legislation presented 'no reason to disregard or disapply fundamental principles of the law of contract or to extend the law of unjust enrichment beyond its proper bounds'.[395]

The Juridical Basis of the Doctrine

The doctrine of frustration is further complicated by the ongoing controversy about the juridical, or theoretical, basis of the doctrine. Lord Wright noted that 'the general nature of the doctrine of frustration has given rise to many irreconcilable explanations'.[396] The essential question, as Furmston points out, 'is whether the courts strive to give effect to the supposed intention of the parties or whether they act independently and impose the solution that seems reasonable and just'.[397] Because the theoretical basis of frustration remains unresolved, it is difficult to predict when and in what circumstances the courts will actually invoke frustration, and this in turn means that the doctrine itself remains inherently uncertain and problematic.[398]

Any attempt to formulate a theoretical basis for the doctrine must first take into account two fundamental characteristics of English contract law. The first characteristic is that English contracts are considered to be absolute in nature, unless they can be otherwise qualified. The second characteristic involves the sanctity of contract, whereby the terms of the contract are considered to be formulated by the parties themselves, and are binding on them by virtue of this exercise of their free will.

When the doctrine of frustration was first formulated by Blackburn J. in *Taylor v Caldwell,* these two features of English contract law were clearly uppermost in his mind. Given the absolute nature of Common Law contracts, a party could escape liability for non-performance only if he could point to a term in the contract which exempted him from liability. In the absence of an express term, this had to be an implied term. But the implied term necessarily had to be one which reflected the joint will of the parties, and which gave effect to their mutual, albeit unexpressed, intention. In *Taylor v Caldwell* Blackburn J. was able to find that the contract before him was not absolute, because there was an implied term which qualified it, and he further found

---

395 (2022) EWCA Civ. 1021, paragraph 143.
396 *Denny, Mott & Dickson, Limited v James B Fraser & Company, Limited* (1944) AC 265, 276.
397 Furmston, op. cit., 713, 714.
398 McKendrick, op. cit. (fn. 226), 34.

that this implied term was one which the parties had implicitly agreed to, as required by the will theory.[399]

The notion that there existed an implied term between the parties therefore became the first basis upon which the doctrine of frustration was formulated. The judgment of Earl Loreburn, in the case of *Tamplin (F.A.) Steamship Co. Ltd v Anglo-Mexican Petroleum Products Co. Ltd.*, exemplifies this approach.[400] In the course of analysing the nature of frustration Earl Loreburn premised his judgment on the traditional understanding that Common Law contracts were absolute in nature, and that a party could be relieved of his contractual obligations, upon the occurrence of a supervening event, only if an appropriate term, either express or implied, could be found in the contract:

> ... a Court can and ought to examine the contract and the circumstances in which it was made, not of course to vary, but only to explain it, in order to see whether or not from the nature of it the parties must have made their bargain on the footing that a particular thing or state of things would continue to exist. And if they must have done so, then a term to that effect will be implied, though it be not expressed in the contract.[401]

This implied term had to be attributed to the parties themselves, because the Court did not have any power to intervene:

> In most of the cases it is said that there was an implied term in the contract which operated to release the parties from performing it, and in all of them I think that was at bottom the principle upon which the court proceeded. It is in my opinion the true principle, for no Court has an absolving power, but it can infer from the nature of the contract and the surrounding circumstances that a condition which was not expressed was a foundation on which the parties contracted.[402]

The finding of an implied term between the parties was therefore an essential aspect of the doctrine of frustration. The theory of the implied term harmoniously reconciled the doctrine of frustration with the doctrines of the absolute nature of contracts and the will theory. By virtue of this theory, the absolute nature of a Common Law contract remained as the starting point in determining liability for breach, unless a term, either express or implied, provided otherwise. An implied term which qualified the contract had to issue from the joint will of the parties, because this upheld the legally binding nature of

399 See pages 168–170 *supra*.
400 (1916) 2 AC 397, 403.
401 Id., 403.
402 (1916) 2 AC 397, 403.

the contract based on the will theory. When therefore the court declared that there was an implied term in the contract, it was only finding a term that the parties themselves had implicitly agreed to, rather than itself intervening to alter the terms of the parties' agreement.[403]

The fundamental problem with the implied term theory, however, was that in the vast majority of cases the parties had never actually addressed their minds to the supervening event which subsequently occurred, and so in reality there could not be an implied term existing between them at the conclusion of their contract with regard to that event. In *James Scott & Sons v Del Sol,* decided in 1922, Lord Sands mocked the theory of the implied term:

> A tiger has escaped from a travelling menagerie. The milkgirl fails to deliver the milk. Possibly the milkman may be exonerated from any breach of contract; but, even so, it would seem hardly reasonable to base that exoneration on the ground that 'tiger days excepted' must be held as if written into the milk contract.[404]

In that same year, in *Russkoe v Stirk*, Lord Atkin recognised that the implied term was no more than a legal fiction, and declared that it was actually a device whereby something 'is imputed by the law to both parties'.[405] Its true nature he described as follows:

> It is not ... what two hardheaded bargainers subjectively agree with: it is to be regarded objectively as the term which the law imputes to two persons as being a term of the contract resulting in its dissolution. But, however that may be, it is sufficient, I think, to say this, that all that the Courts have been concerned with is the question: – Aye or no, have they agreed that the contract shall come to an end? – and if they have agreed that the contract shall come to an end then it appears to me that the consequences that follow, follow as a matter of positive law, and do not follow as a matter of contract express or implied between the parties.[406]

According to Lord Atkin, it was thus the Court, acting behind the legal fiction of the implied term, which decided whether the contract had come to an end through a supervening act of frustration. This was particularly true when the subject matter of the contract had neither been destroyed nor disappeared, but

---

403 See, for example, the comments of Lord Sumner in *Hirji Mulji v Cheong Yue Steamship Co.* (1926) AC 497, at 510: 'Frustration ... is explained in theory as a condition or term of the contract, implied by the law *ab initio*, in order to supply what the parties would have inserted had the matter occurred to them, on the basis of what is fair and reasonable, have regard to the mutual interest concerned and of the main objects of the contract'.

404 (1922) SC 592, 597.

405 (1922) 10 LLLR 214, 217.

406 Id., 217.

rather when there had been a transformation in the surrounding circumstances of the contract, as occurred in *Krell v Henry*.[407]

The theory of the implied term had originally been designed to reconcile the doctrine of frustration with the doctrines of the absolute contract and the sanctity of contract. But if the implied term was no more than a legal fiction which enabled the Court to intervene to terminate a contract, then the Court was not upholding the contractual intentions of the parties, but rather, as McElroy and Williams pointed out, making a new contract for them:

> ... if a court forms the opinion (though in the nature of things that opinion can never be but speculative) that both parties 'contemplated' the continued existence of a 'state of things', the court is justified, by that fact alone, in reading into the contract a condition that if the 'state of things' should cease to exist, the contract is dissolved, even though the contract itself contained no reference whatever to this 'state of things'. In other words, that the Court may, as the result of purely *ex post facto* construction, 'make' a contract for the parties.[408]

In other words, the implied term, which was originally introduced to reconcile the doctrine of frustration with that of the doctrines of the absolute contract and the will theory, could actually be used by the Court to evade those doctrines.[409]

Some other theory was therefore required to reconcile the three doctrines. One such approach was to explain frustration in terms of a total failure of consideration. By virtue of this theory, when a supervening event had rendered performance impossible by one of the contracting parties, the contract was thereby frustrated, because the other party would not receive any consideration in return for the execution of his obligation. This theory was put forward by McElroy, in his book *Impossibility of Performance,* published in 1941:

> ... a party seeks to be excused, not on the ground that performance has become impossible but on the ground that performance of the other

---

407 (1903) 2 KB 740. See pages 177–180 *supra*.
408 McElroy and Williams, op cit., 253.
409 In spite of being heavily criticised, the theory of the implied term continued to be relied upon in subsequent cases as the justification for the frustration of a contract. See, for example, *Joseph Constantine Steamship Line Limited v Imperial Smelting Corporation Limited* (1942) AC 154, per Viscount Simon L.C., at 163, 164; *British Movietonews Ld. v London and District Cinemas Ld.* (1952) AC 166, per Viscount Simon L.C., at 183, and per Lord Simonds, at 187; and *Port Line Ltd. v Ben Line Steamers Ltd.* (1958) 2 QB 146, per Diplock J, at 162.

party's promise has become impossible and that there is, in consequence, no longer any consideration for the performance of his own promise.[410]

However, as pointed out by Lord Simon in the 1981 case of *National Carriers Ltd v Panalpina (Northern)*, a total failure of consideration arises relatively rarely in frustration cases, and thus it cannot provide an adequate basis for a comprehensive explanation of frustration:

> Though such [i.e. a total failure of consideration] may be a feature of some cases of frustration, it is plainly inadequate as an exhaustive explanation: there are many cases of frustration where the contract has been partly executed.[411]

Yet another theory which was proposed as an alternative to the implied term was the theory of the foundation of the contract. In *Taylor v Caldwell* Blackburn J. had referred to the ongoing existence of the subject matter as the 'foundation of what was to be done'.[412] Vaughan Williams L.J. had likewise declared in *Krell v Henry* that 'if the contract becomes impossible of performance by reason of the non-existence of the state of things assumed by both contracting parties as the foundation of the contract, there will be no breach of the contract thus limited'.[413]

Although Blackburn J. and Vaughan Williams L.J. had both referred to the 'foundation of the contract' only as a subsidiary aspect of the implied term, which was the actual basis for their respective decisions, the 'foundation of the contract' theory was subsequently developed as a separate approach in its own right for determining whether or not a contract had been frustrated. This was first done in 1916 by Viscount Haldane L.C., in the case of *Tamplin (F.A.) Steamship Co. Ltd v Anglo-Mexican Petroleum Products Co. Ltd*.[414] Viscount Haldane declared that when the possibility of performance is dependent 'on the continued availability of a specific thing, and the availability of that thing comes to an end by reason of circumstances beyond the control of the parties' the occurrence of that event may be 'of a character and extent so sweeping that the foundation of what the parties are deemed to have had in contemplation has disappeared and the contract itself has vanished with that foundation'.[415] This theory, as Treitel points out, 'has the merit of simplicity as it does not involve speculation as to the intention of the parties or value judgments in

---

410 Roy Granville McElroy *Impossibility of Performance* Cambridge: At the University Press, 1941, 75.

411 *National Carriers Ltd v Panalpina (Northern) Ltd.* (1981) AC 675,702. See also the comments of Lord Hailsham LC in this regard, at page 687.

412 (1863) 3 B& S 826, 833; 122 ER 309, 312.

413 (1903) 2 KB 740, 749.

414 (1916) 2 AC 397.

415 Id., 406.

seeking a 'just solution'.[416] It thus appears to reconcile neatly the doctrine of frustration with the doctrines of absolute contract and sanctity of contract.

The theory of the foundation of the contract was thereafter espoused in a number of cases.[417] In *WJ Tatem, Limited v Gamboa*, decided in 1939, Goddard J. declared that the foundation of the contract theory 'seems to me to be the surest ground on which to rest the doctrine of frustration, and I prefer it to founding it on implied terms'.[418] In 1942, Viscount Simon L.C. cited the theory, in *Joseph Constantine Steamship Line, Limited v Imperial Smelting Corporation, Limited*, as one of the three possible bases for a finding of frustration.[419]

But the theory was criticised by Lord Hailsham L.C. in *National Carriers Ltd. v Panalpina (Northern) Ltd.*, on the ground that the descriptive words of the theory, such as 'foundation', 'fundamental' and 'adventure' were themselves too nebulous to provide any real guidance as to when a contract should be discharged for frustration.[420] Treitel elaborates on this criticism by pointing out any doubt as to what constitutes the 'foundation' of the contract 'can, in the last resort, be resolved only by construing the contract. If this is so, there is no practical difference between the 'foundation' theory and the 'implied term' theory in its objective sense. Indeed, exponents of the one sometime use the language of the other'.[421]

Eventually, some judges came to acknowledge that when the courts made a finding of frustration they were actually imposing their own solution on the parties' contractual relationship, and were doing so simply on the basis of what was 'just and reasonable' in the circumstances. This theory is referred to in various ways, among which are the 'just and reasonable approach' and the 'just solution'. Lord Wright was an advocate of this theory, declaring in an extrajudicial address that it was the judge, on the basis of what was just and reasonable in the circumstances, who decided whether there was frustration or not:

> The truth is that the court or jury as a judge of fact decides the question in accordance with what seems to be just and reasonable in its eyes. The judge finds in himself the criterion of what is reasonable. The court is

---

416 Treitel, op. cit., 647.

417 The dicta of Viscount Haldane LC was cited with approval by Pickford LJ, with whom Bankes LJ and Sargant J concurred, in *Countess of Warwick Steamship Company v Le Nickel Société Anonyme* (1918) 1 KB 372, at 376.

418 (1939) 1 KB 132, 137.

419 (1942) AC 154, at 163: 'The doctrine of discharge from liability by frustration has been explained in various ways – sometimes by speaking of the disappearance of a foundation which the parties assumed to be at the basis of their contract, sometimes as deduced from a rule arising from impossibility of performance, and sometimes as flowing from the inference of an implied term'.

420 (1981) AC 675, 688.

421 Treitel, op. cit., 647.

in this sense making a contract for the parties, though it is almost blasphemy to say so.[422]

Lord Denning was another advocate of this approach. In *British Movietonews Ld v London and District Cinemas Ld.* he declared as follows:

> In these frustration cases, as Lord Wright said, the court really exercises a qualifying power – a power to qualify the absolute, literal or wide terms of the contract – in order to do what is just and reasonable in the new situation.[423]

He then went on to assert that the courts had the power to reread the words of a contract in a qualified manner in order to ensure a just and reasonable outcome:

> The judgments show that, no matter that a contract is framed in words which taken literally or absolutely, cover what has happened, nevertheless, if the ensuing turn of events was so completely outside the contemplation of the parties that the court is satisfied that the parties, as reasonable people, cannot have intended that the contract should apply to the new situation, then the court will read the words of the contract in a qualified sense; it will restrict them to the circumstances contemplated by the parties; it will not apply them to the uncontemplated turn of events, but will do therein what is just and reasonable ...

> This does not mean the courts no longer insist on the binding force of contracts deliberately made. It only means that they will not allow the words, in which they happen to be phrased, to become tyrannical masters. The court qualifies the literal meaning of the words so as to bring them into accord with the true scope of the contract. Even if the contract is absolute in its terms, nevertheless if it is not absolute in intent, it will not be held absolute in effect.[424]

This passage reveals the tensions inherent in attempting to ground the doctrine of frustration on a juridical basis. The problem is how to reconcile the doctrines of the absolute contract and the will of the parties with that of frustration. Earlier judgments had frequently discussed the application of frustration on the basis that it had to be reconciled with these two doctrines. A good example is the statement of Lord Sands, who declared that the implied term was a 'pious fiction': 'a fiction because it does not correspond with anything

---

422 Robert Alderson Wright (Baron of Durley) *Legal Essays and Addresses by the Right Hon. Lord Wright of Durley* Cambridge: Cambridge University Press, 1939, 259.
423 (1951) 1 KB 190, 200.
424 Id., 201, 202.

that was in the minds of the parties at the time; pious because it seeks to do homage to a very sacred legal principle, the sanctity of contract'.[425] But in *British Movietonews* Lord Denning attempted to develop the just and reasonable approach in a manner which would enable the court to remake the parties' contract simply when it considered it just and reasonable to do so, thereby effectively denying the doctrines of absolute contract and sanctity of contract.

The House of Lords emphatically repudiated Lord Denning's proposition. In doing so, Lord Simonds employed this forthright language:

> But I must at least dissent from the suggestion of the learned Lord Justice that the court, whether it is exercising its function in construing a document or in applying the law of frustration to particular circumstances, "really exercises a qualifying power ... in order to do what is just and reasonable in the new situation." Nor can I accept the theory, which appears to underlie his judgment, that in recent cases ... there has been some development of this branch of the law, which would justify such a proposition as that just cited.[426]

The House of Lords thereby reaffirmed the doctrines of the sanctity of contract and the absolute contract. A court was not entitled to qualify an absolute and literal contract in order to do what it considered just and reasonable.[427] In the 1999 case of *Eridania SpA v Rudolf A Oetker (The 'Fjord Wind')*, Moore-Bick J. endorsed this approach when he refused 'to have regard to some wider considerations of justice and fairness than the earlier authorities would otherwise suggest'.[428]

A fifth theory is that of the 'true construction of the contract'. By virtue of this theory, a court would seek to determine whether frustration had occurred by construing the terms of the contract in order to determine if their meaning could extend to the new circumstances which had arisen as a result of the supervening event. If they could not be so construed then the contract has been frustrated by the supervening event. The construction theory, as McKendrick points out, 'commands most judicial acceptance'.[429] In the

---

425 *James Scott & Sons v Del Sol* (1922) SC 592, 596. A more recent case which reaffirms both the doctrine of the absolute contract and that of the sanctity of contract is *Eurico SpA v Philip Brokers (The Epaphus)* (1987) 2 Lloyd's Rep. 215, discussed *supra* at page 157.

426 *British Movietonews Ld. v London and District Cinemas Ld.* (1952) AC 166, 188. Consider also the following comments of Viscount Simon L.C., at page 184: 'When the authorities referred to by Denning L.J. as justifying the proposition that judges now exercise a wider power in these matters than they did some years ago are examined it will be found that they do not support any such notion'.

427 McKendrick, op. cit. (fn. 226), 33.

428 (1999) LLLR. 307 329.

429 McKendrick, op. cit. (fn. 226), 33.

National Carriers case, for example, Lord Hailsham L.C. declared that it was the formulation which he personally preferred.[430]

The genesis of this theory may be found in the *Tamplin* case, when Earl Loreburn posed the question 'What is the true meaning of this contract?'[431] From this early beginning, the theory thereafter developed into a separate juridical approach to frustration. In the 1944 case of *Denny, Mott & Dickson Ltd. v James B. Fraser & Co. Ltd.*,[432] Lord Porter noted that there were three separate approaches to a finding of frustration in English law:

> Whether this result follows from a true construction of the contract or whether it is necessary to imply a term or whether again it is more accurate to say that the result follows because the basis of the contract is overthrown, it is not necessary to decide.[433]

But in this same case, Lord Wright did decide which of the three approaches was the correct one, and endorsed the true construction of the contract:

> The data for decision are, on the one hand, the terms and construction of the contract, read in the light of the then existing circumstances, and on the other hand the events which have occurred.[434]

The construction theory was also put forward by Viscount Simon L.C. in *British Movietonews Ltd v London and District Cinemas Ltd.*:

> If, on the other hand, a consideration of the terms of the contract, in the light of the circumstances existing when it was made, shows that they never agreed to be bound in a fundamentally different situation which has now unexpectedly emerged, the contract ceases to bind at that point – not because the court in its discretion thinks it just and reasonable to qualify the terms of the contract, but because on its true construction it does not apply in that situation.[435]

The theory was then articulated by Lords Reid and Radcliffe in the case of *Davis Contractors Ltd v Fareham Urban District Council.*[436] *Davis Contractors* thereafter became the benchmark case which is habitually referred to with

---

430 *National Carriers Ltd. v Panalpina (Northern) Ltd.* (1981) AC 675, 688. See page 225 *infra* for a more detailed discusssion of Lord Hailsham L.C.'s comments.
431 *Tamplin (F.A.) Steamship Co. Ltd v Anglo-Mexican Petroleum Products Co. Ltd.* (1916) 2 AC 397, 404.
432 (1944) AC 265.
433 (1944) AC 265, 281.
434 Id., 274, 275.
435 (1952) AC 166, 185.
436 (1956) AC 696. See page 182–183 *supra* for the facts of *Davis Contractors*.

reference to the construction theory, and has been referred to again and again in subsequent cases.

Lord Reid began his judgment by stating that it was 'necessary to consider what was the true basis of the law of frustration'. [437] He referred to the three theories set out by Lord Porter in the *Denny, Mott* case.[438] He rejected the theory of the basis of the contract being overthrown on the grounds that it was not a question of law,[439] and rejected the implied term theory by pointing out its artificiality: 'I think it would be difficult to say that a reasonable man in the position of the party who opposes unsuccessfully a finding of frustration would certainly have agreed to an implied term bringing it about'.[440] Lord Reid then endorsed the construction theory, and set out his understanding of the theory:

> It appears to me that frustration depends, at least in most cases, not on adding any implied term, but on the true construction of the terms which are in the contract read in light of the nature of the contract and of the relevant surrounding circumstances when the contract was made.[441]

The appeal of the construction theory, as set out by Lord Reid, is that it avoids the Scylla of the fictitious implied term, on the one hand, and the Charybdis of judicial interference, on the other. When the court has resort to the construction theory it does not imply a term to which the parties themselves had not actually turned their minds, nor does it 'qualify' the contract which the parties have made. It therefore cannot be accused of acting as an 'officious bystander intruding on the parties'.[442] The theory is thus able to reconcile the doctrine of frustration with the doctrines of the absolute contract and sanctity of contract. In this regard the court respects the actual terms of the agreement which the parties have themselves consented to, i.e. it upholds their joint will. Moreover, Lord Reid noted that the construction theory was not necessarily connected to the 'just and reasonable' approach. Quoting Viscount Simon L.C. from the *British Movietonews case*, he noted that the application of the construction theory did not necessarily mean that the court would find that 'it was just and reasonable to qualify the terms of the contract, but because on its true construction it does not apply in that situation'.[443] Thus, by doing no more than

---

437 (1956) AC 696, 719.

438 See page 219 *supra*.

439 (1956) AC 696, 719.

440 Id. 720.

441 Id., 720, 721. Lord Reid also subsequently declared that '[t]he question is whether the contract which they did make is, on its true construction, wide enough to apply to the new situation: if it is not, then it is at an end': Id. 721.

442 *National Carriers v Panalpina (Northern) Ltd.* (1981) AC 675, 687 (per Lord Hailsham LC).

443 *Davis Contractors Ltd v Fareham Urban District Council* (1956) AC 696, 721, quoting Viscount Simon L.C. from *British Movietonews Ltd v London and District Cinemas Ltd.* (1952)

construing the terms of the contract, the court upholds the doctrine of the absolute contract. This is because it simply determines, through the process of construction, whether the agreement which the parties have entered into is or is not an 'absolute' contract. It does this by analysing whether the terms that the parties themselves have agreed to are wide enough to include the supervening event, or whether their agreement is a qualified contract, in that on a proper construction of its terms those terms are found to exclude the supervening event. This understanding of the construction theory therefore would seem to be the theory best suited to reconcile the doctrine of frustration with the doctrines of the absolute contract and the sanctity of contract.

Lord Radcliffe, like Lord Reid, was highly critical of the implied term approach, pointing out that it was in most cases a logical absurdity to assume that the parties had implied a term into their contract, when in reality this could not have been so, given that the supervening event had been unforeseen at the time of the conclusion of the contract.[444] Lord Radcliffe dismissed the implied term theory in colourful language, saying that its effect was to reduce the contracting parties to 'disembodied spirits' and that 'their actual persons should be allowed to rest in peace'.[445] He then endorsed the construction theory as the correct basis on which to proceed, in the following memorable passage:

> ... frustration occurs whenever the law recognizes that without default of either party a contractual obligation has become incapable of being performed because the circumstances in which performance is called for would render it a thing radically different from that which was undertaken by the contract. *Non haec in foedera veni*. It was not this that I promised to do.[446]

However, Lord Radcliffe did not separate the construction theory from the just and reasonable approach, as had Lord Reid. Instead, he prefaced his definition of the construction theory by noting that in place of the 'disembodied spirits' of the contracting parties 'there rises the figure of the fair and reasonable man. And the spokesman of the fair and reasonable man, who represents after all no more than the anthropomorphic conception of justice, is and must be the court itself'.[447] In other words, Lord Radcliffe was in effect linking the construction theory to the 'just and reasonable' approach, and declaring that

---

AC 166, 185. See page 219 *supra*. This is also the conclusion of McKendrick, op. cit. (fn. 226), 33.

444 *Davis Contractors Ltd v Fareham Urban District Council* (1956) AC 696, 728.

445 Id., 728.

446 Id., 729. This passage was previously set out at page 183 *supra*.

447 *Davis Contractors Ltd v Fareham Urban District Council* (1956) AC 696, 728.

it would be the court who would decide what was 'fair and reasonable' in the process of construing the contract.

The problem with this approach, however, is that the construction theory might then become simply a façade behind which the courts actually do intervene to alter the terms of the parties' contract, and by doing so do not uphold the doctrines of the absolute contract and the sanctity of contract. Construction is then no longer simply a process by which the court determines the ambit of the contractual words used by the parties themselves, but rather becomes a device whereby the court achieves a result which, in its opinion, is 'fair and reasonable'.

Recently yet another juridical basis for the doctrine of frustration has been put forward, in the case of *Canary Wharf v EMA*.[448] The presiding judge, Smith J., has styled this theory 'performance rendered radically different by fundamental change of circumstances'.[449] It will hereafter be referred to as the 'radically different' theory. The phrase 'radically different', as seen above, had originally been coined in 1956 by Lord Radcliffe, and had traditionally been understood to operate within the context of the construction theory.[450] However, relying upon dicta from *National Carriers Ltd v Panalpina (Northern) Ltd*,[451] Smith J. asserted that the radically different theory was actually a separate and distinct theory, and that it, rather than the construction theory, 'best encapsulates the essence of the doctrine of frustration'.[452] In this regard, Smith J. relied upon the statement of Lord Roskill:

> What is sometimes called the construction theory has found greater favour. But, my Lords, if I may respectfully say so, I think the most satisfactory explanation of the doctrine is that given by Lord Radcliffe in *Davis Contractors Ltd v Fareham Urban District Council*...[453]

Lord Roskill's statement appeared on its face to differentiate the construction theory from the radically different theory, and Smith J. contrasted the two theories by declaring that there was indeed a 'material difference' in how the two theories 'work in their application'.[454]

In order to demonstrate how this was so, Smith J. proceeded first to analyse the construction theory and then to distinguish it from the radically different theory. Smith J. noted that the construction theory 'involves ascertaining precisely which obligations each party did and did not assume' and then determine whether 'the contract makes sufficient provision for the subsequent

---

448 (2019) EWHC 335 (Ch).
449 (2019) EWHC 335 (Ch), paragraph 28(5).
450 (1956) AC 696, at 729; (1956) 2 All ER 145, at 160. See page 221 *supra*.
451 (1981) AC 675; (1981) 1 All ER 161.
452 (2019) EWHC 335 (Ch), paragraph 27.
453 (1981) AC 675, 717; 1 All ER 161, 188.
454 (2019) EWHC 335 (Ch), paragraph 26(5).

frustrating event'.[455] If it does so, 'the contract will prevail, and there will be no discharge'.[456] But, according to Smith J., although 'the true construction of the contract may be relevant to the question', it was 'not of itself the test for frustration'.[457] This was because 'even a sophisticated contract which, on its face, appears to make provision for all subsequent vicissitudes, may find itself defeated by the truly unforeseen'.[458] 'The weakness of the construction theory', Smith J. declared, 'is that it assumes – wrongly – that construction or interpretation of the contract can resolve every problem'.[459] But in point of fact it cannot do so, and it is actually the radically different theory, rather than the construction theory, which must be utilised in order to determine whether there has been frustration:

> Whether a contract is frustrated depends upon a consideration of the nature of the bargain of the parties when considered in the light of the supervening event said to frustrate that bargain. Only if the supervening event renders the performance of the bargain 'radically different', when compared to the consideration in play at the conclusion of the contract, will the contract be frustrated.[460]

In order to apply the radically different theory, it was necessary to ascertain the parties' 'common purpose' when entering the contract.[461] This common purpose was not to be found by reciting the individual terms and conditions of the contract, but rather involved something which was 'much more elemental, that cannot necessarily be captured in their contract…',[462] In other words, finding the common purpose involved an examination of factors which would not fall within the construction theory.[463] These additional factors, according

---

455 Id., paragraph 27(4). Smith J. acknowledged that in many cases 'there may be little difference in outcome between the construction theory, and the "performance is radically different" test': (2019) EWHC 335 (Ch), paragraph 26(5).
456 Id. (2019) EWHC 335 (Ch), paragraph 27(4).
457 Id., paragraph 26(5).
458 Id., paragraph 26(5).
459 Id., paragraph 26(5), fn. 38.
460 Id., paragraph 27.
461 Id., paragraph 29.
462 Id., paragraph 29.
463 Sutherland, op. cit., 191, 192. The construction theory limits the interpretation of a contract to 'the meaning which the document would convey to a reasonable person having all the background knowledge which would reasonably have been available to the parties in the situation in which they were at the time of the contract'. It 'includes absolutely anything which would have affected the way in which the language of the document would have been understood by a reasonable man', but 'excludes from the admissible background the previous negotiations of the parties and their declarations of subjective intent': *Investors Compensation Scheme Ltd v West Bromwich Building Society* (1998) 1 WLR 896, at 912, 913 (per Lord Hoffmann).

to Smith J., had been enumerated by Rix L.J., in *Edwinton Commercial Corp v Tsavliris Russ (Worldwide Salvage and Towage) Ltd (The Sea Angel)*:

> In my judgment the application of the doctrine of frustration requires a multi-factorial approach. Among the factors which have to be considered are the terms of the contract itself, the matrix or context, the parties' knowledge, expectations, assumptions and contemplations, in particular as to risk, as at the time of the contract, at any rate so far as there can be ascribed mutually and objectively, and then the nature of the supervening event, and the parties' reasonable and objectively ascertainable calculations as to the possibilities of future performance in the new circumstances.[464]

By virtue of this 'multi-factorial' approach, Smith J. concluded that he could legitimately take these additional factors – viz. the parties' knowledge, expectations, assumptions and contemplations – into consideration, when deciding whether the parties had had a common purpose and whether that common purpose had been frustrated by the intervention of a supervening event which had rendered their common purpose 'radically different'. He noted that these additional factors 'might very well arise out of the previous negotiations of the parties and their declarations of subjective intent'.[465] Although such matters could not be taken into account under the construction theory,[466] they were 'relevant in the case of frustration' under the radically different theory, by virtue of their inclusion as the third factor in the dicta of Rix L.J.[467] The radically different theory thus widens the juridical basis upon which frustration may be determined. As Smith J. notes, the consideration of these additional factors as permitted by the radically different theory meant that it was 'possible – notwithstanding the true construction of a contract – for that contract nevertheless to be discharged if the common purpose of the bargain (which I have found to be something beyond the true construction of the contract) is frustrated'.[468]

Smith J. fashioned his radically different theory essentially upon the authority of a single quote from *Panalpina*, viz. the statement of Lord Roskill, reproduced above, which appeared to differentiate the construction theory from

---

464 (2007) EWCA Civ 547, paragraph 111.
465 (2019) EWHC 335 (Ch), paragraph 32.
466 Id., paragraph 32. See page 223, fn. 463 *supra*.
467 (2019) EWHC 335 (Ch), paragraph 32.
468 Id., paragraph 244. The claimant Canary Wharf had argued that common purpose should be equated with the construction theory: (2019) EWHC 335 (Ch), paragraph 30. This was rejected by Smith J, who applied the radically different theory. However, the EMA was not able to convince Smith J. that there had been a common purpose which had been frustrated, even under his more liberal radically different theory: (2019) EWHC 335 (Ch), paragraphs 244–248.

the test put forward by Lord Radcliffe.[469] Relying on Lord Roskill's statement, Smith J. was able to articulate his radically different theory as a separate and distinct juridical basis for frustration. But it is highly unlikely that Lord Roskill actually meant to differentiate the construction theory from Lord Radcliffe's statement. Lord Roskill stated that 'there is, I venture to think, little difference between Lord Radcliffe's view and the so-called construction theory'.[470] In other words, he was stating that they were essentially one and the same.

Lord Hailsham L.C. took a similar view. He referred to the radically different test made by Lord Radcliffe and declared that this 'is the formulation I personally prefer'.[471] But he actually situated this statement within the wider context of the construction theory:

> Another theory ... is that the doctrine is based on the answer to the question, 'What, in fact, was the true meaning of the contract"?' This is the 'construction theory'. In *Davis Contractors Ltd v Fareham Urban District Council* ... Lord Radcliffe put the matter thus, and it is the formulation I personally prefer:[472]

This is also true of Lord Simon. Although Lord Simon referred to 'the theory of the radical change in obligation' he did so by equating it with the construction theory, so that the two were in his opinion identical:

> the 'theory of a radical change in obligation' or 'construction theory" (which appears to be the one most generally accepted today.)[473]

Lord Wilberforce did not even refer to Lord Radcliffe's statement. He enumerated the various juridical bases of frustration, including the construction theory, but did not make mention of a radically different theory.[474] Lord Russell did not address the matter of the juridical bases of frustration at all.

A close reading of Lord Radcliffe's judgment makes plain that he, like Lord Reid, was actually endorsing the construction theory in his judgment. A comparison of their two judgments demonstrates that this is so. Lord Reid set out his understanding of the construction theory in the following passage:

> It appears to me that frustration depends, at least in most cases, not on adding any implied term but on the true construction of the terms which

---

469 See page 222 *supra*.
470 (1981) AC 675, 717; (1981) 1 All ER 161, 188.
471 Id., 688; Id., 166.
472 Id., 688; Id., 166.
473 Id., 702; Id., 176.
474 Id., 693; Id., 170.

are, in the contract, read in light of the nature of the contract and of the relevant surrounding circumstances when the contract was made.[475]

Lord Radcliffe sets out his approach in a passage which is remarkably similar to that of Lord Reid:

All that anyone, arbitrator or court, can do is to study the contract in the light of the circumstances that prevailed at the time when it was made and, having done so, to relate it to the circumstances that are said to have brought about its frustration.[476]

It is evident from these two passages that both judges were endorsing the construction theory. It is within the context of the construction theory that the two judges then describe in divergent language the changed circumstances which would bring about the frustration of the contract. Lord Reid declared that the contract would be terminated by frustration 'on the emergence of a fundamentally different situation'.[477] He also declared that for frustration to occur, the supervening event must transform the obligation into 'a job of a different kind from that contemplated in the contract'.[478] Lord Radcliffe declared that frustration will occur because 'a contractual obligation has become incapable of being performed because the circumstances in which performance is called for would render it a thing radically different from that which was undertaken by the contract'.[479] Both judges are describing the changed nature of a supervening event which transforms the contractual obligation into something outside the terms of the contract. Lord Radcliffe states that the circumstances must render the obligation 'radically different'; Lord Reid that the obligation must have become 'fundamentally different' or 'a job of a different kind'. Both judges clearly situate their respective tests to determine the consequences of the supervening event within the context of the construction theory.

That this is so was recognised by Dillon L.J. in the 1986 case of *Notcutt v Universal Equipment Co (London) Ltd*.[480] Dillon L.J. understood both Lord Reid and Lord Radcliffe to be adhering to the construction theory. He conflated their two judgments into a single and comprehensive assessment, which he termed 'the test to be satisfied':

If the unexpected event produces an ultimate situation which, as a matter of construction, is not within the scope of the contract or would render

---

475 *Davis Contractors Ltd v Fareham Urban District Council* (1956) AC 696, 720, 721; (1956) 2 All ER 145, 153.
476 Id., 730; Id., 161.
477 Id., 723; Id., 155.
478 Id., 724; Id., 156.
479 Id., 729; Id., 160.
480 (1986) 1 WLR 641.

performance impossible or something radically different from that which was undertaken by the contract, then it is unjust that the contracting party should be held to be still bound by the contract in those altered circumstances. I approach the facts of this case on the footing that the test to be satisfied is that explained by Lord Reid and Lord Radcliffe...[481]

Smith J. justifies his advocacy of the radically different theory on the basis that the construction theory would not be able to resolve every problem which might arise, because even 'a sophisticated contract' might 'find itself defeated by the truly unforeseen'.[482] It was thus only by resort to the radically different test that it could be determined whether a contract had been frustrated.[483] But, in Peel's opinion, this analysis misconstrues the purpose and function of the construction theory. Peel points out that the construction theory is simply 'an exercise in the allocation of risk', with two possible outcomes.[484] On the one hand, if the risk of an event is found to have been assigned under the terms of the contract to one or the other of the contracting parties, the terms of the contract will govern, and failure to perform by that party will result in breach of contract. On the other hand, if the risk is found not to have been assigned to either party, the contract may be frustrated, if the event in question is, as Lord Radcliffe declares, 'radically different from that which was undertaken'.[485] 'The conclusion that performance is radically different', Peel emphatically asserts, 'is determined by the construction of the contract ('that which was undertaken'); it is not a recognition of its limits'.[486]

There is an additional problem with Smith J.'s theory. Smith J. quotes from Rix L.J., who had declared in *The Sea Angel* that 'the doctrine of frustration requires a multi-factorial approach'.[487] On the basis of this authority, Smith J. asserts that the radically different theory allows a judge to enquire 'as to the parties' "common purpose", as discernible from a multiplicity of factors, including the parties' 'knowledge, expectations, assumptions and contemplations'.[488] This permits the judge to consider 'the previous negotiations of the parties and their declarations of subjective intent'.[489] Such enquiries go far beyond the scope permitted under the construction theory, which limits the

---

481 Id., 647.
482 (2019) EWHC 335 (Ch), paragraph 26(5).
483 Id., paragraph 27.
484 Peel, op. cit., 609.
485 *Davis Contractors Ltd v Fareham Urban District Council* (1956) AC 696, 729; (1956) 2 All ER 145, 160.
486 Peel, op. cit., 609.
487 *Edwinton Commercial Corporation v Tsavliris Russ (Worldwide Salvage & Towage) Ltd (The "Sea Angel")* (2007) EWCA Civ 547, paragraph 111. The full statement of Lord Rix is reproduced at page 224, *supra*.
488 (2019) EWHC 335 (Ch), paragraph 32. See Sutherland, op. cit., 193.
489 (2019) EWHC 335 (Ch), paragraph 32.

judge to an interpretation of the terms and conditions of the contract in the context of the facts when the contract was concluded, and which excludes pre-contractual negotiations. The radically different theory thus considerably expands the scope of the doctrine of frustration.

But as Al-Rikabi points out, 'the reference to the "parties' knowledge, expectations, assumptions and contemplations" was not intended, and should not be understood, as permitting reliance on pre-contractual negotiations that would not normally be admissible in construing the terms of the contract'.[490] This is because Rix L.J. did not make his statement with regard to the admissibility of pre-contractual negotiations. The issue in *The Sea Angel* involved the question of whether a delay of approximately three months towards the end of a time charter of twenty days, caused by reason of the unlawful detention of the vessel by port authorities, would amount to frustration.[491] The defendant had submitted that the 'critical or main and in any event overbearing test to apply' in determining whether there had been frustration was to compare 'the probable length of the delay with the unexpired duration of the charter'.[492] In other words, the defendant was arguing that a single factor would be decisive when determining whether there had been frustration of the time charter. Rix L.J. did not accept this argument, declaring that 'the development of the law shows that such a single-factored approach is too blunt an instrument'.[493] Instead, he adopted a '"multi-factorial" approach'.[494] The reference which Rix L.J. made to the 'parties' knowledge, expectations, assumptions and contemplations' involved factors which were to be taken into account when determining whether the delay constituted frustration. They were not part of some third component which would enable the judge to consider pre-contractual negotiations, as Smith J. asserted. In *The Sea Angel*, Rix L.J. was actually applying the construction theory.

It would therefore appear that the radically different theory put forward by Smith J in *Canary Wharf v EMA* may not be a valid theory. As the appeal launched by the EMA was abandoned when it was able to find a subtenant for the premises, it remains to be seen whether the radically different theory represents a legitimate development in the doctrine of frustration, or whether it will be rejected by a superior court.[495]

---

490 Zahra Al-Rikabi 'Revisiting *Canary Wharf v EMA*: Applying the "Radically Different" Theory of Frustration' (2021) *Butterworths Journal of International Banking and Financial Law* 122, 123.

491 (2007) EWCA Civ 547, paragraph 1.

492 Id., paragraph 117.

493 Id., paragraph 118.

494 Id, paragraph 111.

495 It should be noted that in the case of *Barclays Bank Plc v Veb/Rf* (2024) EWHC 1074 (Comm) Smith J.'s radically different theory was the test adopted by the High Court to determine whether frustration had occurred with regard to the performance of an arbitration agreement. Applying the multi-factorial approach advocated by Smith J., Deputy Judge

The English courts have struggled for well over one hundred years to reach a satisfactory juridical basis for the doctrine of frustration, and it can be concluded from the above discussion that this has not yet been achieved, although the construction theory comes closest to doing so. But according to Treitel, the absence of juridical connectivity is actually of no practical significance.[496] This is because the courts have narrowed the ambit of frustration to the point that, apart from actual impossibility, it will only occur when there has been a radical change in circumstances which renders the obligation different in nature, and not merely more onerous or expensive to perform.[497] This will occur very rarely, and therefore discussion of the juridical bases of the doctrine becomes largely academic. The narrowness of the doctrine, as McKendrick points out, means that whether the courts can intervene on the basis of the 'just and reasonable' approach will not actually arise in the great majority of cases, because frustration will be held not to apply to the circumstances of the case.[498]

French law does not suffer from the logical incoherence which characterises frustration in English law. To begin with, there is no concept of the absolute contract in French law. A party simply cannot enter into a contract in which the contractual obligation which he has undertaken cannot be performed by reason of impossibility: *impossibilium nulla obligatio*. There can be no contract in those instances in which the contractual obligation of the party is or has become impossible. Thus the issue of the absolute contract does not arise in French law.

The second issue, viz. the reconciling of the concept of *force majeure* with the doctrine of the sanctity of contract, or *l'autonomie de la volonté* as it is known in French, likewise does not give rise to the theoretical problems which exist in English law. There is a significant difference between *l'autonomie de la volonté*, on the one hand, and the will theory, on the other, even though the will theory originated from its Civil Law equivalent.[499] Whereas the will theory postulates that the consequences of a contract should be derived from the will of those who made it, this is not so with the theory of *l'autonomie de la volonté*.[500] Although *l'autonomie de la volonté* was paramount in French contractual law during the nineteenth century, and has since remained one of the most important aspects of French contractual law, it was actually superimposed upon Roman foundations, and functioned subject to the original

---

John Kimball K.C. concluded that performance of the arbitration agreement in the changed circumstances was not radically different from what the parties had originally envisaged, and therefore did not amount to frustration. He also found that frustration had not occurred because the parties had foreseen the risk involved. See paragraphs 38–55 of the judgment.

496 Treitel, op. cit., 649.
497 See, for example, the dicta of Viscount Simon , at page 184, fn. 225 *supra*.
498 McKendrick op. cit. (fn. 226), 38.
499 See pages 158 *supra*.
500 Nicholas, op. cit. (fn. 13), 948, 949.

Roman law framework.[501] As Nicholas notes, comparativists 'habitually point to the contrast between Roman law and modern systems – whether Common law or Civil law – that the Romans had a system of typical contracts (supplemented by the *stipulatio*, which was a method of contracting rather than a contract), whereas the moderns have a unitary system of contract'.[502] But the French law of contract has been influenced by its Roman law forebear in a way which differentiates both Roman law and French law, on the one hand, from the Common Law, on the other. As seen in Chapter 1, the discrete Roman law contracts each had their own particular rules.[503] Although French law developed a general law of contract, it nevertheless continued to preserve the specific contract types in the *Code civil*, each of which remains subject to rules derived from the specific Roman law contract types, which set out 'the essential elements of that type of contract, and the rights and duties of the parties to them'.[504] As a result, '[t]he parties freely make their agreement, but the law will, as far as possible, categorise that agreement as a specific typical contract, and the rights and duties of the parties will be seen as flowing from that categorisation rather than from the agreement itself'.[505] In other words, much of the content of a French contract is governed by pre-existing rules, as was the case in the Roman law of contracts. This is the case with *force majeure*. The concept of *force majeure* is a mandatory rule, which governs the binding nature of the general law relating to contracts, but from which there can be derogation with regard to various specific contracts. The approach of both Roman and French law is thus altogether different from that of the Common Law.

The Risk of Loss

The doctrine of frustration was initially formulated in the decision of *Taylor v Caldwell* in order to mitigate the harshness of the rule in *Parradine v Jane*, and was to a considerable degree inspired by and patterned after *vis maior* and *force majeure* in Roman and French law. But whereas in both Roman and French law the occurrence of *vis maior* and *force majeure* render a contract void *ab initio*, Blackburn J. ruled in *Taylor v Caldwell* that the contract would be terminated from the point at which the frustrating event occurred.

Blackburn J. ruled in this way because this enabled him to distribute the losses which resulted from the frustrating event more or less equally between the two parties. Once performance by the defendant music hall owners became impossible as a result of the fire the contract was terminated at this point, so

---

501 Id., 949. See also Cartwright, op. cit., 59–63.
502 Nicholas, op. cit. (fn. 13), 949.
503 See page 16 *supra*.
504 Nicholas, op. cit. (fn. 13), 949.
505 Id., 949.

that the defendants were excused from providing a music hall as stipulated in the contract, the plaintiffs were excused from having to pay the rental costs of the music hall, and neither party was entitled to sue for non-performance of the obligation due to them. The plaintiffs bore the loss of being unable to stage the performances and the defendants bore the loss of not receiving the rental fees. As Treitel points out, '[t]his division of the two risks operates as a kind of loss-splitting'.[506]

This ruling by Blackburn J. meant that the two contracting parties were still obliged to perform their contractual obligations which fell due prior to the occurrence of the frustrating event, and were only relieved of their contractual obligations which fell due after the frustrating event. The development of the rule relating to the risk of loss was thus qualitatively different in English law than it was in French law. The basic position in French law was that when *force majeure* occurred, the contract would generally be rescinded *ab initio*, and the law would attempt to put both parties back into the position at which they would have been prior to the conclusion of the contract.[507] In some situations, such as a lease, this was not possible, and in those situations the lease would be terminated from the point of the intervention of *force majeure*, with neither party being under any further obligation.[508] When loss was inevitable the law then had to determine who was to bear the loss. French law therefore developed the two rules of *res perit debitori* and *res perit domino*.[509] But the basic rule was that, in the event of *force majeure*, the contract would be considered to have come to an end *ab initio*, and the parties would, to the fullest extent possible, be restored to their original positions.[510]

The approach of English law, on the other hand, was completely different. When frustration occurred, the contract would be terminated at that point in time. The parties would not be restored to their original position, but rather would bear the losses that they had incurred up to the point in time of the supervening event. When the performances of the contracting parties fell due at the same time, this approach would bring about a more or less equal

---

506 Treitel, op. cit., 46.

507 See pages 89–90 *supra*.

508 See pages 88–89 *supra*.

509 See pages 127–132 *supra*.

510 In French law, under the previous regime, when the creditor had already performed his part of the contract he was entitled to be reimbursed for what he has already done, on the basis of the doctrine of cause viz. that each obligation is the cause of the other. This meant that when one obligation disappeared as a result of *force majeure* the doctrine of cause removed the obligation for the counter-performance. As a result the counter-performance did not need to be performed, and if it had already been performed, the creditor was entitled to restitution: see page 88 *supra*. Under the current regime, Article 1218 specifies that in the event of *force majeure*, the contract is terminated by operation of law, and both parties are released from their obligations under the conditions set out in Articles 1351 and 1351-1. (*Si l'empêchement est définitif, le contrat est résolu de plein droit et les parties sont libérées de leurs obligations dans les conditions prévues aux articles 1351 et 1351-1'*.)

distribution of loss between them. In such circumstances, as Treitel notes, 'the person to whom the thing or service was to be supplied cannot recover damages in respect of the benefit that he expected to derive from it', while the prospective supplier cannot recover the agreed remuneration or price'.[511]

However, problems arose with this approach when the contract stipulated that the respective performance of the two parties was to occur at different points in time, and frustration occurred after performance of one of the parties but before performance by the other. Given that frustration released both parties from their obligations from the point in time that it occurred, the first party would bear the loss of his obligation, since it had occurred prior to the frustrating event, whereas the second party would be released from his obligation, since it had not yet arisen when the frustrating event occurred.

This approach meant that there could be a resulting hardship to one of the parties, which would not have occurred in French law. This can be seen from the notorious case of *Chandler v Webster*.[512] The plaintiff had agreed to rent a room from the defendant for the purpose of viewing the coronation, for the price of £141.15s, which was payable immediately. The plaintiff paid £100 upon the conclusion of the contract, and so still owed the defendant £41.15s when the contract was terminated due to the supervening event of frustration, viz. the sudden illness of the king. The plaintiff thereupon claimed reimbursement of the £100 in quasi-contract, on the basis that the defendant had not provided him with a room, which amounted to a total failure of consideration.

The Court of Appeal rejected this argument. As the doctrine of frustration, unlike *force majeure*, does not terminate a contract *ab initio*, but rather does so only from the occurrence of the frustrating event, it could not be said that there had been a total failure of frustration. An action in quasi-contract was therefore inadmissible. Collins MR explained the decision of the Court as follows:

> If the effect were that the contract was wiped out altogether, no doubt the result would be that money paid under it would have to be repaid as on a failure of consideration. But that is not the effect of the doctrine; it only releases a party from further performance of the contract. Therefore the doctrine of failure of consideration does not apply.[513]

The plaintiff could not therefore recover the £100 which he had already paid, because there had not been a total failure of consideration. Moreover, as the plaintiff's obligation to pay the amount agreed upon, i.e. £141.15s, had fallen

511 Treitel, op. cit., 47.
512 (1904) 1 KB 493.
513 (1904) 1 KB 493, 499. This of course is precisely what happens when *force majeure* takes place. The *force majeure* 'wipes out the contract', i.e. it renders it void *ab initio*, thereby requiring both parties to be restored to their original positions. See pages 89–90 *supra*.

due under the terms of the contract prior to the frustrating event, not only could he not recover the £100 he had already paid, but he was also required to pay the defendant the remaining £41.15s, even though he received nothing in return.[514] The rule that the losses were to lie where they had fallen before the frustrating event could thus clearly work a hardship on one of the contracting parties when their contractual obligations fell due at different points in time.

Moreover, the rule that parties were only relieved of their obligations which fell due after the frustrating event meant that in cases which were essentially the same the loss would not be borne in a uniform manner, but would rather simply depend on when the obligations of each of the contracting parties came due. This meant that whether a particular party bore the loss of frustration was basically fortuitous rather than consistent and predictable. This varying effect can be seen by contrasting the contract in *Krell v Henry* with that in *Chandler v Webster*, both of which were 'coronation cases' and which were both frustrated by the sudden onset of the King's illness. But this same frustrating event produced very different consequences in the two cases. In *Chandler v Webster* the Court ordered the contracting party renting the room to pay the full amount agreed upon, because the contract stipulated that full payment was due immediately upon the conclusion of the contract. In *Krell v Henry*, on the other hand, the contracting party renting the room was relieved of his obligation to pay the agreed amount, because the announcement that the procession had been postponed occurred before the agreed time of payment. 'Given that a frustrating event, by definition, is an unforeseen event, it was perverse', as McKendrick observed, 'to select the date of the frustrating event as the date for ascertaining the rights of the parties'.[515]

The decision in *Chandler v Webster* 'caused general dissatisfaction and was severely criticised in legal circles'.[516] However, the opportunity to redress the consequences of the decision did not arise until 1942, in the case of *Fibrosa Spolka Acyjna v Fairbairn Lawson Combe Barbour Ltd*.[517] In July 1939 a contract had been concluded between the appellants, a Polish company, and the respondents, an English company, whereby the English company agreed to manufacture and deliver to the Polish company certain machinery, at a cost of £4,800. £1,000 was paid in advance. The contract was frustrated before the machinery could be delivered, by the outbreak of war in September 1939. As a result, the appellant had paid £1,000 to the respondents but received nothing in return at the point in time that the contract was terminated by the occurrence of the supervening event. The Polish company argued that there had

---

514 (1904) 1 KB 493, 497.
515 Ewan McKendrick 'The Consequences of Frustration – The Law Reform (Frustrated Contracts) Act 1943' 51, 53 in Ewan McKendrick (editor) *Force Majeure and Frustration of Contract* London: Lloyd's of London Press Ltd., 1991.
516 Furmston, op cit., 730.
517 (1943) AC 32; (1942) 2 All ER 122.

been a total failure of consideration, but the ruling in *Chandler v Webster* precluded this submission. Under the rule in *Chandler v Webster*, the deposit had been paid by the Polish company under a then valid contract, and therefore when the contract was subsequently frustrated by the outbreak of war the loss fell on the Polish company. The Polish company could not recover in quasi-contract, because the contract had not been void *ab initio*, and therefore there had not been a total failure of consideration.

In order to change the rule with regard to the apportionment of loss, which it considered to be manifestly unjust, the House of Lords decided to overrule *Chandler v Webster*, which it did unanimously.[518] It did so by redefining the notion of consideration with regard to quasi-contracts. Viscount Simon L.C. distinguished the meaning of consideration in a contractual sense from its meaning in a quasi-contractual sense:

> In English law, an enforceable contract may be formed by an exchange of a promise for a promise, or by the exchange of a promise for an act – I am excluding contracts under seal – and thus, in the law relating to the formation of contract, the promise to do a thing may often be the consideration. But when one is considering the law of failure of consideration and of the quasi-contractual right to recover money on that ground, it is, generally speaking, not the promise which is referred to as the consideration, but the performance of the promise. The money was paid to secure performance and, if performance fails the inducement which brought about the payment is not fulfilled.[519]

The Court was thus able to hold that an action in quasi-contract for total failure of consideration could indeed be relied upon in these circumstances, in order to recover monies paid during the life of the contract before the supervening event of frustration occurred. This finding enabled the Polish company to recover the £1,000 it had paid to the English company.

This decision went some way to mitigating the harshness of the rule which had been established in *Chandler v Webster*. However, it did so only in cases in which there had been a total failure of consideration. It did not, and could not, redress those situations in which there was only a partial failure of consideration, because it was blocked from doing so by the 1867 precedent of *Appleby v Myers*.[520] Moreover, although it gave redress with regard to the claim

---

518 In this regard see the hypothetical example set out by Lord Atkin, involving the sale of a horse which dies before delivery: (1943) AC 32, 50-51; (1942) 2 All ER 122, 130.

519 (1943) AC 32, 48; (1942) 2 All ER 122, 129.

520 (1867) LR 2 CP 651, at 660–661; (1861–1873) All ER Rep 452, 458–459. In this case the plaintiffs had contracted to erect machinery for the defendant in his factory. The plaintiffs had agreed to complete the entire work on the machinery, and to be paid once this had been done. A fire destroyed the factory before the plaintiffs completed the work. The Exchequer Court held that the fire constituted a frustrating event, thereby relieving both parties of fur-

of the Polish company, the English company had also suffered consequential loss as a result of the frustration, because it was left with a partially completed industrial product, on which it had expended considerable time and money, and for which it had received no compensation. Lord Simon adverted to these ongoing problems in his judgment:

> He may have incurred expenses in connexion with the partial carrying out of the contract which are equivalent, or more than equivalent, to the money which he prudently stipulated should be prepaid, but which he now has to return for reasons which are no fault of his. He may have to repay the money, though he has executed almost the whole of the contractual work, which will be left on his hands. The results follow from the fact that the English common law does not undertake to apportion a prepaid sum in such circumstances...[521]

Although the decision in the *Fibrosa* case removed the injustice which was occasioned by the decision in *Chandler v Webster*, it clearly had not, and actually could not, address all of the issues concerning the apportionment of loss which might arise in such situations, as seen above.

As a result, the matter was submitted in May 1937 to the Law Revision Committee. The Committee was asked to consider '[w]hether and, if so, in what respect the rule laid down or applied in *Chandler v Webster* (1904) 1 KB 493 requires modification'.[522] After examining the rule, the Committee made a damning assessment, declaring that 'a rule of law which, in the absence of a breach of contract by either party, awards all the advantages of the contract to one party and all its disadvantages to the other, is *prima facie* suspect. But this is the result which the existing rule is calculated to produce'.[523] It recommended that the law be altered as follows:

1) Money paid by the one party to the other in pursuance of the contract shall be recoverable, but subject to a deduction of such sum as represents a fair allowance for expenditure incurred by the payee in the performance of or for the purpose of performing the contract. In fixing the amount of such deduction the Court shall include an allowance for overhead expenses but shall also take into account any benefits accruing to the payee by reason of such expenditure, and the amount recovered shall not exceed the total of

---

ther performance. It further held that there could be no recovery for the partial performance of the plaintiffs, given that the contract required that the entire work be completed before payment. See also *Cutter v Powell* (1795) 6 TR 320; 101 ER 573.

521 (1943) AC 32, 49; (1942) 2 All ER 122, 129–130. In this regard see also the comments of Lord Atkin, at pages 54–55; 132, and Lord Russell, at page 56; 133.

522 7th Interim Report, Cmd 6009 (1939), 3.

523 Id., 3.

any money so paid or agreed to be paid under the contract. Loss of profit shall in no case be taken into consideration.

2) When at the moment of frustration the contract has been performed in part and the part so performed is severable, these rules shall apply only to that part of the contract which remains unperformed, and shall not affect or vary the price or other pecuniary consideration paid or payable in respect of that part of the contract which has been so performed.

3) For the purpose of these recommendations no regard shall be had to amounts receivable under any contracts of insurance.[524]

These recommendations formed the basis of the *Law Reform (Frustrated Contracts) Act* 1943 c. 40. The *Law Reform (Frustrated Contracts) Act* is comprised of only three sections. Section 1 is entitled 'Adjustment of rights and liabilities of parties to frustrated contracts', and contains six subsections. Section 2 is entitled 'Provision as to application of this Act', and contains five subsections. Section 3 sets out the short title and interpretation of the Act. The Act is limited in its application, by virtue of subsection 1(1), to those cases in which 'a contract governed by English law has become impossible of performance or been otherwise frustrated, and the parties thereto have for that reason been discharged from the further performance of the contract ...'.[525] The wording of subsection 1(1) – contracts which have 'become impossible of performance or been otherwise frustrated' – necessarily excludes contracts which contain an initial impossibility. Such contracts may be instances of a common mistake between the contracting parties, or they may be instances of an absolute contract deliberately so drafted.[526] The Act itself does not define 'frustration'; this thus remains within the purview of the Common Law.[527]

The Act has made several alterations to the Common Law. These alterations are set out in subsections 1(2) and 1(3) of the Act.[528] They were designed to enable a contracting party to recover money paid even though there had not been a total failure of consideration, and to be compensated, in certain circumstances, for partial performance. As seen above, apart from a total failure of consideration, the Common Law did not permit a party to recover monies paid in advance, nor did it permit a party to recover for partial performance.

---

524 Id., 7, 8.
525 *Law Reform (Frustrated Contracts) Act* 1943 c. 40, section 1(1).
526 See the references to the creation of an absolute contract containing an impossible term, done deliberately, at pages 157–158 *supra*.
527 McKendrick, op. cit. (fn. 315), 56.
528 Subsections 1(4) and 1(5) address the meaning of 'expenses', and direct the Court to disregard sums payable under a contract of insurance, respectively. Subsection 1(6) 'enables the court to make an award not only against the recipient of the valuable benefit but also against a person who has assumed obligations under the contract in consideration of the conferring of a benefit on another person, whether that person is a party to the contract or not': Treitel, op cit., 608.

Because losses must lie where they fall upon the occurrence of the frustrating event, a contracting party could not recover in either of these situations prior to the enactment of the Act.[529]

Subsection 1(2) addresses the right to recover money paid before the occurrence of the frustrating event. The first part of subsection 1(2) reads as follows:

> All sums paid or payable to any party in pursuance of the contract before the time when the parties were so discharged (in this Act referred to as 'the time of discharge') shall, in the case of sums so paid, be recoverable from him as money received by him for the use of the party by whom the sums were paid, and, in the case of sums so payable, cease to be payable.[530]

This provision entitles a contracting party to recover monies paid or payable under the contract prior to the occurrence of the frustrating event. In this regard, it confirms the decision in *Fibrosa*. However, subsection 1(2) extends the right to recover beyond those cases in which there had been a total failure of consideration to those in which there had been partial consideration, which had not been possible under the Common Law. The provision limits such claims to those payments made before the parties were discharged by the occurrence of the frustrating event.

This extended right of recovery for monies paid can, however, be offset by the other contracting party in a counterclaim for expenses incurred in the performance of the contract. This is set out in the second paragraph of section 1(2):

> Provided that, if the party to whom the sums were so paid or so payable incurred expenses before the time of discharge in or for the purpose of the performance of the contract, the court may, if it considers it just to do so having regard to all the circumstances of the case, allow him to retain or, as the case may be, to recover the whole or any part of the sums so paid or payable, not being an amount in excess of the expenses so incurred.[531]

An offsetting claim will be limited to those expenses which were incurred prior to the frustrating event. The wording of the proviso gives the court a

---

529 This state of affairs was cogently pointed out by Lord Atkin in the *Fibrosa* case: 'That the result of the law may cause hardship when a contract is automatically stayed during performance and further right to performance is denied to each party is incontrovertible. One party may have almost completed expensive work. He can get no compensation. The other party may have paid the whole price, and if he has received but a slender part of the consideration he can get no compensation': (1943) AC 32, 54–55; (1942) 2 All ER 122, 132.

530 *Law Reform (Frustrated Contracts) Act* 1943.c. 40, subsection 1(2).

531 Id., subsection 1(2).

considerable discretion – it may allow a contracting party who has incurred expenses to retain or recover 'the whole or any part of the sums so paid or payable' when 'it considers it just to do so having regard to all the circumstances of the case'.[532]

This paragraph, like the paragraph which precedes it, goes to redressing the limitations of the Common Law. As seen above, the House of Lords had ruled in the *Fibrosa* case that the Polish company was able to recover the money it had paid in advance on the basis of a total failure of consideration.[533] The English company, on the other hand, was left saddled with a partially completed piece of specialised heavy machinery, on which it had expended considerable time and money, but was unable to recover any of the sums it had expended prior to the supervening event. The judges acknowledged the inequity of this result, but were unable to grant any relief, as this was beyond the power of the court.[534] Section 1(2), however, now enables the court to make such an adjustment, 'if it considers it just to do so, having regard to all the circumstances of the case'.

The 1995 case of *Gamerco SA v ICM/Fair Warning (Agency) Ltd.*[535] provides an example of the application of subsection 1(2), both with regard to amounts paid and payable before discharge and with regard to expenses incurred prior to discharge. The plaintiffs, a Spanish corporation, entered into a contract with the defendants, the corporate persona of the rock group Guns N' Roses, in order to promote a rock concert. The concert was to be held on 4 July 1992, in a stadium in Madrid. On 30 June Spanish engineers declared that the stadium was potentially unsafe. The local authorities then banned all use of the stadium on 1 July and revoked the permit which the plaintiffs had obtained to conduct the concert. The parties became aware of these actions on 2 July. They were unable to find an alternative stadium, and the concert was cancelled on 3 July. The Spanish plaintiffs had already paid US$412,500 on account, and still owed the English defendants a balance of US$362,500 under the terms of the contract, when the permit was cancelled. Both parties had incurred expenses in preparation for the concert, the plaintiffs in the amount of some US$450,000 and the defendants US$50,000.

The court found that the contract had been frustrated by virtue of the withdrawal of permission by the Spanish authorities. Both parties were therefore discharged from the time of the frustrating event. Had the Common Law still applied to this case, the losses would have lain where they had fallen when the contract was discharged, so that the defendants would have been entitled to retain the US$412,500 which had already been paid, and would also have been entitled to claim the remaining US$362,500, as this amount had actually

---

532 Id.
533 See page 234 *supra*.
534 See pages 234–235 *supra*.
535 (1995) 1 WLR 1226.

accrued under the contract on 30 June, but had not yet been paid when the contract was discharged. Moreover, each of the parties would have had to bear as a loss the expenses which they had incurred prior to the discharge, i.e. expenses of US$450,000 by the plaintiffs, and US$50,000 by the defendants.

This, however, was not the result which obtained, by virtue of the application of section 1(2) of the Act. The first part of subsection 1(2) declared that all monies paid or payable prior to the occurrence of the frustrating event were, in the instance of monies already paid, to be repaid, and in the instance of monies payable, to cease to be payable. This, meant, as Garland J. found, that the plaintiffs were entitled, at the moment of discharge, to be repaid the amount of US$412,500 which they had already paid, and were not required to pay the US$362,500 which was payable under the contract.

The first part of section 1(2) mandated the recovery of sums paid before the discharge of the contract and further mandated that sums payable before discharge ceased to be payable, so that these amounts simply had to be repaid (or ceased to be payable) in the event of the contract being frustrated. No discretion was permitted in the application of the first part of section 1(2). The second part of subsection 1(2) dealt with expenses which the parties had incurred prior to the occurrence of the frustrating event. Unlike the first part of section 1(2), the second part did give the judge a discretion to determine whether the party to whom such sums had already been paid or were payable could offset the repayment of those sums by the whole or part of the expenses which he had incurred. This offsetting of expenses would be determined on the basis that the court 'considers it just to do so having regard to all the circumstances of the case'.[536]

As seen above, both parties in the *Gamerco* case had incurred expenses in preparation for the concert. Subsection 1(2) permitted a claim for expenses to be offset only against sums which had been paid. The expenses of the plaintiff, viz. some US$450,000, were therefore not claimable under the Act. The defendants, who had incurred US$50,000 in expenses, claimed that they should be able to offset their expenses against the sum already paid to them by the plaintiffs. The court, however, exercised its discretion to prevent the defendants from offsetting their expense of US$50,000, or any part thereof, from the amount to be repaid to the plaintiffs. It noted that neither party 'was left with any residual benefit or advantage'[537] and stated that it had 'particular regard to the plaintiffs' loss'.[538] 'The emphasis', as McKendrick observes, was 'thus placed on the "broad nature" of the discretion which the court enjoys and the imperative to do justice on the facts of the case'.[539]

536 *Law Reform (Frustrated Contracts) Act 1943* c. 40, subsection 1(2).
537 (1995) 1 WLR 1226, 1235.
538 Id., 1237.
539 McKendrick, op. cit. (fn. 234), 304. For a critical analysis of Garland J.'s decision not to award any amount to the defendants for the expenses they had incurred, see J.W. Carter and

Whereas subsection 1(2) was designed to reapportion monetary losses in the event of frustration, subsection 1(3) was designed to address valuable benefits which could accrue to one contracting party when the other party was able only partially to fulfil his contractual obligation, as a result of a supervening event which discharged the contract. The Common Law doctrine of strict performance prevented a contracting party who was unable to perform his obligation in its entirety from recovering any part of the performance, even if he had been unable to complete his performance due to the intervention of a frustrating event.[540] The effect of this doctrine was to confer a valuable benefit *gratis* on the other party. Subsection 1(3) was designed to enable redress in such a situation. The subsection reads as follows:

> Where any party to the contract has, by reason of anything done by any other party thereto in, or for the purpose of, the performance of the contract, obtained a valuable benefit (other than a payment of money to which the last foregoing subsection applies) before the time of discharge, there shall be recoverable from him by the said other party such sum (if any), not exceeding the value of the said benefit to the party obtaining it, as the court considers just, having regard to all the circumstances of the case and, in particular –
>
> a) the amount of any expenses incurred before the time of discharge by the benefitted party in, or for the purpose of, the performance of the contract, including any sums recoverable by that party under the last foregoing subsection, and
> b) the effect, in relation to the said benefit, of the circumstances giving rise to the frustration of the contract. [541]

This subsection now undoes the effects of the Common Law doctrine of strict performance when frustration has resulted in the discharge of the contract before completion of the party's obligation, by permitting that party to make a claim for any valuable benefit which has been conferred on the other party prior to discharge. A claim of this nature will be subject to the discretion of the court, which must consider whether such a claim is 'just, having regard to all the circumstances of the case'. In this regard, the court must take two matters 'in particular' into account. These two matters are set out in subsections (a) and (b), viz. any expenses incurred before the time of discharge by

---

Gregory Tolhurst 'Gigs N' Restitution – Frustration and the Statutory Adjustment of Payments and Expenses' (1996) 10 *Journal of Contract Law* 264, 268–270.

540 See *Cutter v Powell* (1795) 6 TR 320; 101 ER 573; *Appleby v Myers* (1867) LR 2 CP 651; (1861–1873) All ER Rep. 452.

541 *Law Reform (Frustrated Contracts) Act* 1943 c. 40, subsection 1(3).

the benefitted party, and the impact which the circumstances of the frustrating event have had on the value of the benefit.[542]

Subsection 1(3) was first applied in the case of *BP Exploration Co. (Libya) Ltd. v Hunt (No. 2)*.[543] The defendant Hunt had been granted an oil concession in Libya, but lacked the resources, equipment and expertise to explore and develop the concession. He therefore entered into an agreement with the plaintiff, BP Exploration, which did possess these attributes. The defendant assigned to the plaintiff a half share in the concession, and the plaintiff agreed to explore, develop and operate the whole of the concession entirely from its own resources and at its own expense, thereby assuming the risks of the venture. The plaintiff also agreed to pay the defendant 'farm-in' contributions of two million American dollars and four million barrels of Iranian oil. If the exploration and development of the concession resulted in the production of oil in commercially viable quantities, the operating expenses would then be borne equally by the plaintiff and the defendant. Moreover, the plaintiff would then receive three-eighths of the defendant's half share of the oil produced, until 125 percent of the 'farm-in' contributions and one-half of the costs of exploration and development had been recovered. These reimbursement payments were to be made in oil.

The exploration of the concession led to the discovery of an extremely large and lucrative oil field. This led to the erection of wells and the building of a pipeline and the generation of considerable profits for BP Exploration and Hunt. In 1971 the Government of Libya was overthrown in a revolution, and the new government, led by Muammar Gaddafi, expropriated the plaintiff's half share in the oil field. Two years later, the Libyan Government also expropriated the half share of the defendant. Neither party received adequate compensation. When the expropriation of its half share took place in 1971, the plaintiff had recovered approximately half of its costs from the defendant under their agreement.

The plaintiffs argued that the contract had been frustrated by the expropriation of its half share, and claimed such sums of money as the Court considered just, under section 1(3) of the Act, for the benefits which the defendant had received from the plaintiff for its performance of the contract prior to its frustration. The case was decided at first instance by Goff J.[544] Goff J. found that the contract had indeed been frustrated by the actions of the Libyan

---

542 Id., subsection 1(3)(a)(b).

543 (1979) 1 WLR 783 (QBD); (1982) 1 All ER 925 (HL).

544 *BP Exploration Co. (Libya) Ltd. v Hunt (No. 2)* (1979) 1 WLR 783; (1982) 1 All ER 925. Baker notes that '(t)he case was fortunate in its judge, Robert Goff J.', as 'readers will be grateful for the clarity of Goff J.'s judgment'. Baker then adds that Goff J. 'not only set a precedent in law reporting by drafting the W.L.R. headnote himself, but at the same time reworked the relevant part of *Goff and Jones* (2nd ed. (1978), appendix) to accommodate his judgment': J.H. Baker 'Frustration and Unjust Enrichment' (1979) 38 *Cambridge Law Journal* 266, 268.

Government. He then analysed subsection 1(3) in detail and held that the sub-section should be applied in a three-step process. First, the 'valuable benefit' referred to in the subsection had to be identified.[545] Second, the benefit had to be valued.[546] Third, the Court had to make an assessment of a 'just sum'.[547] The relevant benefit, Goff J. stated, must in all cases 'have been obtained by the defendant by reason of something done by the plaintiff'.[548] The valuation of the benefit was contingent on subsection 1(3)(b), which 'makes it plain that the plaintiff is to take the risk of depreciation or destruction by the frustrating event'.[549] Goff J. therefore concluded that the value of the benefit 'must surely be measured upon the benefit as at the date of frustration', so that it was the end product which constituted the benefit.[550] In making an assessment of the just sum Goff J. noted that the 'principle underlying the Act is prevention of the unjust enrichment of the defendant at the plaintiff's expense'.[551] This would be calculated in much the same way as a claim in restitution:

> ... where (as in the case of a benefit conferred under a contract thereafter frustrated) the benefit has been requested by the defendant, the basic measure of recovery in restitution is the reasonable value of the plain-tiff's performance – in a case of services a quantum meruit or reasonable remuneration, and in a case of goods, a quantum valebat or reasonable price.[552]

But, as Goff J. pointed out, when the actual benefit received by the defendant was less than the just sum to which the plaintiff would otherwise be entitled, the Court was limited by subsection 1(3) to awarding a sum which was no more than equal to the defendant's benefit.[553]

At the time of the frustration of the contract, the plaintiff had paid the defendant some 9 million dollars, had spent about 87 million dollars on explo-ration and development and had recovered approximately 62 million dol-lars.[554] Goff J. calculated that the defendant had received a 'valuable benefit' of approximately 85 million dollars.[555] However, he awarded the plaintiff a just sum of only 35 million dollars. He arrived at this sum by adding the amount

---

545 *BP Exploration Co. (Libya) Ltd. v Hunt (No. 2)* (1979) 1 WLR 783, 802; (1982) 1 All ER 925, 940.
546 Id., 802–805; Id. 940–943.
547 Id., 805–806; Id. 942–943.
548 Id., 802; Id., 940.
549 Id., 803; Id., 940.
550 Id., 803; Id., 941.
551 Id., 805; Id., 942.
552 Id., 805; Id., 942.
553 Id., 805; Id., 942.
554 *BP Exploration Co. (Libya) Ltd. v Hunt (No. 2)* (1979) 1 WLR 783, 827; (1982) 1 All ER 925, 960.
555 Id., 821, 827; Id., 955, 960.

paid by the plaintiff to the defendant with the sum of 87 million spent by the plaintiff on development and then subtracting the amount of 62 million dollars which the plaintiffs had recovered.[556]

The decision of Goff J. was appealed to the Court of Appeal[557] by both the plaintiff and the defendant, and then to the House of Lords by the defendant.[558] The appeal and cross-appeal were unanimously rejected in the Court of Appeal, and the defendant's appeal, on narrower grounds, was unanimously rejected in the House of Lords. In the Court of Appeal, Lawton L.J. declared that the role of the judge under subsection 1(3) of the Act was simply 'to fix a sum which he considers just'.[559] The Court of Appeal will not ordinarily overturn a trial judge's assessment in this regard:

> What was difficult was the assessment of the sum which the court considered just, having regard to all the circumstances of the case. Save for what is mentioned in paras (a) and (b), the subsection gives no help as to how, or on what principles, the court is to make its assessment as to what factors it is to take into account. The responsibility lies with the judge: he has to fix a sum which he, not an appellate court, considers just. This word connotes the mental processes going to forming an opinion. What is just is what the trial judge thinks is just. That being so, an appellate court is not entitled to interfere with his decision unless it is so plainly wrong that it cannot be just.[560]

McKendrick is critical of this aspect of Lawton L.J.'s judgment. He points out that 'it is regrettable that the Court of Appeal did not establish guidelines to assist trial judges in the exercise of their discretion and to ensure a measure of consistency in decided cases and out of court settlements'.[561]

Section 2 of the Act sets out a number of general provisions relating to its application. Subsection 2(1) limits the application of the Act to contracts which have been frustrated on or after 1 July 1943. Subsection 2(2) declares that the Act binds the Crown. Subsection 2(3) permits contracting parties to exclude the application of the Act by inserting a provision addressing the consequences of frustration. Subsection 2(4) addresses the issue of a contract's severability and its consequences. Subsection 2(5) sets out three types of contract to which the Act does not apply, in subsections (a), (b) and (c). These three types of contract are, respectively, contracts for the carriage of goods by

---

556 Id., 827; Id., 960.
557 *BP Exploration Co (Libya) Ltd v Hunt (No. 2)* (1982) 1 All ER 978.
558 *BP Exploration Co (Libya) Ltd v Hunt (No. 2)* (1982) 1 All ER 986.
559 *BP Exploration Co (Libya) Ltd v Hunt (No. 2)* (1982) 1 All ER 978, 983.
560 Id., 980.
561 McKendrick, op. cit. (fn. 234), 305. See also the criticisms of Charles Mitchell, Paul Mitchell and Stephen Waterson (editors) *Goff & Jones on Unjust Enrichment* (tenth edition) London: Thomson Reuters, 2022, 542–543.

sea or a charterparty,[562] contracts of insurance and certain contracts for the sale of goods. Subsection 2(5)(c) specifies two such types of contracts, viz. '[a]ny contract to which section seven of the *Sale of Goods Act, 1893*' applies, and 'any other contract for the sale, or for the sale and delivery, of specific goods, where the contract is frustrated by reason of the fact that the goods have perished'.[563]

The exception of contracts referred to in section 7 of the *Sale of Goods Act 1893* will be analysed first. Section 7 of this Act, which has now become section 7 of the *Sale of Goods Act 1979*, reads as follows:

> Where there is an agreement to sell specific goods and subsequently the goods, without any fault on the part of the seller or buyer, perish before the risk passes to the buyer, the agreement is avoided.

By virtue of its wording, section 7 of the *Sale of Goods Act* applies only to an agreement to sell, not to a contract of sale. Consequently, the exception set out in subsection 2(5)(c) of the *Law Reform (Frustrated Contracts) Act*, as it pertains to the *Sale of Goods Act 1979*, also only applies to agreements to sell and not to contracts of sale. It is therefore necessary to differentiate between the two. Section 2 of the *Sale of Goods Act 1979* defines the two types of agreement. A contract of sale, according to subsection 2(4), occurs 'when the property in the goods is transferred from the seller to the buyer' whereas an agreement to sell occurs, according to subsection 2(5), when 'the transfer of the property in the goods is to take place at a future time or subject to some condition later to be fulfilled'. The essential difference between the two resides in the moment at which the transfer of the property in the goods takes place. This is important because the passing of the risk ordinarily occurs at the same time as the transfer of the property, as noted in subsection 20(1) of the Act:

> Unless otherwise agreed, the goods remain at the seller's risk until the property in them is transferred to the buyer, but when the property in them is transferred to the buyer the goods are at the buyer's risk whether delivery has been made or not.

The wording of subsection 20(1) enables the contracting parties to agree to transfer the risk of the goods to a time separate from that of the transfer of the property in the goods. If this occurs, section 7 of the *Sale of Goods Act* will not apply and the buyer will bear the loss. But unless the parties agree to such an arrangement, the risk, by virtue of section 20(1), will be borne by the seller until the property in the goods is transferred to the buyer. Section 7 will apply

---

562 Subsection 2(5)(a) excludes time charterparties and charterparties by way of demise from the class of charterparty.
563 Subsection 2(5)(c).

in such situations, so that if the goods 'perish' before transfer occurs, the contract will be avoided and the seller will bear the loss.

The term 'perish' is not defined in the Act. The perishing of goods will include not only the physical destruction of the goods, but also cases in which the goods have become unfit for the purpose, as occurred when a shipment of dates was contaminated by sewage.[564] However, if the goods have not perished, and the contract has been frustrated for some other reason, section 7 will not apply. This occurred in *Re Shipton, Anderson & Co v Harrison Bros & Co.*, in which the government requisitioned goods after the agreement had been made.[565] Subsection 7 is also limited to 'specific goods'. 'Specific goods' are defined in section 61(1) to mean 'goods identified and agreed on at the time a contract of sale is made, and includes an undivided share, specified as a fraction or percentage of goods identified and agreed on as aforesaid'.

The consequence of exempting agreements to sell specific goods which perish from the provisions of the *Law Reform (Frustrated Contracts) Act* has been 'to fragment the law'.[566] When a contract is discharged pursuant to frustration all amounts paid or payable by the buyer to the seller prior to the occurrence of the supervening event must be reimbursed, by virtue of section 1(2) of the *Law Reform (Frustrated Contracts) Act*. Moreover, the Court has the discretion, under section 1(2) of the Act, to set off such expenses as the seller has incurred prior to the discharge, as it considers just in all the circumstances. However, when frustration occurs under section 7 of the *Sale of Goods Act* the buyer cannot recover such amounts, nor can the Court exercise a discretion to set off any part of the seller's expenses, because section 2(5)(c) of the *Law Reform (Frustrated Contracts) Act* specifies that section 1(2) of the Act does not apply. In other words, the losses lie where they fall.

Likewise, when a valuable non-monetary benefit has been obtained by one of the contracting parties as a result of a supervening event which prevents completion of performance, section 1(3) of the *Law Reform (Frustrated Contracts) Act* gives the Court a discretion to award a sum which it considers just in all the circumstances to the other party, up to the value of the benefit. But this will not occur in situations in which specific goods have perished, because section 2(5)(c) of the Act exempts section 7 of the *Sale of Goods Act* from the provisions of section 1(3).[567] Thus in cases in which specific goods have perished, the losses continue to lie as they have fallen, and the apportioning provisions

---

564 *Asfer & Co. v Blundell* (1896) 1 QB 123.

565 (1915) 3 KB 676.

566 Aubrey L. Diamond 'Force Majeure and Frustration Under International Sales Contracts' 165, 170 in Ewan McKendrick (editor) *Force Majeure and Frustration of Contract* London: Lloyd's of London Press Ltd., 1991.

567 As Diamond points out, it will be rare that a party will obtain a benefit in situations in which specific goods perish before the risk of loss passes to the buyer: Diamond, op. cit., 170. However it is not impossible, as seen in the case of *Blackburn Bobbin Co v Allen* (1918) 2 KB 467.

of section 1(2) and section 1(3) of the *Law Reform (Frustrated Contracts) Act*, which were designed to mitigate some of the harsher consequences of the Common Law regime, will not apply.

Section 2(5)(c) of the *Law Reform (Frustrated Contracts) Act* also refers to a second type of contract of sale which is exempt from the provisions of the Act. The section refers to this type of contract as follows: 'any other contract for the sale or for the sale and delivery of specific goods, where the contract is frustrated by reason of the fact that the goods have perished'.[568]

The meaning of this part of section 2(5)(c) remains obscure, as Diamond forcefully asserts:

> No one knows what the last part of section 2(5)(c) means, or whether it is possible for a contract of sale to be frustrated by the perishing of the goods without section 7 of the Sale of Goods Act applying.[569]

Furmston attempts to explain this part of the section by noting that the wording refers to cases in which specific goods have perished when the risk has already passed to the buyer, either in a contract of sale or an agreement to sell. He asserts that in such circumstances, if the specific goods perish before delivery and without fault of the seller, the buyer must bear the loss.[570] But as Treitel points out, it is difficult 'to see how such a contract could be frustrated by the perishing of goods; the hypothesis that risk had passed would seem to exclude frustration'.[571] Treitel speculates that it may be that 'the point of excepting such a case from the 1943 Act is to make it clear that the buyer is liable for the whole price and that there is no power to order restitution, or to allow or award, anything in respect of expenses'.[572]

It is difficult to understand why agreements for sale, but not contracts of sale, have been excluded from the operation of the *Law Reform (Frustrated Contracts) Act* when frustration is in issue, particularly as there does not seem to be any reason why this is so.[573] The Act should apply to all contracts for the sale of goods which have been terminated by frustration.

Section 7 of the *Sale of Goods Act 1979* specifies that an agreement to sell specific goods is discharged when the goods perish without fault on the part

---

568 Section 2(5)(c).
569 Diamond, op. cit., 170.
570 Furmston, op. cit., 739.
571 Treitel, op. cit., 631, 632.
572 Id., 632. Treitel elaborates on this point as follows: 'Where goods are destroyed after the risk has passed to the buyer, the contract is not discharged by the destruction of the goods: the statement that risk has passed means that the buyer must pay the price even though the goods have been destroyed, and that the seller is under no further liability in respect of his inability (in consequence of the destruction) to deliver them': Treitel, op. cit., 82.
573 Furmston, op. cit., 739

of either the seller or the buyer, before the risk passes.[574] In such circumstances the contract is frustrated and the loss will be borne by the seller. But section 7 applies only to specific goods. When the goods are 'non-specific' or 'generic' in nature and perish, the question then is whether a contract for the sale of generic goods is frustrated and subject to termination by virtue of frustration.

English law does not specifically address goods as being either generic or fungible in nature.[575] The Sale of Goods Act instead refers to 'unascertained goods', which are goods usually sold simply by description. Such goods are governed by section 16, which reads as follows:

> Subject to section 20A below, where there is a contract for the sale of unascertained goods no property in the goods is transferred to the buyer unless and until the goods are ascertained.

In other words, the effect of section 16 is that title to unascertained goods will not be transferred to the buyer while such goods remain unascertained. Should the goods perish by a supervening event, the seller cannot claim that there has been frustration, and cannot obtain relief under the law. This is because the seller had contracted only to supply goods of a certain description, and is therefore still contractually bound to do so. Consequently, he must obtain replacement goods of the same nature, quality and quantity in the marketplace. If he does not do so, he will be liable in damages for breach of contract.[576]

Section 16 is qualified by section 20A, subsection (1) of which reads as follows:

> This section applies to a contract for the sale of a specified quantity of unascertained goods if the following conditions are met –
>
> a) the goods or some part of them form part of a bulk which is identified either in the contract or by subsequent agreement between the parties; and
> b) the buyer has paid the price of some or all of the goods which are the subject of the contract and which form part of the bulk.

By virtue of section 20A, goods which qualify under this section will not be considered to be unascertained goods, provided 'that 'the buyer has paid the price for some or all of the goods which are the subject of the contract and which form part of the bulk'. The title to such goods will be transferred to the

---

574 'Specific goods' are defined in section 61(1) to mean 'goods identified and agreed on at the time a contract of sale is made, and includes an undivided share, specified as a fraction or percentage of goods identified and agreed on as aforesaid'.

575 Treitel, op.cit., 89.

576 Id., 92.

buyer when he has paid the price, and he will bear the risk of loss should they perish. However, if the buyer has not yet paid the price, the conditions set out in section 20A will not have been met, and the goods will therefore still be considered as unascertained.[577]

The approach of English law to unascertained goods is substantially similar to that of French law. As has been seen, the traditional position of the former French law was that there could not be *force majeure* with regard to generic goods, because in the event that such non-specified goods were destroyed, the seller could obtain replacement goods of the same nature, quality and quantity in the marketplace. In other words, in the event that such goods remain unspecified, they cannot perish. The current French law is much less clear on the matter of generic goods, and consequently remains to be resolved by the courts. However, it is likely that the same approach will be taken under the new regime with regard to generic goods.[578]

Summary

The historical development of the English legal system was unique in Europe in that it did not derive from Roman law. The Common Law is thus fundamentally different from continental European Civil Law. There was no pre-existing source of authority in the Common Law, and the law developed primarily as a result of judge-made law, within the procedural framework of the forms of action. The law was and remains pragmatic in nature, addressing actual problems as and when they arise on a case-by-case basis. As a result, the Common Law lacks an overarching logical structure and interconnected legal principles.

Throughout much of its history, the law of contract remained an unimportant and undeveloped area of the Common Law. But the law of contract came into its own in the nineteenth century, with the advent of the Industrial Revolution. The sudden intensity of commercial dealings transformed the law of contract during this period into an extremely important area of the law. The emerging law of contract was conceived of essentially in commercial terms, and consequently was characterised by commercial features such as consideration and the absence of good faith. This commercially oriented law of contract developed in the pre-existing context of the absolute contract. The absolute contract had become a fundamental part of the law of contract in the seventeenth century, with the decision of *Paradine v Jane*.[579] The absolute contract prescribed that liability for non-performance was absolute. This meant, apart from the exception of contracts of a strictly personal nature, that there could

---

577 Treitel, op. cit., 77, 78.
578 See pages 130–132 *supra*.
579 (1647) Aleyn 26, Style 47, 82 ER 519, 897.

be no escape from liability in the event that a supervening event rendered performance impossible.

It was only with the 1863 decision of *Taylor v Caldwell*[580] that a way was devised to avoid the consequences of the absolute contract. The circumventing of the absolute contract required that an implied term be found which limited the absolute liability of the contracting parties. The implied term had to emanate from the will of the parties, in order to satisfy the exigencies of the will theory. This, however, created problems, because in most cases the implied term was a fiction; the parties had never actually turned their minds to the event which occurred. This gave rise to what has become known as the 'juridical problem', i.e. on what basis might the Court terminate a contract for frustration which would satisfy the component elements of an English contract. This problem has never been resolved in a satisfactory manner.

In *Taylor v Caldwell*, Blackburn J. purported to introduce the doctrine of frustration into the English law of contract by patterning it upon the concepts of *vis maior* and *force majeure*. But given the significant differences between *vis maior* and *force majeure*, on the one hand, and the doctrine of frustration, on the other, it is doubtful that he actually did so. The new English doctrine required the finding of an implied term, which was not necessary in either Roman or French law. Moreover, *vis maior* and *force majeure* pertain to the obligation of the debtor, who is released from performance by its occurrence, whereas in English law frustration affects the whole contract, which can be terminated by either party and which comes to an end from the time of the supervening event.

Frustration did originally emulate *vis maior* and *force majeure* by requiring that the subject matter of the contract be destroyed, or that performance be otherwise rendered impossible by the supervening event. But in the 1903 decision of *Krell v Henry*[581] the doctrine progressed to address the matter of *rebus sic stantibus*, and in so doing explicitly repudiated the requirement of impossibility that was a necessary aspect of *vis maior* and *force majeure*. *Krell v Henry* has never been overturned, although subsequent cases narrowed its ambit to situations in which the change in circumstances was so fundamental that it made the contract one of a radically different kind. In other respects, however, the doctrine has continuously expanded in case after case, to the extent that it has now become ubiquitous, applying even to leases, which, given the proprietary interest of the tenant, were traditionally considered to be outside its purview.

In *Taylor v Caldwell*, Blackburn J. had ruled that the losses would lie where they fell at the point at which the supervening event had terminated the contract. However, successive cases were unable to develop a coherent approach to the allocation of loss which would be equitable in all circumstances on the

---

580 (1863) 3 B & S 826; 122 ER 309.
581 (1903) 2 KB 740 (CA).

basis of this approach. Eventually it became necessary to enact the *Law Reform (Frustrated Contracts) Act*, in order to correct the problems created by the case law. The legislation, however, has proven to be extremely complex, and fragments the application of the doctrine of frustration in ways which are not easily explainable. The Act has been subject to considerable criticism on the basis that the contract, whatever its nature or subject matter, should be subject to the same law.

Conclusion

'For my thoughts are not your thoughts, neither are your ways my ways', saith the Lord. 'For as the heavens are higher than the earth, so are my ways higher than your ways, and my thoughts than your thoughts'. *

Isaiah 55:8, 9

This Conclusion will round out the comparative analyses which have been brought to bear throughout this book with some final observations, relating primarily to the contrasting characteristics of the French and English legal systems and the impact which this has had on their approach to supervening events. Supervening events in contract law, as seen throughout this book, have been dealt with by Roman, French and English law in significantly different ways. These different approaches are the products of the wider legal context within which they have been formulated. They can therefore only be understood by examining the historical development and general character of each of the three systems, and then by examining each system's respective law of contract, which has been a fundamental part of this study. As this book has shown, there is an ineluctable relationship between the wider legal context and the way in which supervening events are dealt with in that legal system.

French law was derived to a very large degree from Roman law, and the French law of contract almost exclusively so. This law was originally drawn from the *Corpus Iuris*. But the French law which developed from the *Corpus Iuris* was qualitatively different from its progenitor and is characterised by attributes which differ significantly from Roman law. Roman law was the product of practical men, the Praetors and the jurists, who were motivated primarily by pragmatic considerations to resolve actual problems as and when they arose. They were not interested in formulating general principles or abstract concepts, which do not form a part of Roman law. Roman law was consequently a system of specific and discrete legal categories, which functioned casuistically through the resolution of individual cases in a pragmatic manner.

French law, on the other hand, although drawn from the *Corpus Iuris*, was elaborated primarily in an academic context. Standard academic methodologies,

---

* Webster's Bible (Isaiah 55: 8, 9). See www.blueletterbible/org/web/Isaiah 55.

DOI: 10.4324/9781003533450-5

involving processes of generalisation, conceptualisation and logical analysis, were brought to bear on the study of the *Corpus Iuris*. As a result French law developed into a legal system which was scholastic and conceptual in nature, and which works by way of definitions and distinctions.[1] This academic character, as Nicholas points out, 'was never lost, and has to a large extent been transmitted to the modern civil law'.[2]

By virtue of its reliance on the *Corpus Iuris*, French law has traditionally operated within the context of a pre-existing source of legal authority, where the legal rules and principles are to be found. This source of authority was originally the *Corpus Iuris*. When the *Code civil* was enacted in 1804, the Code then became the authoritative and exclusive source of authority. The *Code civil* is a closed and complete system, in which logically coherent principles and legal rules regulate and resolve whatever legal problems may arise. The law precedes the facts, and works by a deductive process, whereby the general principles and abstract concepts set out in the Code are interpreted and utilised to resolve individual legal problems.[3]

In contrast to French law, English law was influenced very little by Roman law, and instead developed largely as an independent, indigenous legal system. There was no pre-existing source of authority in the Common Law comparable to the *Corpus Iuris* or the *Code civil*. Instead, the Common Law operated by means of the writ system, which provided only a procedural framework for the bringing of an action. Each writ set out a particular form of action, briefly describing the type of dispute and setting out the procedure and method of trial for its resolution. These procedures differed from writ to writ, depending on the nature of the dispute in question. The rules of law were formulated incrementally by the courts on a case-by-case basis. Consistency was maintained by the rule of precedent.

The forms of action set out in the writ system were originally designed to address actual and recurring societal problems. In other words, the approach to legal problem solving in English law was, from the very beginning, one of pragmatism.[4] This pragmatic approach strongly influenced the subsequent development of English law, and came to be one of its primary characteristics.

---

1 R.C. van Caenegem *The Birth of the English Common Law* (second edition) Cambridge: Cambridge University Press, 1988, 88.

2 Barry Nicholas *An Introduction to Roman Law* Oxford: Clarendon Press, 1962, 47.

3 Barry Nicholas *The French Law of Contract* (second edition) Oxford: Clarendon Press, 1992, 4; van Caenegem, op cit. (fn. 1), 88, 89; Thomas Mackay Cooper 'The Common Law and the Civil Law – A Scot's View' (1950) 63 *Harvard Law Review* 468, 470.

4 David has noted that 'English law is, in many respects, closer to Roman law than the Romanist laws themselves are today, in the sense that it has duplicated, though quite autonomously, the same general evolution': René David and J.E.C. Brierley *Major Legal Systems in the World Today* (third edition) London: Stevens, 1985, 31. A comparison of Roman law and English law does reveal some striking similarities. In this regard see Obrad Stanojevic 'Roman Law and Common Law – A Different Point of View' (1990) 36 *Loyola Law Review* 269.

As a result, whereas the Civil Law is an academically oriented system, constructed in a logically coherent and interconnected manner, the Common Law is a practitioner-oriented system, in which the judges address legal problems as and when they arise, in a practical and pragmatic fashion, with little regard for any overarching theoretical basis or foundation.[5] Consequently, the facts precede the law in the Common Law. It is an open system of law, in the sense that it is never complete and is in a state of continuous development.[6] As van Caenegem notes, the Common Law 'moves empirically from case to case, from one reality to another.'[7]

The English law of contract developed in a very different manner from both the Roman and the French laws of contract. Whereas the law of contract was an extremely important part of Roman and French law, contract law in England remained undeveloped throughout much of the history of the Common Law. The very different attention given to contract law in the French and English legal systems reflects their academic and pragmatic orientations. The Roman law of contracts was the most important and innovative part of Roman law, and so exerted a particular fascination on French legal scholars. As a result the law of contractual obligations became the dominant component of the evolving French law, and consent became the defining characteristic of all French contracts.[8] In England, on the other hand, contracts were, from a practical point of view, by and large unimportant in a society which was rural and agrarian in nature. As a result, contract law was neglected and remained undeveloped during much of the history of the Common Law.

Contract law only became an important part of the English legal system in the nineteenth century, in response to the commercial demands arising from the advent of the Industrial Revolution. Consequently, the law of contract was not understood in terms of a consensual agreement, as in France, but rather as a commercial bargain. The English contract was legally binding as much by the necessary exchange of valuable consideration as it was by the mutual consent of the parties. Moreover, whereas in the French law of contract, liability for contractual breach was contingent on the fault of the debtor, in the Common Law

---

5 Legrand notes that '[t]he courts have made it clear ... that systematisation is associated with useless theorising': Pierre Legrand 'European Legal Systems Are Not Converging' (1996) 45 *International and Comparative Law Quarterly* 52, 65. In this regard the statement of Griffiths L.J., in *ex parte King*, is illustrative: 'The common law of England has not always developed on strictly logical lines, and where logic leads down a path that is beset with practical difficulties the courts have not been frightened to turn aside and seek the pragmatic solution that will best serve the needs of society': (1984) 3 All ER 897, 903 (CA). See also the statement of Lord Halsbury LC in *Quinn v Leathem*: '... a case is only an authority for what it actually decides. I entirely deny that it can be quoted for a proposition that may seem to follow logically from it. Such a mode of reasoning assumes that the law is necessarily a logical code, whereas every lawyer must acknowledge that the law is not always logical at all': (1901) 1 AC 495, 506 (HL).

6 Nicholas, op. cit. (fn. 3), 4; van Caengegem, op cit. (fn. 1), 88, 89; Cooper, op. cit., 470.

7 van Caenegem op. cit. (fn. 1), 88.

8 See pages 41–43 *supra*.

this was not so. The starting point in the English law of contract was the absolute contract, by which contractual liability was absolute. This meant, first, that a contract could legitimately set out obligations which were impossible to fulfil, and secondly, that a contracting party could be held liable although not at fault.

The very different historical context of the Civil Law and the Common Law, and the resultant very different general characteristics of each system which this different historical context has produced, have had a crucial impact on the way in which each of the two legal systems has dealt with the issue of supervening events. *Force majeure* in French law is at once derived from *vis maior* but also differs in important respects from *vis maior*. *Force majeure* retains the basic elements of *vis maior,* in that the debtor must prove that a supervening event has rendered his performance impossible, without fault on his part. In this regard *vis maior* and *force majeure* share the same common features. Both concepts constitute the antithesis of contractual liability, and therefore provide a debtor who has not performed his contractual obligations with a legitimate defence.

But whereas *vis maior* never went beyond the stage of individual and discrete instances, *force majeure* was transformed into an abstract legal concept. This occurred first by academic scholars such as Domat and Pothier, and was then set out in former Articles 1147, 1148 and 1302 of the *Code civil*. Although *force majeure* was not originally defined in the *Code civil*, its essential attributes, viz. that it be irresistible, unpredictable and external in nature, were inferred from the wording of former articles 1147 and 1148. The revised articles have now set out a definition of *force majeure* in current Article 1218. In both the former and the revised articles *force majeure* has been defined as an abstract and generalised legal concept, the elements of which are linked to each other in a logical and interconnected manner. As is characteristic of the Civil Law, the law addressing *force majeure* precedes the facts of any particular case, and this pre-conceived and abstractly defined concept will be utilised in order to resolve deductively any actual disputes involving non-performance and supervening events.

A concept comparable to *force majeure* was simply not possible throughout much of the history of the English law of contract, by virtue of the absolute contract. A defendant could only escape liability if he had inserted an explicit exculpatory provision into his contract; otherwise he would be liable for non-performance. But by the mid-nineteenth century, it was increasingly recognised in legal circles that non-performance of the absolute contract, when occasioned by a supervening event, made for an inequitable loss allocation, as only one party bore all of the losses.[9]

---

9 In *J. Lauritzen AS v Wijsmuller BV (The 'Super Servant Two')*, Bingham L.J. explained the reasoning behind the development of the doctrine: 'The doctrine of frustration was evolved to mitigate the rigour of the common law's insistence on literal performance of absolute promises ... The object of the doctrine was to give effect to the demands of justice, to achieve a just and reasonable result, to do what is reasonable and fair, as an expedient to escape from injustice where such would result from enforcement of a contract in its literal terms after a significant change in circumstances': (1990) LLLR. 1, 8 (CA).

As is the wont of English law, the solution to this problem came by way of judicial decision, whereby a judge addressed the specific issue before him, in order to resolve the particular problem at hand. This is precisely what Blackburn J. did in the landmark case of *Taylor v Caldwell*,[10] introducing a loss-splitting formula which would be borne by both parties. In so doing he devised a way to circumvent the consequences of the absolute contract.

Blackburn J.'s formulation of the new doctrine was initially limited to resolving the problem of allocation of losses when the subject matter of the contract had been destroyed. But from this first case the doctrine of frustration thereafter gradually expanded, as judge after judge enlarged the doctrine incrementally, with the resolution of the specific problem which came before each of them. In *National Carriers Ltd. v Panalpina (Northern) Ltd.* Lord Roskill, after outlining the continuous development of the doctrine, commented as follows:

> My Lords, I mention these matters for three purposes: first to show how gradually but also how extensively the doctrine has developed; second to show how, whenever attempts have been made to exclude the application of the doctrine to particular classes of contract, such attempts, though sometimes initially successful, have in the end uniformly failed; and third … the doctrine has, at any rate in the last half century and indeed during and since the 1914–18 war, been flexible, to be applied whenever the inherent justice of a particular case requires its application.[11]

The concept of frustration has thus developed in accordance with the nature of the Common Law. The facts precede the law, and the law is formulated on a case-by-case basis, by means of empiricism and inductive reasoning. Consequently, the concept of frustration has been constantly evolving. As Smith J. observed, '[t]here is no *numerus clausus*, no limited class of frustrating event'.[12]

The problem with formulating the law on a case-by-case basis, however, is that no general theory may emerge 'which would give an overview of the structure and purpose of the law'.[13] Judges deal with the specific problems which come before them, and do not necessarily consider the wider implications of their decisions. As Watson points out, judges can be in a difficult position when it comes to making law:

10 (1863) B&S 826; 122 ER 309.

11 (1981) AC 675, 712; (1981)1 All ER 161, 184. See pages 190–191, 220 and 223 *supra* for a discussion of this case.

12 *Canary Wharf (BP4) T1 Limited v European Medicines Agency* (2019) EWHC 335 (Ch), paragraph 41.

13 R.C. van Caenegem *An Historical Introduction to Private Law* Cambridge; Cambridge University Press, 1992, 172.

As lawmakers, they are not in a position to consider the legal institution as a whole. And a case when it comes before the bench may arrive at the wrong moment; the law may already be too settled to be easily redirected; or it may be so underdeveloped as to provide little guidance for a judgment which itself will determine the future growth of the law.[14]

As a result the law on a particular matter may not develop in a logical or coherent fashion. The series of English cases which attempted to develop the law with regard to the allocation of loss exemplifies this problem. In order to mitigate the inequitable consequences of the absolute contract, Blackburn J. had ruled in *Taylor v Caldwell* that the contract be terminated when the supervening event occurred and that the losses to the parties lie where they fell at that point in time. This formula ensured that the losses incurred by the parties were divided more or less equally between them. But it did so only because their respective contractual performances occurred at the same time. Blackburn J. did not foresee that his solution would not be equitable when performance by the parties did not occur at the same time. This became apparent in *Chandler v Webster*.[15] By following the precedent set in *Taylor v Caldwell*, the Court was necessarily obliged to render an inequitable decision. Although the holding in *Chandler v Webster* was subsequently modified in the *Fibrosa* case,[16] the House of Lords was stymied from formulating a comprehensive solution which would apply in all possible situations, by virtue of the earlier precedents of *Cutter v Powell*[17] and *Appleby v Myers*.[18] Eventually this state of affairs could only be untangled by the enactment of the *Law Reform (Frustrated Contracts) Act 1943*.[19]

French law has not been beset by problems of this order.[20] This is because in French law *force majeure* already exists as an abstract and generalised concept, independent of specific case law. In other words, the law precedes the facts. But this can and does lead to problems of a different order. Those prob-

---

14 Alan Watson 'Roman Law and English Law: Two Patterns of Legal Development' (1990) 36 *Loyola Law Review* 247, 248.

15 (1904) 1 KB 493. See pages 232–235 *supra* for a discussion of this case.

16 *Fibrosa Społka Acyjna v Fairbairn Lawson Combe Barbour Ltd.* (1943) AC 32; (1943) 2 All ER 122. See pages 233–235 *supra* for a discussion of this case.

17 (1795) 6 Term Rep. 320; 101 ER 573.

18 (1867) LR 2 CP 651; (1861–1873) All ER Rep. 452. See page 234, fn. 520 *supra* for a discussion of *Appleby v Myers*.

19 See pages 235–248 *supra*.

20 In French contract law, the law precedes the facts. Thus, when *force majeure* occurs, the pre-existing law mandates that the contract ordinarily be rescinded *ab initio*. Should either of the contracting parties have expended any amounts or performed their obligations in whole or in part under the contract, the pre-existing law mandates that those expenses be reimbursed in order to put the parties into the position they were in before the conclusion of the contract. When loss must fall on one of the parties, the pre-existing rules of *res perit debitori* and *res perit domino* apply to indicate which party will bear the loss. See pages 89–90 and 127–129 *supra*.

lems involve the calling into question of the very attributes of the concept itself. This has occurred at various points in the evolving understanding of *force majeure*. The concept was originally thought to comprise three essential elements, viz. exteriority, irresistibility and unforeseeabilty, which were purportedly set out in the wording of former Articles 1147 and 1148.[21] But this was then challenged by Antonmattéi, who asserted that irresistibility alone was sufficient to give rise to *force majeure*.[22] Antonmattéi's thesis was adopted by the *Cour de cassation* and became the accepted understanding of the essential elements of *force majeure*. Subsequently, in revised Article 1218, yet another formulation of the concept was adopted, whereby *force majeure* must comprise the elements of irresistibility and unforeseeability, but need not include the element of exteriority.[23] When the law precedes the facts, as occurs in the Civil Law, the very foundation of the concept itself may be called into question.

In the nineteenth century, the judges and practitioners of the Common Law were eager to seek guidance for the rapidly evolving English law of contract from both French law and Roman law. As has been seen above, the works of Pothier, and in particular his *Traité des Obligations*, were an extremely important source of inspiration in this regard.[24] Roman law was also frequently referred to, as can be seen from comments made in 1843 by Tindell C.J.:

> The Roman law forms no rule, binding in itself upon the subject of these realms: but, in deciding a case upon principles, where no direct authority can be cited from our books, it affords no small evidence of the soundness of the conclusion at which we have arrived, if it proves to be supported by that law, the fruits of the researches of the most learned men, the collective wisdom of ages and the groundwork of the municipal law of most of the countries in Europe.[25]

In *Taylor v Caldwell* Blackburn J. had made much of Roman and French law in his judgment, in order to introduce a principle comparable to *vis maior* and *force majeure*. But although Blackburn J. purportedly relied on Roman and French law, the differences between English law, on the one hand, and the Roman and French laws, on the other, were so considerable that it cannot be said that he actually patterned the doctrine of frustration on the doctrines of *vis maior* and *force majeure*. Instead, he relied upon the existence of the implied term as the central element in his new doctrine. Because the absolute contract was the starting point in English contract law, and because the will

---

21 See page 83 *supra*.
22 See page 83 *supra*.
23 See pages 87–88 *supra*.
24 See pages 142–145 *supra*.
25 *Acton v Blundell* (1843) 12 M & W 324, 353; 152 ER 1223, 1234.

theory required that the terms of a contract comprise only those terms which the parties had freely agreed to, a contracting party could avoid liability only if he could point to a term in the contract which exempted him from liability. If no explicit term could be found in the contract, the absolute nature of the contract might nevertheless be circumvented by finding that there was an implied term. This would satisfy the requirements of the will theory, as the implied term would be understood to have been agreed to by the parties themselves, even though they had not explicitly so stated in the contract. It was essentially on this basis that Blackburn J. constructed his doctrine of frustration.

In the English law of contract the will theory, and in the French law of contract the *théorie de l'autonomie de la volonté*, both require that the terms of the contract emanate from the will of the contracting parties. But whereas in French law the implied term was rejected on the grounds that it did not proceed from the will of the parties, in English law the very opposite result obtained, with the implied term being recognised on the grounds that it did proceed from the will of the parties.

Reliance on the existence of an implied term in English law, however, was in most cases simply a fiction. Although the implied term was usually a fiction, it was considered to be a 'pious fiction', as Lord Sands declared,[26] because it was the means by which the component elements of an English contract, involving the absolute contract and the will theory, could be reconciled with the doctrine of frustration. But throughout the twentieth century, there was increasing opposition to the implied term as the basis for a finding of frustration. This has led to what is known as the 'juridical problem', i.e. how does a court justify its decision that frustration has occurred. Any theory which seeks to replace the implied term must begin from the absolute contract, and must be one which does not result in the court rewriting the terms of the contract. Various theories have been put forward over the years but, for one reason or another, have not generally been found to be satisfactory. The theory which has gained most favour amongst English judges is the construction theory, which was cogently articulated by Lords Reid and Radcliffe in the benchmark case of *Davis Contractors Ltd v Fareham Urban District Council*.[27] Like the implied term theory, the construction theory is able to reconcile the component elements of an English contract, but, unlike the implied term theory, does so in a way which does not involve a fiction. This theory, however, has been criticised by Smith J., in the case of *Canary Wharf (BP4) T1 Limited v European Medicines Agency*.[28] Smith J. has argued that the construction theory cannot adequately identify supervening events which constitute frustration, and he has proposed as an alternative the radically different theory. The juridical problem thus continues to give rise to conceptual issues.

---

26 *James Scott & Sons v Del Sol* (1922) SC 592, 596. See pages 213 and 217–218 *supra*.
27 (1956) AC 696; (1956) 2 All ER 145.
28 (2019) EWHC 335 (Ch).

The juridical problem does not exist in French contract law, because in French law there is no concept of the absolute contract. A French contract will not be valid if the obligations contained therein cannot be performed by reason of impossibility. Moreover, when performance is rendered impossible, without fault on the part of the debtor, the debtor is released from his undertaking, by reason of *force majeure*. The debtor simply cannot be held liable in French law for an obligation which has become impossible without fault on his part. Because there is no such thing as an absolute contract in French law, there is no need to find an implied term in the contract.

The very different nature and structure of the Civil Law and the Common Law have also had a direct bearing on their different responses to the issue of *rebus sic stantibus*, i.e. how to deal with a contract when performance was still possible but when the surrounding circumstances have become significantly altered, so as to change fundamentally the nature of the contract. Neither the Civil Law nor the Common Law originally made provision for such an occurrence. But the reasons for not recognising *rebus sic stantibus* were very different in the two systems.

In French law the *Code civil* represents the exclusive legal authority for the subject matters which it addresses. Because the articles of the Code are the only source of law those articles constitute the only basis for the resolution of all legal problems. The French courts must therefore interpret the appropriate article or articles of the Code in order to arrive at a resolution of the specific case before them.[29] Although the generality of the articles in the Code should theoretically provide a solution to all problems, in reality codified law simply 'cannot provide for or regulate all the cases which might arise in practice.'[30] When the issue of *imprévision* arose in the nineteenth century, French law was unable to provide a solution for precisely this reason, as shown in the decision of the *Cour de cassation* in the *Canal de Craponne* case.[31] The case hinged on the proper interpretation of former Article 1134. The Court decided that the wording of the article did not permit the termination or revision of contracts involving *imprévision*. As a result a party bound by contracts which had been entered into some three hundred years earlier, and which required the irrigation of farmland for what had become an utterly derisory payment, was precluded from obtaining relief at law. The codified law was unable to provide a solution, because its wording could not be interpreted to address this type of problem.

---

29 David and Brierley, op. cit., 77.
30 John Cartwright *Contract Law: An Introduction to the English Law of Contract for the Civil Lawyer* (fourth edition) Oxford: Hart Publishing, 2023, 40; van Caenegem, op. cit. (fn. 13), 171.
31 Cass. Civ. 6 mars 1876; 1876.1.161; D. 1876.1.193, note Giboulot. (*Syndicat des arrosants de Pélisanne c. de Gallifet e.a.*) Reproduced in part in Rudden op. cit., 412. See pages 81–82 *supra* for a discussion of this case.

Unlike French law, there is in the Common Law no pre-existing and exclusive source of legal authority such as the *Code civil*, whose wording prescribes the content and extent of the law. Common Law judges instead formulate rules of law on a pragmatic and case-by-case basis, in order to resolve the actual problem at hand. Initially the Common Law did not provide relief in situations in which the nature of the contract had fundamentally changed. But this failure to do so was predicated on the absolute contract, whereby a defendant would be held liable for non-performance in all circumstances.

However, once Blackburn J. had devised a way in *Taylor v Caldwell* to circumvent the absolute contract, and thereby to enable a contracting party to terminate the contract when a supervening event had occurred, the issue of whether a fundamental change in circumstances would be recognised as coming within the doctrine of frustration was inevitably bound to arise at some point. It did so in 1903 in the case of *Krell v Henry*.[32] Faced with a situation in which the contract was still capable of performance, but in which the surrounding circumstances had fundamentally changed, the Court of Appeal decided that the doctrine of frustration would be available to discharge a contract not only in cases of physical or commercial impossibility,[33] but also in cases in which the nature of the contract had fundamentally changed.[34] Although the decision in *Krell v Henry* was the subject of considerable criticism, it has never been overturned. Subsequent cases, such as *Davis Contractors Ltd v Fareham Urban District Council*,[35] have defined much more precisely when a contracting party may invoke frustration even though the contract is still capable of performance. As a result, there is in the Common Law one doctrine of frustration, which addresses both cases of impossibility of performance and cases in which the nature of the contract has fundamentally changed.

This is in marked contrast to the Civil Law. When the French law of contract was revised in 2016, Article 1195 was included to address situations involving *imprévision*. But unlike the Common Law, which has combined into a single doctrine of frustration the cases of impossibility of performance and cases in which the nature of the contract has fundamentally changed, the concepts of *force majeure* and *imprévision* have been kept strictly separate and distinct in the revised articles of the *Code civil*. This differentiation of the two concepts into two separate categories reflects the essential character of the Civil Law. French law gradually developed from Roman law by a process of systematisation, which extended over several centuries. It is of the very nature of the Civil Law to systematise legal concepts into a logical and orderly structure.[36] As a

---

32 (1903) 2 KB 740.
33 *Taylor v Caldwell* (1863) B&S 826; 122 ER 309; *Jackson v Union Marine Insurance Co Ltd* (1874) LR 10 CP 125.
34 See pages 177–180 *supra* for a discussion of this case.
35 (1956) AC 696; (1956) 2 All ER 145.
36 As Cooper notes, in the Civil Law tradition 'the instinct is to systematize': Cooper, op.cit., 470.

result the parameters of *force majeure* have been conceptualised and precisely delineated in Articles 1218, 1351 and 1351-1, and those of *imprévision*, as a separate and distinct concept, in Article 1195. The procedure to be followed if the matter is one of *force majeure* differs entirely from the procedure to be followed if the matter is one of *imprévision*.

In the Common Law, on the other hand, impossibility of performance and fundamental change of circumstances both come within the single doctrine of frustration, so that if one or the other is found to constitute frustration, the same procedure will apply, viz. that either party may terminate the contract, which will take place from the occurrence of the supervening event. The allocation of loss will be governed in both cases by the *Law Reform (Frustrated Contracts) Act 1943*, as is explicitly indicated by the wording of the Act.[37]

The Civil Law instinct for systematisation has affected the categorisation of *force majeure* and *imprévision* in yet another way, which further differentiates the French approach to supervening events from the English approach. French law is divided into two fundamental parts, viz. private law and administrative law. A legal matter will be handled entirely by one or the other of the two parts, depending on its characterisation. The substantive laws of each part are not premised on the same basis, as the private law operates on the principle of equality and administrative law on the principle of the priority of the public interest. These two substantive bodies of law are applied in separate court systems, and do not always reflect the same legal principles, given their different orientations.[38] Both *force majeure* and *imprévision* are now addressed both by private law and by administrative law. But because the orientation of the two parts of the law is not premised on the same basis, *force majeure* in private law is not dealt with in the same manner as in administrative law, nor is *imprévision* dealt with in private law as it is in administrative law. In other words, there are four separate legal categories which address supervening events in French law.

This structural dichotomy in French law between private and administrative law does not exist in English law. Legal issues involving the public authorities are dealt with in the same courts as private law matters, and are resolved by the same legal principles. There is no counterpart in English law to the special and different provisions of French administrative law with regard to contracts. In the Common Law the same law applies to all contracts, both private and public.[39] Contracts between private individuals and the State will be subject to the same principles as those that govern contracts between private individuals. Given that the same Common Law of contract applies both to the public and

---

37 The opening clause of section 1(1) of the Act declares as follows: 'Where a contract governed by English law has become impossible or been otherwise frustrated...'. By including the words 'or been otherwise frustrated' the Act applies to those situations in which the nature of the contract has been fundamentally changed.

38 See pages 39–40 *supra*.

39 See page 139 *supra*.

the private domains, and given further that the doctrine of frustration includes both impossibility of performance and a fundamental change in the nature of the contract, there is consequently a single, common doctrine of frustration which applies in all circumstances.

The English and French approaches to the issue of *rebus sic stantibus* are also conditioned by the very different understanding in the two systems of what a contract is and does. In the French context, a contract is understood to be a consensual agreement, whereas in the English context it is a commercial bargain. As Harris and Tallon note, 'the two systems take different views about moral arguments. French law gives greater weight to evaluating the behaviour of the parties, whereas English law … is primarily interested in the exchange of economic value achieved by the contract'.[40] This different understanding of the nature of a contract can be seen in the approach which each system takes with regard to *rebus sic stantibus*. The decision in *Krell v Henry* had created unease in legal circles, because it was thought to undermine the certainty of contract, and consequently subsequent decisions dramatically narrowed its scope. In *Davis Contractors Ltd v Fareham UDC* Lord Radcliffe declared that frustration could only be invoked when the change in the contractual obligation was such 'that the thing undertaken would, if performed, be a 'radically different thing from that contracted for'.[41] The change had to be so 'radically different', in the words of Rix L.J. in *Edwinton Commercial Corporation v Tsavliris Russ, The Sea Angel*, that it amounted to 'a break in identity between the contract as provided for and contemplated and its performance in the new circumstances'.[42] The cases have emphasised that the increased onerousness of contractual performance will not enable a contracting party to invoke frustration.[43]

By way of contrast, French law has made onerousness the test for determining whether a contract may be revised or terminated for *imprévision*. Article 1195 declares that a contracting party can invoke the procedures set out therein when 'a change of circumstances not foreseen (*imprévisible*) at the time of the conclusion of the contract renders performance excessively onerous…'.[44] Clearly this test is less exacting than the test in English law. The English test requires that performance be transformed into that of a 'different

40 Donald Harris and Denis Tallon' Conclusion' 379, at 385, in Donald Harris and Denis Tallon (editors) *Contract Law Today: Anglo-French Comparisons* Oxford: Clarendon Press, 1989.

41 (1956) AC 696, 727.

42 (2007) 2 All ER Comm. 634, 664, 665.

43 In *Davis Contractors* Lord Reid observed that 'the job proved to be more onerous but it never became a job of a different kind from that contemplated in the contract': (1956) AC 696, 724. In *The Sea Angel* Rix LJ declared that 'mere incidence of expense or delay or onerousness is not sufficient': (2007) 2 All ER Comm. 634, 664, 665.

44 '*Si un changement de circonstances imprévisible lors de la conclusion du contrat rend l'exécution excessivement onéreuse …*'. See pages 95–108 *supra* for a discussion of the introduction of *imprévision* into the *Code civil*.

kind', whereas French law requires only that contractual performance have become 'excessively onerous'. The much more rigorous English test reflects the commercial orientation of English contract law, which places an extremely high premium on contractual certainty for commercial purposes. The less rigorous French test, on the other hand, reflects the moral dimensions of French contract law. The moral aspects of French contract law ensure that it places a premium on evaluating the behaviour of the contracting parties as well as addressing any inequalities which may exist between them.[45] The statements of the then Minister of Justice, Mme Christiane Taubira, at the launch of the official consultation process for the *Projet d'ordonnance* on 23 February 2015 reflect this moral dimension. Mme Taubira declared that one of the three reforming themes of the revised articles would be the protection of the weaker party.[46] This consideration certainly played a part in the introduction of Article 1195, which was designed to protect a weaker contracting party who finds himself in a situation of contractual disequilibrium as the result of *imprévision*.

The procedure adopted in each of the two jurisdictions when contractual performance has fundamentally changed also reflects the different understanding of the nature of the contract. French contracts are consensual in nature. This is reflected in the procedure set out in Article 1195, which emphasises the importance of the consent of the parties in the possible readjustment of the contract. Because *imprévision* arises when performance has become 'excessively onerous' the contract may still be salvageable if the parties can consent to renegotiated terms. The procedure of Article 1195 is therefore designed to encourage them to do so. It is only at the very last stage, when the parties have demonstrated through fruitless negotiations that they are unable to agree on anything, that the judge will then intervene in order either to readjust or to terminate the contract.

The outcome in English law is entirely different. Because the English test of frustration for change of circumstance is so much more exacting than the French test, requiring the contract to become 'different in kind' rather than simply more onerous (even 'excessively' so), the original contract between the parties can no longer exist when this occurs, and thus there must be termination.

To conclude, the historical development of the Civil Law and the Common Law has made for fundamentally different legal systems, which are characterised much more by dissimilar attributes than by similar ones, and which operate in profoundly different ways. These broad differences have significantly influenced the approach taken by the French and English laws of contract to supervening events. Some commentators have concluded that the differences

---

45 Harris and Tallon, op. cit., 385, 386.
46 *Dépêches JurisClasseur – Actualités* Jeudi 26 Février 2015 – Civil – Réforme du droit des contrats: l'avant-projet soumis à consultation, 1.
   http://www.web.lexisnexis.fr/depeches-jurisclasseur/depeche.26-02-2015/03.

between French and English law are so profound that they result in two wholly different ways of thinking, and that these separate and distinct *mentalités* can never be reconciled.[47] Whether this is so or not remains debatable. But it is certainly true that there is not, and never has been, any common understanding in Roman, French and English law about what exactly constitutes an act of God and how the law should respond to it. Apart from all else, this must itself surely be reckoned as an act of God.

---

47 Cooper, op. cit., 470; Legrand, op. cit., 60–64.

Bibliography

Addison, Charles G. *A Treatise on the Law of Contracts* (2nd edition, volume 1), London: W. Benning and Co. Law Booksellers, 1849.

Alpa, Guido. 'Réflexions sur le Projet Français de Réforme du Droit des Contrats' (2015) 4, *Revue Internationale de Droit Comparé* 878.

Al-Rikabi, Zahra 'Revisiting *Canary Wharf v EMA*: Applying the "Radically Different" Theory of Frustration' (2021), *Butterworths Journal of International Banking and Financial Law*, 122.

Anon 'Life and Writings of Pothier' (1834) 12, *American Jurist and Law Magazine* 341.

Antonmattéi, Paul-Henri *Contribution à l'étude de la force majeure*, Paris: Librairie Générale et de Jurisprudence, 1992.

Atiyah, P.S. *The Rise and Fall of Freedom of Contract*, Oxford: Clarendon Press, 1979.

Austin-Baker, Richard 'Implied Terms in English Contract Law' (Chapter 10) 225, in Larry A. DiMatteo, Qi Zhou, Severine Saintier, and Keith Rowley (editors) *Commercial Contract Law: Transatlantic Perspectives*, Cambridge: Cambridge University Press, 2013.

Austin-Baker, Richard *Implied Terms in English Contract Law* Cheltenham and Northampton, Mass. Edward Elgar, 2011.

Bacon, Francis *Maxims of the Law* (Volume IV of *The Works of Francis Bacon*), London: C. Baldwin, Printer, 1819 (first published in 1597).

Baker, J.H. 'Frustration and Unjust Enrichment' (1979) 38, *Cambridge Law Journal* 266.

Baker, Sir John *An Introduction to English Legal History* (5th edition), Oxford: Oxford University Press, 2019.

Barnes, W. '*Hadley v Baxendale* and Other Common Law Borrowings from the Civil Law' (2005), 11. *Texas Wesleyan Law Review* 627.

Beale, Hugh and Christian Twigg-Flesner 'ÇOVID-19 and English Contract Law' 461, in Ewould Hondius, Marta Santos Silva, Andrea Nicolussi, Pablo Salvador Coderch, Christiane Windehorst and Fryderyk Zoll (editors) *Coronavirus and the Law in Europe*, Cambridge: Intersentia, 2020.

Bédard, Julie 'Réflexions sur la Théorie de l'Imprévision en Droit Québécois' (1997) 42, *McGill Law Journal*, 761, 769.

Bénabent, Alain *Droit des Obligations* (20e édition), Paris: LGDJ, Lextenso, 2023.

Boczek, Boleslaw Adam *International Law: A Dictionary* Lanham, MD: Scarecrow Press, 2005.

Boix, Arnaud 'Bail Commercial et loyers Covid: la Cour de cassation a tranché dans l'intérêt des bailleurs' (11 juillet 2022). https://www.village-justice.com/articles/bail-commercial-loyers-covid-juin-2002-cour-cassation-vient-trancher-dans,43129.html.

Borghetti, Jean Sébastien 'Non-Performance and Change of Circumstances under French Law' 509 in Ewould Hondius, Marta Santos Silva, Andrea Nicolussi, Pablo Salvador Coderch, Christiane Windehorst and Fryderyk Zoll (editors), *Coronavirus and the Law in Europe*, Cambridge: Intersentia, 2020.

Boucard, Hélène 'The Curious Process of Reforming France's Law of Obligations' (2015) 1, *Montesquieu Law Review* 1.

British Institute of International and Comparative Law 'Breathing Space – Concept Notes on the Effect of the Pandemic on Commercial Contracts'. https://kwww.biicl.org/projects'breathing-space-concept-notes-on-the-effect-of-the-pandemic-on-commercial-contracts?cookiesset=1&ts=1713781018.

Buckland, W.W. '*Casus* and Frustration in Roman and Common Law' (1933) 46, *Harvard Law Review*, 1281.

Buckland, W.W. and Arnold McNair *Roman Law and Common Law: A Comparison in Outline* (2nd edition, revised by F.H. Lawson), Cambridge: Cambridge University Press, 1965 (1st edition published in 1936).

Byles, Sir John Barnard 'The Preface to the First Edition', in *A Treatise on the Law of Bills of Exchange* (12th edition), London: H. Sweet, 1876.

Carbonnier, Jean *'Droit Civil: Les Obligations'* (22e édition), Paris: Presses Universitaires de France, 2000.

Carbonnier, Jean *Essais sur les Lois* (2e édition), Paris: Defrenois Ouvrages 1995.

Carbonnier, Jean *Les Obligations* (Tome 2), Paris: Presses Universitaires de France, 2004.

Carey, Peter Stafford 'A Course of Lectures on the Law of Contract: Lecture I' (1845) 4, *The Law Times*, 563.

Carter, J.W. and Gregory Tolhurst 'Gigs N' Restitution – Frustration and the Statutory Adjustment of Payments and Expenses' (1996) 10, *Journal of Contract Law*, 264.

Cartwright, John *Contract Law: An Introduction to the English Law of Contract for the Civil Lawyer* (4th edition), Oxford: Hart Publishing, 2023.

Casu, Gatien 'Le Projet d'Ordonnance Portant Réforme du Droit des Contrats' Deuxième Partie' *La Gazette: L'Actualité Juridique et Politique de la Faculté de Droit, Université Lyon III Jean Moulin* 1. http://www.unjf.fr/cours/liste-des-cours/magazine-d-actualites-juri.../8315-le-projet-d'ordonnance-portant-reforme-du-droit-des-contrats-deuxieme-partie.

Catala, Pierre (English translation by John Cartwright and Simon Whittaker) *Proposals for Reform of the Law of Obligations and the Law of Prescription* 12. http://www.justice.gouv.fr/art_pix/rapportcatatla0905-anglais.pdf.

Chaline, Olivier *L'Année des Quatre Dauphins,* Paris: Flammarion, 2009.

Champalaune, Carole 'Réforme du droit des contrats: 3 questions à Carole Champalaune' (12 mars 2015). www.textes.justice.gouv.fr/dossiers-thematiques-10083/loi-du-170215-sur-la-simplification-du-droit-des-contrats-3-questions-a-carole-champalaune-27931.html.

Chantepie, Gael et Mathias Latina *La Réforme du Droit des Obligations,* Paris: Editions Dalloz, 2016.

Cicero, Marcus Tullius *On Duties* (edited by M.T. Griffin and E.M. Atkins), Cambridge: Cambridge University Press, 1991.

Cicognani, Amleto Giovanni *Canon Law* (2nd edition, translated by Joseph M. O'Hara and Francis Brennan), Philadelphia: The Dolphin Press, 1935.

Cohen, Morris R. 'The Basis of Contract' (1933) 46, *Harvard Law Review*, 553.

Cooper, Thomas Mackay 'The Common Law and the Civil Law – A Scot's View' (1950) 63, *Harvard Law Review*, 468.

Danzig, R. '*Hadley v Baxendale*: A Study in the Industrialisation of the Law' (1975) 4, *Journal of Legal Studies*, 249.

David, René *English Law and French Law*, London: Stevens & Sons, 1980.

David, René *Le Droit Français* (Tome 1), Paris: R. Pichon et R Durand-Auzias, 1960.

David, René and J.E.C. Brierley *Major Legal Systems in the World Today* (3rd edition), London: Stevens, 1985.

Dawson, John P. *The Oracles of the Law* Westport, Connecticut: Greenwood Press, Publishers, 1968.

de Cruz, Peter *Comparative Law in a Changing World* (3rd edition), London: Routledge-Cavendish 2007.

Deckert, Katrin 'Le droit des contrats en général et la force majeure en particulier à l'épreuve de la crise de la Covid-19' (12 avril 2021). https://www.cciparis-idf.fr.

Deleau, Olivier 'Les Positions Françaises à la Conférence de Vienne sur le Droit des Traités' (1969) 15, *Annuaire Français de Droit International*, 7.

Demogue, René *Traité des Obligations en Général: Source des Obligations* (Tome V), Paris: Librarie Arthur Rousseau, 1925.

Dépêches JurisClasseur – Actualités Jeudi 26 Février 2015 – Civil – Réforme du droit des contrats: l'avant-projet soumis à consultation, 1.

Diamond, Aubrey L. 'Force Majeure and Frustration Under International Sales Contracts' 165, in Ewan McKendrick (editor) *Force Majeure and Frustation of Contract*, London: Lloyd's of London Press Ltd., 1991.

Digest of Justinian (Latin text edited by Theodor Mommsen, with the aid of Paul Krueger; English translation edited by Alan Watson), Philadelphia: University of Pennsylvania Press, 1985.

Domat, Jean *The Civil Law in Its Natural Order* (volume 1, translated by William Strahan), Boston: Charles C. Little and James Brown, 1850; reissued by Fred B. Rothman & Co., Littleton, Colorado: 1980.

Domat, Jean *Les Loix Civiles dans Leur Ordre Naturel* (Tome I, 2e édition), Paris; Chez Pierre Aubouïn, Librairie de Messeigners les Enfans de France, Pierre Emery & Charles Clouzier – Quay des Agustins à l'Ecu de France, 1697.

Dondero, Bruno 'Le blog de Professeur Bruno Dondero – Le Projet d'ordonnance portant réforme du droit des contrats' (23 février 2015). http://brunodondero.com /2015/02/26/le-projet-dordonnacne-portant-reforme-du-droit-des-contrats/.

du Plessis, Paul J. *Borkowski's Textbook on Roman Law* (6th edition), Oxford: Oxford University Press, 2020.

Dupichot, Philippe 'Sur le Projet de Réforme du Droit Français des Contrats', *Projet de Réforme du Droit des Contrats: Regards Croisés* 32. http://www.gide.com/.../dep247_article_philippedupichot_mai2015_O.pdf.

Dupin, M. 'Dissertation sur la Vie et les Ouvrages de Pothier' iii – cl, in Robert Joseph Pothier (M. Dupin: éditeur) *Oeuvres de Pothier: Traité des Obligations* Paris: Pichon-Bechet, Successeur de Bechet Ainé, Librairie, 1827.

European Contract Code www.eurcontracts.eu/site2/docs/EuropeanContr.pdf.

Evans, William David *A Treatise on the Law of Obligations, or Contracts (An Appendix to Pothier on Obligations)* (volume 2), Philapdelphia: Robert H. Small, 1853.

Fabre-Magnan, Muriel *Droit des Obligations (1 - Contrat et engagement unilatéral)* (6me édition), Paris: Presses Universitaires de France, 2021.

Fairgrieve, Duncan and Nicole Langlois 'Frustration and Hardship in Commercial Contracts: A Comparative Law Perspective' (2020), *Jersey and Guernsey Law Review* 142.

Fauvarque-Cosson, Bénédicte 'The French Contract Law Reform in a European Context' (2014), *ELTE Law Journal* 1, 2. http://eltelawjournal.hu/french -contract-law-reform-european-context/.

Feenstra, Robert *Fata Iuris Romani,* Leyde: Presse Universitaire de Leyde, 1974.

Fenet, P.A. *Recueil Complet des Travaux Préparatoires du Code Civil* (Tome treizième), Osnabrück: Otto Zeller, 1968 (réimpression de l'édition 1827).

Fontana, D. *Is Christianity Good for You?* Alresford, Hants: John Hunt Publishing Ltd., 2009.

Fouché, Marie Laure 'Les Règles Spéciales Dérogent aux Règles Générales'. https:// fouche-avocat.fr/les-regles-speciales-derogent-aux-regles-generales/.

Fouchet, Yves 'Projet d'ordonnance portant réforme du droit des contrats: Réponse de la CCI Paris Ile-de-France à la consultation ouverte par la Chancellerie, Rapport présenté par Yves Fouchet et adopté le7 mai 2015. http://www.cci-paris-idf.fr/... /reforme-droit-des-contrats-fou1505.pdf.

Frazer, Andrew 'The Employee's Contractual Duty of Fidelity' (2015) 131, *Law Quarterly Review* 53.

Fuller, Lon L. *The Morality of Law* (revised edition), New Haven: Yale University Press, 1969.

Furmston, Michael *Cheshire, Fifoot, & Furmston's Law of Contract* (17th edition), Oxford: Oxford University Press, 2017.

Gide Loyrette Nouel 'Covid-19 and commercial rents: the French Supreme Court rules in favour of lessors in the frame of three Court decisions dated 30 June 2022' (19 July 2022). https://www.gide.com/en/news/covid-19-and-commercial -rents-thefrench-suprem-court-rules-in-favour-of-lessors-in-the-frame.

Giffard, A.-E. et Robert Villers *Les Obligations dans le Droit Romain et dans l'Ancien Droit Français* Paris: Dalloz, 1970.

Glenn, H. Patrick *Legal Traditions of the World* (5th edition), Oxford: Oxford University Press, 2014.

Goodwin, Albert 'A Re-Evaluation of the "Aristocratic Revolt"' 12, in James Friguglietti and Emmet Kennedy (editors) *The Shaping of Modern France* Toronto: The MacMillan Company, Collier-MacMillan Canada, Ltd., 1969.

Gordley, James *The Philosophical Origins of Modern Contract Doctrine,* Oxford: Clarendon Press, 1991.

Gordley, James and Arthur Taylor von Mehren *An Introduction to the Comparative Study of Private Law,* Cambridge: Cambridge University Press, 2006.

Greig, D.W. and J.L.R. Davis *The Law of Contract,* Sydney: The Law Book Company Limited, 1987.

Grotius, Hugo *De Jure Belli ac Pacis Libri Tres* (translated by Francis W. Kelsey), Oxford: The Clarendon Press, 1925.

Haeri, Kami and Mahasti Razavi 'La Prévision dans le contrat, la prévision dans le procès', *Gazette du Palais* (mercredi 29, jeudi 30 décembre 2010), 14.

Hall, C.G. 'An Unsearchable Providence: The Lawyer's Concept of Act of God' (1993) 13, *Oxford Journal of Legal Studies* 227.

Halpérin, Jean-Louis. *L'Impossible Code Civil* Paris: Presses Universitaires de, France, 1992.

Hardy, Marine et Jean-Baptiste Olivo 'Est-il possible de renégocier son contrat si le prix de l'énergie est devenu trop onéreux?' (samedi 18 février 2023). https://www.village-justice.com/articles/est-possible-renegocier-son-contrat-prix-energie-est-devenu-trop-onereux,45236.html.

Harris, Donald and Denis Tallon 'Conclusion' 379, in Donald Harris and Denis Tallon (editors) *Contract Law Today: Anglo-French Comparisons,* Oxford: Clarendon Press, 1989.

Harris, Donald and Denis Tallon (editors) *Contract Law Today: Anglo-French Comparisons,* Oxford: Clarendon Press, 1989.

Herbert, A.P. 'Dahlia, Ltd. v Yvonne (Act of God)' 314, in *Uncommon Law,* London: Methuen & Co. Ltd., 1935.

Holmes, O.W., Jr., *The Common Law* Project Gutenberg, 1881. https://www.gutenberg.org.

Hondius, Ewoud and Hans Christoph Grogoleit. *Unexpected Circumstances in European Contract Law,* Cambridge: Cambridge University Press, 2011.

Horne, Alistair. *The Age of Napoleon,* London: Phoenix, 2005.

Horowitz, Morton J. 'The Historical Foundations of Modern Contract Law' (1974) 87, *Harvard Law Review* 917.

Hubrecht, G. *Droit Civil* (15ᵉ èdition), Paris: Sirey, 1993.

Ibbetson, David. 'Historical Introduction' 1, in M.P. Furmston (editor) *Cheshire, Fifoot and Furmston's Law of Contract* (17th edition), Oxford: Oxford University Press, 2017.

Ibbetson, D.J. *A Historical Introduction to the Law of Obligations,* Oxford: Oxford University Press, 1999.

Ibbetson, D.J. 'Natural Law and Common Law' (2001) 5, *Edinburgh Law Review* 4.

Institutes of Justinian (5th edition, translated by J.B. Moyle), Oxford: Clarendon Press, 1913.

Jacquot, Pascal - Dalloz-Actualité (Edition du 22 septembre 2022) 'Covid et Perte de la Chose Louée: Premier Arrêt au Fond' (25 mai 2021). https://www.dalloz-actualite.fr.

Jolowicz, H.F. 'Academic Elements in Roman Law' (1932) 48, *Law Quarterly Review* 171.

Jones, William *An Essay on the Law of Bailments,* London: J. Nichols, 1781, reprinted New York and London: Garland Publishing Inc., 1978.

Kelly, Cliona '*Paradine v. Jane*: A Doctrine of Absolute Contractual Liability?' (2004) 12, *Irish Student Law Review* 64.

Kelly, J.M. *A Short History of Western Legal Theory,* Oxford: Clarendon Press, 1992.

Kitson, Frank. *Prince Rupert: Admiral and General at Sea,* London: Constable, 1998.

Kitson, Frank. *Prince Rupert: Portrait of a Soldier,* London: Constable, 1994.

Lacoste, Margot et Christophe Sciot-Siegrist. 'Baux commerciaux et état d'urgence sanitaire: commentaire des arrêts de la Cour de cassation du 30 juin 2022', *Le Monde du Droit* (5 juillet 2022). https://www.lemondedudroit.fr/decryptages/82579-baux-commerciaux-..e-sanitaire-commentaire-arrets-courdecassation-30-juin-2022.html.

Larroumet, Christian, Sarah Bros. *Droit Civil: Les Obligations: Le Contrat (Tome III: 1re partie: Conditions de formation)* (10e édition), Paris: Economica, 2021.

Latina, Mathias '*L'imprévision* Blog Réforme du droit des obligations (Le blog Dalloz dédié à la réforme du droit des obligations)' http://reforme-obligations.dalloz.fr /2015/03/23/limprevision/.

Lawson, F.H. *A Common Lawyer Looks at the Civil Law,* Ann Arbor: University of Michigan Law School, 1953, Reprinted by William S. Hein & Company Buffalo, 1988.

Lebigre, Arlette *La Justice du Roi,* Bruxelles: Editions Complexe, 1995.

Legrand, Pierre 'European Legal Systems Are Not Converging' (1996) 45, *International and Comparative Law Quarterly* 52.

Legrand, Pierre 'Judicial Revision of Contracts in French Law: A Case Study' (1988) 62, *Tulane Law Review* 963.

Legrand, Pierre 'The Impossibility of Legal Transplants' (1997) 4, *Maastricht Journal of European and Comparative Law* 111.

Lorant, Philippe, Arnaud Raynouard et Adélie Grimaldi (Deloitte. Société d'Avocats) 'Théorie de l'imprévision: que retenir de l'application de l'article 1195 du Code civil par le Tribunal de commerce de Paris ?' (13 février 2023), 1. https://blog .avocats.deloitte.fr/theorie-de-limprevision-que-retenir-de-lapplication-de-larticle -1195-du-code-civil-par-le-tribunal-de-commerce-de-paris.

MacMillan, Catherine 'Covid-19 and the Problem of Frustrated Contracts' (2021) 32, *King's Law Journal* 60.

Maine, Sir Henry *Ancient Law* (10th edition), London: John Murray, Albemarle Street, W., 1920.

Mainguy, Daniel 'Le Blog de Daniel Mainguy: La Réforme du Droit des Contrats et des Obligations' http://www.daniel-mainguy.fr/article-la-reforme-du-droit-des -contrats-et-des-obligations 15/06/2015.

Maitland, F.W. *Equity,* Cambridge: At the University Press, 1936.

Maitland, Frederick W. *The Forms of Action at Common Law,* Cambridge: At the University Press, 1936.

Marsh, P.D.V. *Comparative Contract Law: England, France, Germany,* Aldershot: Gower Publishing, 1993.

McElroy, Roy Granville. *Impossibility of Performance* Cambridge: At the University Press, 1941.

McElroy, Roy Granville and Glanville Williams. 'The Coronation Cases – I' (1941) 4, *The Modern Law Review* 241.

McKendrick, Ewan, 'Brexit, Uncertainty and the Doctrine of Frustration' (2019) 34, *Journal of International Banking Law and Regulation* 199.

McKendrick, Ewan, 'The Consequences of Frustration – The Law Reform (Frustrated Contracts) Act 1943' 51, in Ewan McKendrick (editor) *Force Majeure and Frustration of Contract,* London: Lloyd's of London Press Ltd., 1991.

McKendrick, Ewan. *Contract Law* (14th edition), London: Red Globe Press, 2021.

McKendrick, Ewan. 'Frustration and Force Majeure – Their Relationship and a Comparative Assessment' 27, in Ewan McKendrick (editor) *Force Majeure and Frustration of Contract,* London: Lloyd's of London Press Ltd., 1991.

McMeel, Gerard 'Pillans v Van Mierop (1765)' 23, in Charles Mitchell and Paul Mitchell (editors) *Landmark Cases in the Law of Contract,* Oxford and Portland: Hart Publishing, 2008.

Mercadal, Barthélemy *Réforme du Droit des Contrats* LeVallois: Editions Francis Lefebvre, 2016.

Merryman, J.H. *The Civil Law Tradition,* Stanford: Stanford University Press, 1985.

Mignot, Marc. 'Commentaire Article par Article de l'Ordonnance du 10 février 2016 portant réforme du droit des contrats, du régime général et la preuve des obligations (VI)' *Petites Affiches*, No. 67, 04/04/2016, 5.

Ministère de la Justice *Projet de réforme du droit des contrats* (juillet 2008). http:/www .chairejib.ca/files/sites/38/2010/07/reforme_all.pdf.

Ministère de la Justice République Française *Projet d'ordonnance portant réforme du droit des contrats, du régime général des obligations et de la preuve des obligations.* http:// www.justice.gouv.fr/publications/j21_projet_ord_reforme_contrats_2015.pdf.

Mitchell, Catherine 'What Does Covid-19 Teach Us About English Contract Law?', *Cambridge Core,* (Published online by Cambridge University Press) (8 February 2024), 1. https://www.cambridge.org/core/journals/legal-studies/article/what -does-covid19-teach-us-about-english-contract-law/700EE330C37F60F6C37 F60CF0707B07B7EEBF9E.

Mitchell, Charles, Paul Mitchell and Stephen Waterson (editors). *Goff & Jones on Unjust Enrichment* (10th edition), London: Thomson Reuters, 2022.

Moore, Anthony P., Scott Grattan and Lynden Griggs. *Real Property Law* (6th edition), Sydney: Thomson Reuters (Professional) Australia Limited, 2016.

Nicholas, Barry. *The French Law of Contract* (2nd edition), Oxford: Clarendon Press, 1992.

Nicholas, Barry. *An Introduction to Roman Law,* Oxford: Clarendon Press, 1962.

Nicholas, Barry. 'Rules and Terms – Civil Law and Common Law' (1974) 48, *Tulane Law Review* 946.

Nicholas, Barry. 'The Obligation to Disclose Information – The English Report' 166 in Donald Harris and Denis Tallon (editors) *Contract Law Today: Anglo-French Comparisons,* Oxford: Clarendon Press, 1989.

Niort, Jean-François *Homo Civilis, Contribution à l'Histoire du Code civil français (1804 – 1965),* Presses universitaires d'Aix-Marseille, 2015, 526.

Osborne Clarke 'Covid 19 lockdowns & commercial rents' (4 July 2022). https:// www.osborneclarke.com/insights/covid-19-lockdowns-commercial-rents.

Parry, Sir David Hughes *The Sanctity of Contracts in English Law* London: Stevens & Sons Limited, 1959, Reprinted London: Sweet & Maxwell, Littleton, Colorado: Fred B Rothman & Co., 1986.

Pédamon, Catherine and Radosveta Vassileva. 'Contractual Performance in COVID-19 Times: Does Anglo-French Legal History Repeat Itself?' (2021) 29, *European Review of Private Law* 3.

Peel, Edwin *Frustration and Force Majeure* (4th edition), London: Thomson Reuters, trading as Sweet & Maxwell, 2022.

Perillo, J.M. 'Robert J Pothier's Influence on the Common Law of Contract' (2005) 11, *Texas Wesleyan Law Rev* 267.

Peyron, Jean-Marc. 'La destruction partielle d'un immeuble devenu impropre à la destruction du bail entraîne la résiliation de plein droit du bail' (14 juin 2018). lexplicite.fr/la-destruction-dun-immeuble-devenu-impropre-a-la-destination-prevu e-au-bail.

Pothier, Robert Joseph. (M. Dupin: éditeur) *Oeuvres de Pothier: Traité des Obligations,* Paris: Pichon-Bechet, Successeur de Bechet Aîné, Librairie, 1827.

Pothier, Robert Joseph (M. Dupin: éditeur) *Oeuvres de Pothier: Traité du Contrat de Vente* (Tome deuxième), Paris: Béchet Aîné, Librairie, 1824.

Pothier, Robert Joseph. *Treatise on the Contract of Sale by R.J. Pothier* (translated by L.S. Cushing), Boston: Charles C. Little and James Brown, 1839.

Pothier, Robert Joseph. *A Treatise on the Law of Obligations, or Contracts* (volume 1, translated by William David Evans), Philadelphia: Robert H. Small, 1826.

Potter, Harold. *An Historical Introduction to English Law and Its Institutions* (2nd edition), London: Sweet & Maxwell Limited, 1943.

Prichard, A.M. *Leage's Roman Private Law*, London: MacMillan & Co Ltd., 1961.

Rapport au Président de la République relative à l'ordonnance no 2016-131 du 10 février 2016 portant réforme du droit des contrats, du régime général et de la preuve des obligations.

Réformer le droit des contrats, Présentation en Conseil des ministres le 25 février 2015, Lancement d'une grande consultation. www.justice.gouv.fr/publication/j21dp _projet_ord_reforme_contrats_2015.pdf.

Robinson, O.F., T.D. Fergus and W.M. Gordon *European Legal History* (2nd edition), London: Butterworths, 1994.

Rosher. Peter 'Fears Over French Contract Law Rewrite Largely Overblown, Says Expert Outlaw.Com' *Legal News and Guidance from Pinsent Masons.* http://www .outlaw.com/en/articles/2015/may/fears-over-french-contract-law-rewrite-are -largely-overblown-says-expert/.

Rouhette, Georges 'The Obligatory Force of Contract in French Law' 38, in Donald Harris and Denis Tallon (editors) *Contract Law Today: Anglo-French Comparisons,* Oxford: Clarendon Press, 1989.

Rowan, Salène. *The New French Law of Contract,* Oxford: Oxford University Press, 2022.

Rudden, Bernard. *A Sourcebook on French Law* (3rd edition), Oxford: Clarendon Press, 1991.

Rudden, Bernard. 'Pothier et la *Common Law*' 91, in Joël Monéger, Jean-Louis Sourioux et Aline Terrasson de Fougères (éditeurs) *Robert-Joseph Pothier, d'hier à aujourd'hui,* Paris: Economica, 2001.

Ryan, K.W. *An Introduction to the Civil Law,* Brisbane: The Law Book Co. of Australasia Pty. Ltd., 1962.

Scalise, Ronald J. Jr. 'Classifying and Clarifying Contracts' (2016) 76, *Louisiana Law Review* 1064.

Schiavone, Aldo *The Invention of Law in the West,* Cambridge, Massachusetts: The Belknap Press of Harvard University Press, 2012.

Simpson, A.W.B. 'Historical Introduction' 1 in M.P. Furmston (editor) *Cheshire, Fifoot and Furmston's Law of Contract* (16th edition), Oxford: Oxford Univeristy Press, 2012.

Simpson, A.W.B. 'Innovation in Nineteenth Century Contract Law' 171 in A.W.B. Simpson *Legal Theory and Legal History,* London: The Hambleton Press, 1987.

Simpson, A.W.B. *Invitation to Law,* Oxford: Basil Blackwell Ltd., 1988.

Soulier Avocats 'Reform of French Contract Law – Ratification Law Published on April 21, 2018: General Presentation' (30 May 2018), 1. http://www.soulier-avocats .com/en/reform-of-french-contract-law-ratification-law-published-on-april-21 -2018-general-presentation/.

St Augustine *Exposition on the Book of Psalms (Psalm 5, paragraph 7)* Christian Classics Ethereal Library. www.ccel.org/ccel/schaff/npnf108.toc.html.

Stanojevic, Obrad. 'Roman Law and Common Law – A Different Point of View' (1990) 36, *Loyola Law Review* 269.

Stein, Peter, *Roman Law in European History,* Cambridge: Cambridge University Press, 1999.

Stoffel-Munck, Philippe. 'La Réforme en Pratique: La Résiliation pour Imprévision' (2015), *AJ Contrats d'Affaires* 262.

Sutherland, Jamie. 'Leases, Brexit and Frustration' (2019) 23, *Landlord & Tenant Review* 191.

Swadling, William 'The Judicial Construction of *Force Majeure* Clauses' 3 in Ewan McKendrick (editor) *Force Majeure and Frustration of Contract* London: Lloyd's of London Press Ltd., 1991.

Swain, Warren. 'Contract as Promise: The Role of Promising in the Law of Contract. An Historical Account' (2013) 17, *Edinburgh Law Review* 1.

Tanney, Anthony. 'Leases and the Doctrine of Frustration' (2021) 25, *Larsen & Toubro Review* 59, 59.

Teeven, K.M. *A History of the Anglo-American Common Law of Contract*, New York: Greenwood Press, 1990.

Terré, F. (dir.) *Pour une réforme du droit de la responsabilité civile*, Dalloz, 2011.

Terré, F. (dir.) *Pour une réforme du droit des contrats*, Dalloz, 2009.

Terré, F. (dir.) *Pour une réforme du régime général des obligations*, Dalloz, 2013.

Thibierge, Louis. 'l'Impossibilité d'exécuter' *Blog Réforme du droit des obligations (Le blog Dalloz dédié à la réforme du droit des obligations)* at page 1. http://reforme-obligations.dalloz.fr/2015/04/28/limpossibilite-dexecuter/.

Thibierge, Louis. 'Quel champ d'application pour l'article 1195 du Code civil?' (12 septembre 2022). Lagbd.org/Quel_champ_d_application_pour_l'article_1195_du_Code_civil.

Thier, Andreas. 'Legal History' 15, in Ewoud Hondius and Hans Christoph Grigoleit (editors) *Unexpected Circumstances in European Contract Law*, Cambridge: Cambridge University Press, 2011.

Thomas, P.J. *Introduction to Roman Law*, Deventer: Kluwer Law and Taxation Publishers, 1986.

Treitel, Sir Guenter. *Frustration and Force Majeure* (3rd edition), London: Sweet & Maxwell, 2014.

Twiggs-Flesner, Christian. 'A Comparative Perspective on Commercial Contracts and the Impact of Covid-19 – Change of Circumstances, *Force Majeure*, or What?', in Katharina Pistor (editor) *Law in the Time of COVID – 19* (volume 155, p. 161), 2020. https://scholarship.law.columbia.edu.books/240.

Unidroit Principles of International Commercial Contracts www.unidroit.org/english/principles/contracts/principles 2010/integralversionprincipes2010-e.pdf.

van Caenegem, R.C. *An Historical Introduction to Private Law*, Cambridge: Cambridge University Press, 1992.

van Caenegem, R.C. *Judges, Legislators, and Professors*, Cambridge: Cambridge University Press, 1987.

van Caenegem, R.C. *The Birth of the English Common Law* (2nd edition), Cambridge: Cambridge University Press, 1988.

Vidal, José *Théorie Générale de la Fraude en Droit Français*, Paris: Librairie Dalloz, 1957.

Viollet, Paul *Histoire du Droit Civil Français*, Darmstadt: Scientia Verlag Aalen, 1966 (réimpression de la 3me édition du '*Précis de l'Histoire du Droit Français*', Paris, 1905).

Vogenauer, Stefan. 'The Avant-projet de réforme: An Overview' 3 in John Cartwright, Stefan Vogenauer and Simon Whittaker (editors) *Reforming the French Law of Obligations*, Oxford: Hart Publishing, 2009.

Vrankin, Martin. *Western Legal Traditions,* Sydney: The Federation Press, 2015.

Warren, Samuel. *A Popular and Practical Introduction to Law Studies,* London: A. Maxwell, 1835.

Watkin, Thomas Glyn. *An Historical Introduction to Modern Civil Law,* Aldershot: Dartmouth Publishing Company Limited/Ashgate Publishing Ltd., 1999.

Watson, Alan. *Roman Law and Comparative Law,* Athens, Georgia: The University of Georgia Press, 1991.

Watson, Alan. 'Roman Law and English Law: Two Patterns of Legal Development' (1990) 36, *Loyola Law Review* 247.

Watson, Alan. *The Spirit of Roman Law,* Athens, Georgia: The University of Georgia Press, 1995.

Wright, Robert Alderson (Baron of Durley), *Legal Essays and Addresses by the Right Hon. Lord Wright of Durley,* Cambridge: Cambridge University Press, 1939.

Yearbook of the International Law Commission, 1966, volume II: Draft Articles on the Law of Treaties with Commentaries, 1966 – Text adopted by the International Law Commission at its eighteenth session, in 1966, and submitted to the General Assembly as a part of the Commission's report covering the work of that session (at para. 38).

Zimmermann, Reinhard. *The Law of Obligations,* Oxford: Oxford University Press, 1996.

Zweigert, K. and H. Kötz. *An Introduction to Comparative Law* (3rd revised edition, translated by Tony Weir), Oxford: Clarendon Press, 1998.

Index

For Product Safety Concerns and Information please contact our
EU representative GPSR@taylorandfrancis.com Taylor & Francis
Verlag GmbH, Kaufingerstraße 24, 80331 München, Germany